THE ARDEN SHAKESPEARE

THIRD
General Editors: Richard
and David
Associate General
George Wa

KING
HENRY VI
PART 1

THE ARDEN SHAKESPEARE

* Second series

THE ARDEN SHAKESPEARE

KING HENRY VI PART 1

Edited by
EDWARD BURNS

The general editors of the Arden Shakespeare have been
W. J. Craig and R. H. Case (first series 1899-1944)
Una Ellis-Fermor, Harold F. Brooks, Harold Jenkins and
Brian Morris (second series 1946-82)

Present general editors (third series)
Richard Proudfoot, Ann Thompson and David Scott Kastan

This edition of *King Henry VI, Part 1*, by Edward Burns,
first published 2000 by The Arden Shakespeare

Editorial matter © 2000 Edward Burns

Arden Shakespeare is an imprint of Thomson Learning

Thomson Learning
Berkshire House
168-173 High Holborn
London WC1V 7AA

Typeset in Ehrhardt by
Multiplex Techniques Limited, Orpington, Kent
Printed in Italy
by
Milanostampa S.p.A.

British Library Cataloguing in Publication Data
A catalogue record for this book is available from the British Library
Library of Congress Cataloguing in Publication Data
A catalogue record has been requested

ISBN 0-17-4435509 (hbk)
NPN 9 8 7 6 5 4 3 2 1
ISBN 1-903436-43-5
(paperback)
NPN 9 8 7 6 5 4 3 2 1

The Arden website is at
http://www.ardenshakespeare.com/

The Editor

Edward Burns is Senior Lecturer in the Department of English Language and Literature at the University of Liverpool. His publications include *Restoration Comedy: Crises of Desire and Identity* (1987), *Character; Acting and Being on the Pre-Modern Stage* (1990), *Shakespeare's Richard III* (forthcoming), an edition of *Five British Romantic Plays* (with Paul Baines, 2000) and a collection of commissioned essays *Reading Rochester* (1994). He is the official dramaturg of the Chester Mystery Cycle; his modern performing text (1987), a three night cycle, is produced at the Cathedral every five years.

For

Alan Brookes

and in memory of

Nicholas Brooke

1924 – 98

CONTENTS

LIST OF
ILLUSTRATIONS

GENERAL EDITORS'
PREFACE

The Arden Shakespeare is now over one hundred years old. The earliest volume in the first series, Edward Dowden's *Hamlet*, was published in 1899. Since then the Arden Shakespeare has become internationally recognized and respected. It is now widely acknowledged as the pre-eminent Shakespeare series, valued by scholars, students, actors and 'the great variety of readers' alike for its readable and reliable texts, its full annotation and its richly informative introductions.

We have aimed in the third Arden edition to maintain the quality and general character of its predecessors, preserving the commitment to presenting the play as it has been shaped in history. While each individual volume will necessarily have its own emphasis in the light of the unique possibilities and problems posed by the play, the series as a whole, like the earlier Ardens, insists upon the highest standards of scholarship and upon attractive and accessible presentation.

Newly edited from the original quarto and folio editions, the texts are presented in fully modernized form, with a textual apparatus that records all substantial divergences from those early printings. The notes and introductions focus on the conditions and possibilities of meaning that editors, critics and performers (on stage and screen) have discovered in the play. While building upon the rich history of scholarly and theatrical activity that has long shaped our understanding of the texts of Shakespeare's plays, this third series of the Arden Shakespeare is made necessary and possible by a new generation's encounter with Shakespeare, engaging with the plays and their complex relation to the culture in which they were – and continue to be – produced.

THE TEXT

On each page of the play itself, readers will find a passage of text followed by commentary and, finally, textual notes. Act and scene divisions (seldom present in the early editions and often the product of eighteenth-century or later scholarship) have been retained for ease of reference, but have been given less prominence than in the previous series. Editorial indications of location of the action have been removed to the textual notes or commentary.

In the text itself, unfamiliar typographic conventions have been avoided in order to minimize obstacles to the reader. Elided forms in the early texts are spelt out in full in verse lines wherever they indicate a usual late twentieth-century pronunciation that requires no special indication and wherever they occur in prose (except when they indicate non-standard pronunciation). In verse speeches, marks of elision are retained where they are necessary guides to the scansion and pronunciation of the line. Final -ed in past tense and participial forms of verbs is always printed as -ed without accent, never as -'d, but wherever the required pronunciation diverges from modern usage a note in the commentary draws attention to the fact. Where the final -ed should be given syllabic value contrary to modern usage, e.g.

> Doth Silvia know that I am banished?
> (*TGV* 3.1.221)

the note will take the form

221 **banished** banishèd

Conventional lineation of divided verse lines shared by two or more speakers has been reconsidered and sometimes rearranged. Except for the familiar *Exit* and *Exeunt*, Latin forms in stage directions and speech prefixes have been translated into English and the original Latin forms recorded in the textual notes.

COMMENTARY AND TEXTUAL NOTES

Notes in the commentary, for which a major source will be the *Oxford English Dictionary*, offer glossarial and other explication of verbal difficulties; they may also include discussion of points of theatrical interpretation and, in relevant cases, substantial extracts from Shakespeare's source material. Editors will not usually offer glossarial notes for words adequately defined in the latest edition of *The Concise Oxford Dictionary* or *Merriam-Webster's Collegiate Dictionary*, but in cases of doubt they will include notes. Attention, however, will be drawn to places where more than one likely interpretation can be proposed and to significant verbal and syntactic complexity. Notes preceded by * involve editorial emendations or readings in which the rival textual claims of competing early editions (Quarto and Folio) are in dispute.

Headnotes to acts or scenes discuss, where appropriate, questions of scene location, Shakespeare's handling of his source materials, and major difficulties of staging. The list of roles (so headed to emphasize the play's status as a text for performance) is also considered in commentary notes. These may include comment on plausible patterns of casting with the resources of an Elizabethan or Jacobean acting company, and also on any variation in the description of roles in their speech prefixes in the early editions.

The textual notes are designed to let readers know when the edited text diverges from the early edition(s) on which it is based. Wherever this happens the note will record the rejected reading of the early edition(s), in original spelling, and the source of the reading adopted in this edition. Other forms from the early edition(s) recorded in these notes will include some spellings of particular interest or significance and original forms of translated stage directions. Where two early editions are involved, for instance with *Othello*, the notes will also record all important differences between them. The textual notes take a form that has been in use since the nineteenth century. This comprises, first: line reference, reading adopted in the text and closing square bracket; then: abbreviated reference, in italic, to the earliest edition to adopt the accepted reading, italic semicolon and noteworthy alternative reading(s), each with abbreviated italic reference to its source.

Conventions used in these textual notes include the following. The solidus / is used, in notes quoting verse or discussing verse lining, to indicate line endings. Distinctive spellings of the basic text (Q or F) follow the square bracket without indication of source and are enclosed in italic brackets. Names enclosed in italic brackets indicate originators of conjectural emendations when these did not originate in an edition of the text, or when this edition records a conjecture not accepted into its text. Stage directions (SDs) are referred to by the number of the line within or immediately after which they are placed. Line numbers with a decimal point relate to entry SDs and to SDs more than one line long, with the number after the point indicating the line within the SD: e.g. 78.4 refers to the fourth line of the SD following line 78. Lines of SDs at the start of a scene are numbered 0.1, 0.2, etc. Where only a line number and SD precede the square bracket, e.g. 128 SD], the note relates to the whole of a SD within or immediately following the line. Speech prefixes (SPs) follow similar conventions, 203 SP] referring to the speaker's name for line 203. Where a SP reference takes the form e.g. 38+ SP, it relates to all subsequent speeches assigned to that speaker in the scene in question.

Where, as with *King Henry V*, one of the early editions is a so-called 'bad quarto' (that is, a text either heavily adapted, or reconstructed from memory, or both), the divergences from the present edition are too great to be recorded in full in the notes. In these cases the editions will include a reduced photographic facsimile of the 'bad quarto' in an appendix.

INTRODUCTION

Both the introduction and the commentary are designed to present the plays as texts for performance, and make appropriate reference to stage, film and television versions, as well as introducing the reader to the range of critical approaches to the plays. They discuss the history of the reception of the texts within the theatre and scholarship and beyond, investigating the interdependency of the literary text and the surrounding 'cultural text' both at the time of the original production of Shakespeare's works and during their long and rich afterlife.

ACKNOWLEDGEMENTS

My thanks are due to Jessica Hodge, for her adept and humorous diplomacy in the co-ordination of this edition, as indeed to everyone at the publishers, who have been a real pleasure to work with. Linden Stafford, the copy-editor, has demonstrated not only superb skills and breadth of knowledge, but an astounding intuitive ability to spot links missing in my arguments, although present at earlier, often unwritten, stages in their gestation. Our phone calls have been a lively and unpredictable part of my life over the last year or so, not least in the behaviour of cats and builders at both ends of the line. Much thanks.

The general editors, Richard Proudfoot, George Walton Williams, Ann Thompson and David Scott Kastan have all had invaluable input into the development of the edition. The first two in particular have proved stimulating and entertaining to work with – sometimes to the point of exasperation (more than probably mutual), but the process has been highly rewarding. Some residue of unresolved disagreement can be found in the note to Appendix 1; but the main point is that I feel we have all three become excited in exploring the complexities and problems of a play far too often overlooked. My main motivation for trying to do an Arden was to learn, and I certainly have.

In my own department at Liverpool, Antoinette Renouf gave advise on corpus linguistics, Bernard Beatty on matters ecclesiastical and Brian Nellist on matters canine, with much else. Jonathan Bate and Nick Davis gave encouragement and advice on versions of the Introduction, as did, invaluably and from a general reader's point of view, my neighbour Jane Kitovitz. Liverpool has a long tradition of Shakespeare editing, and it has been a privilege to talk about what I was doing with N.W. Bawcutt and Philip Edwards. Finally, Steve Newman witnessed the very last moment of my work on the typescript, and that very moment spotted a mistake.

The staff of the British Film Institute, the Reading Room of the Theatre Museum, Covent Garden, the Library of the Shakespeare Institute at Stratford, the Rare Books and Manuscript Rooms at the British Library, the Picture Library of the Museum of London and the staff of Special Collections and Colin Morgan in the University of Liverpool Library, have all been invaluably helpful.

Material in this edition has been presented at a number of seminars and conferences: at the Liverpool postgraduate drama seminar; the conference on Literary Theory and Editing, again at Liverpool; the Northern Renaissance Seminar at Keele; the CESR *table ronde* at Tours (on more than one occasion!), at Salzburg and at the Shakespeare Association of America at Cleveland, Ohio. Thanks to all who participated in these events, and to (in order) Richard Cowler, Kelvin Everest, Marion Wynne-Davies, Andre Lascombes and his incomparable team, Holger Klein, and Michael Hattaway, for inviting me. Thanks also to Michael Hattaway, Patricia Parker and Gary Taylor for instructive and supportive discussion at these and other events.

The edition is dedicated, with their permission, to two people whose friendship was as valuable as it was entertaining over the time I worked on the edition. To Alan Brookes (to mark his survival of his own wars in France) and, sadly now as a memorial, to the late Professor Nicholas Brooke. Memories of his and Julia's hospitality, and especially of the halting but gastronomically highly rewarding journey we made in his venerable DCV back from Tours, following in the hoofsteps of Miss d'Arc, will colour pleasurably my own sense of what this edition means to me.

Edward Burns
Liverpool

INTRODUCTION

'HAREY THE VJ' ON STAGE AT THE ROSE

Talbot revived

Unusually in the case of an Elizabethan play we have what seems
to be a first-hand description of *1 Henry VI* on stage. A passage in
Thomas Nashe's *Piers Penniless his Supplication to the Devil*, published in the summer of 1592, describes the effect and great
popular success of a play with a central role for the English commander Talbot. This is a reference to an event that Nashe can
expect to be fresh in the minds of the fashion-conscious young
male readership at whom his pamphlet is aimed:

> what if I proove Playes to be no extreame; but a rare exer-
> cise of vertue? First, for the subject of them (for the most
> part) it is borrowed out of our English Chronicles,
> wherein our forefathers valiant acts (that have line long
> buried in rustie brasse and worme-eaten bookes) are
> revived, and they themselves raised from the Grave of
> Oblivion, and brought to pleade their aged Honours in
> open presence: than which, what can be a sharper
> reproofe to these degenerate effeminate dayes of ours?
>
> How would it have joyed brave *Talbot* (the terror of
> the French) to thinke that after he had lyne two hundred
> yeares in his Tombe, hee should triumphe againe on the
> Stage, and have his bones newe embalmed with the teares
> of ten thousand spectators at least (at severall times),
> who, in the Tragedian that represents his person, imagine
> they behold him fresh bleeding.

I will defend it against any Collian, or clubfisted Usurer of them all,[1] there is no immortalitie can be given a man on earth like unto Playes. What talke I to them of immortalitie, that are the onely underminers of Honour, and doe envie any man that is not sprung up by base Brokerie like themselves? They care not if all the auncient houses were rooted out, so that, like the Burgomasters of the Low-countries, they might share the government amongst them as States, and be quarter-maisters of our Monarchie. All Artes to them are vanitie: and, if you tell them what a glorious thing it is to have *Henrie* the fifth represented on the Stage, leading the French King prisoner, and forcing both him and the Dolphin to sweare fealty, I, but (will they say) what do we get by it? Respecting neither the right of Fame that is due to true Nobilitie deceased, nor what hopes of eternitie are to be proposed to adventrous mindes, to encourage them forward, but onely their execrable luker, and filthie unquenchable avarice.

(Nashe, 1.212–13)

As the fullest account of a play in the Shakespeare canon by an Elizabethan writer, this is disappointing in its lack of specifics. What did it look like? Who was the actor playing Talbot? How did he say the lines? Later on in this same pamphlet Nashe says that 'Not *Roscius* nor *Æsope*, those admyred tragedians that have lived ever since before Christ was borne, could ever performe more in action than famous *Ned Allen*' (Nashe, 1.215). Edward Alleyn seems the most likely actor to have created the role of Talbot. He had created the leading roles in Marlowe's plays and in 1588 moved from the disbanded Lord Admiral's Men to Lord Strange's Men. When Nashe's pamphlet was published Alleyn

---

1 McKerrow (Nashe, 212, n.29) glosses 'Collian' in this passage as a variant of 'cullion', meaning scoundrel (its literal meaning is 'testicle'). It thus parallels 'club-fisted Usurer', a money-lender with a tight grasp on his money, as a term of contempt.

and Lord Strange's Men were on tour, as government fears of civil rioting, followed by an outbreak of plague, forced the closure of the theatres from 23 June 1592 (Chambers, 2.44–5). We don't know their repertory but they may well have taken *1 Henry VI*, if it was their play; we know they had performed at the Rose with a repertoire that included a 'harey the vj'. Henslowe, the owner and manager of the theatre, had, as we can learn from interpreting his 'diary' in the context of recent excavation of the site of the Rose, rebuilt his theatre in 1592, very possibly 'making ready for the arrival of Edward Alleyn with his bigger plays and bigger audiences' (Eccles, 28). For all its limitations as documentary evidence, Nashe's description does give us an account of the dynamics of an audience's response to a star actor in a role designed to exploit and articulate his charisma.

On the other hand this passage may describe the performance of a lost and otherwise unrecorded play on the same subject. The play on the life of Henry the Fifth mentioned later is, of course, not Shakespeare's; it may be a description of *The Famous Victories* and/or it may be a garbled version of Prince Edward's victorious entrances at 4.9 and 5.1 of *Edward III*. Only one text of *1 Henry VI* comes to us from Shakespeare's theatre. In 1623, seven years after Shakespeare's death, John Heminge and Henry Condell, former acting colleagues of his in a later company, the Chamberlain's Men (Chambers, 2.228–9), put together a collection of texts ascribable to him which we now call 'the First Folio', usually referred to in this volume as F. We do not know for certain what their sources were. It is unlikely that any of their materials would have come directly to them from Shakespeare himself. In earlier accounts of this text the assumed source is referred to unflatteringly as 'foul papers'.[1] The likelihood that

---

1   The phrase 'foul papers' has sometimes been used as a term for miscellaneous papers and actors' copies, for example, not necessarily authorized by Shakespeare, as well as for the author's rough drafts, any of which could have been sources for F. This may explain the apparent confusion of some of its texts (Greg, 430). But this last point is conjecture, and still controversial (Baldwin, 152–9; Taylor & Jowett, 239–43).

the play remained unrevived means that Heminge and Condell probably used a thirty-year-old collection of papers, in the handwriting of people largely unknown to them, several or all of whom had died before Heminge and Condell set to work.

The editor's task is largely that of presenting a text in a way that clarifies it for the modern reader and actor. F's text was arrived at from documents relating to a long-past theatrical event. Whether or not one believes – as I do (see pp. 73–83) – that this event was in some degree collaboratively devised, the one surviving text shows signs of indecision and confusion which no other direct evidence can help us to disentangle. My practice with punctuation and stage directions has been – given the lack of other evidence – to interpret F with minimum interference; F seems to me to work better in many places than previous editors have often allowed. I suspect that a prejudice against either the play or the state of F's text, or both, has induced a freedom of emendation that would not have been taken with other, more securely canonical, plays.

For the moment at least, I will leave open the matter of how far the play is Shakespeare's. This is a recurrent and complex controversy; but I feel I should alert the reader now to the fact that the Introduction will refer to the author(s) of *1 Henry VI* as 'the dramatists'.

As far as identification of the play goes, I take the view, suggested by Henslowe's date and Nashe's description, that *1 Henry VI* is 'harey the vj' and so Nashe's Talbot play, and that it was new when Henslowe presented it on 3 March 1592. This might seem at first sight uncontroversial, but, for reasons I shall return to later in this Introduction, it forms a challenge to the idea that this play was the first part to be written of a three-part 'cycle', in that this late dating would mean that the play was written and first performed after what are now most generally known as Parts *Two* and *Three*. With several other recent commentators, I take the view that the play is what in the Hollywood terms of the late twentieth century is known as a 'prequel', a dramatic piece

4

that returns for ironic and challenging effect to the narrative roots of an already familiar story.[1] There is in fact nothing in *1 Henry VI* that we need to know to follow the story of Parts *Two* and *Three*. Indeed, those plays can be seen to be stronger without it. The two narratologically later but, according to available evidence, earlier-written plays work as a bipartite presentation of history in a sequence of individual tragic fates. The opening of this two-parter, like that of *King Lear* or Marlowe's *Edward II*, presents the nominally most powerful figure, the King, making a fatal error, a personally wilful but communally catastrophic choice. In *2 Henry VI* it is the handing over of French territory in exchange for the dowerless Margaret; as in *King Lear* or *Edward II*, an impulsive individual act initiates an apparently unstoppable spiral of violence. Detaching *1 Henry VI* from the other two plays allows us to isolate its tone, to see its differences from the other histories in theatrical style and in its attitude to the events portrayed. As a form the 'prequel' is inherently ironic; it depends on the audience having a knowledge of the outcome of events that the characters depicted as living those events do not themselves possess. Where in the two other plays we are aware of characters condemned and condemning themselves to apparently irredeemably catastrophic

---

1　Taylor (199–200, n.14) gives as examples of the 'prequel' Thomas Dekker's *The First Introduction of the Civil Wars of France* (1599), Henry Chettle's *The Rising of Cardinal Wolsey* and Thomas Middleton's *The Widow* (*c*. 1616). There is evidence of what may be a prequel to Thomas Kyd's *The Spanish Tragedy*: performed in 1592 at the Rose, but now probably lost, it was recorded by Henslowe as the 'comodey of Jeronymo' and staged the day before 'Jeronymo'. Plays were never performed twice running, but two-part plays were presented over successive days. A play called *The First Part of Jeronimo* was published in 1605, its intent presumably satirical, but it cannot be necessarily identified with Henslowe's record, which might be an equivalent or a variant of the same 'prequel', or a lost 'first part' to precede Kyd's (Edwards, 137–8). Notable modern examples of the prequel are provided by the proliferation of films in George Lucas's *Star Wars* series (beginning in 1977, and continuing at the time of writing). For present-day audiences the dynamic of the prequel tends to be that of a popularized Freudian psychology – hence the tongue-in-cheek delving back into Alfred Hitchcock's film *Psycho* (1960) in a sequence of later films, the 'traumatic' flashbacks in *Batman Forever* (1995), and other 'backward' constructions of fantasy and horror cycles in the unserious search for an 'explanation' of events.

courses of action or inaction, here moments of decision are opened up to the spectator with a sense of the farcically unpredictable, of the self-aggrandizing littleness of individuals manufacturing for themselves and for their nations a 'fame', a heroic identity, in the face of a universe characterized from the beginning of the play as conditioned by a loss of purpose and by the governance of accident.

So, in this edition *1 Henry VI* is a free-standing piece, designed originally to draw on audience knowledge of the two earlier plays for ominous and ironic effect, but enjoyable on its own as a witty and spectacular piece of physical theatre. The tone and concerns of this play become clearer when we take it on its own. I shall deal with alternative interpretations of the evidence later in the Introduction (see pp. 69–73). For me the play is not so much a component of a historical epic as an ironic meditation on what history is, and as such it constantly exposes the gratuitousness of the signs and symbols which allow us to think we know history. Conflict in the play takes place on the level of a combat between signs whose rootedness in purposive communal history has been lost, and whose meaning is to be re-forged in conflict and in individual self-assertion. However 'natural' the metaphors involved – in the family tree, the language of flowers, the beastliness of war, to cite examples to which I shall return (p. 52ff) – we are constantly drawn to pay attention to the construction of those metaphors, to the strain of their elaborations and the fault-lines that open up in them.

In the passage from *Piers Penniless*, Nashe reminds us that a major concern of the play is the nature of the heroic and the complexities of our relationship to it. We are both an audience sharing the experience of the play in a present moment and at the same time 'posterity', a group of people who exist significantly later than the events the play presents, constructed as witnesses and judges by its theatrical form, but given by hindsight a troubled and ironic sense of the outcome. For Nashe the important thing about theatre is that it brings the remembered

6

and the written to life in a present moment of spectatorship, a moment shared in a highly charged space between the spectator and that accomplished rhetorician/actor who revives the past by his ability to activate imagination through language. Nashe uses a metaphor of 'buried' to make a bridge towards an imaginative revival which is a kind of rebirth or resurrection, if not of the historical individual, of those ideals to which the performance points:

> our forefathers valiant acts (that have line long buried in rustie brasse and worme-eaten bookes) are revived, and they themselves raised from the Grave of Oblivion, and brought to pleade their aged Honours in open presence.
>
> (Nashe, 1.212)

The response of the spectators to Talbot is simultaneously to open his wounds, by going back into the past and confronting his death, and to save him, or preserve his memory at least, in a kind of brine of salt tears.

Dating and identifying the play from Henslowe's 'diary'

Philip Henslowe, businessman and entrepreneur, built, owned and managed several of the earliest public theatres in England, including the Rose and the Fortune. The volume usually, and misleadingly, known as *Henslowe's Diary*, now kept in Dulwich College, London, is actually a kind of account book, started by Philip's brother John in 1576 to keep accounts of a mining and smelting business. Then at some point it was taken over by Philip, who made entries in it until 1609. Though still basically a record of business activities, it includes personal memoranda, spells and cures, folk wisdom and formulae of popularized magic. The list of plays performed, of props and costumes bought, of writers and actors paid and lent money, has provided a major resource in dating and ascribing plays, even though the 'diary's' clipped pragmatic manner means that the help it provides in visualizing and reconstructing staging is frustratingly limited. Page 7 of Henslowe's volume is headed 'In the name of god A men 1591 / beginge the 19 of febreary my / lord stranges mene A ffoloweth / 1591' (Henslowe, 16). ('1591' here is 1592 in terms of a modern calendar; according to the old-style calendar which Henslowe uses, the year begins on 25 March.) What follows is a day-to-day calendar of the plays performed that year at the Rose theatre by a company under the patronage of Lord Strange – hence 'my lord stranges mene'. About a third of the way down the page a line reads 'ne-Rd at harey the vj the 3 of marche 1591 . . . iij^{li} xvj^s 8d'. Henslowe puts 'ne' in the margin before his first mention of a number of plays on his list. Entrance charges to the theatre seem to have been higher on these occasions (Henslowe, xxix–xxx). One way of reading this is that it is an abbreviation that marks the play as 'new'. If we take it this way, we have a date for the first performance of a play that was one of Henslowe's major financial successes.

'Harey the vj' at the box-office

Henslowe's accounts provide evidence of exceptionally large audiences for the play. 'Harey the vj' received at least seventeen performances between March 1592 and the following January and paid Henslowe £33 12s. 8d. in all. Henslowe always took half the money paid by the audience in the galleries, of which there were probably three. The rest of this and the money paid by those standing in as 'groundlings' went to the company performing. We have no direct evidence of the cost of individual entrance to the Rose in 1592, but in 1599 a German visitor, Thomas Platter, attended performances which may have been at either the Rose or the Globe, and explained the pricing policy in his narrative of his travels;

> The places are built in such a way that they act on a raised scaffold, and everyone can well see everything. However, there are separate galleries and places, where one sits more pleasantly and better, therefore also pays more. For he who remains standing below pays only one English penny, but if he wants to sit he is let in at another door,

where he gives a further penny; but if he desires to sit on cushions in the pleasantest place, where he not only sees everything well but can also be seen, then he pays at a further door another English penny.

(Schanzer, 466).

Andrew Gurr estimates a maximum of 1,654 spectators in the galleries of the Rose (Eccles, 136). At the busiest performance of 'harey the vj', the first (3 March), Henslowe took £3 16s. 8d. i.e. 920 pennies, representing half of the takings paid at two pennies per person. So, if pricing policies were similar to those recorded by Platter, the play could have been attended at this performance by just under a thousand spectators in the galleries alone. The total figure for one performance, when we count the 'groundlings' standing around the stage, could potentially more than double this, and, with 16,344 pennies taken for the galleries at the fifteen recorded performances, Nashe's estimate of 'ten thousand spectators (at severall times)' seems an under-estimation. Henslowe records the contribution to his finances of a major popular success, a play that outperformed, financially, other hits of the season, including Robert Greene's *Friar Bacon and Friar Bungay*, Christopher Marlowe's *The Jew of Malta* and Thomas Kyd's *The Spanish Tragedy*. Such popularity might have determined Nashe's choice of a play (to which, it has often been argued, he contributed) to make his point about the centrality of theatre to London life, in the context of *Piers Penniless*'s polemical defence of theatre as the promulgator of virtue and heroism.

Stage space

As a theatrical spectacle the play makes ingenious use of what was at the time the most sophisticated theatre ever seen in London. The Rose theatre was first built in 1587 on the south bank of the Thames, in the 'liberties' of Southwark. Excavation of the site (1988–9) gave evidence of the rebuilding paid for (as recorded in Henslowe, 9–12) in 1592, shortly before 'harey the vj' was premièred. This involved the addition of a roof over the playing space, thus implying a permanent stage with pillars. Earlier theatres were unroofed and may well have had removable stages to allow them to accommodate bear-baiting and other spectacles. The shape and size of that stage are the most surprising discoveries of the excavation. Our preconceptions of the Elizabethan theatre assume a stage extending out into the audience, like the modern 'thrust' stage, and probably square, or deeper than it is broad. Henslowe, however, when he rebuilt the theatre, maximized audience capacity by making its stage only a little deeper than before, and moved it back. He retained a shape which tapered towards the front in a kind of reverse perspective (Fig. 1). So the modified stage in 1592 was 18 ft 4 in deep, 36 ft 9 in wide at the back, and 26 ft 10 in wide at the front (Eccles, 140–1). It was at about shoulder level with those standing in the pit close to the stage, and the standing space 'around' the stage was slightly raked, though, as we can deduce from the stage shape, most of the standing audience would be facing the front of that stage.

This wide shallow stage makes sense of the arrangement of the figures in a line in the often reproduced drawing of *Titus Andronicus* on stage in 1594, usually attributed to Henry Peacham (*Tit*, 39).[1] That play, also staged at the Rose, opens, as does *1 Henry VI*, with a procession and a funeral rite. Processional scenes, moving laterally across the space, offer one way of making use of what is, to modern eyes, the eccentric shape of the Rose stage. Another effect, used widely in *1 Henry VI*, is of multi-focused action – scenes where several distinct groups of performers occupy the stage, inhabiting different but juxtaposed spaces. These are easier to 'read' on a laterally organized stage, like the Rose's. The effect of the 'reverse perspective' shape is harder to envisage. It makes address to the audience – frequent in

1 Jonathan Bate (*Tit*, 38–43) questions the usual dating of the Peacham drawing, and goes on to suggest it is an 'emblematic' illustration, based on reading, not seeing, the play. This is plausible enough, but unverifiable, and driven by a larger argument about a later than conventional dating of the play.

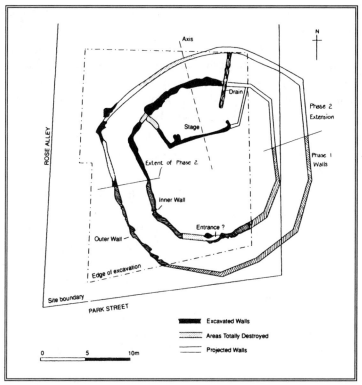

1   Diagram of the Rose stage as rebuilt in 1592

this play, typically coming out of a crowded scene – easier to focus, in that it spreads the audience out in a shallow semicircle, facing the action. It would also push confrontational scenes towards the front of the stage. Characters' entrances would tend to converge centrally and probably only a few feet away from the front, making this the most powerful area of the stage in relation to the audience. By the same token, the actors have quite a long and oddly angled walk to get to such a position. But this works for a play where characters making an entry on stage are frequently energized by aggression. When this is not the case – for

Mortimer, Bedford or the child King – the theatrical emphasis is on their debility.[1]

Excavation cannot of course tell us what was above stage level, let alone how it was decorated. But the evidence, both of the 'De Witt' drawing of the Swan, the only surviving unquestionable contemporary illustration of the interior of a public theatre of the Elizabethan period (Oxford provides a clear reproduction (xxvi)), and of the play texts themselves, points to a playing space 'above', a gallery over the stage to contain musicians, and some action.

> This gallery . . . probably was on a level with the audience's first-storey gallery . . . The Fortune contract asks for a 12 feet high ground-floor gallery and an 11 feet high first-floor gallery. With balustrade, this first-floor gallery would provide access (via ladder) at about 15 feet above the yard. Allowing for the stage's probable height, the climb for Talbot & Co [2.1.28–37] would be about 10 feet. Later in the same scene, the actors playing the French army would have been able to leap over the balustrade, in their shirts, to a 10-feet drop; a reasonable requirement for an athletic actor.
>
> (Eccles, 144).

We may not know what the back of the stage looked like, but we know that in this play the audience's attention is continually being drawn to it, in a sequence of 'siege' scenes, beginning with Gloucester's attempt to gain entrance to the Tower of London. Scenes in the play are mapped against an impressive permanent physical structure, called on to represent large-scale architectural spaces and military arenas. There are probably more scenes 'above' in this play than in any other in the Shakespeare canon.

---

1 R.A. Foakes (141–8) offers a useful summary of the Rose findings. There is evidence for a similarly shaped stage in illustrations to *Roxana* (1632) and *Messalina* (1640); these are easier to interpret in the light of the Rose excavation, and help to suggest that this was a more standard stage shape, with a longer history, than had been assumed (Astington, 149–69).

Indeed every scene until – in effective contrast – the duologue between Mortimer and Richard at 2.5.34–114 fills the stage, draws attention to imaginary spaces beyond it and exploits the vertical as well as the horizontal. This suggests that an exploitation of the stage space's potential for multi-focus action was one of the main reasons for commissioning this highly kinetic piece. At the same time, these examples do not mean that the play is necessarily tied to that setting and unperformable elsewhere. Editors sometimes forget that if a physical situation is described adequately in the dialogue it may be precisely so that it need *not* be replicated in movement or in the scenic depiction of space. The location of particular figures – in the siege of Orleans, for example (1.4.1–68), where the English commanders are above, the Gunner's Boy below, but where we may imagine that the English are in fact in a turret at the end of a bridge on the other side of the river Loire – is so precisely designated by the spoken text that a precisely realized setting is not needed (Fig. 2).

This would allow for a touring production, which might have seemed desirable, given the frequency of summer closures of the theatres at this time and the success of the piece in London,

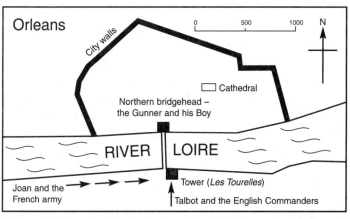

2 Map of Orleans showing the placing of the English army in relation to the bridge over the Loire

although the demands of staging and casting might have strained the resources of a touring company (see Appendix 2.)

The conventions for constructing space that the play's rhetoric activates are ingeniously flexible. On one occasion (2.1 and 2.2) the stage image is turned inside out – the English exit at the back of the stage to signify their entry into Orleans, then, after the French have played a scene in an unidentified space 'outside' the town, the English re-enter from the back with the funeral procession of Salisbury, so establishing the back of the stage as the other side of the wall, the apron stage as the centre of the town. On a later occasion (5.2) the 'above' space, once attention is drawn to it, suddenly 'appears'. Joan Puzel is captured by York, and then Margaret by Suffolk, in a diptych of scenes contrasting two disruptive female figures. Next, when Suffolk asks Margaret's father Reignier for her hand, ostensibly on his king's behalf, Reignier promptly appears 'above' on what is, by his presence, established as the walls of his castle, though until then we had no idea we were anywhere near a castle, let alone his. It is the advantage of a permanent structure that it can, according to a manipulation of the audience's attention, come in and out of view, and fulfil different practical and semiotic functions as action and language activate our sense of it. By having just one figure on it, particularly if that is the semi-comic Reignier, it becomes miniaturized, a kind of storybook castle. In a fully cast and active 'whole stage' scene, like the siege of Orleans, this miniaturization is a kind of scale diagram of a real situation, the depiction of a momentous historical event. The Reignier scene shifts the action of the end of the play towards the comic-erotic. In all these examples the use of stage space establishes the genre of the scene, and so provides a frame for our reading of it: a historical documentary reconstruction (1.4), a comic fabliau (5.2.66–216), a moral emblem of disunity in the scene of York's and Suffolk's failure to help Talbot (4.3). In the case of Joan Puzel's demons, who she tells us are 'under the lordly monarch of the north' (5.2.27) (meaning Satan), if they appear 'above' on the gallery, it becomes an eerie microcosm of a demonic universe (5.2.22–50) – the stage was set up in the north-north-west area of the building, another surprising find. This flexibility comes from the mediation, in the exploitation of a permanent structure, of the non-realist, imaginatively fluent creation of dramatic space inherited from late medieval and earlier Tudor theatre.

Battle scenes and combats

The Rose stage was particularly well adapted to scenes of warfare, and *1 Henry VI* was devised to exploit this. Two elements stand out – virtuoso hand-to-hand combat, and the use of explosions and other pyrotechnic effects.

A military historian's account of the end of the Hundred Years' War would focus on the French shift of tactics and technology, especially their development of a superior artillery. Historically it was this that finally defeated Talbot's attempt to prevent the French from recapturing Bordeaux in 1453 (see Appendix 4). The issue of firepower and of its questionable status in a chivalric world-view is developed in the scene of the Gunner's Boy (1.4.1–68). The linstock he carries across the stage is a burning stick to light a small cannon. No cannon could safely be fired on stage without risk of conflagration or of damage from its recoil. An earlier mishap at the Rose in 1587, the first year of its operation, might have suggested caution. According to one Philip Gawdy, in a rather moralistic letter;

My *Lord* Admyrall his men and players having a devyse in ther playe to tye one of their fellowes to a poste and so to shoote him to deathe, having borrowed their callyvers one of the players handes swerved his peece being charged with bullett missed the fellowe he aymed at and killed a chyld, and a woman great with chyld forthwith, and hurt an other man in the head very soore . . . And yet I fynde by this an old proverbe veryfyed ther never comes more hurte than commes of fooling.

(Rutter, 42).

Presumably, in the interests of safety, the Boy exited with the linstock, and an explosion took place offstage.

The play's extravagant exploitation of theatrical pyrotechnics – in both the literal and the metaphorical sense – is one of its most salient features. Just before Talbot hears of Joan, for example (1.4.96 SD), thunder and lightning – presumably achieved pyrotechnically on the naturally lit Elizabethan stage – signal a blurring between the natural, the ominously supernatural, the diabolic and the straightforwardly militaristic. Such moments both build up Joan Puzel and signal Talbot's confusion as to how to read her, how to interpret, to explain away, her temporary success.

Combats in this play take place between small numbers of clearly identified protagonists. Heraldry is a crucial part of the play's theatrical arsenal, in establishing identity clearly and quickly in these scenes. Displays of swordsmanship were a competing spectacle in the locale in which the plays were produced, and real, not 'prop', swords would be used for the fights; the audience, particularly that part of it which one might take to be interested in the ins and outs of fighting, the young male audience, was likely to be in close proximity to the stage, as groundlings, and so not to be fobbed off with fights as generalized and vestigial as those in some modern productions. English Renaissance duelling practice, in which such an audience could be taken to have a near-professional interest, involved the use of both sword and dagger – for fights involving high-status characters – and was usually blocked on a circle: i.e. each character had to be able to move through 360 degrees while wielding a three-foot-long sword. A stage with the dimensions of the Rose – with a maximum depth of 18 feet 4 inches and, probably, pillars 6 feet or so back, and perhaps as little as 18 feet apart – limits the number of participants and points also to an achieved clarity and precision of effect. Generalized hand-to-hand fighting is never called for; fights between pairs of characters or, on one conjectured occasion (4.4.55.1; but see p. 13), one character fighting three and then rescued by the entry of another, create a sense of battle otherwise amplified by music, explosions and simple charges and chases.

The fights in *1 Henry VI* require two athletic young actors to play John Talbot and Joan Puzel, and demand fighting skills also of the older actors who play Talbot and York and the French commanders, though these are required largely to parry and contain the more active younger figures. This edition proposes the staging of a spectacular fight at 4.4.55.1–4. Such a fight could be a virtuoso show-piece where one actor, centre stage, is attacked by three others, and then unexpectedly rescued by a fourth. Other editions (Ard², Oxf, Cam², for example) have marked an exit for John Talbot after 4.4.55 and the subsequent start of a new scene. This allows directors to get away with a blurred 'shouting and running through smoke' presentation of battle – as recorded, for example, in the 1964 television production of the Royal Shakespeare Company's (RSC) *The Wars of the Roses*. But a fight as this edition presents it is the centre of a scene, not the end of one and the beginning of another. The English Shakespeare Company's (ESC) *Henry VI: House of Lancaster* in the 1980s staged the fight fully and excitingly, accompanied by Tudor liturgical music; it became a theatrical climax, at the end of which Talbot was felled by an offstage pistol shot. In presenting the scene in this volume I have implemented F (additions to F's stage directions, as throughout this volume, are marked by square brackets).

TALBOT
      Then here I take my leave of thee, fair son,
      Born to eclipse thy life this afternoon.
      Come, side by side together live and die,
      And soul with soul from France to heaven fly.
                        Alarum. Exit [Talbot].

[*Enter* ALENÇON, ORLEANS and BURGUNDY *in*] *excursions, wherein Talbot's son is hemmed about* [*by the three Frenchmen, as he goes after his father*], *and* TALBOT [*re-enters and*] *rescues him.*

TALBOT
    Saint George and victory! Fight, soldiers, fight.

(4.4.52–6)

Looked at from this angle the French action of the play is a sequence of spectacular combats. Such combats are not simply interludes, they operate as a kind of syntax, a syntax of action that articulates the narrative and – as in the case of 'the Puzel' – change the conceptual and/or generic terms in which we see action and character.

The context of the performance: company and district

Ferdinando, Lord Strange, was the son and heir of the Earl of Derby, one of the most powerful noblemen of the period who owned extensive properties in the north of England and in the Isle of Man. For a theatre troupe to function on a large scale, it would need a 'patron' of this kind, to meet financial losses, to offer protection to the players when travelling and to provide openings for court performances. For the patron, maintenance of a company supplied prestige and status, but also the basic opportunity to see the kind of plays he wanted when he wanted, particularly on the tours that became increasingly important as outbreaks of plague and official worries about rioting closed the theatres during the summer. The Earl of Derby had hosted performances by the Queen's Men at his seat at Knowsley, north of Liverpool, in 1588, and tours sponsored by him and later by his son took in Leicester, Ipswich, Bristol and Chester, and on occasion got as far north as the borders of Scotland (Chambers, 1.34–5; Chambers, *Stage*, 2.118–24). We can only guess at how far personal taste and political bias influenced the repertory of the companies; Ernst Honigmann points out, for example, the favourable treatment of the Stanley/Derby figure in *Richard III* (Honigmann, 62–4), but the equivalent instance in this play, the presentation of Sir William Lucy, seems to relate to Shakespeare's Warwickshire connections, and for this reason has been used to bolster arguments for his authorship of this part of the play (Cam[2], 64). Some of the plays performed by Strange's Men were large-scale, historically based, extrovert and combative – one of their comic pieces was a version of *The Taming of the Shrew*, a play equally knockabout in style. In 1577 Lord Strange and his father witnessed the last recorded performance of one of the Chester plays, after Elizabeth's banning of the cycle (*REED*, 124). It was put on specially for them 'at the hie Crosse' by the Mayor of Chester. His, or their, choice, the Shepherds' play, is another lively fight-based piece, but it may have been also the safest choice from a religious point of view, as Mary and Jesus are only represented at the end of a play which could have been performed without them. Even so, this event is evidence that the Earls of Derby were interested, not only in theatre generally, but in the medieval and Catholic traditions of the north-west of England.

Ferdinando, Lord Strange, died two years after the London performance of *1 Henry VI*, in mysterious circumstances variously ascribed to witchcraft and to the intrigues of Catholics, whom he had opposed (Rosen, 305–9). The company was taken over for a short time by his widow as 'The Countess of Derby's Men'.

The location of the theatre and the reputation and history of the district feed back more directly into *1 Henry VI*, and into what we can assume as audience response. Southwark from the early Middle Ages onwards had a reputation – from the point of view of the City of London and the court at Westminster – for lawlessness. It was exempt from control by the City, which it faced across the river, and it offered easy routes southward towards the Channel and Europe. Also, it was controlled by various clerical authorities, often in uneasy relation to each other (D.J. Johnson, 33–5). Those most immediately relevant to our play were the bishops of Winchester, of whose magnificent

3 The rose window, all that remains of the palace of the bishops of Winchester in Southwark

palace, then linked to the river by a landing stage, only a wall with a rose window now remains (Fig. 3).

The area was governed by ecclesiastical courts, who imposed punishments and ran their own gaols. Henry VIII's dissolution of the monasteries and his sequestration and reassignment of property previously owned by the Catholic Church (the Winchester property had by this time passed to Cardinal Wolsey) demonstrated the monarch's determination to achieve supremacy, and in 1550 his son Edward VI was able to bring Southwark under City legislature. But, largely for reasons of geographical location, Southwark remained hard to police until at least the eighteenth century – which is partly why the playhouses were built there. The area remained notorious for its prostitutes and brothels (one was called 'The Cardinal's Hat'). Other groups allowed more freedom in Southwark than in the City, both in the Middle Ages and at the time of the writing of this play, were European settlers, particularly Lombards, engaged in financial services, and Flemings (governed, relevantly to this play, by the Dukes of Burgundy), often involved in the cloth and leather trades. The historical reason for Gloucester's attack on the Tower (1.3) was to secure Southwark against the hostility of the City towards its foreign population (Griffiths, 73–81). A threat of riots against immigrants may have been a subsidiary reason for the closure of the theatres, ostensibly on account of the plague, shortly after the first performances of this play in June of 1592. In 1593 or 1594, the Master of the Revels (see p. 71) required a scene of anti-alien rioting to be removed from the manuscript of the play *Sir Thomas More* (Gabrieli & Melchiori 17–20).[1] In *Sir Thomas More* rioting is

---

1 The authorship controversy in the case of *Sir Thomas More* is at least as tangled as the issues surrounding *1 Henry VI*. A recent edition describes it on its title-page as 'A play by ANTHONY MUNDAY and OTHERS Revised by HENRY CHETTLE, THOMAS DEKKER, THOMAS HEYWOOD AND WILLIAM SHAKESPEARE', and gives a lucid summary of arguments for the identification (Gabrieli & Melchiori, 12–17). But, for a range of conflicting positions on this issue, collected into a single volume, see Howard-Hill *passim*.

explicitly presented; in *1 Henry VI* violent action is likewise presented, but its motives are occluded.

The audience's historical memory would fill in the gaps. The surviving printed sources of this play are Hall's *The Union of the Two Noble and Illustre Families of Lancaster and York* (1548) and Holinshed's *Chronicles*, available to the dramatists in the second edition of 1587. Holinshed drew on Hall, but he elaborated some of the material, particularly that involving Jeanne la Pucelle (the form I use for the historical figure represented in the play as Joan Puzel). This is where the play most clearly uses Holinshed's account; the commentary cites and discusses sources as they arise, and, though I have tended to the view that Hall is the major source, this has been disputed, and the controversy has a bearing on interpretation of the political tendency of the *Henry VI* plays.[1] We should also perhaps be sceptical about accounts of sources which imply a one-to-one adaptation of a single text. The playwrights and their audience are at the same distance in time from the late Middle Ages as the late twentieth century is from the high Victorian period. The fifteenth century was similarly distant but also present, in its monuments and myths, and in a kind of dialectic with a later period fascinated with it, and defining itself against it. Through sources now lost, or through intelligent reading of the sources available, the Tudor chroniclers and dramatists reconstructed much of the anxiety produced by the loss of France and the subsequent civil war, an anxiety re-emerging in their own culture towards the loomingly predictable end of Elizabeth's reign. The play's focus on mob-violence, on the threat of popular rebellion and clashes between rival bourgeois and aristocratic interest groups common to both periods, is a development of material present to the dramatists not simply

1   For Hattaway, Holinshed, the more 'popular' writer, is a more important source than the contrastingly 'official' Hall, and this is significant for what Hattaway sees as the subversive and populist tendency of the three plays (Cam^2, 55–7). I tend towards the more traditional view (as reflected in Bullough) that Hall is the major source, with Holinshed used largely as a quarry for juicy bits about Joan Puzel.

in their chronicle sources but in the oral history and traditions of the part of London in which they worked.

PUZZLING AT JOAN

From chronicle to play

The play reorganizes its major sources to create a dramatic structure spanned by two opposing warriors, Talbot and Jeanne la Pucelle.[1] Events as described in the sources are altered in the play to extend the career of both figures across the span of the English/French conflict, and to make those careers more closely parallel in time. (This edition has adopted 'Joan Puzel' for the character's name from the alternatives offered by F – see Appendix 1 and General Editors' note on it – but the Introduction and commentary use 'Jeanne' when referring to the historical figure, and 'Joan' in reference to texts that use this form. Similarly, though the edition adopts 'Dolphin' as Charles's title, I use 'Dauphin' for the historical figure.) The play assigns battles to Joan Puzel and to Talbot, at the expense of the importance of other commanders. The complex disaster of the Lancastrian loss of France is compressed in the play into a sequence of sieges, first Orleans, then Rouen and then Bordeaux. This action creates a clear structure of spectacular conflict to contain a more confusing strand of the play, the inscrutable, the necessarily various and chaotic depiction of the decline of royal power in England, and the move towards civil war.

1 For Jonathan Bate (Bate, *Genius*, 111) the contrast between Joan and Talbot is a symptom of Shakespeare's theatrical development, a token of his move away from the more monolithic structures of Marlowe. But the authorship controversy makes this hard to support; one would then have to argue that, whatever the evidence of non-Shakespearean authorship of the Joan Puzel material, the plan of the play was Shakespeare's. This is not only impossible to demonstrate, but could be challenged by Greene's interest in 'two-protagonist' structures, as for example the alternating attention paid to Friar Bacon and Margaret in Greene's *Friar Bacon and Friar Bungay*. Emrys Jones (Jones, 14) makes the parallel but more sustainable point that '*1 Henry VI* is almost a copy-book product of this rhetorical method of study. Such a training in the writing of *controversiae*, the devising of situations which could be broken down into a structure of division and opposition . . . [is] essentially . . . antipathetic to the single unchallenged way of looking at things, or to the single hero. Marlowe's *Tamburlaine*, by contrast, invites us – compels us – to contemplate its hero and accept him'.

The struggle between Gloucester and Winchester for power over the infant King, and so for control over the kingdom itself, and then the articulation of Richard's claim to the throne, may seem initially like a kind of puzzling subplot to the more extrovert military action. But as the play develops, and the military action is concluded with the deaths of both Talbot and Joan Puzel, the political action in England emerges with an ominous logic connecting *1 Henry VI* to the other histories.

I note divergences from historical events (as the twentieth century attempts to establish them) in the commentary as they arise, but a chronological table of the historical events indicates the play's manipulation of them:

1422	Death of Henry V.	(–1.1)
1427	Bedford sails to France, with a company including Talbot.	(1.1)
1428	Salisbury besieges Orleans. Jeanne relieves Orleans.	(1.4, 1.5)
1429	Talbot captured at Patay.	(–1.1)
	Henry the Sixth crowned at Westminster.	(1.1+)
1430	Jeanne captured.	(5.2)
1431	Henry crowned in France. Jeanne burned.	(4.1, 5.4+)
1432	Henry returns to England. Peace negotiations at Cambrai.	(5.3)
1435	Bedford dies. Franco–Burgundian treaty.	(3.2, 3.3)
1436	York appointed regent of France.	(4.3)
1439	Somerset appointed 'lieutenant and governor general of the war' (see Appendix 4).	(4.3)
1442	Proposed marriage of Henry to the daughter of Armagnac.	(5.1)
1444	Suffolk in France to arrange the marriage of Henry and Margaret, daughter of Reignier, King of Naples.	(5.2)
1445	Henry and Margaret marry.	(5.4+)
1448	French siege of Le Mans; the English concede Maine to the French.	(*2H6*)

1449 The French take Rouen. Talbot is captured,
      then released.   (3.2, 1.1)
1453 The French recapture Bordeaux. Death of Talbot. (4.4)

So the historical Jeanne's career was over long before Talbot's death, and before the start of York's regency in France. Disaster did not strike England so soon after the death of Henry V, nor was the marriage to Margaret so much the final seal on a set of defeats as an attempt to stave them off. Both Talbot and the English possessions in France survived the marriage by some years. Where the chronicles impose order on the chaos of historical fact in gnomic and sententious formulations of cause and effect, the dramatists shift the sequence of events around, allowing the audience certain interpretative possibilities and placing characters in suggestive contrasts and parallels.

Jeanne la Pucelle/Joan Puzel

The first choice an editor has to make with regard to la Pucelle is how to give her name. The historical figure on whom the character is based always called herself 'Jeanne la Pucelle'. The writers of the Tudor chronicles adopted but also distorted that title. The word *pucelle*, as Marina Warner points out, is powerful in emphasizing both virginity and incipient sexuality, and Warner suggests that Jeanne, always aware of her symbolic and iconographic role, chose it for this reason.

> *Pucelle* means 'virgin,' but in a special way, with distinct shades connoting youth, innocence and, paradoxically, nubility. It is the equivalent of the Hebrew *'almah*, used of both the Virgin Mary and the dancing girls in Solomon's harem in the Bible. It denotes a time of passage, not a permanent condition. It is a word that looks forward to a change of state. In Old French, it was the most common word for a young girl; in Middle French, *damoiselle* began taking over. By Joan's day *vierge* was also sometimes added to *pucelle* to clarify the meaning of

chastity; this shows the underlying ambiguity of the word
. . . It may derive from *pulcra* (beautiful), corrupted into
pulcella, which in Latin was used humorously and affec-
tionately for young girls, or, even more aptly, from *pulla*,
giving *pullicella*, a little animal.

(Warner, 22)

The French verbal ambiguity, of which Warner argues Jeanne was
in control, coarsens in English into a sexual joke. In English,
'pucelle' means virgin, 'puzel' means whore. The two English
words can be used in performance to create a double perspective
on Joan; she can be played as fully aware of her own implicit ambiguity. The BBC Shakespeare production of 1982 illustrates this
well in a sly unscripted look to the camera, at the end of Joan's first
scene, after she has 'won' the Dolphin.

Talbot's punning – 'Puzel or Pussel, Dolphin or dogfish'
(1.4.106) – is crudely xenophobic (for arguments for retaining
F's 'Dolphin' rather than modernizing it as 'Dauphin', see
Appendix 1). But pucelle/puzel is a notably unstable term, persistently teased at in the play. It hardly makes sense to think of
F's play with the word 'pucelle' as punning; it is more like the
exposure of a set of shifting and overlapping connotations gen-
erated from one variously spelt word, and this uncertainty of
naming points to an important aspect of the construction of the
figure of Joan, especially as there is a further pun available in the
puzzle of Joan la Pucelle – on pizzle, an Elizabethan term for
penis. The woman in man's clothes wielding a sword is a pucelle
with a pizzle, and therefore a puzzle. The play expands the figu-
ration implicit in the term to create in one role a summation of
binary categories normally seen as discrete – saint/witch, peas-
ant/gentry, villain/hero, man/woman, virgin/whore.

So the 'puzel' is constructed out of irreconcilable opposites.
She/he cannot be read as a substantive realist character, a unified
subject with a coherent single identity. If she establishes a
subjectivity, it is as performer, as a robustly comic presence,

speaking out to the audience and undercutting the heroic identities conferred on her. The critical controversies surrounding the depiction of Jeanne as Joan Puzel can perhaps be contained if we see the figure of the puzel/pucelle as a kind of optical paradox as well as an embodied word-play, as a trick of point of view, like the anamorphic figure that can be read one way as a young woman, the other as a hag. Shakespeare uses this idea himself when he has Cleopatra say of Antony 'Though he be painted one way like a Gorgon, / The other way's a Mars' (*AC* 2.5.116–17).

Looked at in one way, from the beginning of the play, Puzel is a saint; in another, retrospectively, after we have seen her address her demons in 5.2, she's a witch. She is perceptible in succession as ugly (as a dark-haired, sunburnt peasant) and beautiful (the spiritual 'sun' of the Virgin Mary having had the opposite effect on her to its material counterpart). She rhetorically creates this effect herself. She says, of the Virgin:

> In complete glory she revealed herself.
> And, whereas I was black and swart before,
> With those clear rays which she infused on me,
> That beauty am I blest with, which you may see.
>
> (1.2.83–6)

This moment of rhetorical self-creation seems to reflect and contain the contradictory accounts of the sources (see 1.2.86). However, in presenting this ambiguity as created by the character herself within the stage moment, the dramatists strengthen our sense of her rhetorical power, and of her artful construction of the 'puzzle' of herself.

The puzzle of androgyny

The only picture of Jeanne made in her lifetime (though not drawn from life) emphasizes her femaleness (the most striking aspect of her military career, after all) by endowing her, in profile, with a prominent bosom (Fig. 4).

4 The only likeness of Jeanne made in her lifetime, from the *Chronicle of Paris*; the text reads '*Mardi x^e jour de May, fu rapporté et dit à Paris ... que dimanche dernier passé les gens du dauphin en grant nombre après plusieurs assaulz estoint entrez dedens la bastide que tenoient Guillaume Glasdal et autres capitaines et gens d'armes anglois ... devant la ville d'Orléans...*'

In the play, Joan Puzel's body – in the first performances that of a young male actor in military dress – is constructed both in the language she uses of herself and in that used of her, as insistently female and consistently sexualized. Alençon subverts the sanctity of her initial self-presentation by sexualizing her rhetorical skills: 'These women are shrewd tempters with their tongues' (1.2.123), as he puts it in the scene where she wins over the Dolphin, a scene riddled with *double entendre*. But the play, typically, shifts and shuffles the perspectives it allows. Burgundy's 'Pray God she prove not masculine ere long' (2.1.22) at the start of the scene where she appears to have been caught in bed with the Dolphin (2.1.49ff) draws attention to her ambiguous gender. Joan Puzel and the Dolphin, we are told in F at another point, have been 'iugling'. This has been either modernized as 'juggling' or emended to 'ingling', the second being a specifically homosexual term (see 5.3.68n.).

These semi-comic scenes work like a more raucous version of those moments in *Twelfth Night*, *As You Like It* and *Cymbeline* where the performer's linguistic construction of the feminine is played off, for the first audiences at least, against the visual evidence of a male performer. But Joan Puzel is different from Viola forced to fight a duel, or Rosalind fainting at the sight of Orlando's blood, or Imogen, alone in Wales and forced to imagine defending herself with a sword she herself is frightened of. In the later plays a stereotyped assumption of gender difference (man = strong, woman = weak) is used to create the character's femininity (whatever the gender of the performer), while here the actor has licence to draw on his/her own attributes of athleticism and aggression, and thereby to include them in the construction of the character. In counter-balance to and in contradiction of this, the female body becomes a subversive inside that disrupts the religious and 'martial outside' (*AYL* 1.3.120) with bawdy and grotesque results. In her final scene Joan Puzel shifts rapidly between a set of contradictory claims – that she is a virgin, that she is pregnant – in ways that both focus on and make unknowable a female body created rhetorically by a male actor.

Joan Puzel's very fleshiness provides a focal point for a play of androgyny – as puzzle, danger, threat – which other characters react against, and against which they can be read. Her disruptive equivalent in the English scenes is the Cardinal of Winchester. At one point he is called 'Winchester goose' (1.3.53), a term for the prostitutes who plied their trade in the area around the Rose theatre, and his red robes allow him to be aligned with the 'whore of Babylon' as a 'scarlet hypocrite' (1.3.56). As a bastard, hypocrite, celibate man, he is the representative of a church that is presented by Gloucester as a disruption of the properly virile rule of Henry V. Henry VI is a child king, a virgin and a beardless boy, ageing, historically, from four in his first scene (3.1) to ten at his coronation (4.1), and to twenty-two in the last scene of the play (5.4), when he seems to experience, belatedly, his first stirrings of sexual desire. Michael Hattaway suggests that he was played by a boy actor (Cam[2], 63). Though an adult actor has been used for the role in twentieth-century productions, a boy could originally have played this role (and even conceivably have doubled it with that of Margaret). Margaret emerges directly after Joan's final exit, and so initially may seem like a properly feminine corrective to the disruptive Puzel; but the King's childlikeness and her sexuality are in a dangerous configuration, possibly embodied in the same actor. We cannot be certain that a child was cast here, that an actor in a main role would take on another for one scene or that 'doubling' can necessarily be read as significant. (See Appendix 2.) But if the play ends by reinstating a binary definition of sexual identity it is in a context where doing so bodes badly for the story of Parts *Two* and *Three*.

Another puzzle – saint or witch?

Joan Puzel has a series of one-to-one fights with male figures, each of which raises the question or alters the frame of what she is and what power she represents. She wins over the Dolphin, not by the mysterious and still unexplained secret that the historical Jeanne revealed to her Dauphin, but in a one-to-one combat that ends in at least a metaphoric image of the woman on top.

CHARLES

> Then come, o' God's name. I fear no woman.

JOAN

> And while I live I'll ne'er fly from a man.
> > *Here they fight and Joan Puzel overcomes.*

CHARLES

> Stay, stay thy hands. Thou art an Amazon
> And fightest with the sword of Deborah.

JOAN

> Christ's mother helps me, else I were too weak . . .

CHARLES

> Meantime look gracious on thy prostrate thrall.
>
> > (1.2.102–17)

Typically for the play, an unexpected but important transition in its frame of reference is made in an entertainingly extrovert and active way. Joan Puzel parallels Spenser's female warrior Britomart in the quality of unexpectedness and paradoxical reversal governing her fights, taking their outcome into a puzzling and exciting ambiguity. When Britomart defeats Guyon, Spenser's narrator comments:

> Great shame and sorrow of that fall he tooke;
> > For never yet, sith warlike armes he bore,
> > And shivering speare in bloudie field first shooke,
> > He found himselfe dishonored so sore.
> > Ah gentlest knight, that ever armour bore,
> > Let not thee grieve dismounted to have beene,
> > And brought to ground, that never wast before;
> > For not thy fault, but secret powre unseene,
> That speare enchaunted was, which layd thee on the greene.
>
> > (*FQ*, 3.1.7–15)

The effect of this on Guyon parallels Talbot's reaction to his first fight with Joan Puzel – 'My thoughts are whirled like a potter's wheel' (1.5.19). The action is 'wheeled' round and left facing somewhere else, while it is left uncertain what shape if any the potter's wheel is forming. The woman warrior, particularly when her sex is not definitely known, is an agent of confusion. In Spenser the narrator feels moved to step in to reassure Guyon that his honour has not been lost. In the case of both Joan Puzel and Britomart the confusion is a metaphysical as much as a military matter. Britomart's spear is 'enchaunted'.Though she must be pretty adept simply to wield it, 'enchantment' conveniently allows both participants to maintain their honour – he has not been defeated by superior prowess, and she can be read in terms of the allegorical value of the spear as representing her virtue. Joan Puzel's case is slightly different.

Both women enact the heroic narrative convention of the discovery of a weapon, which confirms the finder's identity and gives them their mission, a mission partly symbolized by what is engraved on it, in Joan Puzel's case the *fleurs-de-lis* (for Britomart see *FQ*, 3.3.60). Unlike Britomart's spear, Joan Puzel's sword, found in St Katherine's churchyard, is not presented as magical. Most productions have presented an athletic, determined Joan, but the emphasis on comedy in the role has fluctuated widely, with, in the recorded versions, Brenda Blethyn's sly complicity with the audience at one extreme (BBC, 1982), and Francesca Ryan's earnest peasant warrior at the other (English Shakespeare Company). The ESC version uses an eerie flute melody to accompany Joan's interventions; her first defeat of Talbot, a cartoon-like Boer War warrior with an eye-patch and a handlebar moustache (Michael Fenner), is a quasi-magical charming of him with her sword, where he collapses without its touching him or its even being offered aggressively, thus emphasizing his fear of her and her instinctive ability to exploit this. Other scenes in the production allow her to defeat her enemies by skill. The historical Jeanne apparently never fought hand-to-hand, and indeed claimed at her trial that she had never killed anyone (Warner, 68); her force, both to her supporters and to her opponents, was largely as a symbol.

The re-creation of Jeanne la Pucelle as magical, earthy and witch-like is one of the major reasons why the play, if read as a libellous representation of a real historical person, known since 1920 as Saint Joan (Tillyard, 162), enjoys an uneasy position on the edge of the Shakespeare canon. From Joan Puzel's first entrance the play establishes a conflict of 'readings' of Jeanne; it is the English, largely Talbot, who name her unequivocally as a witch. The appearance of the demons (5.2.28.1) when Joan Puzel summons and interrogates them at the point of her defeat can seem disappointing to a modern audience in its apparent reductiveness, by suggesting that Talbot was right all along.

Michael Hattaway follows A.W. Schlegel in reading this and the scene after her capture as stages in a progressive psychological deterioration (Cam², 24–5; for Schlegel, see Bate, *Romantics*, 366–7). In a performance that took the stage directions literally the demons would be physically there, in the material world of the play, and would express themselves in appealingly graphic gesture. The ESC production avoided the problem by rewriting the lines (5.2.29–44) as an invocation to Mary (see Appendix 3, p. 317), but the inclusion of 'I'll lop a member off' (5.2.36) presents the Virgin in a somewhat unorthodox light. In the Royal Shakespeare Company's full-text performance (1977–8) several shadowy hooded figures appeared at the back and sides of the stage while Joan, spotlit, addressed her lines to the auditorium. In the same company's *The Plantagenets* (1988–9) the dead soldiers rose slowly to sitting position, as the demons 'possessed' them, and then, as Joan's power waned, the corpses fell back, as the demons abandoned them to death again. One of the most startling of the classical sources for Renaissance depictions of magic, Lucan's *Pharsalia*, has the witch Erichtho animate corpses on the battlefield, in order to gain prophetic information from demons speaking through their mouths (Lucan, 6.619–825). This intelligent working of the scene, like the demons' names that Joan shouted out to a crucifix-wielding English private in an onstage burning, flamboyantly supplemented what was otherwise a one-dimensionally hearty reading of the role.

There is nothing in F to suggest that the demons can simply be seen as external manifestations of an internal conflict, as one can, for example, see the good and bad angels in *Dr Faustus*. But Joan Puzel's invocation of them is private, observed only by us, the audience, and in this it is generically unconventional. That she has no witnesses but the audience keeps open the possibility of staging the scene as psychological allegory. The painting of Joan on the battlefield that the eighteenth-century entrepreneur John Boydell commissioned from William Hamilton for his 'Shakespeare Gallery' shows a decorously skirted and incongruously Britannia-like Joan, with figures, called 'Furies' in the original picture title, painted as if they were a kind of storm-cloud, both emanating from and supporting her (Fig. 5).

In this way the moment is transposed from the medieval to the classical, from a Christian demonology to a post-Cartesian psychology of 'the passions', where the demons can be presented as graphic expressions of Joan's emotions of anger and fear.[1] The BBC television presentation of part of the play in its *Age of Kings* series (see Appendix 3) negotiates this brilliantly by focusing in on Joan's (Eileen Atkins's) eyes, while a white-clad female 'demon' (who may equally well be Joan's inner, more vulnerable, or at least more identifiably feminine, self) dances in identical image in both her pupils. This interpretation uses the resources of an early development of televisual style to create a conceptual space in which the ambiguities of the scene can be kept open.

The later BBC version of a nearly complete text (1982) has a brightly lit Joan on her knees addressing the camera, in the middle of a battle staged semi-comically in what looks, typically for this production, like a school gym – right down to the parquet floor, which Joan, the admirably comic and energetic

1 George Romney is recorded as having painted Emma Hamilton, the mistress of Admiral Nelson, '*in the Character of the Maid of Orleans*', as a companion piece to his portrait of her as Cassandra, both for Boydell's Shakespeare Gallery. Nothing more is known of the picture; perhaps, while the linking of the classical and the Christian prophetesses is interesting, the choice of model was felt to be inappropriate (Friedman, 134–5).

Painted by Willm Hamilton, R.A.

First Part of
KING HENRY VI.
Act 5, Scene 4.
Joan la Pucelle & Fiends.

Engraved by Anker Smith.

Published Jany 1 1795 by J.& J. Boydell Shakspeare Gallery Pall Mall & N.º 90 Cheapside London.

5 'Joan la Pucelle and Fiends', from John Boydell's *Graphic Illustrations of the Dramatic Works of Shakespeare* (1803)

Brenda Blethyn, has to scrabble at as she summons the demons from under the earth.

Magic and history: women and men, words and bodies

To ask whether Jeanne is fairly represented as Joan Puzel begins to seem self-evidently cranky when we imagine asking the same question about Richard III or Macbeth. Perhaps embarrassment at the play's presentation of Joan Puzel is a kind of critical refuge from a larger embarrassment – what is magic doing in this and other Elizabethan history plays anyway? Shakespeare and his colleagues at the time of writing this play are working from an idea of history which includes legend, fable and the supernatural. The genre of the history play does not obey the imperative to realism that it might later. For the Elizabethans, history, legend and magic were not so strictly defined in opposition to each other as they were for a literate early seventeenth-century playgoer – the readership of F, for example, to whose compilers *Cymbeline* may have presented a problem of classification such that it ended up among the tragedies. The Elizabethan viewpoint isn't the result of the unthinking inheritance of a jumble of beliefs. *1 Henry VI*, by its openness to different ways of telling historical tales, is enabled to juxtapose versions of events and ways of reading them. Joan Puzel exposes some of the fault-lines in the Tudor narrative of history. She disrupts the whole idea of historical representation at a very basic level, so that the issue is not that of the particular truth to history but the larger question of what historical truth is, and who has power to determine it.

The play is informed by a clash between two readings of events – broadly describable as French/Catholic/Magical/ Female and English/Protestant/Rational/ Male. From the perspective of the second grouping, anything unexpected has to be described as magic, as in the opening scene: 'shall we think the subtle-witted French / Conjurers and sorcerers, that, afraid of him, / By magic verses have contrived his end?' (1.1.25–7).

When a woman is involved, this is called witchcraft. In the *Henry VI* plays and *Richard III*, magical knowledge is associated with women; purposeful but unthinking (and seldom constructive) action with men. Joan Puzel combines the two readings of events. She and her demons emerge as markers of another kind of history, to be set against the heroic patrilinear narrative which Talbot seeks to affirm.[1] It is part of her force in the play, a centrality created by an ahistorical manipulation of the sequence of events, that with the death of Henry V the heroic myth has failed the English anyway. Her success is to some extent a symptom of that failure. Talbot's rhetoric enforces on the play a structure of heroic deeds commemorated in fame, as a pattern of history that survives and binds together individual mortalities. But Joan

---

1 Feminist and cultural criticism of the 1970s established Joan, and the implicit contrast between 'her' and the male figures, as the central interest of the play, the dramatization of a cultural myth of gender conflict. I put 'her' in inverted commas, but in many such readings Joan represents the female in an uncomplicated way. For Marilyn French, for example: 'The subsurface, "mythic" war waged in this play is a war against women, identified with sexuality: it is a war against the outlaw feminine principle' (French, 47). Leslie Fiedler makes a parallel point: 'Talbot is a provincial hero and Joan a universal myth, a figure of inexhaustible archetypal resonance. Even inside the play he cannot touch her; they exist, as it were, in different dimensions, and she fades from his solidity like a dream' (Fiedler, 58). Most of the interesting writing on this play has focused on this contrast, but with different interpretations of both its complicity in misogyny and the nature of gender division. Coppélia Kahn, for example, says of David M. Bevington's study of the play (Bevington, 51–9): 'He appears to accept the traditional categories of male and female roles at face value, whereas I see them as projections of male anxieties, consciously presented as such by Shakespeare' (Kahn, 55, 11n.). Kahn identifies the importance in the play of masculine identity as defined by father-son relations; Joan instances the opposite of this, not only in her femaleness, but in her final rejection of her own father (Kahn, 47–56). But Gabriele Bernhard Jackson calls Kahn's position (as quoted here) 'surely counsel of desperation'; her own detailed historicist presentation of the continuity between the idea of the witch and the idea of the Amazon in the context of Joan's presentation concludes that the play 'locates itself in areas of ideological discomfort' (Jackson, 47, 65). Phyllis Rackin and Jean E. Howard have more recently developed an account of the history plays in terms of their formation of an idea of nationhood out of these kinds of gender division and sexual anxiety (Howard & Rackin, 47–64). It is disappointing to see a recent, self-consciously conservative, account of Shakespeare's career by Harold Bloom reinstating the earlier view that the Talbot/Joan opposition is basically the crude jingoism of an inept and dispensable play, listed in that volume's chronology as, at 1589, Shakespeare's first. But even in this reading Joan emerges at the centre of the play's interest, if at the cost to plausibility of being described as Shakespeare's creation, and a precursor of Falstaff (Bloom, 44–6). The Falstaff comparison had been made earlier by Edward Berry (Berry, 20).

Puzel's doubleness, her outsider status and her powers of illicit knowledge can re-weave or tear the rhetorical fabric of history.

The contrast between an ageing injured male figure and a magical untrustworthy female figure, embodied primarily in Talbot and Joan Puzel, is amplified through other characters. The basic opposition can be traced back to Ovid, where, in *Metamorphoses*, 7, Medea is contrasted not so much to Jason as to Aeson, his father, and to Pelias, another old king, whose daughters she tricks into killing him. Golding, in moralizing the tale in his epistle, skirts Ovid's emotional empathy with Medea, to present it thus:

> The good successe of Jason in the land of Colchos, and
> The dooings of Medea since, doo give too understand
> That nothing is so hard but peyne and travel doo it win,
> For fortune ever favoreth such as boldly doo begin:
> That women both in helping and in hurting have no match
> When they too eyther bend their wits . . .
>   Also there is warning given of this,
> That men should never hastely give eare too fugitives,
> Nor into handes of sorcerers commit their states or lyves.
>   (Golding, *Epistle*, 143–54)

The female sorcerer represents a different idea of historical continuity from that represented by the purposive, forward-moving male warrior or the aged patriarch – she has access to a knowledge of past, present and future, and to a powerful language in which to activate that knowledge, scrambling or reworking the pattern of action in a way that her opponents see as a kind of cheating. We learn from the demon scene (5.2) that magic helps Joan Puzel 'cheat' by allowing her to know what will happen next. The demons don't, however, give her their strength and influence when she asks for it. She asks 'this once', emphasizing that this is a unique and exceptional request; they still refuse her. Magic is a dramatic expression of the anxiety of those within a historical moment, of the magician and of those who consult him or her.

Male heroic figures on the other hand represent the continuity of heroic history; they are both its progenitors and its memorials. A repeated visual motif in the play is the isolation on stage of a male figure who reminds us in his physical state of a history that is, literally, marked on him. The dying Mortimer is one example, and, though the emphasis on his captivity and the physical disability caused by it is the dramatists' own, the intense focus on the body and on Mortimer's compromised and limited movement renders an essentially static scene powerfully physical, and instates the male body as the primary witness of historical narrative.

MORTIMER

> Direct mine arms – I may embrace his neck,
> And in his bosom spend my latter gasp.
> O tell me when my lips do touch his cheeks,
> That I may kindly give one fainting kiss.
> And now declare, sweet stem from York's great stock,
> Why didst thou say of late thou wert despised?

RICHARD

> First, lean thine aged back against mine arm,
> And in that ease I'll tell thee my disease.

> > (2.5.37–44)

The grotesque details of Salisbury's wounding (1.4.68SD–93) and, later (3.2.39.1–54), the display of the sick Bedford embody wounded English integrity, challenging whatever French town is under siege. Behind this may lie the opening image of the play, the dead King's hearse. These figures enact the spectacle that Coriolanus so wished to avoid – to be seen and read as a piece of heroic history, not as an individual but as the summation of one's deeds (*Cor* 2.1.146–56) – but they are also emblems of the obsolescence of English power.

Talbot's initial reaction to Joan Puzel is a reassertion of power from within his body, hyperbolically made at the expense of that body's fabric:

> Heavens, can you suffer hell so to prevail?
> My breast I'll burst with straining of my courage
> And from my shoulders crack my arms asunder,
> But I will chastise this high-minded strumpet.
> *They fight again.*

$$(1.5.9–12)$$

That this masculine self-assertion carries with it a kind of pathos is part of the play's sense that history cannot be operated in so simply. Magic, riddles and puzzles are an intrinsic part of its structure. Scene by scene and in the historiography that the play constructs over all, the rhetoric and action are shaped by the presentation and solution of riddles, the reading of puzzling and dangerous signs, the making and answering, normally the ironical answering, of invocations. The play's opening invocation of heavenly forces is to be answered, not by heavenly rescue, but by news of the failure of the English forces (1.1), just as Joan Puzel's invocation of hellish forces, at the point of her defeat, is to be met by the silent and unhelpful demons (5.2). Talbot and the Countess of Auvergne (2.3) are riddles, puzzles to each other, the riddle solved by Talbot's invocation of his men – ironic, again, but for once successful on the English side. Other crucial scenes – Richard discovering his own history in the scene with the dying Mortimer (2.5), the devising of the red and white roses as a symbol to be read politically (2.4) or, fatally in the young Henry's case, treated as meaningless (4.1.152–4) – and almost all the crucial encounters between characters turn on the making and undoing of riddles: who? why? what? when? History is, to those living it, a riddle to be untied. Magic seems to offer a solution, as both a way of operating on the present and a way of formulating the riddle of past and future.

The Puzel of fame: Jeanne and the court of Burgundy

Marina Warner points out that it was the transcripts of Jeanne's trial that established her voice and shaped for the nineteenth and twentieth century a sense of her mystifying but unquestionable saintly integrity (Warner, 5). But these documents only became available in print in the 1840s. Before that a French explorer of the legend, let alone an English one, would be struck by the contradictoriness and multiplicity of roles assigned to the historical figure. Jeanne's trial as a heretic and subsequent burning at the stake in 1431 was followed in 1456 by a successful tribunal, instigated by the French, to reinstate her as a heroine.

This in itself creates the ambiguity of her subsequent fame. The authors of *1 Henry VI*, ignorant of the details of the trial, present a simple picture. George Bernard Shaw, in a play written in 1923, three years after Jeanne's canonization, developed the voice that we find in the transcripts. Carl Dreyer's famous silent film, *La Passion de Jeanne D'Arc* (1928), establishes Jeanne's integrity with equal power by the actress Falconetti's gaze. But in the Elizabethan play we have Joan Puzel at her most cacophonous and devious, dragged from the battlefield to an improvised *auto-da-fé*. By this stage in the play all the issues raised by trial and revisionist tribunal have been played out by other means. Jeanne's canonization in 1920, after beatification in 1909, was at least partly the outcome of her long-delayed elevation to national symbol – a role that, supplanting St Denis, the Dolphin offers her in the play (1.5.67–8). It could not have happened, or at least the demand for it could not, if the transcripts had not been available, and if a sense of French national identity was not reasserting itself, within the uneasy relation between the Church and the Republic:

Both the beatification and the canonisation were responses to pressure from groups like the Action Française who wished the Vatican to make a firm stand against the rapid secularisation of France and the spread of unbelief in the Christian world in general. Yet at the same time, Joan was once more a figure who bridged division: the French Catholics who, at Leo XIII's suggestion, adopted the

> pragmatic solution of *le Ralliement*, and recognised the
> Republic as the *de facto* government of France and thus
> accepted the idea of working with it, saw in Joan a symbol
> that Church and state could work together.
>
> (Warner, 264)

Jeanne's role as an embodiment of French nationalism obscures the fact that France as we now know it did not exist as a nation when Jeanne was alive. It is a sign of how far the nationalist politics of both France and England have obscured our sense of this history that readers and directors tend (especially in productions of *Henry V*) to see Burgundy as just another French noble, while the films on the topic – including the most recent at the time of writing, the long and in almost every other respect historically scrupulous *Jeanne la Pucelle* (Jacques Rivette, 1994) – leave the Burgundians unidentified, in the interest of a more simply nationalistic Anglo-French conflict. An exception here is the ESC's adaptation of the play, which reassigned (and even invented) lines to build up the character of Burgundy, creating a soliloquy to prepare for his change of sides. (See Appendix 3.) Historically, according to Huizinga, 'the court of the dukes of Burgundy . . . was more pompous and better arranged than that of the kings of France . . . A splendid court could, better than anything else, convince rivals of the high rank the dukes claimed to occupy among the princes of Europe . . . It was boasted that the Burgundian court was the richest and best regulated of all' (Huizinga, 39). The trial of Jeanne is in itself testimony to the Burgundian court's sense of itself.

That the politics of the historical alliance were still alive for Shakespeare is shown in the shift of sympathies for the 'Burgundy' figure between the Elizabethan histories and *King Lear*. In the latter, Burgundy – mocked twice by Lear's references to the wine associated with the area, first when he assigns 'the vines' to France and the less manly 'milk' to Burgundy, then when he characterizes Burgundy as 'waterish' (*KL* 1.1. 84, 260) – is less perceptive than France in his estimate of Cordelia's quality. *King Lear* is a Jacobean play, written after the accession to the English throne of the Scottish King James VI. France was the Scots' traditional ally, as Burgundy was of England. In the Elizabethan plays, the Burgundy figures are dignified and shrewd. In *Henry V* Burgundy is presented as the reconciler of the English and the Valois, and allowed both a serious presentation of the state of war-torn France and a joking complicity with Henry in his wooing of Katherine (*H5* 5.2.278–312). F's text of *1 Henry VI* unhistorically keeps Burgundy on the French side until the end of the action (see 5.2.50.1n.) He is dramatically a more substantial figure than the Valois and Angevin French, his side-changing a token of independence.

Huizinga in *The Waning of the Middle Ages* – a title that would fit this play well – describes a kind of cultural anxiety, operating across the interlinked courts of western Europe in the mid-fifteenth century. The Burgundian court of that period parallelled the later Tudor court in its investment in propaganda and chronicle, and in its maintenance of power through the conspicuous display of wealth. Hall used Burgundian sources, and so the myth of one court informs another. Both courts try to find a place for themselves in 'history'; hence their commitment to chronicle, which lies behind the existence of this set of plays. For both courts the ideas of fame and of the heroic are a characteristic concern, and *1 Henry VI* creatively extrapolates from its sources to develop concerns common to its own period and to that it depicts.

Jeanne and the female worthies, Talbot and the male

Huizinga points out that 'The life of a knight is an imitation; that of princes is so too, sometimes' (Huizinga, 69). In this play characters continually place themselves, or are placed by others, in relation to famous forebears. For both the Burgundian court and the late Elizabethan, a certain anxiety about history shows itself in a codification of patterns of individual fame in the figures of 'the nine worthies'. The cult of the nine worthies (or, given its French origins, *les neuf preux*) 'is found for the first time in a work of the beginning of the fourteenth century, *Les Voeux du Paon*, by Jacques de Longuyon . . . there are Hector, Caesar, Alexander, Joshua, David, Judas Maccabaeus, Arthur, Charlemagne, Godfrey of Bouillon' (Huizinga, 69–70). They represent heroism and its can-onization in human memory through 'fame'; not only were they represented in texts, frescos and tapestries at the Burgundian and other French courts, but they formed a masque at Henry VI's coro-nation: 'On the occasion of his entry into Paris . . . the English king . . . is preceded by all the eighteen worthies of both sexes' (Huizinga, 70).

The first three figures, in both genders' lists, are classical, the next from the Old Testament, the last three Christian. The lists are not completely stable – substitutions can occur, particularly, for nationalistic reasons, within the last three, and lists of the classical heroes can also include Pompey the Great, Theseus and Hercules. When in *Love's Labour's Lost* Shakespeare has the schoolmaster Holofernes, the curate Nathaniel, the page Moth, the peasant Costard and the verbose Spanish courtier, Armado, present a curtailed and awkward masque of the worthies to the courts of the King of Navarre and the French Princess, they demonstrate the distance between the heroic world and the mundane world that all the characters must learn to accept and inhabit; unwittingly at first, but with a certain pathos for at least Armado, who impersonates Hector: 'The sweet war-man is dead and rotten . . . beat not the bones of the buried. When he breathed, he was a man' (*LLL* 5.2.657–9). 'Fame, that all hunt after in their lives' is invoked by the King of Navarre in the first lines of the play as a conquering of death, in his case by study, but the play finds this unworkable, not least in the appearance of Marcadé, the messenger of the French King's death, at the end of a 'masque' already interrupted by the contradictorily benign but equally deflating news that Armado has fathered a child. 'Worthies, away', as Berowne puts it, 'The scene begins to cloud' (*LLL* 5.2.716). In *1 Henry VI* the schema of the worthies can again be seen to fall athwart the action and characters of the play. The Countess of Auvergne's identification of Talbot with Hector initially backfires when she fails to be impressed by his physical stature, but it is undercut, and the whole tradition implicitly ironized, by his knowledge of what his heroism ultimately consists in: the strength of the English army and its loyalty to him (2.3). Individual heroism is a myth, if a strategically necessary one, and his awareness of this makes Talbot closer to the audience.

The French in this play are characteristically more flamboyant and less thoughtful in drawing on *les neuf preux*. In the case of the female worthies, as with the male group, the Old Testament figures are more stable, tending to be any three of Esther, Judith, Deborah or Jael. The classical selection could include Tomyris, Artemisia, Semiramis, Lucretia, Virginia and the Amazons Hippolyta and Penthesilea; the Christians, Saints Helena, Brigid and Elizabeth. Jeanne herself was either seen as surpassing these – and the classical figures, at least, among the male group – or included as one of them. Holinshed points out that in the tribunal to reinstate her she was 'likened to Debora, Iahell, and Iudith' (Holinshed, 3.172). In the first poem written about Jeanne, Christine de Pisan's *Ditié de Jehanne D'Arc* (1429), she is described as superior to both male and female worthies, surpassing Joshua, Gideon, Esther, Judith, Deborah, Achilles and Hector (*Ditié*, st.25–8, 36). In *1 Henry VI*, she is compared to several of these figures, and the Countess of Auvergne compares herself to another, Tomyris (2.3.6). Margaret, Henry VI's queen, was to join the ranks of the female worthies in the seventeenth century; her management of a weak husband put her there. Perhaps *2* and *3 Henry VI* helped establish this image (Wright, 628–43).

The Dolphin expresses his admiration for Joan Puzel in a series of apparently unrelated types, a confusion of Christian, Old Testament and classical:

> Stay, stay thy hands. Thou art an Amazon
> And fightest with the sword of Deborah.
>
> (1.2.104–5)

> Helen, the mother of great Constantine,
> Nor yet Saint Philip's daughters were like thee.
> Bright star of Venus, fallen down on the earth,
> How may I reverently worship thee enough?
>
> (1.2.142–5)

Rather than confirming our sense of Joan Puzel's heroic stature, this unthinking heroic rhetoric inevitably sets itself up for farcical undercutting by reversals in the action, and sceptical comment from other characters. It undermines the tradition, especially in contrast to Talbot's awareness of heroism's limits. Instead of instating her in a heroic pantheon, it points to the confusion that the figure of Jeanne/Joan Puzel introduces into the whole business of heroic historiography.

Joan Puzel and the miraculous body of Mary

The rhetoric Puzel uses of herself is biblical rather than historical, and refers persistently to the Catholic doctrines associated with the Virgin Mary. To fend off her sentence of death she uses a language which combines a primal sense of the female body with a religious language of the transcendent body, derived from the cult of Mary.

> No – misconceived, Joan of Aire hath been
> A virgin from her tender infancy,
> Chaste and immaculate in very thought,
> Whose maiden-blood, thus rigorously effused,
> Will cry for vengeance at the gates of heaven.
>
> (5.3.49–53)

A little later she claims she is pregnant. In her case this is a contradiction, but in Mary's, according to the Catholic doctrine, virginity and pregnancy are miraculously non-contradictory. When Joan Puzel uses the phrase 'the fruit within my womb' (5.3.63) to describe her pregnancy, she makes explicit reference, by echoing Elizabeth's words to Mary, to one of the linchpin doctrines of the Catholic cult of the Virgin, a cult particularly powerful in both France and England at the time of the historical Jeanne, and a central target for Protestant English attacks on Catholicism in the Tudor period (see 5.3.63n.). Joan Puzel and her connection with the miraculous are presented as duplicitous, and so, by extension, are the Catholic doctrines to which she alludes, and which in dramatic terms she 'stands in for'. Talbot's rhetoric is correspondingly Protestant. His biblical references are all from the Old Testament (a source less fully used by Catholics) and speak of stoicism and individual faith. The main figure Talbot is aligned with is Samson, the exemplar of a man who defends his country and suffers for it through individual faith and effort. Historically, of course, Talbot was as Catholic as Jeanne. But for an Elizabethan Protestant audience the play's use of religious sources strikes a recognizably bellicose note, to direct and maintain the sympathies of an audience whose contemporary experience of war would be as Protestants opposed to Catholics, whether Irish, Spanish or French.

In this context opposed interpretations of events exhibit an opposed sense of what meaning is. Joan Puzel, in however burlesque a form she may be presented, dramatizes the possibility of a world-view in which the divine or the demoniacal can directly intervene in the mundane and so, in overriding the physical, validate her aspiration and the French cause. For Talbot this is a nonsense. Conversely, the English commanders of Jeanne's own time were brutally straightforward in accounting for her powers. Warner quotes Bedford as referring, in a report to the government of London in 1433, to 'a disciple and limb of the Fiend, called the Pucelle, that used false enchantment and sorcery' (Warner, 111). Talbot has more the mentality of an Elizabethan rationalist; nonetheless, he refers to Joan as a witch, indicating some significant insecurity in his rational stance. (The audience presumably shares his uncertainty at least until the fiends appear to Joan at 5.2.28.1.) Reginald Scot in the *Discovery of Witchcraft* (1584) demonstrates a robust rational refusal to allow for the magical or miraculous, and so condemns the persecution of witches as both ludicrous and unjust. In suggesting, but not insisting, that Joan Puzel is a witch, Talbot's position is somewhere between that of a humane Protestant sceptic like Scot and the panic of those magistrate witch-hunters whom Scot wrote his book to oppose and who required the notion of witchcraft to validate and demonstrate their own authority.[1] When Talbot proposes that drawing blood from Joan Puzel would be a way of defeating her were she a witch (1.5.6–7) it shows, at an early moment, how his rationalism is vulnerable to current superstition.

SHADOW AND SUBSTANCE

Heraldic beasts and the human animal

The characters' attempts to explain events to themselves and to each other draw often on analogy to animals and to hunting. Such

---

1 A recent study by Deborah Willis places the Joan figure in the context of the Elizabethan witch-hunts, making the interesting point that the apparently farcical idea of Joan's pregnancy links her into a nexus of social and psychological forces, focusing on motherhood, which seem to have lain behind the small-scale local persecutions (Willis, 100–1). Kurt Tetzeli von Rosador places the play, and others by Shakespeare and other dramatists which deal with magic, in the context of a crisis of 'royal charisma' and the Catholic threat, and sees Joan as an embodiment of fears signalled at the very opening of the play (Rosador, 'Magic', 8–9). Rosador expands this argument in an article that appeared slightly later, relating the play to Greene's *Friar Bacon and Friar Bungay*, and expanding on the Marian context (Rosador, 'Sacralizing', 37–45). Richard Hardin, in what is basically a thorough and alert investigation of the sources, presents both the anti-chivalric and the Catholic aspects of Joan's magic, as does John D. Cox, relating the play to Marlowe's *Dr Faustus* (Cox, 57–64). Hardin ends by placing his account in the context of the anthropological interpretation of the scapegoat, drawing on Fiedler (Hardin, 32–5); Fiedler himself claims that the play's apparent vilification of Joan imaginatively reinstates the historical Jeanne's participation in 'the underground cult of the Great Goddess . . . the ancient rites of the mother' (Fiedler, 62–3). This academically unfashionable linking of witchcraft to the existence of a suppressed pan-European woman-centred cult has been re-argued more recently by Carlo Ginzburg (Ginzburg, 1989, trans. 1992).

analogies are continuous with the symbolic practices of the late Middle Ages – heraldry, hunting narratives, beast fable. Like historical and biblical typology, these are ways of thinking about the meaning and value of human action in a context where the end of that action – and so its value as determined by degrees of success or failure – cannot be immediately obvious in itself.

References to animals crowd into Talbot's reaction to his first defeat by Joan Puzel, to fill the vacuum of his incomprehension:

> So bees with smoke and doves with noisome stench
> Are from their hives and houses driven away.
> They called us, for our fierceness, English dogs;
> Now like to whelps we crying run away.
> *A short alarum.*
> Hark, countrymen – either renew the fight
> Or tear the lions out of England's coat.
> Renounce your soil, give sheep in lions' stead;
> Sheep run not half so treacherous from the wolf,
> Or horse or oxen from the leopard,
> As you fly from your oft-subdued slaves.
> *Alarum. Here another skirmish [in which the English*
> *attempt to enter Orleans].*
>
> (1.5.23–32)

Proverbial wisdom about the behaviour of animals, as codified in medieval or Renaissance bestiaries, is used in both periods as a measure of human behaviour. Talbot's examples here seem to create a sense of confusion: first the English are harmless (doves) or useful and industrious (bees) and the French are an unpleasant, inanimate and guilefully used force, like smoke or bad smells. Then the French identification of the English as dogs leads Talbot into trying to rally his soldiers, his hunting dogs. They do not fulfil what is expected of them, and the heraldic idea of the lion from England's shield is called in as a bitterly ironic contrast to the 'sheep' that the men, presumably in blindly following each other in flight, have become. The loyalty of a hunting dog to a careful master is the desired model of obedience here. The Talbot family were associated with a particular type of dog, known for its loyalty and its hunting instincts, to which they gave their name. (Whether it could strictly be called a breed in the modern sense is debatable. In any case, it is not extant as a breed today.) The frontispiece of a manuscript collection of French romances presented by Talbot to Margaret of Anjou shows him with a 'Talbot' dog at his side (Fig. 6).

If a dog is associated with 'Englishness' it is to evoke and to nationalize the bestiaries' association of the dog with fidelity, and so to underline Talbot's own 'dogged' courage. The logic breaks down when he calls the sheep's flight 'treacherous'. Treachery is an exclusively human attribute. Here Talbot calls his men worse than beasts. The taunting challenge to the English soldiers is to stand and fight, and thus to prove that they are not naturally inferior to the French.

In later scenes the battles are still imaged as a hunt; the English, however, are no longer now the hunters, but the hunted:

> O negligent and heedless discipline –
> How are we parked and bounded in a pale –
> A little herd of England's timorous deer
> Mazed with a yelping kennel of French curs.
> If we be English deer, be then in blood:
> Not rascal-like to fall down with a pinch,
> But rather, moody-mad and desperate stags,
> Turn on the bloody hounds with heads of steel
> And make the cowards stand aloof at bay.
> Sell every man his life as dear as mine
> And they shall find dear deer of us, my friends.
>
> (4.2.44–54)

A mixture of heraldic and zoological associations provides Talbot with his conceptual clue to the maze of the French battle action, a means to reduce it to a more manageable set of associations than those of the heroic tradition or of magic. Talbot initially invokes beast analogy in a confused and derisive expression of his own

50

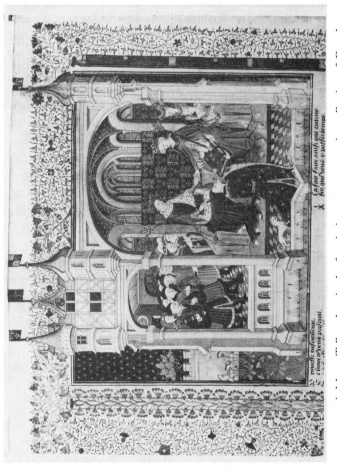

6 Talbot shown accompanied by a Talbot dog, in the frontispiece to a manuscript collection of French romances which he presented to Margaret of Anjou

sense of defeat; but it becomes the vehicle, when that defeat finally faces him, of the pathos of his recognition that battle is a ritualized destruction, like the killing of hemmed-in deer, and that the values of loyalty and contained aggression which his military project shares with the hunt must be finally played out as persistence in the face of overwhelming odds. This, in the end, is a more truthful image of his situation in the present than that provided by analogy to a historical past.

Family trees

The action of *1 Henry VI* has its source in individual characters' sense of genealogy; conflicts between characters are shaped by the transmission of rights and titles across complex family relationships. Instead of providing a large-scale family tree in an appendix, in the ensuing section I embed stages of a tree diagram into an explanatory account of the relationships involved and of their significance for this play.

The 'tree' as metaphor: the claim to the throne of France

The English claim to the French throne, based on the assertion that it could be inherited through the female line, can be represented diagrammatically. By surviving her brothers, Isabella – according to

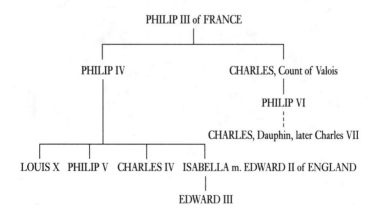

the English – inherits the French throne as the daughter of Philip IV, despite the survival of a son of Philip's younger brother Charles. The anonymous play *Edward III* (1596) uses the 'tree/flower' trope to establish Edward's claim to the French throne:

> only Isabel
> Was all the daughters that this Philip had,
> Whom afterward your father took to wife;
> And from the fragrant garden of her womb
> Your gracious self, the flower of Europe's hope,
> Derived is inheritor to France.
>
> (*E3* 1.1.11–16)

Isabel's womb is a sacralized point of origin, and 'the flower of Europe's hope' suggests that Edward is the natural efflorescence of a communally held wish. The garden/womb metaphor dignifies the idea of female succession – on which the English claim to the French throne depends – to protect it from misogynist readings from both sides, and perhaps also from reflections on the career of Isabel herself, as presented in Marlowe's *Edward II*. Later on in the scene, this 'counsel' has a natural, vegetal, effect on Edward's resolution: 'like to fruitful showers' it 'Hath added growth unto my dignity' (*E3* 1.1.42–3). The same issue is more laboriously presented in the second scene of *Henry V* (1.2.4–114).

The 'family tree', as a visual and verbal metaphor, is more than simply a graphic convenience. Metaphors of growth, of organic wholeness and interrelatedness organize it and condition our response to what it presents. Its origin is medieval, its sources biblical. At the beginning of the first book of Chronicles in the Old Testament lines of descent and genealogy are laid out, in ways that are used later (in relation to the New Testament) to show that Jesus comes from the 'line' of David, originating in the ancestor Jesse. The metaphor of the 'tree' is not present in the biblical text, but later visual representations of this 'line' in stained-glass windows or manuscript illuminations or pageants organize the lines of descent into the 'Jesse tree', an out-branching tree with portraits of individuals at points where, in terms of the growing dynasty, they spring from and/or feed back into its growth. One such accompanied the historical Henry VI in his triumphal entry into the City of London after his coronation in Paris.[1]

The strain of accommodating the actual complexities of medieval dynastic politics to the 'tree' model shows in what we are familiar with as 'the family tree' when it tries to accommodate in a single visual image the dynastic action of a history play. The conventional rendering of dynastic politics in a single family tree (familiar from editions of Shakespeare's histories) may clarify family relations for the modern reader; but the very certainties of the image work to obscure the fact that in the plays competing genealogies are put into the mouths of characters claiming titles that are in dispute. Even with issues of legitimacy simplified and marriages dealt with summarily, several such trees are needed to accommodate the relationships depicted and alluded to in a single text, and the reader is left mentally to superimpose one pattern on another. Some kind of three-dimensional model would probably be more adequate, but then again simplification, for political purposes, is the point of the exercise. An architectural or game-based metaphor, like Gothic vaulting or chess, would when visualized have more room for the facts of the shape of a medieval dynasty and its evolution, but it would not carry the same connotations of natural legitimacy; it would have a nasty taint of human fabrication about it. Mary Midgeley accounts for the attractiveness of the tree idea by comparing it to other vegetal organizations – the strawberry plant is her example – to point out how the tree introduces ideas of height and lowness, which morally and socially inflect it (Midgeley, 158).

---

1 Part of the attraction of the 'Jesse tree' as a visual presentation of genealogy is that the 'root', the origin of the line – Edward III, or whoever – is represented at the top, the apex of the diagram, and so presides over and validates what happens 'below' it. For discussion of the Jesse tree at Henry's entrance into the City, see Ormrod, 100–1, and Osberg, 213–32.

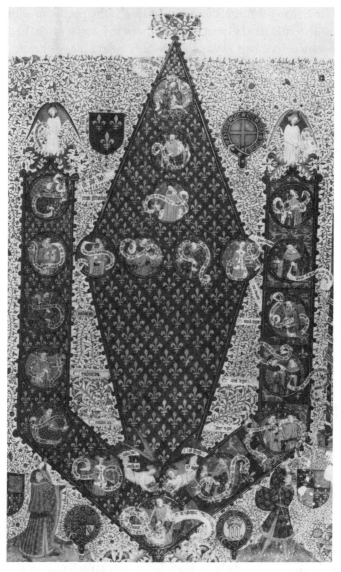

7 The tree of succession represented as a *fleur-de-lis* in an illustrated manuscript presented by the Talbot family to Margaret of Anjou

In *1 Henry VI*, the French claimants to the throne base their case on a rule that women cannot inherit in France while there is a possible male heir, so a king's brother would inherit before his daughter, and the descendants of Charles, Count of Valois (represented in this play by his great-great-great grandson the Dolphin) are the true royal line (see p. 52). The English argument is the more tortuous one, presented with almost parodic inelegance in *Henry V*, contending that this rule, the 'Salic law', applies not to France but to a certain part of Germany:

> *In terram Salicam mulieres ne succedant,*
> 'No woman shall succeed in Salic land':
> Which Salic land the French unjustly gloze
> To be the realm of France, and Pharamond
> The founder of this law and female bar.
> Yet their own authors faithfully affirm
> That the land Salic is in Germany.
>
> (*H5* 1.2.38–44)

The 'tree/growth' idea makes a claim hard to explain in terms of moral right or legal practice, and renders it dependent on arcane historical arguments and selective biblical citation, even though it may seem more 'natural'. The illustrated manuscript presented by the Talbot family to Margaret of Anjou represents this tree of succession as the *fleur-de-lis* itself (Fig. 7).

The 'tree' as metaphor: the claim to the throne of England

In 2.5 of this play Mortimer recounts to Richard his sense of a genealogically derived right to the English throne. Like the English claim to France, Mortimer's link into this tangled skein of inheritance is through the female line – 'by my mother I derived am / From Lionel, Duke of Clarence, third son / To King Edward the Third' (2.5.74–6) – and, like the claim to France, it can be made real only by military force. Mortimer's claim, and the relative positions of Richard II and Bolingbroke/Henry IV can be presented diagrammatically.

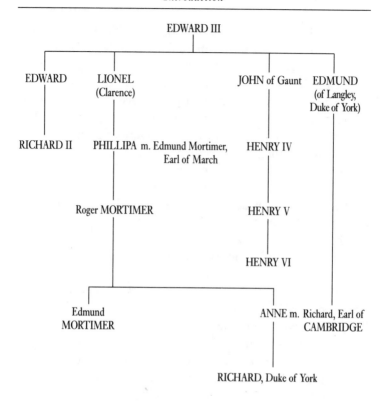

EDWARD III

EDWARD — LIONEL (Clarence) — JOHN of Gaunt — EDMUND (of Langley, Duke of York)

RICHARD II — PHILLIPA m. Edmund Mortimer, Earl of March — HENRY IV

Roger MORTIMER — HENRY V

HENRY VI

Edmund MORTIMER — ANNE m. Richard, Earl of CAMBRIDGE

RICHARD, Duke of York

Mortimer dies at the end of this scene (for the complex question of which historical 'Mortimer' this figure represents, see note on 'List of Roles', p. 110); his line ends, but he has passed on to York, whose mother Anne is Mortimer's sister, a narrative of succession, a place in a dynastic history, which, in *3 Henry VI*, leads to York's death.

The rose garden

Many Shakespearean plays contain a scene which is familiar to us whether we have read or seen the play or not. Perhaps surprisingly in so little performed a play, *1 Henry VI* contains such a scene. The choosing of the red rose and the white (2.4), which we tend to think is historical, is actually the creation of the dramatists. It provides a legend of origin for the civil war.[1] Preserved in *Richard, Duke of York*, an adaptation in 1817 of material from all three *Henry VI* plays (and some from Chapman) put together for Edmund Kean (see Appendix 3), it was, with versions of the following two scenes, the only part of the play revived until the twentieth century, and it provides the subject of numerous illustrations and history paintings. The picture in John Boydell's gallery, by his son Josiah, shows a rambling wild briar rose, in insidious apposition to a sturdy English oak (Fig. 8). Other illustrations (and most productions) present a formal garden, with cultivated roses, in which the red and the white are on different bushes (see 2.4.30n.).

The red rose had been the symbol of the house of Lancaster since the thirteenth century: 'sprung from the same stem as Edward I's golden rose, [it] was a badge of the house of Lancaster from the time of Earl Edmund "Crouchback" (son of Henry III) who died in 1296' (Scott-Giles, 136). York had a wide variety of heraldic symbols to draw on, including the white ostrich feather of his grandfather Edmund Langley; he does not seem historically to have used the white rose symbol to the extent that Hall and the dramatists, in the interests of symmetry, represent. His personal badge was 'the silver falcon and gold fetterlock . . . his hopes of obtaining the crown were symbolised by showing the fetterlock open, so that the falcon was no longer locked up' (Pinches, 106). Richard of York adopted the rose, as a pair of trees on his shield, from the Mortimers, in order to emphasize his line of descent and so his claim to the throne. The marriage of the red rose and the white is the climax of Hall's chronicle, symbolizing the end of the civil wars and the establishment of the Tudor dynasty. This is the

---

1   B.J. Sokol, in a forthcoming article (*N&Q*) kindly sent to me in typescript by RP, links this scene with the well-publicized refurbishment of the Inner Temple gardens in 1591. As well as establishing a contemporary reference apt to the popular tone of the play, this strengthens the case for its identification with Nashe's Talbot play, and so its status as a 'prequel'. Camden mentions that before the rose badges were adopted, 'a white Rose-tree at Longleete, bare upon one branch a faire white rose on the one side, and as faire a red rose on the other; which might as well have beene a foretoken of that division ...' (Camden, 180.11.12–15).

8 The Temple Garden scene, from John Boydell's *Graphic Illustrations of the Dramatic Works of Shakespeare* (1803)

crowning blossom of the family tree. Hall may well be drawing on the role of the red rose and the white in alchemical tradition; one stage of the transmutation of base metals into gold is the 'alchymical marriage' in which the king of the red rose is joined to the queen of the white rose (Roberts, 82–6).

It may be simply coincidence that George Ripley's *The Compound of Alchemy* was written for York's eldest son, Edward IV, though no doubt its printing in 1591, as one of the first printed texts on the topic in English, put alchemical ideas into the currency of late Elizabethan writing. Hall, earlier, could draw on such ideas to strengthen the sense of the dynastic marriage as inevitable and beneficent; the rose garden setting of this scene in the play may well be an alchemical allusion to the crucible of a disorder that eventually leads to a resolution perfected in the marriage depicted at the end of *Richard III*, of Richmond (the red rose) and Elizabeth of York (the white). Although modern productions (and, in SDs, many modern editions) carry the rose symbolism on through the two 'subsequent' plays, it plays no part in *2 Henry VI*, and very little in *3 Henry VI* (unless one takes the direction to wear white and red roses 'in their hats' in the entry SDs of 1.1. of the *True Tragedy* as authorial, and relevant to the performance as a whole). This point has been drawn on in the controversy as to the order of the plays' writing (Taylor, 150). The rose motif, rather than being a coherent unifying principle, may be an invention of this later play's ironic interest in origins and in the instability of symbolic systems.

Truth, symbol and meaning in the central sequence

In *1 Henry VI* succession to both the English and the French thrones has lost any of the inevitability or naturalness which the 'tree' analogy implies. The dynastic tree fragments and contestants for possession of it move, as in the rose garden scene, to the perilous use of flowers as badges of combative, dangerously detachable, identities. A sequence of scenes, from 2.3 to 3.1, dramatizes the dangerous gap between signs and the realities to which they point, specifically the realities of power. These centre on the emergence of

Richard Plantaganet, but are heralded by an inset episode, the encounter of Talbot and the Countess of Auvergne.

The Countess episode is, like the rose scene, an invention of the dramatists. It is a kind of fable, a commentary on the puzzles of fame and identity that condition other strands of the play. Initially, the Countess is disappointed in Talbot. Before his entrance she has exultingly anticipated a visual experience to fit verbal report ('the man / Whose glory fills the world' (2.2.42–3)), but she is disappointed by his diminutive stature as compared to the heroic physique she has imagined. His demonstration to her that in his case at least size does not matter follows on her drawing of the shadow/substance distinction familiar in Shakespeare, and also in Greene (for especially striking examples, see *R2* 4.1.287–99, *TGV* 4.4.115–20 and Greene's *Friar Bacon and Friar Bungay*, 6.128–30), in a context that suggests 'witchcraft by a picture' and so aligns the Countess both with Joan Puzel and with the sorceresses of medieval romance.

> Long time thy shadow hath been thrall to me;
> For in my gallery thy picture hangs.
> But now the substance shall endure the like.
>
> (2.3.35–7)

But Talbot can turn the distinction to his own advantage. He knows that the 'substance' of which he is 'shadow' is not inherent in his individual heroic identity; rather, it is he who has become the symbol of an English army loyal to him, and so they are the substance and he the shadow.

> *Winds his horn. Drums strike up. A peal of ordnance.*
>
> *Enter Soldiers.*
>
> How say you, madam? Are you now persuaded
> That Talbot is but shadow of himself?
> These are his substance, sinews, arms and strength.
>
> (2.3.59SD–62)

The Countess's belief in the inherently heroic, which, if inherent in a single being, can be possessed and controlled, has backfired on her. The episode ends in comic celebration, in feasting and drinking. The Countess herself can see the joke. In her poised antithesis of 'less' and 'more' she gracefully admits her naïvety while returning to her initial point – Talbot is more impressive than he appears:

> I find thou art no less than fame hath bruited,
> And more than may be gathered by thy shape.
>   (2.3.67–8)

The 1982 BBC version conveys this well, in casting a Countess significantly taller than Talbot, and in creating images of her that combine the military, the religious and the erotic.

This temporary resolution is an unusually graceful closure in an action where conflict tends to be disturbingly open-ended. The gap between shadow and substance in the civil dissensions of the English plot marks the rift growing ever nearer to a war more bloody than those in France.

The rose garden scene, which follows this, is unspecific about the cause of the dispute that develops into the conflict between the protagonists. Instead we have the demonstration of a powerful symbolic language in search of, and eventually *producing* rather than *finding*, a reference for itself in action. To set the dispute outside the Temple ('Within the Temple Hall we were too loud; / The garden here is more convenient' (2.4.3–4)) is to set it outside the structure of established law, in a garden that can be read as a kind of Eden, presaging a fall. Gardens figure in other Shakespearean history plays – in *Richard II*, for example (3.4.24–76), and, with more complex situational ironies, the suggestively named Iden's garden in *2 Henry VI* (4.10.1–84) – as images of an imperilled England. We do not know the starting point of the dispute but the subsequent argument turns on Richard Plantagenet's low social status. Richard's father's treachery, his involvement in the last manoeuvre of the anti-Bolingbroke faction in a plot to assassinate Henry V on the eve of his departure to France, has led to Richard's loss of rank. But Warwick uses the tree metaphor – 'Spring crestless yeomen from so deep a root?' (2.4.85) – to assert the status of genealogically derived identity as 'natural', and so overrides Richard's punitive demotion.

The word 'truth' shifts in sense throughout the scene. The 'case of truth' (2.4.2) referred to at the start is never disclosed to us; but by the end of the scene a new and fatal reality has been created in the interaction of unthinking aggression and a loaded language of 'truth'. Richard tries to appropriate the word 'truth' as peculiarly his own by embedding it in a sentence apparently structured to present alternatives, but actually presenting two things which are the same – 'Then say at once if I maintained the truth: / Or else was wrangling Somerset in th'error?' (2.4.5–6). (For further discussion of this line, see 2.4.5–6n., and below, p. 93–4.) When Richard claims truth as 'naked on my side' (2.4.20), we are hurried past any consideration like 'the truth of *what*?' Richard is claiming possession of truth in itself. By instigating the picking of the roses he takes the dispute back into silence, into 'dumb significants' (2.4.26), in order to create a ceremonial of assent. But he also introduces the term 'true-born' (2.4.27), which will rebound on him later in the scene by triggering the taunt from Somerset (2.4.90–3) that Richard's 'true' father, genealogically, was 'untrue' in being condemned a traitor, and so the cause of Richard's loss of his 'true' title.

For Somerset the red rose becomes a badge of 'the party of the truth' (2.4.32). Truth is now factionalized. Meanings for the word – reality/loyalty/status by birth/honesty – spill around the scene too unstably to be resolved by the improvised voting system at the climax of the scene. Somerset stakes his case on a combative redefinition of truth: wearing the badge of the red rose *is* truth, or loyalty – loyalty, to him, involving assent to his definition of reality, 'the truth' in that sense; red rose wearers 'shall maintain what I have said is true' (73). But, whatever the Temple dispute was about, the issue is now the treachery of Richard's father and his own disgraced status.

In this, as in the Countess of Auvergne scene, a gap opens up between sign and substance, which must be bridged by an act of faith, of loyalty, of identification – there by the English soldiers, here by the choosers of the roses. The difference is that 'substance' here is out of sight, initially lost in the shiftingness of the word 'truth' and the 'silence' from which the scene emerges, then remade as an ominous future, still out of sight but coming closer. In both cases the gap between sign and substance is a vacuum that sucks into it the imagination of its witnesses, on stage and in the audience, and in doing so remakes them and redefines their fates.

The next scene fills the gap of 'truth', in narrative terms at least, for Richard, and makes a bridge to his becoming 'York'. Mortimer tells him and us of the events, including Richard's father's treachery, which led to their current position.

> And for alliance' sake, declare the cause
> My father, Earl of Cambridge, lost his head.
>
> MORTIMER
>
> That cause, fair nephew, that imprisoned me.
>
> (2.5.53–5)

The 'cause', an origin, but also a crusade, a mission, replaces the 'case' of the previous scene, and grounds the conflict that emerged there in two or three generations of conflict and disputed succession. Richard's instatement as York in the following scene can seem like an end to conflict, and this is certainly how the child King Henry intends it in 3.1. The King has the power to realign sign and substance, or at least to determine what their relation should be.

> KING
>
> If Richard will be true, not that alone
> But all the whole inheritance I give
> That doth belong unto the house of York,
> From whence you spring by lineal descent.

RICHARD
    Thy humble servant vows obedience
    And humble service till the point of death.

                           (3.1.165–70)

But though 'lineal descent' is reaffirmed in this, it depends on that compromised thing (compromised at least in its relation to Richard), 'truth'. We have seen Richard determined to define truth egotistically, and the hollow overstatement of 'humble servant . . . humble service' can be read as pointing up the insincerity.

    The dispute between Gloucester and Winchester which begins this scene inflects the sign/substance question with a distrust of the 'written', undercutting the authority of, among other things, the second document that Warwick presents later in the scene as a demonstration of Richard's right to the dukedom of York:

          Gloucester offers to put up a bill;
           Winchester snatches it, tears it.

WINCHESTER
    Com'st thou with deep premeditated lines?
    With written pamphlets, studiously devised?
    Humphrey of Gloucester, if thou canst accuse,
    Or aught intend'st to lay unto my charge,
    Do it without invention, suddenly,
    As I with sudden and extemporal speech
    Purpose to answer what thou canst object.

                         (3.1.0.3–7)

Winchester here parallels the move made in the rose garden scene away from the authority of written record to the making of a new reality in debate and conflict, a spontaneous, charismatic, egotistical claiming of power overriding the by now questionably complex and partisan writings and rewritings of law and genealogical lore.

Gloucester characterizes Winchester's flamboyant gesture as an accusation that his own interpretations of events are 'forged', and the double meaning here – of faking and, in fire, making – is returned to by Exeter at the end of the scene.

> This late dissension grown betwixt the peers
> Burns under feigned ashes of forged love
> And will at last break out into a flame:
> As festered members rot but by degree,
> Till bones and flesh and sinews fall away,
> So will this base and envious discord breed.
>
> (3.1.191–6)

'Forged' here does not simply signify 'faking' but the making of a new and ominous reality. Exeter, a survivor of the last reign and, increasingly in this play, its memorializer, realizes that, however the nobles align themselves in terms of a factionalized 'truth', they are all complicit in the 'forging' of a new politics which must involve a new, in this case dangerously loose and volatile, relation of sign to substance.

Henry's childlikeness – successfully created by an adult actor (Alan Howard) in the RSC's complete cycle, and, with special pathos, by Paul Brennan (ESC), but arguably in the original performances played by a child (Appendix 2) – achieves temporary resolutions in a simplicity and directness which in Christian tradition would align him with Christ. But at his coronation in Paris, when Vernon and Basset, followers of York and Somerset respectively, bring the quarrel of the white and red roses into the King's presence, he disastrously demonstrates his naïvety, his ignorance of the power of signs:

> Let me be umpire in this doubtful strife:
> [*Takes the red rose from Basset.*]
> I see no reason, if I wear this rose,
> That anyone should therefore be suspicious
> I more incline to Somerset than York:

> Both are my kinsmen, and I love them both.
> As well they may upbraid me with my crown
> Because, forsooth, the King of Scots is crowned.
>   (4.1.151–7)

He attempts to empty out from the roses any especial significance. But by taking the red rose rather than the white he has given it a meaning that will determine the course of ensuing events. 'Tush, that was but his fancy', the conciliatory Warwick says to an agitated York after the King has left (4.1.178). Fancy is a dangerous faculty with which to operate, when the gap between sign and substance is a vacuum into which events rush.

WHAT IS *HENRY THE SIXTH, PART ONE*? CONTROVERSIES AND (IN)CONCLUSIONS

The 'history cycle', in the Folio and in production
The First Folio is a monument to Shakespeare's reputation, devised by its compilers as an impressive reading experience. They place what is probably Shakespeare's last single-authored play, *The Tempest*, at the beginning and so invite us to read it as a kind of monumental entrance to the volume, a meditation on the art that this particular volume is to celebrate and, unlike the art of magic lost in Prospero's drowned books, to preserve. Their other major interpretative act of ordering is their decision to group all the English histories together in the order, not of their writing, but of the chronology of the events they represent. This has largely determined how they have been read since. For many critics the sequence has represented a largely factual and implicitly patriotic 'national epic' and in the late nineteenth and twentieth centuries directors and theatre managers have built on this idea. Frank Benson's production of the three parts of *Henry VI* at 'The Shakespeare Festival' at Stratford-upon-Avon in 1906 followed on from his company's triumph the previous year with Aeschylus'

Oresteia, and several reviewers made the comparison, largely to Shakespeare's advantage. The anonymous reviewer of *The Herald*, on 4 May, makes a further, more contemporary comparison: 'We should call such a series of plays now a cycle . . . as much to be seen and studied as a whole as the Aeschylean trilogy or the Wagnerian *Ring*'. So Stratford becomes a British Bayreuth, with the history plays as the centre of an equivalent festival of national myth.

This is very much in line with a late eighteenth- and early nineteenth-century sense of Shakespeare as the national genius who spoke for the English and memorialized their history at a crucial stage of the integration of what is now 'Great Britain': the successful defence of England against the Spanish, the eve of the peaceful union of Scotland and England and the time of colonial wars in Ireland. The idea appealed to Samuel Taylor Coleridge so much that he suggested filling in the gaps left by Shakespeare to create a complete panorama.

> . . . it would be desirable that some man of dramatic genius, to which I have no pretensions, should dramatize all those omitted by Shakespeare, as far down as Henry VII. inclusive . . . It would be a fine national custom to act such a series of dramatic histories in orderly succession every Christmas holiday, and could not but tend to counteract that mock cosmopolitism, which under a positive term really implies nothing but a negation of, or indifference to, the particular love of our country.
>
> (Raysor, 1.126)

Coleridge was writing in the aftermath of the French Revolution, and at a time of British opposition to Napoleon. Coleridge had little time for *1 Henry VI* in itself, which he regarded as largely non-Shakespearean (Raysor, 1.127); that he envisaged its theatrical future as part of an adapted sequence has proved prophetic.

Romantic patriotism apart, a twentieth-century appetite for large-scale theatrical experience, for 'epic theatre', however understood, has established the plays as what 'we should call . . . now a cycle'. British productions of *1 Henry VI*, for the stage and television, have all been as part of a much longer historical sequence. Reviewers' and performers' frames of reference have declined in aesthetic dignity over the century, from Wagner and Aeschylus to television soap opera. Helen Mirren, who played Margaret in an uncut *Henry VI* (RSC, 1977), said, 'One isn't playing in three plays, one is playing in a single long play – like a TV serial, or a serialized novel by Dickens' (Potter, 171). Jane Howell, the director of the BBC version of 1982, compares the play, in her preface to the published text, to *Dallas*, a then popular prime-time soap opera, which had raised the profile of the genre by investing a dynastic intrigue plot with glossy melodramatic panache derived ultimately from the Hollywood films of the fifties (Fenwick, 22). Perhaps the popular pleasures of episodic narrative provide a fitter analogy to the early histories than do the nationalist aspirations of high tragic epic. *The Age of Kings* (BBC, 1960) adapted all the histories as a series shown in half-hour episodes on Sunday afternoons. The resulting popular success was highly influential in establishing two staples of British TV drama, the 'classic series' and a form of serial drama self-consciously more 'serious' than the American 'soap'. The idea of the history sequence has been central to the RSC's operations at Stratford, with three major productions directed by the company's artistic directors of the time (Hall/Barton, then Hands, then Noble) and serving to mark, by contrast, changes in the company's style. *1 Henry VI* is almost always cut and adapted to fit the pattern of a 'cycle', the assumption being that the surviving text may be corrupt or chaotic anyway. In Appendix 3 I set out a comparison of the texts of major post-war English-language productions. No producer has yet acted on the evidence that *1 Henry VI* may not belong in a 'cycle' at all.

Problems with Henslowe's reference: dating and identification

At first sight there is no reason to suppose that the play Henslowe records as 'harey the vj' is other than the play I present in this volume as *1 Henry VI*, or that either is other than the play described by Nashe in *Piers Penniless* (see p. 1). We should always bear in mind the paucity and obliquity of the contemporary documentation of Elizabethan theatre. Any supposition we build on such 'evidence' must be precarious, as we cannot quantify what texts and documentation have been lost. But then again we should be suspicious when this uncertainty is evoked to allow room for a view that is in itself subjective, or which confirms a prejudice that can be traced to a later cultural tradition. No traces survive of another play on the topic or of a similar name, and the date that Henslowe gives would fit in well with the pattern of Shakespeare's career so far as we can reconstruct it.

The 'problem' is that to identify the 'lost' text of the Lord Strange's Men's performance as the basis of the text presented thirty years later by Heminge and Condell in F as Shakespeare's would be to date the writing of the play *after* the two plays that F presents as 'The second Part of Henry the Sixt, with the death of the Good Duke HVMFREY' and 'The third Part of Henry the Sixt, with the death of the Duke of YORKE'. Robert Greene, in his *Groatsworth of Wit*, published in September 1592 – the month after *Piers Penniless*, and a few months after Strange's company presented 'harey the vj' at the Rose – includes in an unflattering account of one 'Shake-scene' a parody of one of the most striking lines of *3 Henry VI*. Given that Greene died only a few months after Henslowe recorded the 'ne' performance of 'harey the vj', we must disregard Henslowe's recording of the play as new ('ne') if we wish to place it as written earlier than *3 Henry VI*, which Greene obviously knows well, and expects his readers to know. Furthermore, the versions of the plays that F presents as *2 Henry VI* and *3 Henry VI* were published by Thomas Millington in 1594 and 1595 as 'THE First part of the Contention betwixt the two famous Houses of Yorke and Lancaster, with the death of the good Duke Humphrey' and as 'The true Tragedie of Richard Duke of Yorke, and the death of good King Henrie the Sixt' respectively – which points to a two-part play, popular enough to warrant printing.

There are several ways out of the challenge presented by Henslowe's 'diary' to the idea of a planned three-part 'Henry the Sixth' play. A few plays marked 'ne' were not new when so marked. These entries may be mistakes on Henslowe's part, but another possibility is that 'ne' means that the play was new to the repertory, if not strictly a new play; again, it may have been substantially revised, and so newish. As R.A. Foakes suggests, 'ne' could refer to a play revised and then newly licensed for performance by the Master of the Revels, the Elizabethan court official with responsibility for regulating public performances (Henslowe, xxx–xxxi). This last possibility has the attraction of explaining the higher takings for these performances as at least in part a higher entrance charge – necessary to cover the cost of the licence (at seven shillings, about 25 per cent of the takings of an average single performance, but recuperable in that the granting of a new licence is a good advertisement).

In the case of *1 Henry VI*, the 'new licence for a revision' argument would allow us to see the play as written, in some form, before what were to become Parts *Two* and *Three*, and then substantially revised, probably by an elaboration of the military material to provide a spectacular single-play entertainment for the season, and so 'ne' in these terms. The theory is attractive if one wishes to hold on to the idea of the three plays as a planned sequence, and perhaps also to a characterization of F's text of this part of it as the chaotic revision of a more coherent original. But only an attachment to either of these ideas makes such a reading of the diary entry necessary. While from our position as modern readers, approaching the plays through a tradition that goes back to F, we tend to receive the plays as a cycle, it seems unlikely that the habits of reading and spectatorship which this implies were available to a contemporary audience. Marlowe's *Tamburlaine* set a vogue for two-part plays to which the piece(s) printed in Quarto as *The First Part of the Contention betwixt the Two Famous Houses of York and Lancaster with the Death of the Death of Good Duke Humphrey* and *The True Tragedy of Richard, Duke of York, and the Death of Good King Henry the Sixth* would seem to belong. *Henry VI* would be unique if conceived as a three-parter, and at no point could the dramatists have envisaged performances of the plays in sequence.[1] When, on 8 November 1623, plays not previously printed were registered in preparation for the publication of the First Folio, something was listed as 'The thirde parte of Henry the sixte' (Chambers, 1.139). This must have been our play, the 'third' part in the chronology of its publication, though not in the events which it depicts.

Henslowe was as adept as a Hollywood producer in seeing that the audience of a popular hit can be brought back to look at the roots and causes of what they have been seeing, and so be invited to enjoy the intertextual pleasure of picking up the clues and references forward that are, of course, to the writer and to an audience in the know, really a reference back. For example, a mention of Eleanor, Gloucester's domineering wife, by Winchester, his archenemy (1.1.39), is, in the first scene of the first of three plays,

---

1   Several writers have provided powerful literary arguments that the three parts, and their connection to the sequence of history plays as F presents them, evince an organic coherence in dramatizing a large-scale story of national collapse. These may be unsupported by any evidence from the period as to authorial practice or performance possibility, but it is still plausible that the dramatists are working from a larger vision than their immediate context accommodates. Most accounts of the plays – particularly those written in the ambit of the RSC cycle presentations – leave questions of authorship and of the ordering of the three 'parts' unargued. Among ambitious book-length studies, Edward Berry reads the sequence as an epic of decline, structured through the presentation of the decay of public ceremony, while Emrys Jones explicitly links both particular moments in the plays and the conception of their structure back to Shakespeare's memories of the Corpus Christi cycles, probably seen by him at Coventry, of which his plays become the secular 'Tudor' counterpart (Jones, 31–84). Jones's is a sophisticated argument, which allows Shakespeare to have imagined a cyclic structure, although one which could hardly have been realized in the commercial theatrical environment of the 1590s. David Riggs again does not question the cycle idea but, in evoking a sense of the plays as sophisticated rhetorical exercises, opens them up to a reading less determinate than that of earlier critics like Tillyard, who found organic unity in the plays in their putative pattern of moral cause and effect (Tillyard, 165). Lily B. Campbell, while equally interested in 'the moral patterning of history' (Campbell, 120), finds that the authorship question invites caution, and does not feel the *Henry VI* plays should necessarily be given such close scrutiny as the later more securely ascribed pieces. But more recent studies can refer to 'the existence of a total pattern in Shakespeare's history plays' (Hunter, 233), and be so confident of the place of *1H6* in it that it becomes possible to argue that the Talbot sequence provides a prologue and clue to the 'next' two plays (Leggatt, 11–31). This play in particular is not often served well by 'organic' or 'cycle' readings; when *1 Henry VI* is read as part of a three-part cycle, it can too easily seem a botched version of a more coherent original, or simply a kind of false start.

planted much too early to be of any use as a signal to an audience of what is to follow in Part *Two* – if, that is, we take this play to be part of a dramatic structure designed to be experienced continuously. There is no dramatic follow-up to this in the play itself, and the moment is too glancing to be remembered in anticipation of another afternoon in the theatre. But, if we assume that this play was experienced by its first audiences after they had had a chance to see *The First Part of the Contention*, this reference becomes enjoyable as a teasing suggestion that we might get another look at an impressive character from a play already seen. Elizabethan plays were written for an audience likely to enjoy the business of cross-referencing them to other theatre pieces, to written chronicles and to oral traditions, but this process would be much more *ad hoc* and more flexible than the linear modern experience of the theatrical festival or the television series which inform, consciously or unconsciously, modern accounts of the plays.

Authorship and the genesis of the text

The apparent objectivity of Shakespearean bibliographic and textual scholarship cannot avoid assumptions derived from the more relative and subjective modes of literary judgement and interpretation. Scholars interpret evidence in the light of their prior response to the play as readers, implicit or explicit judgement of its value, and identification of the text as representing one kind of a play or another. Response to 'evidence' is inevitably affected by preconceptions about the value and significance of the texts, about the presumed nature of Shakespeare's project in writing history plays, and indeed about his perceived status as a dramatist in comparison to those contemporaries with whom he may or may not have collaborated on this and other plays.

To make a broad distinction, editors and critics who have valued the play have tended to present it as by Shakespeare, those who haven't see it as by a group of writers who may or may not have included him. Further, scholars of the first persuasion tend to see the three plays as a planned three-part sequence.

This contrast is clearly expressed in the differences between the first two editions of *1 Henry VI* for the Arden Shakespeare. Ard² (Cairncross, 1962) presents powerfully an argument for a single author, Shakespeare, and for a dating which allows for the plays to be written 'in natural sequence' (xxxvii). According to Cairncross,

> there can be little doubt that Shakespeare . . . set himself, and achieved, the ambitious task of staging, in his country's finest hour, its quasi-Biblical story, from the original sin of Henry IV to the grand redemption of the Tudors . . . the unity is there, and Shakespeare has everywhere taken great pains to draw the links tighter.
>
> (Ard², xli)

Cairncross's text proposes much freedom of emendation and of regularization of the verse lines, presumably in order to restore a more 'Shakespearean' sound to a 'corrupt' text. The first Arden (Hart, 1909), however, proceeds on exactly the opposite assumption, based this time on a low estimation of the play:

> All critics, all readers, will probably agree or have agreed that it is one of the least poetical and also one of the dullest of all the plays in the Folio. It is redeemed by few passages of merit – its verse is unmusical, its situations are usually poorly developed – and were it not for the essential interest of the subject-matter, to any English reader it would be unreadable.
>
> (Ard¹, x)

Hart gives one of the fullest accounts of possible co-authorship, placing the play within the Shakespeare/Greene/Peele nexus. His motive for doing so is to give Shakespeare an alibi for what is perceived as an embarrassingly inferior play. Interestingly, the portions he allows Shakespeare – 2.4–5 and 4 – have been ascribed to him in most 'collaborative' readings of the play. Hart's method is based on parallels of verbal detail between *1 Henry VI* and work ascribed to his chosen suspects. While, as a scholarly method, this is unconvincing, and its motives unsympathetic, it may intuit a process of writing and devising more plausible than the assumption of the planned authorship of an epic cycle.

The two most recent editions, Hattaway (Cam²) and Taylor (Oxf), have taken opposed positions on this issue, but inflected their arguments differently from their respective predecessors. Hattaway wishes to see *Henry VI* as an organically designed single-authored epic of England, albeit one with a different, more populist and subversive, agenda than that ascribed to the three-play cycle by Tillyard and his followers. He registers the authorship controversy, in order to say that it doesn't really matter, from the point of view of a reader both post-F and post-structuralist, for whom authorship, however well accredited, is displaced by the independent life of the text. In the *Textual Companion* to the Oxford edition, Taylor offers a complex set of ascriptions of most of the scenes in the play to dramatists other than Shakespeare, some named, some anonymous. A long-delayed article, giving more detail of this argument, finally appeared in 1995 (referred to here as 'Taylor'). I am in broad agreement with his conclusion that the major identifiable contributors to the play are Shakespeare and Nashe, that Nashe is largely responsible for the first act, Shakespeare for the fourth and parts of the second, and that several other writers, now impossible to name, were also involved. I also find attractive his suggestion that these dramatists were involved in the writing of *Locrine* and *Edward III*. I become sceptical as his argument proceeds into statistical detail, and as he seeks to establish more about this 'other' group. While aware that the collaborative versus organically authored controversy tends to become entangled in critical prejudice, Taylor himself exhibits in the 'Nashe' section a willingness to emend no less ready than that of Cairncross in his endeavour to render the play more Shakespearean[1]. I

1 Taylor demotes Winchester from Cardinal to Bishop in 1.3.15 in the interests of narrative coherence, however, rather than from any distaste for Nashe as a dramatist.

myself wish to detach the issue of quality from that of authorship. But consideration of authorship still provides a way into consideration of the concerns and methods of the play. If we accept that the play is collaborative, we need to consider how and how far we can 'unpick' the collaborative text.

The process of collaboration

History plays at this time were often collaborative affairs. One example, chosen almost at random from Henslowe, records a payment 'to geve unto antoney monday & mihell drayton webester & the Rest mydleton [this last name written in as an afterthought] in earneste of A Boocke called sesers ffalle' (Henslowe, 201). A company, or an entrepreneur like Henslowe, might well hit on a likely subject, find a text to work from, and then group together a set of writers, settling their fee and fixing a deadline. There are arguments for identifying the anonymous *Edward III* as at least partly by Shakespeare, and a contribution to *Sir Thomas More* has been plausibly cited as the sole surviving literary manuscript in Shakespeare's hand. Both *Edward III* and *Sir Thomas More* overlap with *Henry VI* in subject matter; it makes sense to see all these pieces, whether we involve Shakespeare in them or not, as the work of a group of writers used to working together on historical material, developing shared interests in a constantly fluctuating, even haphazard, process of collaboration.

Writers working within television, film or radio are familiar with this kind of process. Theatre, however, since the later seventeenth century, has come to be seen as the province of the individual artist who, whether writer or director, dominates and 'authors' the necessarily collaborative process of live performance. This attitude is at least partly the product of the re-creation of Shakespeare from the mid-seventeeth century onwards (Dobson, 13–16, for summary and *passim*) as a great, perhaps for the English Romantics the only great, theatrical genius. Inheriting this idea, we resist the notion of Shakespeare as team-player. But the history play, if we accept his part in these pieces, was a form in which collaborative authorship was more likely to be his practice than in any other genre except – towards the end of his career at least – the romance.

But perhaps early in Shakespeare's career his relation to his collaborators was more fraught. The awkwardness we feel in fitting Shakespeare into scenarios of collaborative authorship may not simply be part of an unquestioning acceptance of the post-Romantic notion of solitary genius; there is contemporary evidence of an uneasy relationship between Shakespeare and his fellow playwrights, his fellow Henslowe employees. In the posthumously published *Greene's Groatsworth of Wit* Robert Greene wrote of

> an upstart Crow, beautified with our feathers, that with his Tygers hart wrapt in a Players hyde, supposes he is as well able to bombast out a blanke verse as the best of you: and beeing an absolute Johannes fac totum, is in his owne conceit the onely Shake-scene in a countrey.
>
> (Greene, F1v)

The piece as a whole is presented as a kind of death-bed confession, put together from Greene's posthumous papers by Henry Chettle. The phrase that parodies *3 Henry VI*'s 'O tiger's heart wrapp'd in a woman's hide' (1.4.137) is set, for emphasis, in a different typeface from the rest, and its original context, as a reproach from the dying and tortured York to the victorious sadistic Margaret of Anjou, makes its citation here particularly pointed. Like Nashe's *Piers Penniless* this pamphlet appeared during the period of 'harey the vj's' phenomenal success, in a context which is further complicated if we assume the three men may have worked together on the play. In the *Groatsworth*, Greene seems to be presenting Shakespeare/Shake-scene as someone who resists or even cheats on the process of collaboration; he thinks of himself as 'the only' and dresses in others' 'feathers'. Perhaps Greene accuses Shakespeare of claiming more credit than was his due for the success of collaborative plays. Perhaps he simply resents a success that seems to him to be unfair, given his own straitened circumstances. Perhaps these two things are continuous with each other. In any case, the context of the passage draws a distinction between the writer as gentleman and scholar, fallen on hard times and profligate ways, and the writers who come out of the less intellectually respectable milieu of the theatre itself. The material Chettle put together moves from a fairy-tale-like story of two brothers, sons of a merchant father, one scholarly ('Roberto'), one business-like, to a comic-erotic tale where the first, having lost his inheritance – all but the 'groat's-worth' of the title – to the second, tries to trick his brother with the help of the courtesan Lamillia, and is tricked in his turn by her. The brother becomes a pimp, and Roberto, after evacuating himself of a misogynistic sonnet behind a hedge, is heard/witnessed:

> On the other side of the hedge sate one that heard his sorrow: who getting over, came towards him . . .
>
> Gentleman quoth hee (for so you seeme) I have by chaunce heard you . . . I suppose you are a scholler, and pittie it is men of learning should live in lacke.
>
> Roberto wondring to heare such good wordes, . . . returnd him thankfull gratulations . . . beseeching his advice how he might be imployed. Why, easily quoth hee, and greatly to your benefite: for men of my profession gette by schollers their whole living. What is your profession, said Roberto? Truly sir, saide hee, I am a player. A player, quoth Roberto, I tooke you rather for a Gentleman of great living, for if by outward habit men should be censured, I tell you, you would bee taken for a substantiall man. So am I where I dwell (quoth the player) . . .
>
> Roberto perceiving no remedie, thought best in respect of his present necessitie, to try his wit, & went with him willingly.
>
> (Greene, D4r–E1r)

The player who involves Greene in writing for the theatre is both his saviour and a kind of devil figure, drawing him into further artistic degradation. The attack on Shakespeare is part of a warning that comes after and out of this narrative;

> To those Gentlemen his Quondam acquaintance,
> that spend their wits in making plaies, R.G.
> wisheth a better exercise, and wisdome
> to prevent his extremities.
>
> (Greene, E4v)

For Greene at least, professional dealings with the likes of Shakespeare have obviously not been happy.

Dividing up the text and ascribing authorship

None of this, of course, helps us to sort out who wrote which bit of the play. This question itself is complicated by what one calls a 'bit' – what units do we split a play into before we subject those units to comparative analysis? We might return here to our collaborating pool of Henslowe employees. Did they each take a section of the plot home, and work on it in isolation? Did they, as their modern equivalents might, sit round a table, sharing ideas and swapping lines until it became unclear who had actually originated what? Many scholarly accounts of authorship assume a solitary experience of creation, either in a rigid parcelling out of responsibility, or in a process of revision, but if we do this we have to decide what the unit of responsibility was. Many studies of authorship also tend to attribute too uniform a significance to act and scene divisions, assuming that a particular writer would take responsibility for an act, individual scene or sequence of scenes. Taylor seems to work from the assumption that plays were parcelled out by the act (Taylor, 153–72); his own discussion of act division elsewhere, however, demonstrates that act division in plays for the public stage became usual only after 1609 (Taylor & Jowett, 3–50). In parcelling out authorial responsibility for sections of *1 Henry VI*, Taylor has to allow for an untidy overlap of act divisions. The evidence points to a variety of ways of dividing up the project, to a kind of piecemeal authorial activity, where the 'units' of textual work assigned to a writer could be determined by any kind of perceived theatrical necessity. We could think of strands through the play that 'belong' to a particular writer, their structural place still open to negotiation when the piece was put together, and, more locally, characteristic episodes that might be perceived as a certain writer's speciality. A law-case of the period records that Thomas Dekker 'wrote two sheetes of paper conteyning the first Act of a Play called The Late Murder in White Chappell, or Keepe the Widow waking, and a speech in the Last Scene of the Last Act of the Boy who had killed his mother' (Carson, 58). This suggests that both division based on act structure and assignment on the basis of character/voice were current. In *Sir Thomas More*, the three pages in Hand D, the hand we think of as Shakespeare's, are only a portion of a scene where Shakespeare's contribution is largely the powerful rhetoric of More's own speeches. If F's *1 Henry VI* is based on a collaborative manuscript including holograph sections by Shakespeare, those sections may well have looked like this (Fig. 9).

Any test of authorship that starts from a splitting of the play into scenes may be starting from the wrong place, as any such attempt to portion out authorial responsibility has already begun from a prior assumption as to what counts as a portion, a unit. I prefer to follow the suggestion of Dekker's 'Boy who had killed his mother', Shakespeare's persuasive More, or the additions to Hieronimo's role in Kyd's *Spanish Tragedy* sometimes ascribed to Jonson,[1] in reading the authorship of *1 Henry VI* in terms of

1   Edwards, in his edition of *The Spanish Tragedy*, gives arguments for and against identifying the scenes, as we now have them, as Jonson's. In summary, the argument *for* is a record of two advance payments by Henslowe to a 'Bengemen Johnson' or 'bengemy Johnsone' in 1601 and 1602 for additions to 'geronymo' or 'Jeronymo' (Henslowe, 182, 203); the argument *against* is that what we have is too unambitious to be what Jonson at this point in his career would have wanted to write, and too slight to warrant the amount Henslowe paid (Edwards, lxi–lxvi). It could be simply that Jonson took the money he needed and fobbed Henslowe off with something less than the impresario expected. But, whatever the case, the example is illustrative of the casual complications of authorship in Henslowe's milieu.

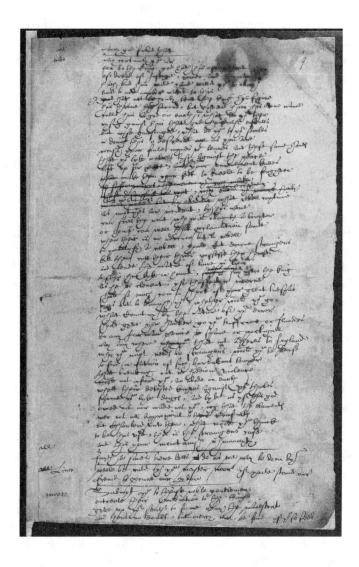

9 Page from the collaborative manuscript of *Sir Thomas More* showing Hand D (Shakespeare?)

strands of rhetorical action which would associate with different dramatists, each supplying something he was particularly 'good at'. Dekker was 'good at' pathos, Shakespeare at politically effective rhetoric, Jonson at an obsessive and more complexly monomaniacal rhetoric than Kyd's. Nashe, if we take the 'Joan Puzel' passages of this play as his, was good at grotesque play with the religious and heroic. But in the absence of external evidence, no certain division of authorship is ever attainable.

I do not believe that we can ever finally know who wrote this or indeed many other plays of the period, nor do I believe that putting a name (or names) to it should determine our sense of the quality and nature of the text. This is not to say that authorship does not matter, and that we should just quietly forget about it. Investigating authorship alerts us to many aspects of the processes that produced the text, and sharpens our questioning of our own critical preconceptions, and those of earlier readers. Computerized study of authorship has, at the time of writing, received much publicity, and may seem to provide something scientific and objective. Many of the plays of the 1590s, however, remain of uncertain authorship. Indeed, there is not a sufficient unambiguously identified corpus of work by any of the writers of the period except Shakespeare and Nashe to provide adequate data for authorship tests (and in Nashe's case the work is largely non-dramatic). So a prior ascription would have to be made on some other basis before enough material could be accumulated. Earlier arguments for authorship (Ard[1], for example) cite George Peele, but there is only a very limited amount of material that we can authenticate as Peele's – of his plays, only *David and Bethsabe* was printed with his name on the title-page. If we accept Robert Greene as a possible contributor to *1 Henry VI*, the Countess of Auvergne episode seems in character – but that is a literary judgement, not a statistical one. No way has yet been devised to compute the complexities of tone and atmosphere that theatrical situation creates around words; but it is through our response to this that we recognize a dramatic 'voice'.

It makes sense to me to see this play as a commissioned piece, based largely on Hall's history, written by a group of writers, among whom Shakespeare took a major part. I take seriously Taylor's argument that this is a collaborative play, in which, on my reading, the Shakespearean strand emerges most clearly in the dynastic 'York' plot and the later scenes for Talbot and his son. The two intersect in plot terms in York's failure to send rescue, and thematically in a concern for genealogy, patrimony and identity. This gradually displaces an 'other-authored' strand initiated in the English-French conflict which begins the play. The crude sexual jokiness of the 'Joan Puzel' passages led many earlier critics to ascribe them to 'some other hand', and so to save Shakespeare from the bad taste of a rebuke to the memory of saintly Joan. But if one disentangles the issue of authorship from the issue of critical value – and the issue of critical value from that of an unironic relation to 'the heroic' required by a post-Romantic reading of 'England's national epic' – then the collaborative process of the play, and the effect of a range of perspectives and attitudes to the heroic and the historical within it, becomes easier to read. Nashe and whoever else may not be poets and playwrights as great as Shakespeare, but they are undeniably lively, distinctive and intelligent, and their contribution may well be as formative as his of the wit and pathos of an exploratory and vividly effective play.

The now lost manuscript which Henslowe owned and Lord Strange's Men worked from to make their performance was, in the unplanned processes of dramatic performance and textual transmission, the genesis of three distinct pieces. The first was 'harey the vj', the great popular success of the 1591–2 season; the second 'The first Part of Henry the Sixt', the first section of a three-part play assembled by Heminge and Condell in F1 to tell the story of the whole of Henry's reign; and the third is *1 Henry VI*, an editorial short title for the edited text. This last, an invention of subsequent editorial process of which the current text is a variant, is inevitably closer to the print of F than to the lost manuscript text used for those original performances. In the context of the authorship controversy, the least questionable labelling of the text would be 'Harry the Sixth, as presented by Lord Strange's Men'. 'Harry the Sixth, by Shakespeare, Nashe and others', would be plausible, if inelegant. But commercial considerations tend to be conservative in reinforcing the familiar; so, however much an edition may present arguments as to authorship and provenance, the familiar title and author-ascription will still be on the cover – otherwise the volume will not sell and so not be profitable to the publisher. This volume is no exception to this process. The title and 'official' author-ascription adopted by this edition are a kind of convention, albeit one established by centuries of editorial and commercial practice. 'Shakespeare's *King Henry the Sixth, Part One*' is, for me, a necessary commercial fiction.

'O for . . .': desire and heroism, wooden O's and emptiness

Though Shakespeare may not have envisaged the serial presentation suggested by F, and adopted in those twentieth-century productions which present the plays as a 'cycle', two scenes at least in *Henry V* acknowledge the narrative of the earlier play. These are the execution of Cambridge, York's father (2.2), and – striking in comparison to *1 Henry VI*, but so apparently pointless without this comparison that it is often cut from productions of *Henry V* – the death at Agincourt, in friendly accord with the dying Duke of Suffolk, of Cambridge's elder brother Edward, the last Duke of York before Richard Plantagenet was reinstated in the title.

> Tarry, my cousin Suffolk!
> My soul shall thine keep company to heaven.
> Tarry, sweet soul, for mine, then fly abreast,
> As in this glorious and well-foughten field
> We kept together in our chivalry.
>
> (*H5* 4.6.15–19)

(The moment is invented by Shakespeare – historically Edward, Duke of York died of heart failure, as his armour was too heavy for him (Edelman, 28–9)). There is a double reference to *1 Henry VI*, in that York's death is placed equivalently in *Henry V* to the death of the Talbots, which it closely echoes (Cam[1], cited at 4.6.11n. in Ard[3]), and contrasts ironically with the conduct of the reinstated Duke of York, whose lack of amity, now in relation to Somerset, leads to Talbot's death and to a defeat as decisive as was the victory at Agincourt. This invented parallel is so complex as to seem almost a private joke, but there are many other examples where the structure of the material underlines the relation between the plays. Burgundy's peace-making speech in *Henry V* (5.2.23–67) parallels closely those with which Joan Puzel wins him over in *1 Henry VI* (3.3.44–85), and Henry's wooing of Katherine is similarly placed structurally to Suffolk's of Margaret. I believe that in *Henry V* Shakespeare returns to the material of the two earlier plays, *1 Henry VI* and *Edward III*, in which he can plausibly be seen to have had a hand, almost to the extent that he constructs the new play in revisionary reference to them. This does not mean that the recollection of *1 Henry VI* which we are invited to make in the Epilogue to *Henry V* necessarily ironizes the preceding play.[1] There is no evidence that *1 Henry VI* was

---

1 Patricia Parker reads *1H6* in relation to *H5* as a pre-existing explanation and ironization of the later play, whose epilogue cues in the audience to a memory of an earlier play and induces them to apply this to later events: 'In the preposterous Shakespeare reversal of the chronological ordering from Holinshed and Hall, these dramatically earlier (though chronologically later) scenes thus already disclose "at full" what is suppressed or only elliptically suggested in the margins of the rebellion scene of *Henry V*' (Parker, 41). The argument is intricately engaged in verbal detail, and depends on those more modern habits of spectatorship which govern our reading of the plays as part of a cycle, and depend on our having texts or films of performance accessible for cross-reference; it seems to me to be unlikely that the audience of *H5* would, or could be expected to, have a close memory of a play from several years earlier which seems to have disappeared from the repertory and was not yet printed; further, given the play's confused authorship and the lack (as far as we know) of author identification in public performances, even a sixteenth-century Shakespeare fan would be unlikely to make the connection. It is possible (and I think more likely) that the connection is private to Shakespeare, and so involves a rethinking of earlier material, not all of it, strictly speaking, authored by himself.

printed or revived in the late 1590s; it is unlikely to have been on the minds of an audience attending *Henry V*. A general knowledge of the story and the experience of attending many plays by different writers on related themes would create a complex cross-referencing different from the modern scholar's linear, text-based, author-centred reading.

Rather, parallels and references to the earlier plays which multiply throughout *Henry V* are symptoms of a reconsideration of their concerns, and perhaps a reassembling by the provident, perhaps exploitative, Shake-scene crow of the borrowed feathers of some years before. *Henry V* reinstates the searching awareness of that gap between sign and substance which in *1 Henry VI* is charted as a slippage towards national disaster, but combines it with *Edward III*'s robust demonstration that heroisms can be created out of a confidence in the production of signs and in the confident extortion of spectatorial assent. If in *Henry V* the same ingredients – tortuously argued genealogies, appeals to heroic typologies of the 'worthies' and others, beast comparisons, erotic-political courtship games, diplomatic rhetoric – tend to construct rather than undermine the heroic, it may be because at the centre of this play there is a king determined to invent a rhetoric of signs, identities and ceremonies which he can control and can use to control events and their meanings. This works from the making of Agincourt, in the St Crispian speech (4.3.18–67), into an icon of English identity (indeed, of anachronistically 'British' identity given Shakespeare's working into the scene of Scots, Welsh and Irish) to the games with badges and leeks that form the comic anticlimax of the battle. There is an obvious contrast here both with his son's fatal inability to intuit the weight of the rose symbolism and with the untroubled confidence of Edward III and the Black Prince in their own iconic meaning. For Henry V, his father's 'buried fear', as Exton calls the murdered Richard II when he presents his body to Henry IV in a coffin (*R2*, 5.6.31), returns to haunt the eve of Agincourt (*H5* 4.1.286–302).

So there is a pathos, an anxiety, at the centre of *Henry V*, which distinguishes it from the extrovert iconizing of *Edward III*, and aligns it more closely with *1 Henry VI*'s sense of the precariousness of the heroic. The emptiness at the heart of *1 Henry VI*, the vacuum left in the absence of a powerful monarch, is a kind of panic consequent on the absence of an authority to validate meanings. The consequence of this is a clash of self-inventing centres of meaning.

Edward III, like *1 Henry VI*, is very much concerned with the construction of individual and group identities through the language of signs. But it suggests potential dissolution only to resolve it into a triumphant emblematization. In *Edward III*, words, deeds and writing are essentially distinct from each other, but capable of coalescing into intense moments of meaning. Audley, the old soldier, hands a weapon to the young Prince Edward:

> Edward Plantagenet, prince of Wales,
> Receive this lance into thy manly hand,
> Use it in fashion of a brazen pen
> To draw forth bloody stratagems in France
> And print thy valiant deeds in honour's book.
> (*E3* 3.3.192–6)

The Prince much later recapitulates this to Audley:

> Thyself art busy and bit with many broils,
> And stratagems forepast with iron pens
> Are texted in thine honourable face.
> (*E3* 4.4.128–30)

This writing on the body, the soldier's body, not only of his own deeds but of the history of his country (a history of which this is the *most* authentic record), is in *1 Henry VI* a kind of defiance to the crazy confusion of meaning encompassing it. In *Edward III* a completeness and explicitness of written signs extends through the play, to the apparently supernatural, as in the prophecy of French defeat. In a full and emblematically exact diagram a flight of ravens imitates the French battle formations ('in triangles and cornered squares, / Right as our forces are embattled' (*E3* 4.5.30–1)). In the subplot where Salisbury's 'pass' through the French lines, given him by Villiers, is first treacherously ignored, but then honoured (*E3* 4.5.64–102), the power of the written word is dramatized; in *1 Henry VI* writing itself is questionable, disruptive, 'forged' (3.1).

In *Henry V*, the old French King remembers the earlier defeat:

> Witness our too much memorable shame
> When Cressy battle fatally was struck,
> And all our princes captived, by the hand
> Of that black name, Edward, Black Prince of Wales;
> Whiles that his mountain sire, on mountain standing
> Up in the air, crowned with the golden sun,
> Saw his heroical seed, and smiled to see him,
> Mangle the work of nature and deface
> The patterns that by God and by French fathers
> Had twenty years been made. This is a stem
> Of that victorious stock.

(*H5* 2.4.53–63)

He invites his court to 'witness' in memory an event which he presents in a powerful verbal icon, an event that the audience of *Edward III* had witnessed in performance. In *Edward III* scenes are often structured around spectatorship and spectacle – offstage events are witnessed, reported, framed, emblematized, most notably the Black Prince's victory at Crécy.

It is important in *Edward III* that King Edward, the Prince's father, watches the battle. His spectatorship confirms that genealogy and individual heroic worth have coincided in a moment of fame, of iconic glory, and this, as the French King's citation of it shows, acquires a power in itself; such memories are part of the English weaponry. In *1 Henry VI* the Talbots, father and son, operate within the same vocabulary, but theirs is an icon of defeat, unwitnessed and ultimately insignificant.

With different degrees of self-consciousness, and with different diagnoses of the heroic status of the events they depict, all three plays present heroic history as in continuity with its representation. In any onstage moment, historical meaning is at issue, the coherence of the dynastic narrative and the value in fame of individual action are at stake. The characters in the history plays continually create narratives to explain their own position, narratives which look both forward and back to their memory or projection of their own history. All these internal narratives, projected by the characters individually and competitively, clash against each other. Sometimes they are couched in terms of prophecy and/or a divine ordering of human affairs, sometimes in terms of *realpolitik*, often drawing on biblical and classical typology to promote their individual 'fame', their status in the eyes of posterity. Often the characters allude to events that span several of the plays, including plays that were yet to be written, probably not even planned. In the context of the theatrical moment of their utterance such allusions can be but partial and provisional. We see 'history in the making', in that we witness a struggle between characters to define what their history is, to determine the meaning and remembered narrative of events over which they have only a constantly thwarted control.

But representation and historical action are the same thing in these plays in that both the action and its re-enactment involve a leap of faith, an extorted assent, to close imaginatively the gap between sign and substance. The Chorus in *Henry V* brilliantly articulates this. The whole business of sign and symbol is theatrical; the stage is a microcosm of larger actions. The first words of the play are 'O for . . .' The stage is an O, a blank, a void to be filled, and so the play is a play of desire, the desire of the audience to fill the void with some imaginative confirmation, and so to create the heroic in a contract enacted within the space between performer and spectator. It is this contrast which Nashe describes in his account of Talbot on stage (see above, p. 1). *Henry V* combines the irony and pathos of the heroic contract in perhaps a more economical way than the earlier play, but *1 Henry VI* makes the later piece possible, and comes closer to it in achievement than is usually allowed. Within the act and its depiction, the resolution, the 'glory', can be held only momentarily, dissolving soon into the realm of reminiscence. The wooden O fades to Joan Puzel's 'circle in the water' (1.2.133).

NOTES ON EDITORIAL PROCEDURES

Punctuation

This edition takes a broadly non-interventionist approach to the punctuation of F, modifying it lightly in order to clarify sense for the modern reader. This, and some points about speech prefixes (SPs) and stage directions (SDs), can be illustrated by a comparison of my text with page 104 in the Histories section of F (2.4.56–2.5.42; TLN 985–1113), reproduced in Fig. 10.

A semicolon as used in modern punctuation can further clarify sentences that F punctuates with commas. So,

> And know vs by these Colours for thy Foes,
> For these, my friends in spight of thee shall weare.
> (TLN 1036–7)

becomes:

> And know us by these colours for thy foes;
> For these my friends, in spite of thee, shall wear.
> (2.4.105–6)

Similarly, a semicolon can be substituted for F's colon, when it would encourage readers and actors to make the connection between the lines (2.4.102–3; TLN 1033–4). These are scenes of argument and self-justification, and the punctuation is designed to carry and clarify long dramatic paragraphs of combative verbal action. In other, more exclamatory sections of the play, full stops can be substituted for commas and semicolons:

104   *The first Part of Henry the Sixt.*

Lawyer. Vnlesse my Studie and my Bookes be false,
The argument you held, was wrong in you,
In signe whereof, I pluck a white Rose too.

Yorke. Now *Somerset*, where is your argument?

Som. Here in my Scabbard, meditating, that
Shall dye your white Rose in a bloody red.

Yorke. Meane time your cheeks do counterfeit our Roses:
For pale they looke with feare, as witnessing
The truth on our side.

Som. No *Plantagenet*:
'Tis not for feare, but anger, that thy cheekes
Blush for pure shame, to counterfeit our Roses,
And yet thy tongue will not confesse thy error.

Yorke. Hath not thy Rose a Canker, *Somerset*?

Som. Hath not thy Rose a Thorne, *Plantagenet*?

Yorke. I, sharpe and piercing to maintaine his truth,
Whiles thy consuming Canker eates his falsehood.

Som. Well, Ile find friends to weare my bleeding Roses,
That shall maintaine what I haue said is true,
Where false *Plantagenet* dare not be seene.

Yorke. Now by this Maiden Blossome in my hand,
I scorne thee and thy fashion, peeuish Boy.

Suff. Turne not thy scornes this way, *Plantagenet*.

Yorke. Prowd *Poole*, I will, and scorne both him and
thee.

Suff. Ile turne my part thereof into thy throat.

Som. Away, away, good *William de la Poole*,
We grace the Yeoman, by conuersing with him.

Warw. Now by Gods will thou wrong'st him, *Somerset*:
His Grandfather was *Lyonel* Duke of Clarence,
Third Sonne to the third *Edward* King of England:
Spring Crestlesse Yeomen from so deepe a Root?

Yorke. He beares him on the place's Priuiledge,
Or durst not for his crauen heart say thus.

Som. By him that made me, Ile maintaine my words
On any Plot of Ground in Christendome.
Was not thy Father, *Richard*, Earle of Cambridge,
For Treason executed in our late Kings dayes?
And by his Treason, stand'st not thou attainted,
Corrupted, and exempt from ancient Gentry?
His Trespas yet liues guiltie in thy blood,
And till thou be restor'd, thou art a Yeoman.

Yorke. My Father was attached, not attainted,
Condemn'd to dye for Treason, but no Traytor;
And that Ile proue on better men then *Somerset*,
Were growing time once ripened to my will.
For your partaker *Poole*, and you your selfe,
Ile note you in my Booke of Memorie,
To scourge you for this apprehension:
Looke to it well, and say you are well warn'd.

Som. Ah, thou shalt finde vs ready for thee still:
And know vs by these Colours for thy Foes,
For these, my friends in spight of thee shall weare.

Yorke. And by my Soule, this pale and angry Rose,
As Cognizance of my blood-drinking hate,
Will I for euer, and my Faction weare,
Vntill it wither with me to my Graue,
Or flourish to the height of my Degree.

Suff. Goe forward, and be chok'd with thy ambition:
And so farewell, vntill I meet thee next.   *Exit.*

Som. Haue with thee *Poole*: Farewell ambitious *Richard.*   *Exit.*

Yorke. How I am brau'd, and must perforce endure
it?

Warw. This blot that they obiect against your House,
Shall be whipt out in the next Parliament;

Call'd for the Truce of *Winchester* and *Glocester*:
And if thou be not then created *Yorke*,
I will not liue to be accounted *Warwicke*.
Meane time, in signall of my loue to thee,
Against prowd *Somerset*, and *William Poole*,
Will I vpon thy partie weare this Rose.
And here I prophecie: this brawle to day,
Growne to this faction in the Temple Garden,
Shall send betweene the Red-Rose and the White,
A thousand Soules to Death and deadly Night.

Yorke. Good Master *Vernon*, I am bound to you,
That you on my behalfe would pluck a Flower.

Ver. In your behalfe still will I weare the same.

Lawyer. And so will I.

Yorke. Thankes gentle.
Come, let vs foure to Dinner: I dare say,
This Quarrell will drinke Blood another day.   *Exeunt.*

*Enter Mortimer, brought in a Chayre,
and Iaylors.*

Mort. Kind Keepers of my weake decaying Age,
Let dying *Mortimer* here rest himselfe.
Euen like a man new haled from the Wrack,
So fare my Limbes with long Imprisonment:
And these gray Locks, the Pursuiuants of death,
Nestor-like aged, in an Age of Care,
Argue the end of *Edmund Mortimer*.
These Eyes, like Lampes, whose wasting Oyle is spent,
Waxe dimme, as drawing to their Exigent.
Weake Shoulders, ouer-borne with burthening Griefe,
And pyth-lesse Armes, like to a withered Vine,
That droupes his sappe-lesse Branches to the ground.
Yet are these Feet, whose strength-lesse stay is numme,
(Vnable to support this Lumpe of Clay)
Swift-winged with desire to get a Graue,
As witting I no other comfort haue.
But tell me, Keeper, will my Nephew come?

Keeper. *Richard Plantagenet*, my Lord, will come:
We sent vnto the Temple, vnto his Chamber,
And answer was return'd, that he will come.

Mort. Enough: my Soule shall then be satisfied.
Poore Gentleman, his wrong doth equall mine.
Since *Henry Monmouth* first began to reigne,
Before whose Glory I was great in Armes,
This loathsome sequestration haue I had;
And euen since then, hath *Richard* beene obscur'd,
Depriu'd of Honor and Inheritance.
But now, the Arbitrator of Despaires,
Iust Death, kinde Vmpire of mens miseries,
With sweet enlargement doth dismisse me hence:
I would his troubles likewise were expir'd,
That so he might recouer what was lost.

Enter Richard.

Keeper. My Lord, your louing Nephew now is come.

Mor. *Richard Plantagenet*, my friend, is he come?

Rich. I, Noble Vnckle, thus ignobly vs'd,
Your Nephew, late despised *Richard*, comes.

Mort. Direct mine Armes, I may embrace his Neck,
And in his Bosome spend my latter gaspe.
Oh tell me when my Lippes doe touch his Cheekes,
That I may kindly giue one fainting Kisse.
And now declare sweet Stem from *Yorkes* great Stock,
Why didst thou say of late thou wert despis'd?

  Rich. Fol.

10 Page 104, sig. k6v, from the Folio text, 2.4.56 – 2.5.42; TLN 985–1113

> Hung be the heavens with black. Yield day to night.
> Comets, importing change of times and states,
> Brandish your crystal tresses in the sky
> And with them scourge the bad revolting stars
> That have consented unto Henry's death –
> King Henry the Fifth, too famous to live long.
> England ne'er lost a king of so much worth.
>
> (1.1.1–7)

As this example shows, I have avoided exclamation marks even
where they might seem apt to a modern reader. They too easily
dictate the way the line is spoken. I have used an exclamation mark
only when it is the simplest way to point the syntax:

> See the coast cleared, and then we will depart.
> Good God, these nobles should such stomachs bear!
> I myself fight not once in forty year.
>
> (1.3.87–9)

F often likes to mark a rhythmic break in the middle of a line, a
caesura, with a comma. For example:

> The argument you held, was wrong in you;
> In signe whereof, I pluck a white Rose too.
>
> (2.4.57–8; TLN 986–7)

I have omitted commas where they do nothing to help the sense of
the line, also commas that seem to be the symptom of a more confusing habit of F, that of marking the end of a phrase with some
kind of stop if it feasibly makes sense at all in isolation – whether
or not the larger sense of the line flows on. The compositor often
seems not to have read on before reaching for a stop:

> Here in my Scabbard, meditating, that
> Shall dye your white Rose in a bloody red.
>
> (2.4.60–1; TLN 989–90)

A dash has the advantage of not imposing any particular tone or phrasing on the actors. Here it also clarifies the sense better than F's commas.

> No, Plantagenet:
> 'Tis not for fear, but anger, that thy cheeks
> Blush for pure shame, to counterfeit our roses –
> And yet thy tongue will not confess thy error.
> (2.4.64–7; TLN 994–7)

Dashes also provide a mode of parenthesis that is clearer than the commas often used for this purpose in F.

> Since Henry Monmouth first began to reign –
> Before whose glory I was great in arms –
> This loathsome sequestration have I had.
> (2.5.23–5; TLN 1093–5)

I have avoided brackets. F uses them, with particular frequency in the Mortimer scene:

> Yet are these Feet, whose strength-lesse stay is numme,
> (Vnable to support this Lumpe of Clay)
> (2.5.13–14; TLN 1083–4)

For a modern reader brackets isolate that part of the text and so can prove inhibiting for actors. I have minimized the use of inverted commas, a convention for marking direct speech unknown to F's compositors, but there are points at which they seem the least mannered way of making sense of the text for modern readers.

F's punctuation can be both inelegant and dramatically apt –

> Then say at once, if I maintain'd the Truth:
> Or else was wrangling *Somerset* in th'error?
> (2.4.5–6; TLN 933–4)

The punctuation here creates a farcical effect, in that the form of Richard's sentence seems to allow for two possibilities, but both are versions of his being in the right. This could be pointed: 'Then say at once – if I maintained the truth, or else: was wrangling Somerset in th'error?' But this is strained, while a dash or commas could lose the comic possibility, by allowing the actor impatiently to pose the same, essentially open, question twice.

F's persistent recourse to commas is equally likely to create an ambiguity of meaning. An example from the page reproduced is perhaps trivial:

> *Keeper.* My Lord, your louing Nephew now is come.
> *Mor. Richard Plantagenet*, my friend, is he come?
> (2.5.33–4; TLN 1104–5)

It would matter to the actors whether Richard or the Gaoler was the *friend* to whom Mortimer refers, but the decision they reach does not substantially affect the sense of the scene. In other places (see 1.5.21n., for example) points of interpretation are at stake, and it seems better to retain F's punctuation; the ambiguity is germane to the dramatic situation.

Stage directions

In adding to and developing the SDs provided by F the editor's aim must be to make things clear for a reader with some basic knowledge of the theatre of the time of the play. I have added as few SDs as seem to me compatible with producing a clear reading text. Often an exit, by modern convention, needs to be supplied. Whatever manuscript F is derived from seems often to have left the timing of an exit as a matter of common sense, and the F compositors, as usual in the period, have not bothered to repair the omission. It would make a difference to the Mortimer scene if the Gaolers left their prisoner alone with Richard, perhaps before 'And now' (2.5.41), which would then constitute tacit permission for a confidential exchange. But then who would carry Mortimer out when he dies? A re-entrance could be supplied after 'Keepers, convey him hence' (2.5.120), which would then become a summons to them to emerge from offstage. I have preferred to leave this kind of decision to directors and actors. Attention to the shape of the stage for which the play was written (see above, pp. 9–15) suggests that exits and entrances may well not have been as clear-cut or as easy to 'time' as on a modern stage, and that if the Gaolers simply withdrew to the back of the stage the audience would 'read' them as 'off'. But even a minimal editorial intervention necessitates a change to F's laconic '*Exit*' at Mortimer's removal. I have respected F's lack of an exit in some places where previous editors have supplied one. In the scene which I have presented as 4.3, I treat Lucy's meetings with York and with Somerset as a continuous action. For more on this, see the discussion of act and scene divisions below (pp. 101–3).

The funeral in 1.1

Sometimes the placing and form of the stage direction decisively affects the shape and tone of the scene. The text of F begins as follows:

Dead March.

Enter the Funerall of King Henry the Fift, attended on by the Duke of Bedford, Regent of France; the Duke of Gloster, Protector; the Duke of Exeter Warwicke, the Bishop of Winchester, and the Duke of Somerset.

But no *exit* is given for the funeral procession at any point in the ensuing scene. The editor has to choose between the following possibilities. First (*a*) the funeral passes across the stage but then immediately exits, thus establishing the onstage situation as that of a group of characters delayed by their own concerns from participating in the ceremony. This has the attraction of an uncluttered stage, and of releasing extras for the subsequent battle scenes. However, references to the 'wooden coffin' (19) and to the presence and possible awakening of Henry's corpse (64) point to the strong visual impact of a coffin and bearers remaining on stage, as does the phrasing of the SD ('*attended on by*' figures who clearly remain). This indicates possibility (*b*), an exit for the funeral at the very end of the scene, by that point abandoned by the mourners. Arguably, this makes their exits too markedly ironic – it verges on the black humour of the interrupted funeral of Henry VI, at the beginning of *Richard III*. Possibility (*c*) is an exit for the funeral, and for Warwick and Exeter, at 'Heralds wait on us' (45). That line, as with possibility (*b*), is then either an admonishment to the lords to follow and so catch up with heralds who have been waiting on – in the sense of waiting for (though admittedly the more expected idiom would be 'await' or 'stay for') – them offstage, or an order to onstage heralds, who have been added in many editions to the opening SD, to *wait on* the nobles as they proceed to the funeral proper; for the difficulties involved in choosing one or the other, see 1.1.45n. This edition opts for (*b*), as preserving the materiality of dead Henry's presence. The sense that the funeral must continue without the chief mourners does not seem inappropriate to the play's attitude to signs and ceremonies (so often to be rendered null or interrupted). The funeral, on the wide and trapezoidally-shaped Rose stage, would have to leave while Winchester spoke his final five lines, but to place the SD before them would misrepresent the situation to the modern reader and lose this juxtaposition, of the burial of the past with the Machiavellian eye to the future of the 'mourners'.

Speech prefixes

F sometimes changes speech prefixes (SPs) after the character has been named or renamed within the dialogue. On the page used as an example (see above p. 91), '*Taylors*' become a single speaking '*Keeper*' (TLN 1070, 1088). This example is not particularly telling in terms of the meaning of the scene. Other names of characters are important in this play as markers of the point they have arrived at in their complicated public careers. The SP '*Yorke*' on the page shown may be in tune with the character's ambitions, but runs ahead of his instatement in that title in the action of the play.

F's stage direction at the start of 2.4 puts it differently, but the first SP immediately contradicts it.

> *Enter Richard Plantagenet, Warwick, Somerset,*
> *Poole, and others.*
> *Yorke.* Great Lords, and Gentlemen,
> What meanes this silence?

The resumption by Richard Plantagenet of his title as the Duke of York should, given its importance to the action, be marked exactly in the SP from that point only, and any earlier use of 'York' in F be replaced by 'Richard'. But it would be unnecessarily confusing to call Talbot 'Earl of Shrewsbury' after this title has been conferred on him (3.4.26), as this particular change has little importance either to the individual character or to the action of the play.

Asides

'Aside' designates a statement assumed not to be heard by other characters on stage but addressed to an audience thus constructed as complicit with individual ambition or resolve. Since Elizabethan times it has been a conventional and familiar stage direction, indicating a variety of possibilities for the actor. At the Rose the compressed irregular hexagon of the stage, the raked standing space for the 'groundlings' on three sides and the several levels of spectators in the galleries produced an open relation to the audience. Actors in this situation would have been able to move flexibly between address to other actors on stage and address to the audience, with no fixed demarcation of stage space between private and public such as the literalizing later theatre of the proscenium arch and painted scenery would define. The BBC's *1 Henry VI* of 1982 constantly makes intelligent and fluent use of the actors' relation to simple, largely static camera positions, to replicate the possibilities of an actor's address to the audience within a non-proscenium arch space. Joan Puzel, at 3.3.85, claps Burgundy heartily on the back for 'Done like a Frenchman' and then, as she walks past him, continues the line directly to the camera for 'turn and turn again', before turning again herself and moving back into the scene (for more detail of the way this convention operates throughout this production, see Willis, *BBC*, 175–86). This is the kind of fast-moving switch of address required by these texts. Such a switch is hard to note clearly within editorial conventions. I have used the SD '*to the audience*' when direct address, aiming at a kind of political complicity, is required. On some other occasions I have used '*to himself*' or '*to herself*', most notably in the Suffolk/Margaret scene (5.2.81–128), which makes great comic/erotic play with the ambiguity, essentially flirtatious, as to what the characters are saying to themselves and what they expect to be heard or half heard or intuited by the other. At some other points I have specified which onstage character is addressed. It is characteristic of the play that most of its scenes are public, though the characters pursue private, even clandestine, ends; the convention of the 'aside' may oversimplify a field of possibilities best left to be worked out by the performers.

Above/within/on the walls.

Several scenes, especially those depicting sieges, require speech from 'within' the Tower of London, or a French town. In an Elizabethan theatre a character who spoke unseen from within might not be easily audible without some strongly visual drawing of attention to focus the auditors. In 1.3, if Gloucester made enough noise and fuss, this would serve the purpose, perhaps providing a comic contrast with the faint voice of Woodville from inside. But often in 'siege' scenes the characters to be understood as 'inside' appear 'above'. F's SD for the capture of Rouen in the third act (3.2.39.1–3) has the victorious French appearing '*within . . . on the walls*'. There '*within*' emphasizes that they have captured and entered the town, neatly combining the two possibilities by suggesting that 'above' is in this context continuous with 'within'. At 1.3.4.1 I have substituted an entrance '*on the walls*' for the 'within' normally supplied by editors. It would be difficult for the start of the scene to have any impact theatrically if the Warders were unseen. By the time Woodville speaks (15) the situation has been established sufficiently for him to speak from behind the door, so F's *'within'* is apt enough there. Antipholus of Ephesus' return to his unwelcoming home in *Comedy of Errors* (3.1) may seem to provide evidence for the opposite, but the scene there is elaborately set up and sustained long enough for the audience to adjust to a comic convention and in any case the play may well have been written for performance indoors.

Lineation and metrical regularity

On the page reproduced as Fig. 10, the end of the rose garden scene is in a more or less metrical sequence, disrupted by a casual-sounding exchange.

> *Yorke.* Good Master *Vernon*, I am bound to you,
> That you on my behalfe would pluck a Flower.
> *Ver.* In your behalfe still will I weare the same.
> *Lawyer.* And so will I.
> *Yorke.* Thankes gentle.
> Come, let vs foure to Dinner: I dare say,
> This Quarrell will drinke Blood another day.
> (2.4.127–33; TLN 1061–7)

To make this regular, three syllables would have to be supplied after 'gentle'. It is of course possible that there was a proper name here that the compositor could not decipher and so simply left out. Against this theory is the lack of any dramatic need for such a name, in contrast to the two other instances where metrically apt proper names have been omitted; in one of the cases at least it seems clearly preferable to supply the missing word. (See 1.1.56n. and 1.4.94n.) An actor could 'play' the gap by indicating that Richard had forgotten the Lawyer's name – this would work, but it would strain a point to notate it (by a dash after 'gentle', for example).

F, especially in the first act, splits some verse lines, particularly at the beginnings of speeches, to avoid turnover. The split is always made at an effective point metrically or in terms of sense, but it would be pedantic to reproduce F's lineation when the evident reason for it no longer applies. The many unmetrical lines are another matter. Pope and many editors since, including Cairncross (Ard²), assume that the verse (often, significantly, taken by them to be Shakespeare's verse) was regular originally but 'corrupted' in the process from initial composition to print, and can be restored by the omission and substitution of particular words. I have tended to resist this. In many scenes the verse moves fluently between rhymed and unrhymed, regular and irregular. I print as irregular verse (and occasionally as prose) those lines which cannot be made to scan without radical surgery. Sometimes I have indicated in the commentary or textual notes where an easy elision, cut or slight reshaping of the line can render it metrical, if that is desired. There are possibilities also of pronouncing words (sounding '-ion' endings as two syllables, for example) in a way that makes the metre more regular. In performance this now seems mannered, and much more distracting than metrical irregularity. Sixteenth- and seventeenth-century blank verse also allowed for the pronunciation of -ed inflections which would not be sounded today. Here I follow Arden practice in noting in the commentary individual instances of divergence from modern pronunciation, but it is not always possible to be entirely certain of the authors' metrical intentions.

But there is a point to be made here about the verbal style of the play, as F preserves it. Lapses into 'prosaic' rhythms can be used in anti-heroic 'plot-laying' moments – the Gunner's scene with his son (1.4.15–17), or the Countess's with her Porter (2.3.1–3), for example – and this, if we take the play to be, not a botched heroic play, but something more achievedly ironic, can be seen (and heard) to be theatrically apt. Actors must find their own way here. 'Many of the emendations suggested for this play', says Norman Sanders, probably with an eye to Ard[2], 'have been aimed at turning flat, mediocre verse into metrically regular flat, mediocre verse' (Sanders, 244). F's text at least allows actors a variety and freedom of spoken rhythm which does something to counter the flatness.

Act and scene divisions

One way in which this edition differs from others is in scene division, particularly in Acts 1 and 4. In F, plays either mark scene divisions consistently or not at all. In Acts 1 and 2 of *1 Henry VI*, however, only the acts and '*Scena Prima*' are numbered, while four scenes are numbered in its '*Actus Tertius*'. Act 4 is headed '*Actus Quartus. Scena Prima*', but '*Scena secunda*' and '*Scena Tertia*' follow only much later, at the points editors usually mark as 5.1 and 5.2. The final scene (5.4 in this edition) is marked '*Actus Quintus*'.

As Taylor has established (Taylor & Jowett, 3–50), plays for the professional stage were not split into formal act divisions, nor performed with gaps between the acts, before about 1610. Only academic and court performances bothered to follow classical precedent by splitting plays into five acts and – as much for social reasons as anything else – having musically accompanied intervals between the acts. In the public theatre the action was continuous, and food and drink were consumed as it went along. The confusion of scene numbering in F's text may support notions of collaborative authorship; Taylor suggests that *1 Henry VI* is perhaps one of only seven plays in F printed from a 'holograph', an original authorial manuscript (Taylor & Jowett, 242).

After an '*Actus Quartus. Scena Prima*', F has no further numbered scenes until a '*Scena secunda*' at the English court, which most editions number as the first scene of a fifth act. F goes on to call the very last scene of the play '*Actus Quintus*'. If this was taken as a misreading or mistranscription of '*Actus Quintus scena quinta*' and the scenes were counted back, the fifth act would start with the scene containing the death of Talbot, assuming that a '*Scena secunda*' implies a '*Scena prima*' before it. In the original perfor-mances, no act break would be marked; if, as happens with other plays from this period (*A Midsummer Night's Dream*, for example) a play written as continuous remained in the repertory after a marking of the five-act structure had become customary, act breaks would have acquired some justification in performance practice. I work from F, which attempted to make sense of thirty-year-old theatrical papers and aim, in my turn, to present a reading experi-ence that makes sense to a modern actor or theatregoer.

Earlier in the Introduction (pp. 9–15), I dealt with the way the text constructs stage space, particularly in its exploitation of the possibilities of the Rose. Two examples will serve to pull together the various strands of my argument about how a printed text can represent and facilitate stage practice, given my sense of the play as a piece of physical theatre, observing a flexible pre-realist con-vention in representing space and time. In both cases this edition produces something radically different from previous presen-tations of F's text.

The scene where Talbot's fate is sealed by York's and Somerset's inability to collaborate to rescue him makes sense as a continuous action, albeit one that non-naturalistically juxta-poses distinct geographical locations.

> Lucy, farewell; no more my fortune can
> But curse the cause I cannot aid the man.
> Maine, Blois, Poitiers and Tours are won away,
> Long all of Somerset and his delay.
> > *Exeunt [all but Lucy].*

LUCY
> Thus, while the vulture of sedition
> Feeds in the bosom of such great commanders,
> Sleeping neglection doth betray to loss
> The conquest of our scarce-cold conqueror,
> That ever-living man of memory,
> Henry the Fifth. Whiles they each other cross,
> Lives, honours, lands and all hurry to loss.

Enter SOMERSET *with his army* [*and a Captain of Talbot's.*]

SOMERSET
It is too late, I cannot send them now.

(4.3.43–54)

Other editions mark a change of scene after 'loss' (1.53), thus necessitating an exit and immediate re-entrance for Lucy (whose entry in F is simply '*another Messenger*').

This edition's 1.5.40 –70 – the Dolphin and Joan Puzel's appearance above to greet the French victory – is usually marked as a separate scene. I take an event continuous with the preceding action, though happening on a different level of the stage, to be still part of the same 'scene', in the spectacular style of a play like this. To some extent this depends (as with the final Talbot sequence in 4.4, conventionally split into separate scenes) on what one makes of '*alarums*' and '*excursions*'. In editorial tradition these, as a punctuation of the action, have marked a place to begin or end scenes. In a play like this, however, they may, rather, act to establish a continuity of action when the stage is empty of speaking participants. The events depicted are more comprehensible as continuous action across the stage space than when split into separate scenes that represent distinct locations (according to the conventions of a later scenic theatre, or of cinema). Oxford goes to the opposite extreme to this edition, in splitting up 1.4 (the 'Gunner's Boy' scene) into different sections, depending on where the characters are standing on stage. However confused the process by which F's text was arrived at, it seems to me that a minimal interference with what it gives us provides the clearest and theatrically most suggestive text.

KING HENRY VI
PART ONE

LIST OF ROLES

LONDON AND THE ENGLISH COURT

Duke of GLOUCESTER	*Protector of the realm, in the minority of the King*	
Duke of EXETER		
Earl of WARWICK		
Bishop of WINCHESTER	*Henry Beaufort, great-uncle to the King, and later Cardinal*	5
Duke of SOMERSET		
WOODVILLE	*Lieutenant of the Tower of London*	
RICHARD Plantagenet	*Later Duke of YORK, and Regent of France*	10
Duke of SUFFOLK	*(William de la Pole)*	
VERNON	*a gentleman of the Inns of Court, who joins the party of Richard Plantagenet*	
Edmund MORTIMER		
KING Henry the Sixth		15
BASSET	*a follower of the Duke of Somerset*	
Three Messengers	*to the funeral of Henry V*	
Two Warders	*of the Tower of London*	
Servingmen	*of Winchester and Gloucester*	
Mayor	*of London*	20
His Officers		
Lawyer	*of the Temple*	
Gaolers	*of Edmund Mortimer*	
Legate	*from the Pope to Winchester*	
	Ambassadors to the English court	25

THE ENGLISH ARMY IN FRANCE

Duke of BEDFORD	*Regent of France*	
Earl of SALISBURY		
Sir John TALBOT	*later Earl of Shrewsbury*	
Sir Thomas GARGRAVE		
Sir William GLANSDALE		30
Sir John FASTOLFE		
Sir William LUCY		
JOHN	*Talbot's son*	

106

Soldier	*at the siege of Orleans*	
Messenger	*to Sir John Talbot*	35
Talbot's Captain		
Messenger	*to York*	
Servant	*to Sir John Talbot*	

Soldiers, two Attendants on Bedford, Guards

THE FRENCH

CHARLES, the Dolphin of France	*crowned by the French as King Charles VII, a title unrecognised by the English*	40
Duke of ALENÇON		
REIGNIER	*Duke of Anjou and Maine, King of Naples and Jerusalem*	
BASTARD of Orleans		45
JOAN Puzel	*a peasant*	
Duke of BURGUNDY		
COUNTESS of Auvergne		
MARGARET	*daughter of King Reignier*	
Master Gunner of Orleans		50
Master Gunner's Boy	*his son*	
Sergeant	*of a band*	
Two Sentinels	*before Orleans*	
Messenger	*to Talbot from the Countess of Auvergne*	
Porter	*to the Countess of Auvergne*	55
Four Soldiers	*at Rouen*	
Watch	*of the City of Rouen*	
Govenor of Paris		
Captain	*of the French forces in Bordeaux*	
Scout		60
Shepherd	*who claims to be Joan Puzel's father*	

Soldiers, Fiends, Herald

LIST OF ROLES The first list appeared in Rowe's edition of 1709. Within the classification I have adopted, the roles are listed in order of speaking. In those cases where I have adopted a form of the name different from that of other editions, or where the form of a name in itself requires further comment, I have presented the discussion in Appendix 1.

1 GLOUCESTER Humphrey (1391–1447), the youngest of Henry V's brothers, the fourth son of Henry IV. His fall from power, as engineered by Margaret and Suffolk, his wife Eleanor's conviction for sorcery and his eventual murder at the instigation of the Cardinal of Winchester form the major part of the action of the first half of *2H6,* which in F is subtitled 'with the death of the Good Duke HVMFREY'. Hall, the major source of this play, fixes the image of the 'good', trusty Gloucester, largely created by Gloucester's own skill in 'self-glorification and propaganda' (Griffiths, 237), through the chronicles and other writings which he commissioned and which lay behind Hall's sources. When Shakespeare returns to him in the later *H5*, his is largely a walk-on role, with several marked appearances, but only five lines. The name is usually, but not invariably, pronounced as two syllables – 'Gloster' – an alternative spelling in F. Exceptions to this are recorded in the commentary.

3 EXETER Thomas Beaufort (d. 1427), uncle of Henry V, and the illegitimate half-brother of Henry IV. With the Bishop of Winchester, he was appointed the young King's guardian. His role is often choric, as observer and 'memory' of Henry V's reign. He is given a similarly central but more military role in *H5*.

4 WARWICK Richard de Beauchamp (1382–1439), who appears in several scenes towards the end of *H5*, though with only one insignificant line. Historically he was Governor of Calais at the time of Agincourt. His son-in-law, Richard Neville, or Warwick 'the

kingmaker', plays a significant role in *2H6* and *3H6*, but he is a very different character from his father-in-law, one whose political ambitions seem diametrically opposed to the conciliatory instincts of the Warwick of this play. Barton & Hall's adaptation of the plays as *The Wars of the Roses* none the less conflates the two characters, and invents material for this play's Warwick in order to link him to the later figure (see Appendix 3). If the plays are read as a planned three-part sequence, it makes sense to assume that the figure is a conflation of father and son (see notes on Mortimer and Somerset), though, as Hall and Barton demonstrate, we would then have to acknowledge that *1H6* draws the character indistinctly. If this option is taken without emending *1H6*, then 'Warwick's' outburst in *2H6* (1.1.116–23) is a dramatically sudden change of temperament, triggered by anger at the deal with Reignier. His claim that he had won the lands now given away suggests that *2H6* builds this aspect at least of the chronologically earlier figure into the later. If, on the other hand, we take *1H6* as a later, free-standing play (see Introduction, pp. 69–73), then the Warwick figure need be no more continuous with that of *2H6* and *3H6* than history and the sources would suggest, and the contrast of peaceable father and irascible wily son has its appeal as ironic comment on later events. But Bullough is perhaps over-confident in his presentation of the two figures as clearly distinct (see index to Bullough, 3.511).

5 WINCHESTER Henry Beaufort (d. 1447), Bishop, then Cardinal, of Winchester. He was the illegitimate son of John of Gaunt, and so Henry VI's great-uncle. As in Gloucester's case, a massively complex historical nexus of rivalry and competition for influence is simplified by Hall's use of partisan sources and by the dramatists' pursuit of heightened contrast. For Hall, he was 'surnamed the riche Cardinall of Winchester, and nether

called learned bishop, nor verteous priest' (Bullough, 3.52). The Bishop's magnificent palace was in that area of London, Southwark, where the theatres themselves were later to stand. It was an area notorious for lawlessness, and so the Bishop is tainted by association of a kind that the dramatists can play on in relation to their immediate audience (see Introduction, pp. 19–22). Gloucester and Woodville in addressing him as 'Cardinal' in 1.3 anticipate his official elevation to that rank, a development not clinched until 5.1. See 1.3.36n. for various ways of reading this.

7 SOMERSET 'Shakespeare, like the chroniclers, conflated two historical personages. John Beaufort, first Duke of Somerset (1403–44) . . . [and] . . . Edmund Beaufort, second Duke of Somerset (1406–55) . . . John Beaufort's younger brother' (Cam², 63). This composite figure, defined by a quarrel with York that one brother inherits from the other, appears as a supporter of the King's party in *2H6* where, in the last moments of the play, Richard, York's son (the future Richard III), kills him in ironic fulfilment of a prophecy. The historical John was rumoured to have committed suicide as a result of his failures in France; 'perhaps . . . he too became aware of his shortcomings' (Griffiths, 458).

8 WOODVILLE Richard Woodville (d. 1441). Hall makes it plainer than does this play that Woodville is of the party of Winchester, who 'cherished hym against the state and worship of the kyng, and of my . . . lorde of Gloucester' (Bullough, 3.49). Historically, Richard Woodville was the grandfather of Elizabeth Woodville, who marries Edward IV, the eldest son of York, in Act 4 of *3H6*. Her daughter married Henry Tudor (Richmond in *R3*) to unite the Yorkists and the Lancastrians, and so founded the Tudor dynasty, a marriage which is both the climax and the *raison d'être* of Hall's chronicle.

9 RICHARD Plantagenet. Given the title and status of Duke of York (1411–60)

in 3.1. This play charts the emergence of the major protagonist of *2H6* and *3H6*. In F *3H6* is subtitled 'with the death of the Duke of YORKE'. Hall presents Richard's instatement as Duke of York as coincident with the death of Mortimer, and so as a crucial dynastic event. This strengthens his retrospective justification of Richard's career. (See notes on King and Mortimer.) The stature accorded York – in determined opposition to weak or overtly villainous adversaries – may well reflect a Yorkist bias in the materials available to Hall. As in the case of Mortimer, the dramatists have exaggerated the extent of Richard's alienation from the court. See 2.4.3n.

11 SUFFOLK William de la Pole, Earl of Suffolk (1396–1450). In *2H6* he has become Margaret's lover, to be killed, like so many of the characters in *2H6* and *3H6*, as the fulfilment of a riddling prophecy. The role, both in *2H6* and in the current play, seems to be an expansion of Hall's more cautious 'THE erle of Suffolke (I cannot saie) either corrupted with bribes, or to[o] muche affectionate to this unprofitable mariage, condiscended and agreed' (Bullough, 3.71), and his later reference to him as 'the Quenes dearlynge' (Bullough, 3.112). There is no historical evidence for this relationship, but, especially given the eight years it took the King and Queen to conceive a child, and the coincidence of the Queen's pregnancy with the King's catastrophic mental breakdown, anti-Lancaster propagandists had ample opportunity to speculate on the paternity of their heir (Griffiths, 719). For further comment on the form and pronunciation of the name, see Appendix 1.

12 VERNON The character seems to be the dramatists' invention: a gentleman studying law at the Inns of Court who proposes that the choosing of roses shall be interpreted as a vote between York and Somerset, and then – whether cynically or not – joins York's party to the extent that the latter can refer to him as his 'servant'. According

to Hattaway, the name occurs in Hall as a companion in arms of Talbot (Cam[2], List of Characters, 64).

14 MORTIMER Edmund, fifth Earl of March (1391–1425). Shakespeare may seem to return to the character in *1H4*, where the marriage of an Edmund Mortimer to the daughter of the Welsh prince Owen Glendower clinches a rebellious alliance against Henry IV. Historically, however, the Edmund Mortimer by whose death Richard inherits the sense of a 'right' to the throne is that particular Edmund's nephew; this second Edmund remained a trusted and powerful courtier, appointed the King's lieutenant in Ireland in 1423 'for nine years, an unusually long term' (Griffiths, 164), before dying of plague two years later. This fictional scene has, however, a reference to a more unlucky Mortimer, John, brother of the rebel, who was imprisoned in the Tower of London and executed on trying to escape, in the same year that the fifth Earl of March, Edmund, died of plague. So the figure in this play is a conflation of three historical Mortimers: the known rebel, his brother the unfortunate prisoner and the (historically loyal) uncle of Richard.

15 KING Henry VI (1421–71) was crowned at nine months old, and his reign encompassed the longest period of civil war in English history. The catastrophe of *2H6* and *3H6*, taken as a diptych, is set up at the very beginning of *2H6*: his giving up the bulk of his possessions in France in exchange for the dowerless Margaret. Towards the end of *3H6* he is murdered in the Tower of London by Richard, the youngest surviving son of York and the future Richard III. Historically, Henry seems to have been an earnest, if rather naïve ruler, until his severe mental collapse in 1453, from which he never fully recovered, and after which he seems to have been a debilitated and largely passive figure (Griffiths, 715–19). Hall dignifies this by presenting him as 'of a meke spirite, and of a symple witte, preferryng peace before

warre, reste before businesse, honestie before profite, and quietnesse before laboure . . . there could be none, more chaste, more meke, more holy, nor a better creature' (Bullough, 3.105). This necessitates a further demonizing of Margaret, and establishes a picture that the plays elaborate. All this leaves open the possibility of the King's sainthood, a posthumous status urgently sought by Lancastrians. Unlike the historical Jeanne la Pucelle, Henry has yet to be canonized, but this campaign has coloured his presentation in chronicle and drama. Huizinga's description of him as 'an imbecile bigot' reflects the historian's partisanship of Reignier and Margaret (Huizinga, 18). In this play Henry ages, in strictly historical terms, from what would be the age of four, if we read 3.1, his first appearance, as taking place in 1426, the date of an uneasy public reconciliation of Gloucester and Winchester, at which the King was present, and at which he knighted several young aristocrats, including York (Griffiths, 79–80), to ten at the time of his coronation in Paris (4.1) and then to twenty-two at the time of the proposed marriage (5.1). Until stirrings of interest are roused in him by Suffolk's description of Margaret in the very last scene of the play, Henry is presented as pre-pubescent. Michael Hattaway suggests that the part was conceived for a boy actor (Cam[2], List of Characters, 63). This casting, obviously attractive if *1H6* is taken as an independent piece, would also work if the play were to be performed as the start of the three-part cycle, though all modern productions have used the same adult actor throughout. If a child were to be cast in a performance of the three parts, the adult actor playing the role in the later two plays could take over at 5.1. See Introduction, p. 30 and Appendix 2. See also notes on Suffolk and Margaret.

16 BASSET An invention of the dramatists, he represents, in his opposition to Vernon, one pole of the Lancaster/

York contention. Unlike Vernon in relation to York, he seems to be of Somerset's 'family'; i.e. a long-standing retainer. Again, the name is taken from Hall, but not the character (Cam[2], List of Characters, 64).

20 **Mayor** If we take the play's chronology as historical fact (which the dramatists themselves of course did not) then the Mayor of London in the scenes in this play was, according to Stowe (2.172), '*John Couentrie*, mercer'. A new mayor was elected from within the business community of the City of London every year, with responsibility to impose the rule of the law within the City's bounds – the City being a relatively small part of what is now central London, separate from and often politically opposed to both Westminster, the seat of government, and Southwark, Winchester's base and, later, the location of the theatres themselves.

21 **Officers** According to Stowe (2.187–8), the Mayor of London had thirty-two officers in all, each with a different function in legislation and in the regulation of trade. The officer in this play is the 'Common Crier', accompanying the Mayor to issue a call to order. Officers would wear a 'livery' or distinct official costume: 'I reade, that the Officers of this Cittie ware Gownes of partie colours, as the right syde of one colour, and the left side of another . . . in the 19. yeare of *Henrie* the sixt, there was bought for an Officers Gowne two yeards of Cloath, coloured Mustard . . . and two . . . coloured blew' (Stowe, 2.189).

26 BEDFORD John (1389–1435), the third son of Henry IV. When Shakespeare presents him in *2H4*, it is in implied comparison to Hal. John is the more dutiful but also colder and more calculating son, who thus seems initially – at least to Falstaff – to offset the liveliness of his brother. Later the play, especially at the scene of the battle of Galtree Forest (*2H4* 4.1), reveals him to be a ruthless, arguably dishonourable military commander, and the comparison can be seen to suggest a

potentially troubling similarity between the two brothers, which foreshadows Hal's rejection of Falstaff. Like others of the English party in the current play, he figures in *H5* in name and silent presence only. In *1H6* he is a significant military leader, but presented more warmly, as a figure of past glories, whose death, in a scene invented by the play, is a reference to Arthurian legend, a marker of a heroic past from which the English can only now decline. (See Introduction, p. 39, and 3.2.93n. and 110n.)

27 SALISBURY Thomas de Montacute (1388–1428). He appears in *H5*, but is used there simply to swell the martial scene and to interject the occasional generalized comment. In the current play he may be a one-scene role, but his surprising shooting by the Master Gunner's Boy and the subsequent onstage exequies are an important marker of the end of England's heroic era.

28 **Sir John** TALBOT John, Earl of Shrewsbury (d. 1453). The play's manipulation of its sources places Talbot's and Joan's parallel and rival careers as the spanning structural narrative of the play. In historical terms her career was well over before his became especially significant. Talbot has the largest number of scenes of any character, and these are invariably carefully constructed to maximize audience focus on a charismatic figure. (See Introduction, pp. 23–4, and Appendix 2.)

29–30 **Sir Thomas** GARGRAVE and **Sir William** GLANSDALE Apart from their presence at the shooting of Salisbury, where Gargrave is also shot, to die offstage (1.4.70), the characters have no other particular significance in the play. Hall has 'Glasdale'. F gives the name only once (1.4.62), with the 'n', and that is the form I have adopted.

31 **Sir John** FASTOLFE In this play the character is derived from an account in Hall of Bedford demoting the knight from the Order of the Garter, to which he had been elected 'the same yere', as punishment for his retreat at the battle

of Meuns, at which Talbot was captured (Bullough, 3.59; see 1.1.134n.). Earlier references to Fastolfe in Hall mention that he was Bedford's 'great Master of his household' (Bullough, 3.47) and list him with Talbot and 'diverse other valiaunt knightes and esquiers' (Bullough, 3.56). The play takes an incident that Hall is at pains to point out as 'out of character' to simplify him in his two appearances a cowardly foil to Talbot and the other English commanders. F calls the character 'Falstaff', but there is little apart from his strategic withdrawals from action to link him with the figure who appears in *1H4*, *2H4* and *MW*, in terms of calculated dishonesty, a liking for drink or physical bulk. A producer of our play might well consider casting in the role an actor who is spectacularly thin. For a discussion of the form of the name adopted by this edition, see Appendix 1.

32 **Sir William** LUCY The name, that of 'the Sheriff of Warwickshire during the reign of Henry VI' (Cam², List of Characters, 64), does not figure in the sources, and this has prompted speculation that the assignment of this name to an authoritative messenger/choric figure was prompted by a connection local to Shakespeare, in that a descendant, Sir Thomas Lucy (1582–1600), was 'a local magnate, of Charlecote, near Stratford-on-Avon' (Cam², List of Characters, 64). This then becomes evidence to those who see the play as collaboratively written to assign at least this part of it to Shakespeare (Taylor, 168).

33 JOHN Talbot's son John (d. 1453) is first mentioned by Hall as part of his father's party in taking Castillon; he is described as 'lord Lisle, by hys wyfe sonne to the sayd erle of Shrewesbury' (Bullough, 3.72). This is to distinguish the legitimate John from 'his [Talbot's] bastard sonne Henry Talbot' (3.73), who also died with Talbot in the vain attempt to retake Castillon. The play expands on Hall's invented dialogue between John and his father to foreground the issue of legitimacy, and so prudently omits Henry, as well as

omitting – in order to heighten the pathos – a surviving legitimate son back in England (Kastan, 21–2).

34 **Soldier** For a discussion of matters of military hierarchy, see Appendix 4.

40–1 CHARLES Dolphin (Dauphin) of France (1403–61). Although the character shares some semi-comic traits with the Dauphin in *H5*, historically the figure in that play is Charles's older brother Louis, who died in 1415. The current play does not emphasize, as does, for example, Shaw's *St Joan* (1923), the coronation of Charles VII at Reims. It confuses chronology to suggest that Charles had been crowned as an immediate response to Henry's death (see 1.1.92n.). None the less, variations in the way the character is named in this play can be seen to depend on this event, and the English response to it (see 5.3.123n.). For more on this, and on the spelling and pronunciation of the title, see Introduction, p. 23, and Appendix 1.

42 **Duke of** ALENÇON Jean, the fifth Duke of Alençon (1409–76). According to Hall, 'THE duke of Alaunson, whiche . . . was late delivered out of Englande, revived again the dull spirites of the Dolphyn, and the fainte hartes of his captaines, promisyng to theim greate victory with litle travail' (Bullough, 3.52). This leads to his success at Le Mans, which the play reassigns to Joan. Though in some sense they are equivalent figures, the play puts him in her shadow – he always appears as one of the group of French commanders.

43 REIGNIER René or Reignier, Duke of Anjou and Maine, King of Naples and Jerusalem (1409–80). The play much expands his role from the sources (but see 3.2.39.3n., and Appendix 2, for comment on this). The keynote of the character is given by Hall's remark: 'callyng hymself kyng of Scicile, Naples, and Hierusalem, hauyng onely the name and stile of the same, without any peny profite, or fote of possession' (Bullough, 3.71). He thus becomes part of a general theme in the play, of the emptiness and controversial legitimacy

of signs and titles. For more on the spelling and pronunciation of the name, see Appendix 1.

45 BASTARD **of Orleans** Jean, Count Dunois (1403?–68). The illegitimate son of Charles, Duke of Orleans. His father, probably now best known to English readers as a lyric poet, appears in *H5*, to be captured at Agincourt and taken into exile to England. The Duke was released, somewhat controversially, in 1440, as part of the Anglo-French peace negotiations. 'This coragious Bastard', as Hall calls the son, was 'in greate authoritie in Fraunce, and extreme enemie to the Englishe nacion' (Bullough, 3.55). The play strengthens his role by making him the figure who introduces Joan Puzel into the action.

46 JOAN **Puzel** Better known to later readers and audiences as 'Joan of Arc' (1412–31); canonized as 'Sainte Jeanne d'Arc' in 1920. On the various versions of the historical Jeanne's name, and on the construction of 'the Puzel' in this edition, see Introduction, pp. 25–7, and Appendix 1.

47 **Duke of** BURGUNDY Philip (1396–1467). The character returns in the last scene of Shakespeare's *H5*, where he acts as peacemaker: 'I have laboured / With all my wits, my pains and strong endeavours / To bring your most imperial majesties / Unto this bar and royal interview' (5.2.24–7). This speech on the physical effect of the war on the land of France has often in performance been reassigned to the King, the Queen or Mountjoy. This is a token of a historical forgetfulness, largely determined by French nationalism, as to the importance of the court of Burgundy in the late Middle Ages. In *1H6* his role as middleman between France and England is worked out to England's detriment; in Hall's account Henry V enjoins the English on his deathbed to keep 'continual peace and amitie with Philip duke of Burgoyn' (Bullough, 3.44), and Burgundy acts as co-regent of France with Bedford, but Joan Puzel, in a scene of the dramatists' invention, persuades him in this play to change loyalties by means of a speech whose rhetorical gambits foreshadow his own in the later play.

48 COUNTESS **of Auvergne** An invented character in an invented episode. There are several parallel scenes in plays of the period and earlier in which an interlude of a comic/erotic kind gives the dramatists space to recap the political themes in a different mode – the King/Countess of Salisbury scenes in *E3*, for example, arguably the product of the same group of playwrights. See Introduction, pp. 61–2.

49 MARGARET The daughter of Reignier, Margaret of Anjou (1430–82) married Henry VI in 1445. She figures largely in *2H6*, *3H6* and *R3*. Her appearance at the end of this play is as an ominous prediction of what an audience who had seen those plays already knew was to occur. There she is Suffolk's lover, York's nemesis, and warrior woman on behalf of Henry VI, whom she seems both to despise and to love. In *R3* she returns to the English court from her exile in France in order to bestow her curses on it; this is unhistorical, as she never returned to England and died the year before Richard's accession. She enters that play as a kind of ghost, while the other characters see her as a witch and prophetess. Her function seems to be as a reminder, an impotent but gloating memorial, of the history dramatized in the previous three plays. Hall describes her as 'a woman of a greate witte, and yet of no greater witte, then of haute stomacke, desirous of glory, and covetous of honor, and of reason, pollicye, counsaill, and other giftes and talentes of nature, belongyng to a man, full and flowyng' (Bullough, 3.105–6). See also notes on Suffolk and King.

61 **Shepherd** Hall calls Joan 'a shepherdes daughter . . . a beggers brat' (Bullough, 3.61). The encounter in which Joan Puzel denies her 'father' is invented, but it may be influenced by Hall's account of 'one, called the shepherd, a simple man, and a sely soule', whom the French also credited with magical powers (Bullough, 3.63).

KING HENRY VI
PART ONE

1.1 *Dead march. Enter the funeral of King Henry the Fifth,*
attended on by the Duke of BEDFORD, *Regent of France;*
the Duke of GLOUCESTER, *Protector; the* Duke of EXETER;
[the Earl of] WARWICK; *the* Bishop of WINCHESTER; *and the*
Duke of SOMERSET.

BEDFORD

Hung be the heavens with black. Yield day to night.

1.1.0.1 *funeral* the coffin and those bearing it. These could be either the nobles
themselves – effective theatrically, but
not representative of medieval or
Renaissance ritual practice, and so
unlikely to be the stage practice the text
implies – or six extras there simply for
this purpose. These figures, wearing
black and hooded, remain as an ominous visual presence, until they remove
the coffin. For a fuller discussion of the
form of the *funeral*, and, most specifically, its exit, see Introduction, pp.
95–6. It is not completely clear
whether we see the delayed and disrupted beginning of the funeral (which
is how the BBC version, for example,
presents it), or the end of the funeral,
as the coffin leaves Westminster Abbey,
as in the first scene of *R3*. But this second option seems dramatically much
less effective. It is an important irony in
the scene that the very concerns raised
by the death of Henry prevent a properly respectful completion of the ritual
of his funeral – from which, whatever
staging option is chosen, most of the
notable figures of the new reign eventually absent themselves.

0.4–0.5 WARWICK . . . SOMERSET Warwick and Somerset do not speak. At this
point, there is no way that they could be
identified by an audience, but it is possible

that they wear their heraldic badges over
their mourning cloaks, in which case the
point is made that the lords who will
later split over the issue of the roses are
here in at least a formal accord.
Depictions of Elizabeth I's funeral in
1603, on the other hand, suggest that
mourners all wore the royal coat of
arms, in which case the characters could
not be identified, and these characters'
names have been put in to indicate that
all the available nobility is present.

1 **heavens with black** The term *heavens*
is often used for the permanent canopy,
supported by pillars, that covered the
central section of the stage of an out-
door Elizabethan playhouse. Such a
canopy is thought to have been decorated with astrological and cosmological
symbols. We have no way of knowing
exactly what the superstructure of the
Rose theatre consisted of, but it seems
likely that the line refers to this kind of
canopy, conventionally hung with black
for tragic plays (Hotson, 142–3). Here
attention is drawn to the theatricality of
'heroic' rhetoric. The English lords may
wish to create a sense of tragedy, but the
line is ambiguous as to whether Bedford
is describing a black-hung stage or
demanding one. In either case, the play
establishes, characteristically, a potential
for bathos in its very first line.

1.1] *(Actus Primus. Scæna Prima.)*   0.4 *the* Earl of WARWICK] *Ard²; Warwicke* F

Comets, importing change of times and states,
Brandish your crystal tresses in the sky
And with them scourge the bad revolting stars
That have consented unto Henry's death –   5
King Henry the Fifth, too famous to live long.
England ne'er lost a king of so much worth.

GLOUCESTER

England ne'er had a king until his time.
Virtue he had, deserving to command,
His brandished sword did blind men with his beams,   10
His arms spread wider than a dragon's wings:
His sparkling eyes, replete with wrathful fire,
More dazzled and drove back his enemies
Than midday sun fierce bent against their faces.
What should I say? His deeds exceed all speech;   15
He ne'er lift up his hand but conquered.

EXETER

We mourn in black, why mourn we not in blood?

---

2 **Comets** Comets were seen as markers of a great man's death. The death of Julius Caesar, as described by Plutarch and reworked by Shakespeare in both *JC* (2.1.44–5 and 2.2.30) and *Ham* (1.1.117), provides a spectacular example.
importing signifying

3 **crystal** transparent; with a symbolic moral sense of clarity and rightness, as opposed to the *bad revolting stars* of the next line

9 **Virtue** The primary sense here is less the more familiar one, of moral goodness, more the theological one, of the power to act, possessed by angels and other supernatural beings. For Renaissance commentators like Machiavelli, virtue (*virtu*) was the capacity to take decisive action, its opposite idleness, or *ozio* (*Discorsi*, 2.2.282–3).

10 **his beams** the sword's, but with a sense also of Henry's personal qualities, as might be conveyed by the *beams* of his eyes

11 **dragon's wings** See, for a later example of the analogy of warrior and fabulous beast, *Cor* 4.1.30. There, too, dragons are not only fearsome but solitary and apocalyptic – they signal the end, in imagery derived from Revelation, 20.2. There may also be a reference to the Welsh/Celtic dragon, linking Henry back to Arthur, son of Uther Pendragon (see 3.2.93n.), and forward to the Tudors, whose dynasty starts from Owen Tudor's marriage to Henry's widow Katherine. 'The red dragon was one of the supporters of the Tudor kings . . . There is some room for doubt whether the dragon in the Royal Arms was really of Welsh origin . . . It was certainly in use by King Henry III' (Fox-Davies, 225–6).

14 **bent** turned

16 **lift** lifted
conquered conquerèd

6 King Henry] Henry *Pope*

Henry is dead, and never shall revive:
Upon a wooden coffin we attend,
And death's dishonourable victory   20
We with our stately presence glorify,
Like captives bound to a triumphant car.
What? Shall we curse the planets of mishap
That plotted thus our glory's overthrow?
Or shall we think the subtle-witted French   25
Conjurers and sorcerers, that, afraid of him,
By magic verses have contrived his end?

WINCHESTER

He was a king, blest of the King of kings.
Unto the French the dreadful Judgement Day
So dreadful will not be as was his sight.   30
The battles of the Lord of Hosts he fought;

19 **wooden** Though the King's coffin is literally *wooden*, with a lead lining (1.1.64), Exeter is bitterly invoking the current colloquial sense of the word as 'dull', 'useless'. See also 5.2.110 and n.

21 **presence** official attendance; with a sense, in reference to both the dead king and to death itself, of *OED* B, 'ceremonial attendance upon a person of superior, esp. royal, rank'

22 **triumphant car** The Romans established the custom of a triumphal entry into Rome by a conqueror in a chariot (*car*), with representatives of the conquered on display as part of the spectacle. Plays of the period capitalize on this frequently; see, for example, Marlowe's *2 Tamburlaine* (4.3) and *Tit* 1.1. Late medieval and Renaissance monarchs imitated the custom. Henry V did not, but after Agincourt he made a public return to London, at Blackheath. This is represented in the later *H5*, as in the sources, as an exemplarily modest affair. When the comparison to Rome is evoked, it is in the dramatists' choice of analogies for a spontaneous civic response that turns the scene into the triumph Henry himself has not

sought (*H5* 5.0.16–28). So the opening scene of this play is an ironic inversion of a triumph Henry never awarded himself in life. Here he is death's trophy, and the English lords the captives following its chariot/hearse.

23 **planets of mishap** planets with unlucky influence

27 **magic verses** Hall presents the French as likely to be taken in by witchcraft, but he sees that as a token of their weakness, not as genuine access to supernatural powers. Here it is in keeping with the excuses that the English characters tend to make for unexpected defeat: see Introduction, pp. 36–7.

28 **King of kings** As a title for Christ this occurs several times in Revelation and the Epistles. See Revelation, 19.16 and 17.14, and 1 Timothy, 6.15.

29 **Judgement Day** Described in Revelation as the last day, on which God will come to judge all mankind. See Revelation, 6.14–17 and 20.11–15.

30 **his sight** the sight of him

31 **battles . . . Hosts** Winchester is aligning Henry with King David, as one who fights 'the battels of the lord' (1 Samuel, 25.28, and 1 Samuel, 18.17;

The Church's prayers made him so prosperous.

GLOUCESTER

The Church? Where is it? Had not churchmen
    prayed,
His thread of life had not so soon decayed.
None do you like but an effeminate prince,   35
Whom like a schoolboy you may overawe.

WINCHESTER

Gloucester, whate'er we like, thou art Protector,
And lookest to command the prince and realm.
Thy wife is proud, she holdeth thee in awe,
More than God or religious churchmen may.   40

GLOUCESTER

Name not religion, for thou lov'st the flesh,
And ne'er throughout the year to church thou goest –

---

the phrase occurs in connection with
other biblical figures, but the Book of
Samuel seems to be a favourite source
of the dramatists).

34 **thread of life** In classical mythology
an individual life is figured as a thread
spun by three sisters, the fates, one of
whom, Atropos, will eventually cut it.
Here, *decayed* emphasizes material
fragility, and the pathos of a premature
death from illness.

37 **Protector** regent. Given the King's
youth in this play, Gloucester has the
responsibility of exercising his authority on his behalf.

38 **lookest** aim

39 **Thy . . . proud** In Hall, Gloucester at
this point illegally married 'the lady
Jacquet or Jacomin . . . whiche was law-
full wife to John duke of Brabant then
livyng, whiche mariage was not onely
woundered at of the common people,
but also detested of the nobilite, &
abhorred of the Clergie' (Bullough,
3.46). John later – 'what with force, and
what with spirituall compulsaries' –
managed to reclaim his wife. It seems

more likely that, *pace* Bullough, the
line is a reference to Gloucester's
equally unfortunate second marriage,
to Eleanor Cobham. Her downfall,
engineered by Suffolk's and Margaret's
manipulation of her ambitious nature,
precipitates Gloucester's (*2H6* 1.2–3.2).
This reference – arguably clumsy, if
this play is read as the first of a planned
sequence – makes more sense if we take
it as later than that which F presents as
'The second Part . . .'; it could be a joking but ominous reminder to an audience   that   already   knows   *The
Contention*, perhaps also as a teaser that
a flamboyantly memorable figure may
be about to appear in this play too. See
Introduction, p. 72.

41–3 Hall, 'This man was . . . more noble
of blodd, then notable in learning, haut
in stomacke, and hygh in counte-
naunce, ryche above measure of all
men, & to fewe liberal, disdaynfull to
hys kynne and dreadfull to his lovers,
preferrynge money before frend-
shippe' (Bullough, 3.109).

33] *Pope; F lines* it? / pray'd, /

118

Except it be to pray against thy foes.

BEDFORD

    Cease, cease these jars and rest your minds in peace.

    Let's to the altar. Heralds wait on us.   45

    Instead of gold we'll offer up our arms –

    Since arms avail not now that Henry's dead.

    Posterity, await for wretched years

    When at their mothers' moistened eyes babes shall

        suck,

    Our isle be made a nourish of salt tears,   50

    And none but women left to wail the dead.

    Henry the Fifth, thy ghost I invocate:

    Prosper this realm, keep it from civil broils,

    Combat with adverse planets in the heavens;

    A far more glorious star thy soul will make   55

    Than Julius Caesar, or bright –

---

43 **Except** unless

45 **Heralds . . . us** See 1.1.0.1n. If this is read as a command to a group of on-stage heralds who have entered with the coffin to prepare to exit with it and with the nobles, it can act as a cue to them, possibly also to Warwick and Somerset, possibly to the whole funeral, to exit at this point; the other characters are interrupted by the Messenger and remain on stage. Or it could be a simple statement of fact, in which *wait on* means 'are waiting for'. A comma in the text after *Heralds* would weight the line towards the first possibility; I have preferred to leave the choice open.

49 **When . . . suck** an unmetrical line, but hard to emend without losing some of the sense, unless *moistened* is emended to 'moist'

50 **nourish** nurse. *Riv* gives a gloss to the French word *nourrice*, a point originally made by Theobald in a footnote opposing Pope's reading; Pope emended *nourish* to 'marish', and some other

editors have followed, on the basis that the word 'nourish' is not used as a substantive elsewhere. F seems stronger, in turning into metaphor the hyperbole of the previous line. The word may be a reminiscence of Henry V's dying exhortation, as presented by Hall: 'And what thynges either I have gotten or you shal obtaine, I charge you kepe it, I commaund you to defend it, and I desire you to norishe it' (Bullough, 3.44–5).

52 **invocate** invoke; call upon in prayer

53 **broils** disturbances

56 **Julius Caesar** Julius Caesar is an example of the mortal hero who becomes a star on his death. The opening of the first book of Lucan's *Pharsalia* promises this fate to Nero – in Marlowe's translation 'thee (seeing thou, being old, / Must shine a star) shall heaven (whom thou lovest) / Receive with shouts' (Lucan (Marlowe), 45–7). Nero seems to be on the writers' mind in a later broken-off line (1.4.94), but the Elizabethan

45 us.] us. *Exit Funeral. Ard²;* us. *Exeunt Warwick, Somerset, and Heralds with coffin. Oxf*   47 not now . . . dead.] *Cam²;* not, now . . . dead, *F*   50 nourish] marish *Pope*

Enter a Messenger.

MESSENGER

My honourable lords, health to you all.
Sad tidings bring I to you out of France,
Of loss, of slaughter and discomfiture.
Guyenne, Champagne, Reims, Rouen, Orleans,   60
Paris, Gisors, Poitiers are all quite lost.

BEDFORD

What sayest thou man, before dead Henry's corse?
Speak softly, or the loss of those great towns
Will make him burst his lead and rise from death.

GLOUCESTER

Is Paris lost? Is Rouen yielded up?   65
If Henry were recalled to life again
These news would cause him once more yield the ghost.

EXETER

How were they lost? What treachery was used?

MESSENGER

No treachery, but want of men and money.
Amongst the soldiers this is muttered: 70
That here you maintain several factions,
And whilst a field should be dispatched and fought

audience might be more likely to expect the metrically apt 'Hercules'. It is of course impossible to establish whether this or some other name was present in the MS and left out by the compositors as illegible, or whether the line is truncated for effect, as a messenger rushes in. See Introduction, p. 100.

59 **discomfiture** total defeat

60–1* This account compresses a number of losses that occurred over a much larger span of time; Paris, for example, was not lost until 1436. *Rouen* is not mentioned in the list in F, but

Gloucester's reference to it at 65 makes it a valid addition. Gloucester pronounces it as two syllables, and the metrical fitness helps here, but in 3.2 and 3.3, scenes set in Rouen, it is pronounced as a monosyllable.

64 **burst his lead** break from the lead lining of his coffin

67 **These news** As late as the mid-nineteenth century *news* could be construed as either singular or plural.

69 **want** lack

70 **muttered** mutterèd

72 **dispatched** speedily concluded

60 Rouen] *Capell; not in F*   61 Gisors] *(Guysors)*   62 sayest] *(say'st)*   man, . . . corse?] man! . . . corse *Staunton*   65 Rouen] *(Roan)*

You are disputing of your generals.
One would have lingering wars, with little cost.
Another would fly swift, but wanteth wings.   75
A third thinks, without expense at all,
By guileful fair words peace may be obtained.
Awake, awake, English nobility,
Let not sloth dim your honours new begot;
Cropped are the flower-de-luces in your arms;   80
Of England's coat one half is cut away.   [*Exit.*]
EXETER
Were our tears wanting to this funeral
These tidings would call forth her flowing tides.

---

73 **generals** Though the basic force of
the line is clear enough, its expression
is ambiguous; *generals* seems to be
used in the sense where it is the opposite of 'particulars', as 74–7 suggests
(see *OED sb.* B 2a, first example 1566),
since technically there is only one
'general' of the army (see Appendix 4,
on military hierarchy), and *disputing
of*, on this reading meaning 'arguing
about', would be awkward in this
sense anyway.

80 **flower-de-luces** The *fleur-de-lis*, a
stylized depiction of a lily flower, has
been long associated with France, but
there is some doubt as to what it originally represented. It is readable as an
iris, which, as Fox-Davies puts it, 'was
known by the name of a lily until
comparatively modern times'. He
continues, 'The fleur-de-lis as the
finial of a sceptre and as an ornament
of a crown can be taken back to the
fifth century. Fleurs-de-lis upon
crowns and coronets in France are at
least as old as the reign of King Robert
(son of Hugh Capet) whose seal represents him crowned in this manner'
(Fox-Davies, 273). The standard

legend, however, interprets the visual
motif as a trio of feathers, brought by
a dove to Clothilde, wife of the pagan
king Clovis, when her husband converted to Christianity after his victory
over the Alemanni (Warner, 167). The
imagined origin of the symbol is thus
also the origin of France as a Christian
nation. The precise context of this
reference is Edward III's incorpora-
tion of the device into the royal coat of
arms, as part of his claim to the sover-
eignty of France: 'upon his new Great
Seal (made in the early part of 1340)
we find . . . "Quarterly, 1 and 4, azure,
semé-de-lis or (for France); 2 and 3,
gules, three lions passant guardant in
pale or (for England)." The Royal
Arms thus remained until 1411, when
upon the second Great Seal of Henry
IV, the fleurs-de-lis in England (as in
France) were reduced to three in number, and so remained as part of the
Royal Arms of this country until the
latter part of the reign of George III'
(Fox-Davies, 274).

83 **her** England's. Theobald's emendation seems unnecessary.

---

74 lingering] *(lingring)*   76 third] third man *F2*   81 SD] *Cam¹*   83 her] their *Theobald*

BEDFORD

Me they concern; regent I am of France.

Give me my steeled coat. I'll fight for France.　　　　85

Away with these disgraceful wailing robes;

Wounds will I lend the French, instead of eyes,

To weep their intermissive miseries.

Enter to them another Messenger.

2 MESSENGER

Lords, view these letters, full of bad mischance.

France is revolted from the English quite,　　　　90

Except some petty towns of no import.

The Dolphin Charles is crowned king in Reims:

---

84 **regent . . . France** According to Hall, 'the duke of Bedforde Regent of Fraunce, no lesse studied then toke payne, not onely to kepe and ordre the countrees and regions by kyng Henry late conquered and gained, but also determined not to leve of from daily warre and continuall travaile till the tyme that Charles the Dolphyn . . . wer ether subdued or brought to dewe obeysance' (Bullough, 3.45–6).

85 **steeled** steelèd; literally, his armour made of steel, but the metaphorical sense of the word, as resolute, ready for action, can be applied to Bedford himself

86 **disgraceful** Passive mourning is dishonourable when action is required.
　　wailing robes hooded black robes worn over black clothes on an occasion of mourning (contemptuously characterized here as *wailing*). Oxf's SD has Bedford remove his at this point, but unless the others follow suit this creates an inappropriately strong visual emphasis on one figure, and, arguably, begins the collapse of the funeral rituals too early.

88 **intermissive** coming regularly at intervals

90 **France is revolted** According to Hall, it was not so much Henry's death as that of Charles VI of France which caused these 'revolts'; 'a greate parte of the nobilitee whiche ether for feare of the puissance of the Englishemen, or for to please and folowe the mynde and appetite of Charles the Frenche kyng, toke parte with kyng Henry against the Dolphyn: Heryng now of the French kynges death, returned from the English part and adjoyned themselfes to the compainie of the Dolphyn, and diligently studied howe to vanquishe and dryve awaie the Englishe nacion out of the territory of Fraunce' (Bullough, 3.46).

91 **import** importance. The stress is on the second syllable.

92 **Dolphin** For this form of the title, see Appendix 1.
　　crowned . . . Reims crownèd. Historically, the Dauphin was not crowned at Reims until 1429, under Jeanne's protection (the form 'Jeanne' is used throughout this edition when the reference is to the historical figure). According to Hall, when Charles heard of his father's death he, 'callyng together the Princes of his faccion,

---

86 robes;] robes. *He removes his mourning robe Oxf* 89 SP] *Rowe; Mess. F* 92 Dolphin] *F throughout;* Dauphin *Rowe*

The Bastard of Orleans with him is joined.
Reignier, Duke of Anjou, doth take his part.
The Duke of Alençon flieth to his side.   *Exit.*

EXETER

The Dolphin crowned king? All fly to him?   96
O whither shall we fly from this reproach?

GLOUCESTER

We will not fly, but to our enemies' throats.
Bedford, if thou be slack, I'll fight it out.

BEDFORD

Gloucester, why doubt'st thou of my forwardness?   100
An army have I mustered in my thoughts,
Wherewith already France is overrun.

Enter another Messenger.

3 MESSENGER

My gracious lords – to add to your laments,
Wherewith you now bedew King Henry's hearse,
I must inform you of a dismal fight   105
Betwixt the stout Lord Talbot and the French.

WINCHESTER

What? Wherein Talbot overcame, is't so?

3 MESSENGER

O no: wherein Lord Talbot was o'erthrown.

caused hymself to bee proclaimed
Kyng of Fraunce' (Bullough, 3.46),
but there is no mention of a coronation
ceremony in Hall.
96 **crowned** crownèd
97 **reproach** source of disgrace or dis-
    credit
105 **dismal fight** battle with an unlucky
    outcome (for the English); the battle of
    Patay (1429, but moved earlier to
    tighten the structure of the play). See
    Introduction, p. 24).
108 **Lord . . . o'erthrown** The event

narrated here is, historically speaking,
subsequent to Jeanne's taking of
Orleans. As with most of the events
alluded to in this scene, narrative continuity and sequence have been
manipulated to create an emblematic
picture of national disaster. The
Messenger's account in itself follows
Hall closely. '[The French] had perfite
knowledge, that the lorde Talbot with
.v. thousand men, was commyng to
Meum . . . And first thei appoynted
their horsemen, whiche were well and

94 Reignier] *Rowe; Reynold F;* René *Oxf*   96 crowned] *(crown'd)*   103+ SP] *Rowe; Mess. F*

The circumstance I'll tell you at more large.
The tenth of August last, this dreadful lord   110
Retiring from the siege of Orleans,
Having full scarce six thousand in his troop,
By three and twenty thousand of the French
Was round incompassed and set upon.
No leisure had he to enrank his men.   115
He wanted pikes to set before his archers,
Instead whereof sharp stakes plucked out of hedges
They pitched in the ground confusedly,
To keep the horsemen off from breaking in.
More than three hours the fight continued,   120
Where valiant Talbot, above human thought,
Enacted wonders with his sword and lance.
Hundreds he sent to hell, and none durst stand him.
Here, there and everywhere enraged he slew.
The French exclaimed the devil was in arms,   125

richely furnished, to go before, and sodainly to set on the Englishemen, or [=ere] thei wer, either ware or set in ordre. The Englishmen commyng forwarde, perceived the horsemen, and, imaginyng to deceive their enemies, commaunded the fotemen, to environe & enclose themselfes about, with their stakes, but the French horsmen came on so fiersly, that the archers had no leyser, to set themselfes in a raie [array]. There was no remedy, but to fight at adventure. This battaill, continued by the space of thre long houres. And, although thenglishmen wer overpressed, with the nombre of their adversaries, yet thei never fledde backe one foote, til their capitain the lorde Talbot, was sore wounded at the backe, and so taken. Then their hartes began to faint, & thei fled' (Bullough, 3.59).

109 **at more large** at greater length
110 **The tenth . . . last** Hall gives a day –

'Saterdaie' – but not a date. The date given in the play would actually antedate Henry V's death, on 1 September 1422, and in any case does not reflect particularly well on the Messenger's haste.

112 **full scarce** *Full* is an intensifier (like 'very'), so the meaning of the phrase is 'only' or 'no more than'. But the contradiction between *full* in its larger meaning and *scarce* could create an oxymoron, to emphasize rhetorically the Messenger's intensity and his listeners' confusion. Holinshed has 'not past *six thousand* men' (3.165), Hall has 'v. thousand men' (Bullough, 3.59).
114 **incompassed** incompassèd
115 **enrank** place in military formation, 'rank'
116 **wanted** lacked
118 **pitched** pitchèd
    confusedly confusèdly
120 **continued** continuèd
123 **stand** withstand, stand against

112 full scarce] scarce full *Rowe*   124 slew] flew *Rowe²*

All the whole army stood agazed on him.
His soldiers, spying his undaunted spirit,
'A Talbot, a Talbot' cried out amain,
And rushed into the bowels of the battle.
Here had the conquest fully been sealed up,   130
If Sir John Fastolfe had not played the coward.
He being in the vanguard, placed behind
With purpose to relieve and follow them,
Cowardly fled, not having struck one stroke.
Hence grew the general wrack and massacre.   135
Enclosed were they with their enemies.
A base villain, to win the Dolphin's grace,
Thrust Talbot with a spear into the back –
Whom all France, with their chief assembled strength,
Durst not presume to look once in the face.   140

BEDFORD
Is Talbot slain? Then I will slay myself,

---

126 **agazed** gazing, but including a variant of aghast or frightened
128 '**A . . . Talbot**' the usual form in
which the soldiers shout support for
their commander, as a kind of rallying
cry. The source is the French *à* meaning 'to'.
  cried crièd
  amain with full force
130 **sealed up** concluded, like a docu-
ment closed over, and authorized, by a
seal of wax
131* **Fastolfe** See note in List of Roles,
(p. 111) and Appendix 1
134 **Cowardly fled** Hall mentions Fastolfe's cowardice, without ascribing
this consequence to it. The English
flight in Hall is general, a panic consequent on Talbot's injury. 'From this
battaill, departed without any stroke
striken, sir Jhon Fastolffe, thesame yere
for his valiauntnes elected into the
ordre of the Garter' (Bullough, 3.59).

See note on Fastolfe in List of Roles
(p.111).
135 **wrack** disaster
136 **Enclosed** Enclosèd
137 ***A base villain** F's 'Wallon' seems to
be either an invention of the dramatists (the sources do not identify the
nationality of the assailant) or a misreading on the part of F's compositors
of a sequence of minims (see 1.3.29n.)
in secretary hand. Walloons, inhabi-
tants of what is now South Belgium,
do not play any role in the fighting as
the sources of the play report it,
though they might strike a contemporary chord as (enforced) allies of the
Spaniards, their rulers at the time the
play was performed. But the Walloons
were the allies of Burgundy – and
therefore of the English – at this point
in the conflict, so a Walloon who
behaved in this way would be outstandingly base. See 2.1.10.

---

128 cried] *(*cry'd*)*   131 Fastolfe] *Theobald; Falstaffe F throughout*   132 vanguard] *(*Vauward*)*
137 villain] *this edn;* Wallon *F*   141 slain? Then] *Theobald⁴;* slaine then? *F*

For living idly here in pomp and ease
Whilst such a worthy leader, wanting aid,
Unto his dastard foemen is betrayed.

3 MESSENGER

O no, he lives, but is took prisoner, 145
And Lord Scales with him, and Lord Hungerford:
Most of the rest slaughtered, or took likewise.

BEDFORD

His ransom there is none but I shall pay.
I'll hale the Dolphin headlong from his throne;
His crown shall be the ransom of my friend. 150
Four of their lords I'll change for one of ours.
Farewell, my masters. To my task will I.
Bonfires in France forthwith I am to make,
To keep our great Saint George's feast withal.
Ten thousand soldiers with me I will take, 155
Whose bloody deeds shall make all Europe quake.

3 MESSENGER

So you had need, for Orleans is besieged.
The English army is grown weak and faint:
The Earl of Salisbury craveth supply

---

146 **Lord Scales ... Hungerford** According-ing to Hall: 'there wer slain above xij. C. and taken .xl. whereof the lorde Talbot, the lord Scales, the lord Hungerford, & sir Thomas Rampston, were the chief' (Bullough, 3.59). Thomas Lord Scales became one of Margaret's most power-ful advisers. He successfully defended the Tower against Cade and his follow-ers, as he is seen doing in *2H6* 4.5, but was killed by Yorkists in 1460, when they took control of London. Hungerford, the treasurer of the realm, was another staunch Lancastrian. Rampston, historically 'Rempston', was the governor of Calais. So the English lost, temporarily at least, four of their most important men.

149 **hale** pull
151 **change** exchange
153 **Bonfires** Bonfires were lit on days of popular celebration, as the next line here implies. See 1.5.51, where, ironi-cally, it is the French who celebrate the failure of the English to capture Orleans in precisely this way. The lit-eral meaning of Bedford's words here is that he intends to burn French cities.
154 **Saint George's** George, a legendary classical warrior and saint (but, given his ahistorical status, now for the Catholic Church no longer a saint), is the patron of England, whose flag bears his blood-red cross. He is figured in Spenser's Red-Cross Knight of *FQ*, 1.

157 for ... besieged] 'fore ... besieg'd *Hanmer*

And hardly keeps his men from mutiny,   160
Since they, so few, watch such a multitude.   *[Exit.]*

EXETER

Remember, lords, your oaths to Henry sworn:
Either to quell the Dolphin utterly,
Or bring him in obedience to your yoke.

BEDFORD

I do remember it, and here take my leave,   165
To go about my preparation.   *Exit.*

GLOUCESTER

I'll to the Tower with all the haste I can,

---

162 **Remember . . . oaths** This moment is stronger if the coffin is still on stage. Exeter is remembering Henry V's dying words, as reported by Hall: 'And my brother of Bedford with the helpe of the duke of Burgoyne I wyll shall rule and be regent of the realme of Fraunce, commaundyng him with fyre and sworde to persecute Charles callyng him selfe dolphyn, to thentent either to bryng him to reason & obeysaunce, or to dryve and expel him out of the realme of Fraunce admonishyng you to lese no tyme, nor to spare no cost in recoveryng that whiche to you is now offered. . . . The noble men present promised to observe his preceptes and performe his desires, but their heartes were so pensive & replenished with doloure that one without wepyng could not beholde the other' (Bullough, 3.44–5). A portion of this speech was spoken by an offstage voice at the beginning of the scene in Barton & Hall's adaptation, *The Wars of the Roses*; see Appendix 3.

163 **quell** suppress; kill, destroy

166 **go about** set about

preparation pronounced as five syllables

167 **Tower** The Tower of London was the repository of the royal armoury. As Protector Gloucester is trying to secure the young King's position against possible opposition. His failure to do so is dramatized in 1.3. In Hall, 'The articles of accusation, and accord, betwene my Lorde of Gloucester, and my lorde of Wynchester' recount Gloucester's grievances against Winchester, as he presented them to the parliament in the King's presence (Bullough, 3.49; 3.1.0.3). Though here Gloucester presents control of the Tower as a necessary preliminary to proclaiming Henry king, Hall presents the proclamation as having been made before this incident, not as a result of Gloucester's individual agency, but as a decision of 'the noblemen', including Winchester. 'The politicke Princes . . . caused yong prince Henry . . . beyng of the age of .ix. monethes or there about with the sound of trumpettes openly to be proclaimed kyng of Englande and of Fraunce' (Bullough, 3.45). Historically, Gloucester's motivation was to procure the services of one 'Friar Randolf', a magician imprisoned in the Tower for his involvement in the magical experiments of Joan of Navarre, Henry IV's second wife (Griffiths, 75–6); but both Hall and this play ignore this in favour of a simpler, more directly personal opposition between Gloucester and Winchester.

161 SD] *Cam*[1]   166 SD] *(Exit Bedford.)*

127

To view th'artillery and munition,
And then I will proclaim young Henry king.   *Exit.*

EXETER

To Eltham will I, where the young King is,   170
Being ordained his special governor,
And for his safety there I'll best devise.   *Exit.*

WINCHESTER

Each hath his place and function to attend.
I am left out; for me nothing remains.
But long I will not be Jack out of office.   175
The King from Eltham I intend to steal,
And sit at chiefest stern of public weal.

> *Exit [Winchester one way. Exit the funeral
> another way, with Warwick and Somerset].*

170 **Eltham** a royal palace, first recorded in use by Henry III in 1270, in what is now Woolwich, south-east London. Some distance across the river from Westminster and the Tower, in what was then a rural area, this was the safest place for the young King, for reasons of both health and security. James I was the last monarch to use it. The great hall and the moat still exist.

175 **Jack . . . office** Winchester's description of himself is a scathingly ironic self-deprecation. The phrase is proverbial (Dent, J23). Hall records that 'the custody of this young prince was apoyncted to . . . Henry Beaufford bishopp of Wynchester' jointly with Exeter, the King's uncle (Bullough, 3.45). The dramatists override this to build for Winchester a villainous and solitary exit. The only evidence of an attempt by Winchester to abduct the King from Eltham, the palace where he spent most of his childhood, is Hall's 'articles of accusation', unsupported claims made by Gloucester: 'ITEM my said lorde of Winchester . . . purposed . . . to set hande on the kynges persone, and to have removed hym from Eltham . . . to Windsore, to the entent to put hym in suche governaunce as hym list' (Bullough, 3.49).

176 ***steal** F has 'send', but Mason's conjecture *steal* seems much better, as a closing rhyme, and as an underlining of Winchester's intent. If 'send' is a misreading, on the compositor's part, it may have been induced by *intend*.

177 **chiefest . . . weal** The stern is the steering position of a boat, the back end, from which the rudder is controlled; Winchester is saying that he will steer public administration, though his place is in the background. *Sit* makes him sound almost comically complacent, and *chiefest* is a self-aggrandizing tautology.

169 SD] *(Exit Gloster.)* 176 steal] *Singer (Mason);* send *F* 177 SD]; *Exeunt Cam¹ Winchester . . . Somerset] this edn*

[1.2]   *Sound a flourish. Enter* CHARLES [the Dolphin],
ALENÇON *and* REIGNIER, *marching with Drum and Soldiers.*

CHARLES

Mars his true moving, even as in the heavens
So in the earth, to this day is not known.
Late did he shine upon the English side:
Now we are victors – upon us he smiles.
What towns of any moment but we have?   5
At pleasure here we lie near Orleans:
Otherwhiles, the famished English, like pale ghosts,
Faintly besiege us one hour in a month.

ALENÇON

They want their porridge and their fat bull-beeves:
Either they must be dieted like mules   10

1.2.1 **Mars . . . moving** Mars was the
Roman god of war. The motions of
the planet Mars were seen as completely unpredictable; the human eye
could find no discernible pattern in
them. Theobald notes that 'The
Revolutions of the Planet *Mars* were
not found out till the beginning of the
17th Century. *Kepler*, I think, the
Person, who first gave Light to
Discovery upon this Subject'. So a
homology became available for 'the
fortunes of war'. The reference continues from the preceding scene the
sense of planetary 'influence', of the
power astrologers believe astronomical
phenomena have over human actions
and fates. Cf. 1.1.2–5.

5   **moment** importance
6   **At pleasure** freely
7   **Otherwhiles** from time to time
8   **besiege** The English *besiege* both the
town of Orleans, from across the river
Loire, and the newly established
French camp, on the other side of
them. The Dolphin refers to the sec-

ond, where he and his forces are. See
diagram of Orleans, Fig. 2, p. 13.
9   **want** lack
fat bull-beeves The association of
the English with beef, particularly in
the context of a nationalistic assertion
of masculinity and courage, is long-
standing. The Elizabethan army
received a ration, every seventh day,
of two pounds of salt beef or two and
a half pounds of fresh (Cruikshank,
88). Whether in this play, in
Hogarth's eighteenth-century painting *The Roast Beef of Old England* or
in the present-day (1999) journalistic
response to continental worries about
the dangers of British beef infected
by BSE, beef is a marker of the line
between England and France. The
French term *les rosbifs* for the English
is still at the time of writing just about
current, though perhaps rather camp.
'Beef-witted' (Nashe, 1.370.18; *TC*
2.1.12) is not a compliment, even in
English.

1.2] *Capell*   0.1 the Dolphin] *this edn*   7 Otherwhiles] The whiles *Capell*   9 bull-beeves] *(*Bul
Beeues)

And have their provender tied to their mouths,
Or piteous they will look, like drowned mice.

REIGNIER

Let's raise the siege: why live we idly here?
Talbot is taken, whom we wont to fear.
Remaineth none but mad-brained Salisbury,   15
And he may well in fretting spend his gall;
Nor men nor money hath he to make war.

CHARLES

Sound, sound alarum, we will rush on them.
Now for the honour of the forlorn French:
Him I forgive my death that killeth me   20
When he sees me go back one foot, or fly.   *Exeunt.*

Here alarum. They are beaten back by the English, with great loss.
Enter CHARLES, ALENÇON *and* REIGNIER.

CHARLES

Who ever saw the like? What men have I?
Dogs, cowards, dastards! I would ne'er have fled,
But that they left me midst my enemies.

REIGNIER

Salisbury is a desperate homicide;   25
He fighteth as one weary of his life.

11 **have . . . mouths** wear nosebags –
bags of hay or other food fastened
around horses' heads, so they can eat
while working
12 **drowned mice** drownèd; proverbial
(Dent, M1237)
13 **raise the siege** See 8n. Reignier means
'end the English siege of Orleans'.
14 **wont** are used
15 **mad-brained Salisbury** Hall presents the decision to besiege Orleans as
follows: 'the erle of Salisburies devise,
(although it semed harde and straunge
to all other, and to hym as it wer a thyng

predestinate very easie) was graunted
and allowed, whiche enterprise was the
finall conclusion of his naturall destiny,
as you shall shortely perceive' (Bullough,
3.54).
16 **fretting . . . gall** Gall is a secretion of
the liver, and is synonymous with bitterness. Reignier says that Salisbury
will expend his *gall* in *fretting*, meaning
impotent worry.
18 **alarum** the normal form in F, made
conventional by subsequent edns, for
'alarm', meaning call to battle
19 **forlorn** lost; desperate

13 live] lie *Hudson (Walker)*   21.1] 1.3 *Oxf*

The other lords, like lions wanting food,
Do rush upon us as their hungry prey.

ALENÇON

Froissart, a countryman of ours, records
England all Olivers and Rolands bred   30
During the time Edward the Third did reign.
More truly now may this be verified,
For none but Samsons and Goliases
It sendeth forth to skirmish. One to ten?
Lean raw-boned rascals – who would e'er suppose   35
They had such courage and audacity?

CHARLES

Let's leave this town, for they are hare-brained slaves,

---

28 **hungry prey** It is the English not the French who are hungry; the epithet is transferred.

29 **Froissart** The French historian of the century previous to that of the events of the play, associated with a golden age of chivalry, now past. His *Chroniques* were written and rewritten between 1360 and 1400. They were translated by Sir John Bourchier, Lord Berners, in 1523–5, and used as a source by the writers of *Edward III*.

30 **Olivers and Rolands** The central figures of the *Chanson de Roland*, an eleventh- or twelfth-century French narrative poem, are devoted friends who die defending Christendom out of loyalty to each other and to Charlemagne. According to Berners's translation of Froissart, 'the erle of Lune, in susteynynge the Castellyans and in exscusynge of them' says that the English troops under the command of the Black Prince, the son of Edward III, at the battle of Najera in 1367, were 'worth a Rowlande or an Olyvere'. Talking of the battle facing them in 1387, Lune continues, 'But the duke of Lancastre hathe none suche . . . nor we shall not fyght agaynst Rowlande nor Olyver'. So the

reference is already in a context of the decline of heroism (Froissart, 4.429). Shakespeare returns to the names, and to some of the themes of the tale, in *As You Like It*: Orlando's name is the Italian form of Roland; his brother is (ironically, given their mutual hostility) Oliver; and their dead father Rowland.

33 **Samsons and Goliases** Samson was a Hebrew warrior (Judges, 14–16) and Goliath the giant champion of the Philistines, killed by the young David (1 Samuel, 17.4–54). (Cf. *E3* 4.6.35–6.) Talbot's account of himself in captivity seems also to allude to the Samson story – see Introduction, p. 47 – but both these figures are, ominously, most famous in defeat, by an adolescent (and often in Renaissance depictions androgynous) male in the one case, by a deceitful seductress in the other: types of Joan and the Countess respectively.

34 **One to ten?** Alençon is expressing his incredulity at the odds – one Englishman to ten Frenchmen.

37 **hare-brained** *OED* cites Hall as its first instance of this expression. Hares have a reputation for reckless or 'mad' behaviour, particularly in spring.

---

30 bred] *Rowe;* breed *F*   37] *Pope; F lines* Towne, / Slaues, /

And hunger will enforce them to be more eager.
Of old I know them; rather with their teeth
The walls they'll tear down than forsake the siege.   40

REIGNIER

I think by some odd gimmers or device
Their arms are set, like clocks, still to strike on;
Else ne'er could they hold out so as they do.
By my consent, we'll even let them alone.

ALENÇON   Be it so.   45

Enter the BASTARD *of Orleans.*

BASTARD

Where's the Prince Dolphin? I have news for him.

CHARLES

Bastard of Orleans, thrice welcome to us.

BASTARD

Methinks your looks are sad, your cheer appalled.
Hath the late overthrow wrought this offence?
Be not dismayed, for succour is at hand: 50
A holy maid hither with me I bring,
Which by a vision sent to her from heaven
Ordained is to raise this tedious siege

41 **gimmers** According to *OED sb.*[1] 3,
gimmer is a 'Corrupt form of GIM-
MAL', meaning 'links, connecting
parts (in machinery) esp. for transmit-
ting motion'. *OED* gives this line as its
first citation of this sense.
42 **still** perpetually, without pause
on perhaps a pun on 'one', to continue
the allusion to clocks
44 **By my consent** with my permission.
In line with Reignier's character in the
play, the phrase has an ironically
courtly tone.
48 **cheer appalled** mood downcast or

darkened
51 **A holy maid** The dramatists introduce Joan Puzel earlier into the action
than did Hall, and they make the
Bastard her patron, to link her into an
action which he had, historically, initiated. In Hall 'She (as a monster) was
sent to the Dolphin, by sir Robert
Bandrencort capitain of Vancolour'
(Bullough, 3.56–7). Hall's account was
later elaborated by Holinshed, to
whose version the play is closer.
53 **Ordained** Ordainèd

38 to be] be *Pope*   41 gimmers] *F (*Gimmors*)*, *Alexander;* Gimmals *F2*   47+ SP CHARLES] *Rowe;*
Dolph. F

And drive the English forth the bounds of France.
The spirit of deep prophecy she hath,   55
Exceeding the nine sibyls of old Rome:
What's past and what's to come she can descry.
Speak, shall I call her in? Believe my words,
For they are certain and unfallible.

CHARLES

Go call her in: but first – to try her skill –   60
Reignier, stand thou as Dolphin in my place.
Question her proudly, let thy looks be stern.
By this means shall we sound what skill she hath.

Enter JOAN Puzel.

REIGNIER

Fair maid, is't thou wilt do these wondrous feats?

JOAN

Reignier, is't thou that thinkest to beguile me?   65

---

54 **forth the bounds** out of the territories, across the borders

56 **nine sibyls . . . Rome** *Sibyl* was a term given to prophetesses of the ancient world. The usual estimate given of their numbers is ten (*OED* 1). They were spread across the Mediterranean world, though the most famous was that described by Virgil in *Eclogue VI*. Later, Christian writers took the words Virgil ascribes to her as a prophecy of Christ. Christine de Pisan, in a poem of praise she wrote after the coronation of Charles at Reims, *Ditié de Jehanne d'Arc* (1429), went so far as to claim that the sibyl had prophesied the coming of Jeanne (*Ditié*, st. 31). To take the number of sibyls down to nine (also the number of the 'worthies' – see Introduction, pp. 43–6) may be to suggest that Joan Puzel is the true tenth.

60 **Go . . . in** 'Unto the Dolphin into his gallerie when first she was brought, and he shadowing himselfe behind, setting other gaie lords before him to trie hir cunning from all the companie, with a salutation, (that indeed marz all the matter) she pickt him out alone, who thereupon had hir to the end of the gallerie, where she held him an houre in secret and private talke, that of his privie chamber was thought verie long' (Holinshed: Bullough, 3.75–6). This tale, with its analogues to tests in folk-tale and witch-trials, is a development of a much simpler description of the meeting made at the historical Jeanne's trial, and debated there as to whether it was tantamount to a claim of supernatural powers and therefore heretical (see Warner, 60).
try test

63 **sound** test

---

60 in:] in. *Exit* Bastard. *Capell*   63.1] *Enter* La Pucelle, *usher'd.* / *Capell; Enter the Bastard of* ORLEANS *with* JOAN LA PUCELLE. *Dyce; Enter* BASTARD *and* JOAN LA PUCELLE *armed Cam²*, *after Oxf*   65 + SP JOAN] *this edn; Puzel.* F

Where is the Dolphin? Come, come from behind.
I know thee well, though never seen before.
Be not amazed, there's nothing hid from me.
In private will I talk with thee apart.
Stand back, you lords, and give us leave awhile.   70

REIGNIER

She takes upon her bravely at first dash.

JOAN

Dolphin, I am by birth a shepherd's daughter,
My wit untrained in any kind of art;
Heaven and Our Lady gracious hath it pleased
To shine on my contemptible estate.   75
Lo, whilst I waited on my tender lambs
And to sun's parching heat displayed my cheeks,
God's mother deigned to appear to me
And, in a vision full of majesty,
Willed me to leave my base vocation   80
And free my country from calamity:
Her aid she promised and assured success.
In complete glory she revealed herself.
And, whereas I was black and swart before,

---

67 **thee** Joan significantly addresses the
Dolphin without ascribing to him any
royal title.

71 The line could be glossed, following
OED dash *sb.* 2 *fig.*, as 'She conducts
herself well, from the first impact she
makes'. But as so often in Joan's scenes
there is a sexual innuendo – *first dash* –
here from a metaphor of horse-riding,
which in itself stems from Hall's
description of Joan, in which boldness
and immodesty are combined: '[she]
was a rampe of suche boldnesse, that
she would course horses and ride
theim to water, and do thynges, that
other yong maidens, bothe abhorred &
wer ashamed to do' (Bullough, 3.56).

75 **estate** social class, place in society

78 **deigned** deignèd
80 **base** low
vocation pronounced as four syllables
84 **black and swart** dark, swarthy. The
distinction here is one of social class,
as 77 alerts us; Joan Puzel there says
that, as a peasant labourer, she has to
the 'sun's parching heat displayed my
cheeks', so she was sunburnt, unlike a
fair-skinned aristocrat or bourgeoise.
The miracle is a physical expression of
her rise in status. *Black* could mean
black-haired, unfashionable at the time
of the play's writing, and so raising the
comic possibility that the Virgin Mary
has given Joan Puzel a miraculous
make-over – or, of course, that she has
dyed her hair herself.

With those clear rays which she infused on me,   85
That beauty am I blest with, which you may see.
Ask me what question thou canst possible
And I will answer unpremeditated;
My courage try by combat, if thou dar'st,
And thou shalt find that I exceed my sex.   90
Resolve on this: thou shalt be fortunate,
If thou receive me for thy warlike mate.

CHARLES
Thou hast astonished me with thy high terms.
Only this proof I'll of thy valour make –
In single combat thou shalt buckle with me,   95
And, if thou vanquishest, thy words are true;

85 **infused** poured
86 **That beauty** The play here allows both Hall's and Holinshed's accounts of Joan's appearance to remain in unresolved apposition, though they contradict each other. For Holinshed, 'Of favour was she counted likesome, of person stronglie made and manlie' (Bullough, 3.75), while, for Hall, 'whether it wer because of her foule face, that no man would desire it, either she had made a vowe to live chaste, she kept her maydenhed' (Bullough, 3.56). The balance of emphasis between the two accounts is controlled by Joan Puzel's powers of rhetorical persuasion. Her rhetoric of self-presentation tends to evoke biblical echoes which combine the erotic and the miraculous. See 'An Excellent Song which was Salomons', as the Geneva Bible called The Song of Solomon: 'I am blacke . . . but comelie . . . Regarde ye me not because I am blacke: for the sunne hathe loked upon me' (1.4–5).
89 **My . . . combat** This play invents the trial by combat. There is nothing to suggest that the historical Jeanne fought hand to hand, or indeed played

more than an advisory and symbolic role in the French victories (Warner, 165–6). The dramatists create an active combative figure with more erotic and comic potential than dignity. Holinshed's Joan is efficient with her sword 'wherewith she fought & did manie slaughters by hir owne hands' (Bullough, 3.75). Bullough (3.26) makes the comparison with Spenser's Britomart (*FQ*, 3), a virtuous woman warrior, whose prowess stems from and is symbolic of her virginity; as with Joan Puzel her weapon (a spear) is itself numinous, possibly sacred, and part of the apparatus of the symbolism of active virtue. See Introduction, pp. 31–2, for further thoughts on this parallel, and on the handling in production of the ambiguity between magical and physical powers in Joan Puzel's case (pp. 32–6).
91 **Resolve on this** come to this conclusion
92 **mate** word with a complex set of meanings, which is why Joan Puzel chooses it; it can mean associate, adversary and equal, or married partner.
93 **high terms** elevated language
95 **buckle** engage

86 with, which you] which you *F2;* with you *Ard²*

Otherwise I renounce all confidence.

JOAN

I am prepared. Here is my keen-edged sword,
Decked with five flower-de-luces on each side,
The which at Touraine, in Saint Katherine's churchyard,   100
Out of a great deal of old iron, I chose forth.

CHARLES

Then come, o' God's name. I fear no woman.

JOAN

And while I live I'll ne'er fly from a man.
Here they fight and Joan Puzel overcomes.

CHARLES

Stay, stay thy hands. Thou art an Amazon

---

97 **confidence** trust, with a sense (*OED* 3) of reliance on divine help

99 **flower-de-luces** Cf. 1.1.80n.

100 **Saint Katherine's churchyard** Hall presents this and the recognition incident in a context of rhetorically stressed mockery of the credulity of the French: 'What should I reherse, how they saie, she knewe and called hym her kyng, whom she never saw before. What should I speake how she had by revelacion a swerde, to her appoynted in the churche of saincte Katheryn, of Fierboys in Torayne where she never had been' (Bullough, 3.57). Holinshed prefaces his account, closer verbally to the play's, with an equally sceptical parenthesis, '(as their bookes make hir)', and presents the incident as 'at the Dolphins sending by hir assignement, from saint Katharins church of Fierbois in Touraine . . . in a secret place there among old iron, appointed she hir sword to be sought out and brought hir, that with five floure delices was graven on both sides' (Bullough, 3.75). There were five *fleurs-de-lis* on

Edward III's coat of arms, to emphasize his claim to the crown of France. Line 100 is metrically irregular (unless *Katherine's* is pronounced Kath'rine's) in a way which seems to me to point to a prosaic undercutting of the heroic stance asserted in more insistent lines elsewhere. Hattaway (Cam[2]), presumably on the same basis, marks this and the following line as an aside.

103 The sexual innuendo introduced here is developed by the French lords throughout the scene, and colours later presentation of Joan Puzel. The language used of her and by her always permits a reading of her activities other than the saintly or the heroic by hinting at sexual significance.

104 **Stay** stop

Amazon The Amazons were a mythical race of women warriors, mentioned by Homer in the *Iliad* as having fought on the Trojan side at Troy. Their leader Penthesilea was often cited as one of the nine 'female worthies' with whom Joan was compared (see Introduction, pp. 45–6).

---

99 five] *Steevens;* fine *F*   100–1] *Aside Cam[2]*   100 churchyard] Church *Pope*   101 great deal] deal *Dyce*   102 come, o'] *(come a); come, a Cam[2];* come on *(Oxf)*   103 fly from a] fly no *F2*   SD *Joan Puzel*] *this edn; Ioane de Puzel F;* la Pucelle *Rowe*

And fightest with the sword of Deborah.   105
JOAN
  Christ's mother helps me, else I were too weak.
CHARLES
  Whoe'er helps thee, 'tis thou that must help me.
  Impatiently I burn with thy desire,
  My heart and hands thou hast at once subdued.
  Excellent Puzel, if thy name be so,   110
  Let me thy servant and not sovereign be.
  'Tis the French Dolphin sueth to thee thus.
JOAN
  I must not yield to any rights of love,
  For my profession's sacred from above:
  When I have chased all thy foes from hence,   115
  Then will I think upon a recompense.
CHARLES
  Meantime look gracious on thy prostrate thrall.

105 **Deborah** another 'female worthy' (see 104n.). She was a prophetess who led Israel against the Canaanites (Judges, 4 and 5). Holinshed's report of the posthumous annulment of Joan's condemnation for witchcraft includes the fact that she was reinstated as 'a damsell divine . . . likened to Debora, Jahell, and Judith' (Holinshed, 171–2), the three 'biblical' female worthies, and again for Christine de Pisan, in the *Ditié*, three biblical seemed the most apt comparison (see Introduction, p. 45).
110 **Puzel** Nobody yet has spoken her name, nor has she named herself; the Dolphin believes it to be Puzel, though it is not clear which of its senses is uppermost in his mind. Though, as a French speaker he hears it as 'pucelle', he is as 'puzzled' as any other character in his encounter with her. See Appendix 1, on naming, and Introduction, pp. 25–7.
113 **yield . . . rights** ambiguous between

the meanings 'yield rights to any' and 'yield to any rites'. F spells it 'rights'.
114 **profession's** Joan Puzel uses the word in *OED*'s sense I 1a, 'The declaration, promise or vow made by one entering a religious order . . . the fact of being professed in a religious order'. So she claims here that she is a kind of nun, given that status *from above*, meaning heaven.
115 **chased** chasèd
117 **prostrate** This implies Joan has 'floored' him, and that he is trying to turn a position of defeat to an expression of gallantry. She wins over – or 'overcomes' – the Dolphin, not by the mysterious and still unexplained secret that the historical Jeanne revealed to her Dauphin, but in a single combat that seems to end in a graphic and sexually inflected image of a woman on top. Joan might imaginably stand or sit astride the Dolphin, to set up the subsequent vein of innuendo.

113 rights] rites *Pope*

REIGNIER

My lord, methinks, is very long in talk.

ALENÇON

Doubtless he shrives this woman to her smock –

Else ne'er could he so long protract his speech.   120

REIGNIER

Shall we disturb him, since he keeps no mean?

ALENÇON

He may mean more than we poor men do know:

These women are shrewd tempters with their tongues.

REIGNIER

My lord, where are you? What devise you on?

Shall we give o'er Orleans, or no?   125

JOAN

Why no, I say. Distrustful recreants!

Fight till the last gasp. I'll be your guard.

CHARLES

What she says I'll confirm. We'll fight it out.

JOAN

Assigned am I to be the English scourge.

---

119 **shrives . . . smock** *Shrives* means hears, as a priest, the confession of sins and imposes a penance. Such a penance might involve publicly wearing only an undergarment (*smock*), or shroud-like sheet to indicate shame – see, for example, Eleanor, Duchess of Gloucester, *2H6* 2.4 – or privately wearing an uncomfortable garment next to the skin. Here, of course, the line conveys a sexual innuendo, 'strips her to her undergarments' (cf. *3H6*, where Richard of Gloucester and Clarence are watching their brother Edward woo Lady Grey (3.2.107–8)).

120 **so . . . speech** This continues the innuendo of the previous line to suggest that the Dolphin is sexually aroused by his 'bout' with Joan.

121 **mean** moderation (*OED sb.*² I 1b)

123 **shrewd** a word with many related meanings. Here its primary use is as an intensifier of *tempters* (in the way that modern colloquial English might use 'real'), but it carries into this other senses, often used in a misogynistic context, of 'cunning' and 'abusive'.

126 **recreants** *OED* B *sb.* 1, 'one who yields in combat; a cowardly or faint-hearted person'

129 **the English scourge** Marlowe's Tamburlaine entitles himself 'the scourge of God' (*2 Tamburlaine*, 5.3.248). There the grammatical form is

125 o'er Orleans] *(o're Orleance);* over Orleans *Rowe;* over Orléans, yea *(Oxf)* 127 I'll] I will *Capell*

This night the siege assuredly I'll raise.   130
Expect Saint Martin's summer, halcyons' days,
Since I have entered into these wars.
Glory is like a circle in the water,
Which never ceaseth to enlarge itself
Till by broad spreading it disperse to nought.   135
With Henry's death the English circle ends:
Dispersed are the glories it included.
Now am I like that proud insulting ship
Which Caesar and his fortune bare at once.

ambiguous: he is both a punishment that those who believe in God may think comes from God and, contradictorily, a challenge to the very idea of God. Here Joan presents herself in a simpler sense, as a scourge of the English, allowing it to be assumed that she has God's sanction.

130 **assuredly** assurèdly
131 **Saint Martin's summer** The festal day of St Martin de Tours – Martinmas – is on 11 November. Unexpectedly warm weather late in the year is called St Martin's summer; it is said that, when his coffin was carried back to Tours along the Loire for burial, trees and flowers bloomed in a second spring. The saint was a Roman soldier, most famous for an act of charity where he cut his cloak in half with his sword to share it with a beggar. He became the Bishop of Tours, in central France, and was a highly revered saint in the Middle Ages.
*halcyons' days** Alcyone was the daughter of Aeolus, the wind-god, who, according to Ovid in his *Metamorphoses*, joined her drowned husband Ceyx in a transformation into kingfishers; or that at least is the species assigned them as the tale is anglicized. Golding has '*The Kings fisher*' as a marginal note to this passage in his translation of 1567. Ovid

tells of a mythical seabird: 'for seven peaceful days in the winter season Alcyone broods upon her nest floating upon the surface of the waters. At such a time the waves of the sea are still; for Aeolus guards his winds' (Ovid, 11.745–8). See also Dent, D116. The idea of the calm sea is developed into the *circle in the water* of 133.

132 **entered** enterèd
135 **nought** The circle idea implies zero, an emptiness, an absence. But it is 'naught' in F, which, though on one level simply an alternative spelling, brings out the sense of evil, or at least of *vanitas*, by opening the possibility of a pun on the more strictly mathematical term.
137 **Dispersed** Dispersèd
138–9 Caesar and his ship are normally referred back to the *Life of Julius Caesar* (Plutarch (North), 781–2), where Caesar emboldens a sea-captain carrying him alone in a boat to Brundisium by telling him that his own personal fate will ensure their survival. The same story is told by Lucan in *Pharsalia*, 5.04–677, where it is inflected differently, given Lucan's hostility to Caesar; this ironic edge is more apt to Joan and the French.

131 halcyons'] *Riv; Halcyons F;* halcyon *F3*   132 entered] *(entred); entered thus F3*

CHARLES

> Was Mahomet inspired with a dove?   140
> Thou with an eagle art inspired then.
> Helen, the mother of great Constantine,
> Nor yet Saint Philip's daughters were like thee.
> Bright star of Venus, fallen down on the earth,
> How may I reverently worship thee enough?   145

ALENÇON

> Leave off delays, and let us raise the siege.

140 **Mahomet** the prophet Muhammad (570–632). Sceptical Elizabethan accounts of his powers, following a medieval tradition, allege that he attracted a dove to appear to speak to him by lodging corn in his ear. The English form 'Mahomet' should be pronounced with stress on the first and last syllable.

140, 141 **inspired** inspirèd

141 **eagle** In both classical and Christian traditions the eagle is associated with divine inspiration, in the classical as the bird of Zeus, which carried the beautiful Ganymede to heaven at his command (a story that was read either sexually or as a spiritual allegory), in the Christian as the emblem of the apostle John, one of the evangelists, and author of the Book of Revelation. The zoological lore that underpins both ideas is the belief that the eagle has eyes which, uniquely, enable it to look at the sun. But here it is also opposed to the dove, the bird of peace, as the bird of war.

142 **Helen** the mother of the Roman emperor *Constantine*, whom she converted to Christianity. She was led by a vision to find, on Calvary, the cross on which Christ was crucified. Many relics identified with this event still survive. She was listed as one of the female 'worthies'. See Introduction, p. 45.

143 **Saint Philip's daughters** Acts, 21.8–9: 'he had foure daughters virgines, which did prophecie'. Although they play no further part in the biblical narrative, they figure in sixteenth- and seventeenth-century debates as to whether women had the power and the right within the Christian Church to prophesy and to write. Nashe refers to them in *The Terrors of the Night* as 'the chast daughters of Saint *Philip*' (1.381.14); chastity in itself, given the way this scene among others presents Joan, would make them *not like* her.

144 **Venus** perhaps a reference back to Mars – whose lover the goddess was – mentioned in the first line of the scene. The legend of Venus come down to earth (to look for Cupid) is retold by Spenser, *FQ*, 3.6.11–28, as the introduction to the description of the garden of Adonis. *Star of* associates Joan Puzel with the planet Venus, which has the double aspect of the morning star, associated in Christian tradition with Lucifer, the challenger of God, as the visible star nearest the sun, and the evening star, which often has erotic connotations, as the first star of the night.

145 a metrically irregular line. Although it could be 'corrected', the metrical pattern gives sexual urgency to Charles' enthusiasm for Joan.

144 fallen] *(falne)*   145 reverently] reverent *Dyce²*

REIGNIER

Woman, do what thou canst to save our honours,
Drive them from Orleans and be immortalized.

CHARLES

Presently we'll try. Come, let's away about it.   149
No prophet will I trust, if she prove false.   *Exeunt.*

[1.3]   *Enter* GLOUCESTER, *with his* Servingmen
                         [*in blue coats*].

GLOUCESTER

I am come to survey the Tower this day:
Since Henry's death I fear there is conveyance.
Where be these warders that they wait not here?
Open the gates, 'tis Gloucester that calls.

[*Enter two* Warders *on the walls.*]

149 **Presently** immediately
1.3.0.2* **blue coats** In contrast to the first
English scene, dominated visually by
physical stillness, and by a preponder-
ance of black, this scene is continuously active, and laid out in broad
colour contrasts that the text is at pains
to specify. Gloucester's men are in *blue*,
Winchester's in *tawny* (47). Winchester
himself, if wearing cardinal's robes, is
dressed in *scarlet* (42); see 47n.
2   **conveyance** used here in its sense as
'furtive or light-fingered carrying off;
stealing' (*OED* 4). The scene expands
on one of the 'articles of accusation,
and accord, betwene my Lorde of
Gloucester, and my lorde of
Wynchester', as presented by Hall
(Bullough, 3.49): 'First, where as he
beyng protector and defendor of this
lande, desired the toure to be opened to
hym, and to lodge hym therein, Richard
Woodevile esquire, havyng at that tyme
the charge of the kepyng of the toure,

refused his desire, and kepte thesame
toure against hym, unduly and against
reason, by the commaundement of my
saied Lorde of Winchester'. The play
builds on the presentation of Winchester at the end of the first scene, to
show Gloucester acting in defence of his
own and the monarchy's interests.
Historically, Winchester's motive in
installing Woodville in the Tower was to
strengthen his position in protecting
foreign merchants based in Southwark,
who had become the victims of attacks
by Londoners (Griffiths, 74–5).
4   **Gloucester** here, and at 6, 62 and (less
clearly) 80, pronounced as three syllables: 'Glou-cest-er'. Otherwise in this
scene the more usual two-syllable pronunciation is used. In modern pronunciation the three-syllable version could
sound awkward in performance.
4.1 **on the walls* For a consideration of
this and other related SDs, see
Introduction, pp. 99–100.

1.3] *Capell*   0.2 *in blue coats*] *Capell*   1 come . . . this day] this day come . . . Tower *Pope*
4.1] *this edn*

1 WARDER
    Who's there, that knocks so imperiously?　　　　5
1 SERVINGMAN
    It is the noble Duke of Gloucester.
2 WARDER
    Whoe'er he be, you may not be let in.
1 SERVINGMAN
    Villains, answer you so the Lord Protector?
1 WARDER
    The Lord protect him – so we answer him.
    We do no otherwise than we are willed.　　　　10
GLOUCESTER
    Who willed you? Or whose will stands but mine?
    There's none Protector of the realm, but I.
    Break up the gates, I'll be your warrantize;
    Shall I be flouted thus by dunghill grooms?
       Gloucester's Men rush at the Tower gates, and
       Woodville, the Lieutenant, speaks within.
WOODVILLE
    What noise is this? What traitors have we here?　　　　15
GLOUCESTER
    Lieutenant, is it you whose voice I hear?
    Open the gates, here's Gloucester that would enter.
WOODVILLE
    Have patience, noble duke, I may not open;
    The Cardinal of Winchester forbids.
    From him I have express commandment　　　　20
    That thou nor none of thine shall be let in.

10, 11 **willed** commanded
11 **willed** willèd
13 **warrantize** guarantee
14 **dunghill grooms** the lowest kind of
servants, those who clear the stable-
yard of horse dung
19 **Cardinal of Winchester** See note on
List of Roles.

5 knocks] knocketh *Theobald*　6 SP] *Cam²; Glost*. 1. *Man. F*　8 SP] *Cam²;* 1. *Man. F*　19 The
Cardinal] My lord *Oxf*　20 commandment] *(commandement)*

GLOUCESTER

Faint-hearted Woodville, prizest him 'fore me?
Arrogant Winchester, that haughty prelate
Whom Henry, our late sovereign, ne'er could brook?
Thou art no friend to God, or to the King: 25
Open the gates, or I'll shut thee out shortly.

SERVINGMEN

Open the gates unto the Lord Protector,
Or we'll burst them open, if that you come not quickly.

Enter, to the Protector at the Tower gates, WINCHESTER,
and his Men in tawny coats.

WINCHESTER

How now, ambitious Humphrey, what means this?

23 Hall describes Henry's refusal to allow
Winchester to be cardinal: 'Whiche
degree, kyng Henry the fifth knowyng
the haute corage, and the ambicious
mynde of the man, prohibited hym on
his allegeaunce once, either to sue for
or to take, meanyng that Cardinalles
Hattes should not presume to bee egall
with Princes' (Bullough, 3.51–2). See
1.3.36n. and 5.1.28–33.

26 **shut thee out** Gloucester is threaten-
ing to have Woodville dismissed from
his position, and so banned from
entering the fortress which he current-
ly governs. The metre suggests a stress
on *thee*.

29 *****Humphrey** When the printer deciphered F's '*Vmpheir*' from Elizabethan
secretary hand he could well have been
working from a chaos of minims (the
short vertical penstrokes which make
up 'u', 'm' 'r' 'i'); the descender of a 'p'
or an 'f' below the line could well have
been the only distinct figure.
Humphrey seems the best reading here,

as 'Umfrey', one of Hall's spellings of
the name, would be very similar to
'Umpheir' in the secretary hand of the
(now lost) playhouse manuscript; then
only '-eir' would be an error, and 'reie'
or 'erie' could have been the MS form.
The word seems to have cross-
fertilized in the printer's mind with
'umpire', a slightly unusual word
which occurs elsewhere in the
Gloucester/Winchester scenes.   F2
ingeniously emends to 'umpire', but
this would imply that Winchester was
accusing Gloucester of ambition in
taking on an arbitrator's role in some
other unspecified dispute; he cannot,
by definition, be 'umpire' in the quarrel between himself and Winchester.
Oxf's 'vizier' is bizarre (see *TxC*, 220;
1.4.29n.). Humphrey is the first name
of the Duke of Gloucester (see note on
List of Roles); Winchester is the only
character who uses it, in a belittling
disregard for Gloucester's title.

28 Or we'll] We'll *Pope*   29 Humphrey] *Theobald; Vmpheir F;* umpire *F2;* vizier *Oxf*

GLOUCESTER

Peeled priest, dost thou command me to be shut out?   30

WINCHESTER

I do, thou most usurping proditor –
And not Protector – of the King, or realm.

GLOUCESTER

Stand back, thou manifest conspirator,
Thou that contrived'st to murder our dead lord,
Thou that giv'st whores indulgences to sin;   35
I'll canvas thee in thy broad cardinal's hat

---

30 ***Peeled** or, possibly, 'pilled'. F has 'Piel'd', and the meaning of these two alternatives is identical in this context: 'threadbare' (*OED* peeled 3a; *OED* pilled 3). The scene's emphasis on costume and rank is extended by Gloucester's mocking Winchester in terms of the humility implied by his status as priest, as opposed to the grandeur of his (at this point) merely self-assigned role (see 36n.). There could also be a reference to Winchester's tonsure, the shaved (*pilled*) crown of a monk or a priest in orders, but this again would be a sarcasm of Gloucester's.

31 **proditor** traitor, or betrayer (*OED*)

34 This is another of the charges in Gloucester's 'accusation' in Hall: 'kyng Henry the fifth, told hym on a time, when our said sovereigne lorde beyng prince, was lodged in the palaice of Westminster in the greate chambre, by the noyes of a spanyell there was on a night a man espied and taken behynd a tapet of the said chamber . . . [who] confessed that he was there by the steryng up and procuryng of my saied Lorde of Winchester, ordained to have slain thesaied prince there in his bedde' (Bullough, 3.50).

35 **indulgences** remission of the punish-

ment due for sin after death, granted by the Church to an individual for acts of charity. As such charity often took the form of a prescribed donation to the Church, anti-Catholic propaganda tended to represent indulgences as simply bought and sold. Usually indulgence was given orally – the only survival in current Roman Catholic practice is in blessings from the Pope – but the use of the plural here suggests that the reference may be to written certificates, purporting to have the Pope's signature or seal, sold by unscrupulous figures like Chaucer's Pardoner in *The Canterbury Tales* (*Riv*, Pardoner's Prologue, fragment VI (group C), 335–6). The licensing of whores in the diocese of Southwark was the bishops' responsibility. See Introduction, pp. 19–21.

36 **canvas** trap in a net, normally used of small birds. As at 42, Gloucester is mockingly demeaning Winchester.
cardinal's hat Cardinals are invested with a broad-brimmed scarlet hat, a stylized version of a pilgrim's hat, and it would seem that Winchester is wearing a version of one in this scene. Gloucester's crediting Winchester with one creates problems in terms of the chronology of his eventual

---

30 Peeled] *Cam²*; Piel'd *F*   to be] be *Pope*   36 cardinal's hat] bishop's mitre *Oxf*

If thou proceed in this thy insolence.

WINCHESTER

Nay, stand thou back – I will not budge a foot.

This be Damascus, be thou cursèd Cain,

To slay thy brother Abel, if thou wilt.   40

GLOUCESTER

I will not slay thee, but I'll drive thee back:

Thy scarlet robes as a child's bearing cloth

I'll use, to carry thee out of this place.

WINCHESTER

Do what thou dar'st, I beard thee to thy face.

GLOUCESTER

What? Am I dared, and bearded to my face?   45

Draw, men, for all this privileged place.

---

installation as a cardinal, presented later in the play, in keeping with Hall's account (see 5.1.28). This contradiction has been used by previous editors as an argument for collaborative authorship (see Introduction, pp. 73–5); Oxf simply emends lines in this scene to avoid the problem. The inconsistency (unlikely to be noticed by audiences, it must be said) comes from the historical Winchester's own position. In Henry V's reign he had been refused leave by the King to bid for or to accept the title of cardinal. If 5.1 represents his public installation – to the consternation of a survivor of the last reign, Exeter (28–33) – this scene could show him laying claim to a title to which he has as yet no right. Gloucester, who makes most of the references to the Cardinal's status, could well be offering a mockery of this 'empty' show; again the ambiguity is typical of the play's interest in the legitimacy and insignia of identity, status and allegiance.

39 **Damascus . . . Cain** The story of Cain and Abel is told in Genesis, 4.8.

Damascus, in present-day Syria, was by tradition the site of Abel's murder by his brother Cain, a legend recorded in Mandeville, *Travels*, among other texts. Gloucester and Winchester are related but less closely; as John of Gaunt's illegitimate son, Winchester is Gloucester's uncle.

cursed cursèd

42 **child's bearing cloth** a large piece of cloth, folded and tied around a woman's body, so that she can carry a child on her back

44 **beard** challenge. Winchester's choice of term carries on the implied questioning of his own masculinity.

46 **privileged** privilegèd. The Tower is 'privileged' in that it is directly under royal jurisdiction, and so, like the Inns of Court, and the royal presence in later scenes, it is exempt from the jurisdiction of the City. As in those cases, the effect of this is to make conflict more, rather than less, volatile. The situation here is especially confusing, given that it is unclear who at this stage can claim to exercise royal power.

Blue coats to tawny coats. Priest, beware your beard;
I mean to tug it and to cuff you soundly.
Under my feet I stamp thy cardinal's hat.
In spite of Pope or dignities of Church,   50
Here by the cheeks I'll drag thee up and down.

WINCHESTER

Gloucester, thou wilt answer this before the Pope.

GLOUCESTER

Winchester goose, I cry, a rope, a rope.
Now beat them hence – why do you let them stay?
Thee I'll chase hence, thou wolf in sheep's array.   55
Out, tawny coats – out, scarlet hypocrite.

47 **Blue . . . coats** 'Blue-coat' is a generic term for a dependant, or servant, of an aristocrat. Winchester's men's *tawny* livery might suggest that his followers are wearing leather jerkins; the word is linked to the idea of 'tanned', burnt and dried by the sun, and this is how it is generally used by Shakespeare, almost always with pejorative overtones, as in, for example, *AC* 1.1.6., *LLL* 1.1.173, *Tem* 2.1.55. It is unusual to have attention so precisely focused on a costume in a Shakespearean text; the meaning here could be that Winchester's servants are dressed in protective leather, like a private militia, or it could refer to the colour, an orangey brown, and so be there simply to denote contrast.

53 **Winchester goose** 'a certain venereal disorder . . . also a prostitute' (*OED* goose 3), a reference particularly apt, given the bishops' licensing of the Southwark brothels. See also Dent, G366, and *TC* 5.11.54, where Pandarus in his epilogue both draws attention to his own diseases and taunts the audience with the possibility of 'Some galled goose of Winchester' being among their company.

rope for hanging or beating, both punishments that would demean Winchester,

but which, from Gloucester's point of view, would fit his illegitimate status

55 **wolf . . . array** from Matthew, 7.15, 'Beware of false prophetes, which come to you in shepes clothing, but inwardly they are ravening wolves'

56 **scarlet hypocrite** The phrase uses the colour of the Cardinal's robes to unite the association of the areas of Winchester's jurisdiction with prostitution and theatre with his own dubious personal reputation. Revelation, 17.3–5, describes the vision of a 'woman sit upon a skarlat coloured beast, full of names of blasphemie . . . And the woman was araied in purple & skarlat'. The Geneva Bible has as its marginal gloss 'The beast signifieth the ancient Rome: the woman that sitteth thereon, the newe Rome which is the Papistrie, whose crueltie and blood sheding is declared by skarlat'. Wolsey in *H8* (3.2.255) is similarly addressed as 'Thou scarlet sin'. There the reference is more clearly anti-Catholic, but here, as in the conflict between Joan Puzel and Talbot, anti-Catholic sentiments are evoked for an Elizabethan audience in a context where both characters would, historically, have been of the same faith.

47 tawny coats] tawny *Pope*   49 I] I'll *F2*   cardinal's hat] bishop's mitre *Oxf*   52 thou wilt] thou'lt *Pope*   56 scarlet] cloaked *Oxf*

Here Gloucester's Men beat out the Cardinal's Men, and enter
in the hurly-burly the Mayor *of* London *and his* Officers.

MAYOR

　　Fie, lords, that you, being supreme magistrates,
　　Thus contumeliously should break the peace.

GLOUCESTER

　　Peace, mayor, thou knowst little of my wrongs.
　　Here's Beaufort, that regards nor God nor king,　　　　　60
　　Hath here distrained the Tower to his use.

WINCHESTER

　　Here's Gloucester, a foe to citizens,
　　One that still motions war and never peace,
　　O'ercharging your free purses with large fines –
　　That seeks to overthrow religion,　　　　　65
　　Because he is Protector of the realm,
　　And would have armour here out of the Tower,
　　To crown himself king and suppress the Prince.

GLOUCESTER

　　I will not answer thee with words, but blows.
　　　　Here they skirmish again.

MAYOR

　　Naught rests for me, in this tumultuous strife,　　　　　70
　　But to make open proclamation.
　　Come, officer, as loud as e'er thou canst.
　　　　[*The Officer gives the*] *cry:*

56.2 *hurly-burly* commotion
57 **Fie** an expression of strong reproof
58 **contumeliously** insolently
60 **Beaufort** Winchester; Beaufort was his family name (see note on List of Roles).
61 **distrained** forced; taken over
63 **still motions** always urges
64 Winchester tries to appeal to the Mayor

by characterizing court levies on him and his fellow citizens as excessive. *Free* does not imply that they are free from court jurisdiction, but that they are generous.
65 **religion** pronounced as four syllables
68 **suppress** make powerless
71 **proclamation** pronounced as five syllables

60 Beaufort] *(Beauford)*　72–72 SD canst . . . *the cry*] *this edn;* canst, cry *F;* canst. *Cry. Ard²;* canst cry. *Hands the officer a paper Cam²*

OFFICER *All manner of men, assembled here in arms this day*
   against God's peace and the King's, we charge and command
   you, in his Highness's name, to repair to your several dwelling   75
   places, and not to wear, handle or use any sword, weapon or
   dagger henceforward, upon pain of death.

GLOUCESTER

   Cardinal, I'll be no breaker of the law:

   But we shall meet and break our minds at large.

WINCHESTER

   Gloucester, we'll meet to thy cost, be sure.   80

   Thy heart-blood I will have for this day's work.

MAYOR

   I'll call for clubs, if you will not away:

   [*to the audience*] This Cardinal's more haughty than
      the devil.

GLOUCESTER

   Mayor, farewell: thou dost but what thou mayst.

WINCHESTER

   Abominable Gloucester, guard thy head,   85

   For I intend to have it ere long.

                     Exeunt [*Winchester, Gloucester and their Men*].

MAYOR

   See the coast cleared, and then we will depart.

   Good God, these nobles should such stomachs bear!

   I myself fight not once in forty year.   *Exeunt.*

---

79 **break our minds** reveal our thoughts
82 **call for clubs** i.e. as a means to separate
the two parties, without taking either
side. See *Tit* 1.1.536, *AYL* 5.2.41.
86 The unmetrical line has a potentially
comic effect; for emendations to something more regular, see the textual
notes.

87 **the coast cleared** The Mayor's language is characterized as rich in cliché
and semi-proverbial phrasing, as also
'should such stomachs bear' and 'not
once in forty year' (Dent, C469, S874).
88 **stomachs** thought to be the seat of
emotion, especially haughtiness; valour; anger, aggression

73 SP] *Hanmer; not in F*   78 Cardinal] Bishop *Oxf*   83 SD] *this edn; Aside Oxf* Cardinal's]
bishop is *Oxf*   86 it ere] it e're be *F3;* ere't be *Capell*

[1.4]   *Enter the* Master Gunner of Orleans *and his* Boy.

GUNNER

Sirrah, thou knowst how Orleans is besieged,

And how the English have the suburbs won.

BOY

Father, I know, and oft have shot at them –

Howe'er, unfortunate, I missed my aim.

GUNNER

But now thou shalt not: be thou ruled by me.   5

Chief master gunner am I of this town –

Something I must do to procure me grace.

The Prince's espials have informed me

How the English, in the suburbs close entrenched,

Went through a secret grate of iron bars   10

1.4.0.1 See 55.1n. for the staging implications of the actions proposed by the
Master Gunner, his Boy and their *piece
of ordnance* (15). The latter may be on
stage at the start of the scene, but is
more likely to be offstage, and that is
the option chosen by this edition.

1   **Sirrah** See 3.1.61n.

2, 9   **suburbs** the outer parts of the town
– here meaning the area beyond the
city walls, on the other side of the river
Loire. The English have won the tower
that guards the main bridge into the
fortified town. The stage represents
the inside of Orleans, the space 'above'
a tower, to be imagined as on the far
side of the river. See Fig. 2, p. 13.

7   **grace** good will; advancement

8   **espials** spies; stressed on second syllable
informed informèd

9   **close entrenched** securely dug in; or
(less likely) 'fortified nearby'

10   **grate . . . bars** This whole scene is very
close to its source in Hall, and is structured by a graphic use of the available
stage space (see Introduction, pp.
12–13). 'In the toure that was taken at
the bridge ende . . . there was a high

chamber havyng a grate full of barres of
yron by the whiche a man might loke al
the length of the bridge into the cite, at
which grate many of the chief capitaines stode diverse times, vieuyng the
cite & devisyng in what place it was best
assautable. Thei with in the citee perceived well this totyng hole, and laied a
pece of ordynaunce directly against the
wyndowe. It so chaunced that the .lix.
daie after the siege laied before the
citee, therle of Salisbury, sir Thomas
Gargrave and William Glasdale and
diverse other, went into thesaid toure
and so into the high chambre, and loked
out at the grate, and with in a short
space, the sonne of the Master gonner,
perceived men lokyng out at the wyndowe, tooke his matche, as his father
had taught hym, whiche was gone
doune to dinner, and fired the gonne,
whiche brake & shevered the yron barres of the grate, wherof, one strake
therle so strongly on the hed, that it
stroke away one of his iyes and the side
of his cheke. Sir Thomas Gargrave was
likewise striken, so that he died within
two daies' (Bullough, 3.55). The

1.4] *Capell*   1 SP] *Cam²; M. Gunner. F*   8   Prince's espials] *(Princes espyals);* Prince' espials *Ard²;*
Prince's 'spials *Pope*   10 Went] Wont *Steevens (Tyrwhitt)*

149

In yonder tower, to overpeer the city
And thence discover how with most advantage
They may vex us with shot or with assault.
To intercept this inconvenience,
A piece of ordnance 'gainst it I have placed,   15
And even these three days have I watched if I could
    see them.
Now do thou watch, for I can stay no longer.
If thou spiest any, run and bring me word,
And thou shalt find me at the Governor's.   19

BOY

Father, I warrant you, take you no care.   *Exit [Gunner].*
I'll never trouble you, if I may spy them.   *Exit.*

Enter SALISBURY *and* TALBOT *on the turrets, with others*[, Sir
    Thomas GARGRAVE *and* Sir William GLANSDALE].

SALISBURY

Talbot, my life, my joy, again returned?

source's 'diverse times' might support
Steevens's emendation of F's '*Went*' to
'Wont', meaning 'are accustomed to'.
15 **piece of ordnance** small cannon. For
its use and placing see 55.1n. and
Introduction, pp. 15–16.
    'gainst aimed at; opposite
21 **I'll . . . you** It is important that the Boy
says these lines after his father has gone
– it shows him set on claiming the glory
for himself, in implicit contrast to the
Talbots, father and son, in 4.4.
21.1 *turrets* The actors enter 'above', on
the gallery at the back of the stage or,
possibly, higher still, in a trumpeter's
'turret' in the roof. But the explicit
description of their situation in the
dialogue – 'on this turret's top' (25) –
would mean that the scene could be

played at stage level and still be understood.
***others** I take the *others* required by F's
SD to be Gargrave and Glansdale.
Other editions introduce non-speaking
extras on to the tower, to some extent
on Hall's authority (the 'diverse other'
of his account (Bullough, 3.55)), but
this is largely so that these can carry the
bodies off at the end of the scene. F
leaves the method of removing the bodies unclear. Corpse-carrying is not so
big a problem to audiences and directors as it is to editors – it makes more
sense for someone to be summoned
on to do it (if the scene takes place on the
apron) or for it to be tactfully managed
at the end of the scene, out of the audience's sight, if it takes place 'above'.

13 They . . . us] Vex us they may *(Ard²)*; They may us vex Oxf   16–17] *this edn;* F *lines* watcht, /
watch, / longer. /   16 have I watched] watch'd *Ard²*   18 spiest] (spy'st)   20SD] this edn.; *Exit.* F
opp. 19   21.1] 1.6 *Oxf*   21.1–2 Sir Thomas . . . GLANSDALE] *this edn;* Sir Thomas GARGRAVE, Sir
William GLANSDALE *and others / Capell;* Glasdale *(Oxf)*

How wert thou handled, being prisoner?
Or by what means got'st thou to be released?
Discourse, I prithee, on this turret's top.   25

TALBOT

The Earl of Bedford had a prisoner
Called the brave Lord Ponton de Saintrailles:
For him was I exchanged and ransomed.
But with a baser man of arms by far,
Once, in contempt, they would have bartered me: 30
Which I, disdaining, scorned and craved death,
Rather than I would be so peeled esteemed.
In fine, redeemed I was as I desired.
But O, the treacherous Fastolfe wounds my heart,
Whom with my bare fists I would execute,   35
If I now had him brought into my power.

SALISBURY

Yet tellest thou not how thou wert entertained.

TALBOT

With scoffs and scorns and contumelious taunts.
In open market-place produced they me
To be a public spectacle to all.   40

---

27 ***Ponton de Saintrailles** The historical Jean Ponton de Xaintrailles was,
like most of Charles's military force,
essentially a freelancer, an Armagnac
captain working towards the acquisi-
tion of lucrative posts (he was eventually made seneschal of Limousin) and
unlikely to stay loyal if Charles was
losing; hence the importance of
Jeanne/Joan in uniting an armed force
less stably organized even than the
English. He was not strictly speaking a
Lord; the title here is a token of respect
paid him by Talbot.
28 **ransomed** ransomèd
31 **craved** cravèd

32 ***peeled** See 1.3.30.n.
33 **In fine** in short, to sum up
38 **contumelious** Cf. 1.3.58 and n.
40 Talbot's capture, as first mentioned in
1.1, and his exchange for Saintrailles are
moved forward chronologically in the
play to place Talbot at Orleans, and so
strengthen that symmetry with Joan's
career which gives the play its organiz-
ing structure. The exhibition of Talbot
in the market-place creates (in report)
an icon of heroic display to parallel the
description of Talbot on stage in
Nashe's *Piers Penniless*, as well as offering
a parallel to the captured Samson in Gaza
(see Introduction, p. 47).

---

24 got'st] *(got's)*   26 Earl] Duke *Theobald*   27 Saintrailles] *this edn; Santrayle F;* Santrailles *Capell*
32 peeled] *this edn;* pil'd *F;* pilled *Capell;* vile *Ard²;* vilde *Pope*   34 Fastolfe] *Theobald;* Falstaffe *F*

151

'Here', said they, 'is the terror of the French,
The scarecrow that affrights our children so'.
Then broke I from the officers that led me
And with my nails digged stones out of the ground
To hurl at the beholders of my shame.   45
My grisly countenance made others fly;
None durst come near for fear of sudden death.
In iron walls they deemed me not secure:
So great fear of my name 'mongst them were spread
That they supposed I could rend bars of steel   50
And spurn in pieces posts of adamant.
Wherefore a guard of chosen shot I had,
That walked about me every minute while,
And if I did but stir out of my bed
Ready they were to shoot me to the heart.   55

Enter the Boy *with a linstock* [*lit and burning, and passes over the stage*].

SALISBURY
    I grieve to hear what torments you endured;
    But we will be revenged sufficiently.
    Now it is supper-time in Orleans.
    Here, through this grate, I count each one

---

46 **grisly** frightening; also with a sense of 'grizzly', grey, ageing, grey-haired
51 **spurn** kick
    adamant in classical and Renaissance tradition, a name attached to whatever was thought to be the hardest existing substance
52 **of chosen shot** hand-picked for their skill with guns
53 **every minute while** continuously
55.1 *linstock* a burning stick to fire a small cannon (the *piece of ordnance*, 15) which could either be centrally on stage, set up at the start of the scene by the Gunner, or, more likely, be assumed to be offstage, with the Boy making an

exit in order to fire it. See *H5* 3.0.32–3: 'the nimble gunner / With linstock now the devilish cannon touches'.
59 **grate** It is possible, though not especially likely, that in the original staging a grate or grille of some sort would be placed on the gallery, or the turret, in setting up the beginning of the scene, and the commanders would speak from behind it. On the modern stage this effect would be easier to achieve, but is not really necessary; the dialogue is explicit enough, the point being that the English have adequate defence against the arrows and stones they expect, but that even an iron *grate* is vulnerable to cannon-fire.

55.1 *lit . . . stage*] *this edn; and exit Ard²*

And view the Frenchmen how they fortify.   60
Let us look in: the sight will much delight thee.
Sir Thomas Gargrave and Sir William Glansdale,
Let me have your express opinions –
Where is best place to make our battery next?

GARGRAVE

I think at the north gate, for there stands lords.   65

GLANSDALE

And I, here, at the bulwark of the bridge.

TALBOT

For aught I see, this city must be famished,
Or with light skirmishes enfeebled.
        Here they shoot [from offstage], and Salisbury
        [and Gargrave] fall down.

SALISBURY

O Lord, have mercy on us, wretched sinners.

60 **fortify** *OED* 2.9, 'to establish a position of defence'
63 **express** specific; explicit
64 **make our battery** attack, implying the setting up of battering rams and other siege machines
65 **there stands lords** F's 'Lords' gives no immediately obvious meaning. T.W. Craik drew my attention to an article by R.J.C. Watt proposing 'Loire' for 'Lords' (Watt, 2–5). Hall describes 'Orliance, standyng on the river of Loyre' (Bullough, 3.54), so the phrase could be in the dramatists' minds. If this were the case, then 'Lords' could then be a compositor's reading influenced by the English lords' own situation. But *lords* does make more sense as the description of a military manoeuvre that the English might be contemplating: in other words, 'let's kill their commanders'. Though the verb *stands* is singular and *lords* is plural, the phrase is acceptable as idiomatic English of the period. There is one further possibility.

Linden Stafford suggests to me that the compositors may have misinterpreted 'toures', meaning towers. The point parallels Watt in that a reminiscence of Hall's 'standyng' would create the missing link, the phrase here being 'a greate toure, standing at thende of the same'. See also 75n.
66 **bulwark** defence, fortification; in the context, whatever prevents the English from getting across the bridge in order to break down the gates of the city
67 **famished** reduced to famine (here as a deliberate military strategy), expressing what the English must do, not a description of the current state of the town. The besieged town is better supplied than its besiegers, whose hunger has been described at 1.2.7.
68 **enfeebled** enfeeblèd; four syllables
68.1 *they shoot* a direction for an offstage crew of pyrotechnicians – very busy people, in this play
69 **O ... mercy** 'Lord have mercy on us' is a common response in the Anglican liturgy (Shaheen, 32).

64 battery] *(Batt'ry)*   65 stands lords] stand lords *F2;* stands Lou *Oxf;* stands Loire *(Watt)*
68.1 shoot] *(shot)   from offstage*] *this edn*   68.2 and Gargrave] *this edn   fall*] *this edn; falls F*

GARGRAVE

   O Lord, have mercy on me, woeful man.   70

TALBOT

   What chance is this that suddenly hath crossed us?

   Speak, Salisbury; at least, if thou canst, speak.

   How far'st thou, mirror of all martial men?

   One of thy eyes and thy cheek's side struck off?

   Accursed tower, accursed fatal hand,   75

   That hath contrived this woeful tragedy.

   In thirteen battles Salisbury o'ercame:

   Henry the Fifth he first trained to the wars.

   Whilst any trump did sound or drum struck up,

   His sword did ne'er leave striking in the field.   80

   Yet liv'st thou, Salisbury? Though thy speech doth fail,

   One eye thou hast to look to heaven for grace.

   The sun with one eye vieweth all the world.

   Heaven, be thou gracious to none alive,

   If Salisbury wants mercy at thy hands.   85

   Bear hence his body – I will help to bury it.

   Sir Thomas Gargrave, hast thou any life?

   Speak unto Talbot, nay, look up to him.

   Salisbury, cheer thy spirit with this comfort;

---

71 **crossed** thwarted

73 **mirror . . . men** model of military conduct

75 **Accursed tower** presumably the inadequately secure tower in which the men are standing when they are killed. But, especially if one takes on the suggestion given in 65n., this could mean a French-controlled tower at the other side of the bridge, from which the cannon shot comes. In staging terms, it seems likely that the shot takes place as from offstage, so either interpretation is equally plausible. See Introduction, pp. 13–16.

   Accursed . . . accursed accursèd

79 **trump** trumpet

84 **gracious** pronounced as three syllables, graciòùs (or *Heaven* as two)

85 **wants** lacks

86 **Bear . . . body** Cairncross (Ard²) moved this phrase to 88 from its position in F at 86, to allow Gargrave to be carried out before the end of the scene. F's order, adopted in this edition, leaves both corpses on stage, and Talbot divided and indecisive in the attention he can pay to the two figures. This is an index of the bathetic collapse of his control.

90 Unlike other truncated lines in F (94, for example) this makes sense dramatically

86] *line transposed to follow 88 Ard² (H. Brooks)*   I will . . . it.] *I'll . . . it. Exeunt some with the body of Gargrave. Ard²*

Thou shalt not die whiles –   90
He beckons with his hand and smiles on me
As who should say, 'When I am dead and gone,
Remember to avenge me on the French'.
Plantagenet, I will; and like thee, Nero,
Play on the lute, beholding the towns burn: 95
Wretched shall France be only in my name.
    Here an alarum, and it thunders and lightens.
What stir is this? What tumult's in the heavens?
Whence cometh this alarum and the noise?

Enter a Messenger.

MESSENGER

My lord, my lord, the French have gathered head.
The Dolphin, with one Joan de Puzel joined –   100
A holy prophetess, new risen up –

without emendation; which does not
mean, of course, that it is necessarily
authorial.

92 **As who** like one who

94 **Plantagenet** Salisbury, as a descendant of Edward III

*Nero F2 has 'Nero like will'. Later
edns used the name, while altering the
exact phrasing. Nero is supposed (to
use a phrase that became proverbial in
English) to have 'fiddled while Rome
burned'. Tacitus (15.38–44) tells of the
burning of Rome during Nero's reign,
of the suspicion that he himself
ordered it in order to make room for a
new city, and of his consequent attempt
to shift blame on to the Christians and
subsequent persecution of them.
Suetonius (38) elaborates the rumour,
in describing Nero in stage costume
singing his poem on the sack of Troy
while watching the city burn. Here

both the sense of Neronian megaloma-
nia and the difference between Talbot
celebrating the end of enemy cities and
Nero burning his own might make the
fit less than perfect, unless one takes it
to imply that Talbot's previous attitude
to the French had been more humane,
less callously Neronian.

96 **only . . . name** by my sole responsibility, or merely at the sound of my
name (cf. 2.1.81)

SD *it . . . lightens* Is this gunfire, a natural storm or a presage of witchcraft?
The ambiguity is particularly effective
in the context of the English paranoia
in the face of (historically) superior
French firepower and what seems like
magic; both magic and artillery are of
course examples of anti-chivalric
cheating (see Introduction p. 16).

99 **gathered head** got together in formation to mount an attack

94 like thee, Nero] *Malone;* like thee, *F;* Nero like will *F2;* Nero-like *Pope*   100 de Puzel] la Pucelle
Cam

Is come with a great power to raise the siege.
Here Salisbury lifteth himself up, and groans.

TALBOT
Hear, hear, how dying Salisbury doth groan:
It irks his heart he cannot be revenged.
Frenchmen, I'll be a Salisbury to you. 105
Puzel or pussel, Dolphin or dogfish,
Your hearts I'll stamp out with my horse's heels
And make a quagmire of your mingled brains.
Convey me Salisbury into his tent – 109
And then we'll try what these dastard Frenchmen
dare. *Alarum. Exeunt.*

[**1.5**] *Here an alarum again, and* TALBOT *pursueth* [CHARLES]
the Dolphin, *and driveth him; then enter* JOAN Puzel
driving Englishmen before her. Then enter TALBOT.

TALBOT
Where is my strength, my valour and my force?
Our English troops retire, I cannot stay them;
A woman clad in armour chaseth them.

---

106 **Puzel . . . dogfish** See Appendix 1
for a discussion of the forms of Joan's
names in the play, and for an account
of the term 'Dolphin'. 'The word dog-
fish covers a variety of small sharks, as
fierce as a pack of wild dogs. They
have a keen sense of smell, and hunt
mackerel, herring and whiting like a
pack of hounds' (Grigson, 184). They
were, and in Britain still are, seen as
cheap low-quality food.
    pussel variant of *pucelle* (virgin), but
with a derogatory sense of 'prostitute';
see Introduction pp. 25–6 and
Appendix 1.
109 **Convey me Salisbury** It seems
unnecessary to emend F's 'me' –

which means 'convey Salisbury for me'
– to 'we', as in Ard². That would imply
that Glansdale, Talbot and the others
are going to lift the bodies themselves,
where here the order is to unspecified
English soldiers, who may have been
with the commanders on the turret, or
who may be summoned from offstage
at this point.
1.5.2 **stay** stop
3 SD *approaches him As in the previous scenes in this act, the stage allows
a split focus, and so it does not necessarily matter whether Joan exits and
re-enters at the beginning of the scene,
or stays on after chasing the English
off, though the speed of the action

---

106 Puzel or pussel] Puzzel or pucelle *Theobald*   109 me] we *Ard² (Vaughan)*   110 then we'll]
then *Ard²*   what these] what *Pope*   1.5] *Capell*   0.2 JOAN Puzel] *this edn;* Ioane de Puzel *F;* Joan
la Pucelle *Theobald*   3 them] men *Cam² (Vaughan)*

Puzel [approaches him].

Here, here she comes. I'll have a bout with thee –
Devil, or devil's dam, I'll conjure thee.   5
Blood will I draw on thee – thou art a witch –
And straightway give thy soul to him thou serv'st.

JOAN

Come, come, 'tis only I that must disgrace thee.
Here they fight.

TALBOT

Heavens, can you suffer hell so to prevail?
My breast I'll burst with straining of my courage   10
And from my shoulders crack my arms asunder,
But I will chastise this high-minded strumpet.
They fight again.

JOAN

Talbot, farewell. Thy hour is not yet come.
I must go victual Orleans forthwith.
*A short alarum: then [Charles passes over the stage
and] enters the town with Soldiers.*
O'ertake me if thou canst – I scorn thy strength.   15

makes the second possibility more
likely. See Introduction, pp. 9–12, for
an account of the shape of the Rose
stage, and its implications for the
action of this play.

5   **dam** mother, used mainly of animals.
Devil's dam is a phrase for a threaten-
ing woman; see *CE* 4.3.51 and *Tit*
4.2.67.
conjure *OED v.* III 8, 'to convey away'

6   **Blood . . . draw** Drawing a witch's
blood was seen as a way of rendering
her powerless. See Introduction,
pp. 47–8.

7   **him thou serv'st** the devil

9   **can . . . prevail** Matthew, 16.18 –

'And the gates of hell shall not preuaile
against it' – in, according to Shaheen
(32), 'all versions but Geneva'

12 **high-minded** arrogant. *OED a.* 2
however, records Greene using it in
Friar Bacon and Friar Bungay in a
meaning closer to the modern, non-
pejorative sense, of 'morally noble'.
So, like so many attempts to describe
Joan, the phrase as a whole is a puzzle.

13 **Thy . . . come** 'his houre was not yet
come' (John, 7.30; see also John, 2.4
and 13.1).

14 **victual** provide with food (pronounced 'vittle')
forthwith immediately

3 SD *Puzel . . . him] this edn; Enter Puzel F; Enter* LA PUCELLE *Ard²; Enter* PUCELLE *with Soldiers
Cam²*   8 + SP JOAN] *this edn; Puzel. F*   14 SD *Charles . . . and] this edn*

Go, go – cheer up thy hungry, starved men,
Help Salisbury to make his testament.
This day is ours, as many more shall be.   *Exit.*

TALBOT

My thoughts are whirled like a potter's wheel,
I know not where I am nor what I do.   20
A witch by fear, not force, like Hannibal,
Drives back our troops and conquers as she lists:
So bees with smoke and doves with noisome stench
Are from their hives and houses driven away.
They called us, for our fierceness, English dogs;   25
Now like to whelps we crying run away.

   A short alarum.

Hark, countrymen – either renew the fight
Or tear the lions out of England's coat.

---

16 **starved** starvèd
19 **whirled** whirlèd
   potter's wheel The making and
   breaking of pots provides a recurrent
   image in the Bible for the vulnerability
   of mankind in relation to God. See, for
   example, Isaiah, 41.25, 64.8 and 30.14;
   Psalms, 2.9.
21 **Hannibal** I have retained F's punctuation, which likens Joan and Hannibal
   to each other; if the comma after
   'force' were left out, the sense would
   be altered, and the two figures opposed
   to each other – Hannibal uses *force*,
   Joan uses *fear*. The reference, however,
   seems to be to Plutarch's life of Fabius
   Maximus, where he describes Hannibal's approach into Italy as follows:
   'Hannibal now burst into Italy . . . and
   smote Rome with dire consternation
   and fear. Signs and portents occurred,
   some familiar to the Romans, like peals
   of thunder, others wholly strange and
   quite extraordinary . . . The consul,
   Gaius Flaminius, was daunted by none
   of these things' (3, 2.2–4). Joan is
   heralded by thunder and lightning, but

Talbot seems less sure than Flaminius.
In this reading, Joan and Hannibal are
working in parallel, as kinds of terror-
ists whose effects, in being explained
away as supernatural, only ascribe
more power to them.
22 **lists** likes
23 **noisome** unpleasant; causing annoyance
25 **English dogs** A particular type of
   hound or hunting dog, the Talbot, is
   associated with the Talbot family. See
   Introduction, pp. 49–50.
26 **whelps** puppies
28 **tear . . . coat** The lions are England's
   heraldic symbol, bearing obvious connotations of nobility and ferocity. 'The
   earliest appearance of the lions in the
   arms of any member of the Royal
   Family in England would appear to be
   the seal of King John when he was
   Prince and before he ascended the
   throne. This seal shows his arms to be
   two lions passant. The English Royal
   crest, which originated with Richard I,
   is now always depicted as a lion statant
   guardant' (Fox-Davies, 173–4).

16 hungry, starved] *this edn;* hungry-starued *F;* hunger-starved *Rowe*

Renounce your soil, give sheep in lions' stead;
Sheep run not half so treacherous from the wolf,   30
Or horse or oxen from the leopard,
As you fly from your oft-subdued slaves.

> *Alarum. Here another skirmish [in which the English*
> *attempt to enter Orleans].*

It will not be, retire into your trenches.
You all consented unto Salisbury's death,
For none would strike a stroke in his revenge.   35
Puzel is entered into Orleans
In spite of us or aught that we could do.
O would I were to die with Salisbury:
The shame hereof will make me hide my head.

> *Exit Talbot. Alarum. [The English sound a] retreat*
> *[and exeunt. The French sound a] flourish.*

Enter on the walls [JOAN] Puzel, [CHARLES the] Dolphin,
  REIGNIER, ALENÇON *and Soldiers.*   [1.6]

JOAN
 Advance our waving colours on the walls.   40

---

29 **give . . . stead** 'Give up your proper
emblem, substitute sheep for lions.'
30 **Sheep . . . treacherous** The metaphor may derive from Hall: 'The lorde
Talbot like a capitain, without feare or
dred of so great a multitude, issued out
of his Bastile, and so fiersly fought with
the Frenchemen, that they not able to
withstande his puyssaunce, fled (like
shepe before the Wolffe) again into the
citee, with greate losse of men and
small artilerie' (Bullough, 3.58).
Treacherous is an odd and perhaps pur-
posefully absurd choice of word here:
sheep aren't being treacherous when
they flee wolves. Talbot is reacting egotistically, or patriotically, or both – his
men are being treacherous to him, to
his mission for England, when they act
on an animal imperative to survival.
31 **leopard** pronounced as three syllables
with stress on first and third
32 **subdued** subduèd
39 SD *flourish* here both an answer to the
English retreat, and a heralding of
Joan's and the Dolphin's appearance
'above'; it thus forms a link in the
action, which makes a scene division
unhelpful. As a *flourish* is normally
used to herald royalty, it is a riposte
here to English denials of the
Dolphin's kingly status.
40 **Advance** raise

---

29 soil] *(Soyle); style Dyce;* shield *Vaughan* 32 SD *in . . . Orleans] this edn; Here enter Soldiers to*
another skirmish. Cam² 36 entered] *(entred)* 39 SD.1 *The . . . a] this edn* SD.2 *and . . . a] this edn*
39.1 SCENE VI. *Capell*

Rescued is Orleans from the English.

Thus Joan de Puzel hath performed her word.

CHARLES

Divinest creature, Astraea's daughter,

How shall I honour thee for this success?

Thy promises are like Adonis' garden,   45

That one day bloomed and fruitful were the next.

France, triumph in thy glorious prophetess.

Recovered is the town of Orleans;

More blessed hap did ne'er befall our state.   [10]

REIGNIER

Why ring not out the bells aloud throughout the town?   50

Dolphin, command the citizens make bonfires

And feast and banquet in the open streets,

To celebrate the joy that God has given us.

---

41 In this scene *Orleans* is generally trisyllabic, but this line would scan better with a disyllabic *Orleans* and *Rescuèd*.

43 **creature** three syllables, stressed on first and third
Astraea's The 'last of the immortals', Astraea is the goddess of justice, whose departure from the earth begins the Iron Age, in the mythical history described by Ovid at the beginning of his *Metamorphoses* (1.149–50). Her return would be the condition of a new Golden Age, and it is this that the French see presaged in Joan, rather as official Elizabethan mythography projected it onto Elizabeth.

45–6 **Adonis' . . . next** The classical source of Adonis' garden is Plato's *Phaedrus* (276b), where the emphasis on quick generation implies ephemerality. But the sense of miraculous fecundity is developed by later writers into an expression of the underlying Platonic doctrine of the permanence of basic forms and species; Spenser's *FQ*, 3 for

example, a text that offers parallels to this play at other points, develops the garden into a strong rebuke to the earthly false paradise of the Bower of Bliss of 2.12.

49 **blessed** blessèd
hap accident

52 **feast and banquet** According to Hall, who seems generally interested in matters of eating at this point in his narrative: 'AFTER this siege thus broken up, to tel you, what triumphes wer made in the citee of Orleaunce, what wood was spente in fiers, what wyne was dronke in houses, what songes wer song in the stretes, what melody was made in Tavernes, what roundes were daunced in large and brode places, what lightes wer set up in the churches, what anthemes, wer song in Chapelles, and what joye was shewed in every place, it were a long woorke and yet no necessary cause. For thei did, as we in like case would have dooen, and we beeyng in like estate would have

41 English] English wolves *F2*   43 + SP CHARLES] *Rowe; Dolph. F*   45 garden] gardens *Hanmer*
50] *Pope; F lines* alowd, / Towne? /   out the bells] bells *Ard² (Steevens)*

ALENÇON

All France will be replete with mirth and joy,
When they shall hear how we have played the men.   55

CHARLES

'Tis Joan, not we, by whom the day is won:
For which I will divide my crown with her,
And all the priests and friars in my realm
Shall in procession sing her endless praise.   [20]
A statelier pyramis to her I'll rear   60
Than Rhodope's or Memphis' ever was.
In memory of her, when she is dead,
Her ashes, in an urn more precious
Than the rich-jewelled coffer of Darius,

doen as thei did' (Bullough, 3.58–9).

55 **played the men** acted bravely; an ironic choice of phrase, given Joan's sexual ambiguity

60 **pyramis** pyramid. This reading seems likely in relation to the following line. But *pyramis* could also at this time denote the kind of structure now termed 'obelisk', a reading that, given the obelisk's phallic shape and the sexual innuendo of the exchanges between the Dolphin and Joan, has its attraction in relation to the verb *rear*.

61 **Rhodope's or Memphis'** Rhodope, the name of a mountain range in Thrace, is a mistake, or a more euphonious substitution, for Rhodopis, whose story is told by Herodotus, 2.134–5: '[Mycerinus] . . . left a pyramid . . . Some Greeks say that it was built by Rhodopis, the courtesan, but they are in error'. Rhodopis was the lover of Sappho's brother, Charaxus of Mytilene. According to Herodotus the memorial she designed for herself was in fact 'a great number of iron ox-spits'. These are still, he says, to be seen at Delphi. Marlowe seems to be

working from a similar confusion as to the exact reference and form of the name in *1 Tamburlaine*, when the protagonist tells Zenocrate that she is 'Brighter than is the silver Rhodope, / Fairer than whitest snow on Scythian hills', though he seems to be imagining Rhodope as a river, and shifting the mountainous idea to Scythia (1.2.88–9). The pyramid at Memphis in Egypt is described by Herodotus at 2.8. It is also cited in *1 Tamburlaine* (4.2.103–4) as comparable in magnificence to Damascus, which Tamburlaine is about to conquer: 'the shadows of Pyramides, / That with their beauties graced the Memphian fields'. Dyce emends *or* in this line to 'of', but this extends, rather than clarifies, the confusion.

64 **coffer of Darius** Darius was the king of Persia, in the fifth century BC, who like his son Cyrus tried but failed to conquer Greece. Though his death is registered by Herodotus, there is no description of his coffin, which the context here suggests might be meant by *coffer*; the word

Transported shall be at high festivals 65
Before the kings and queens of France.
No longer on Saint Denis will we cry,
But Joan de Puzel shall be France's saint. [29]
Come in, and let us banquet royally, 69
After this golden day of victory. *Flourish. Exeunt.*

2.1 *Enter [on the walls] a [French] Sergeant of a band,
with two Sentinels.*

SERGEANT

Sirs, take your places and be vigilant.
If any noise or soldier you perceive
Near to the walls, by some apparent sign
Let us have knowledge at the court of guard.

1 SENTINEL

Sergeant, you shall. *[Exit Sergeant.]*
Thus are poor servitors, 5
When others sleep upon their quiet beds,
Constrained to watch in darkness, rain and cold.

could also apply generally to Darius' 'coffers' of riches (see textual notes for Steevens's conjecture, which can accommodate this reading, for which, in Herodotus and elsewhere, he was legendary. In *The Terrors of the Night* Nashe writes: '*Darius* . . . before his fatall discomfiture, dreamt hee saw an Estrich with a winged crowne over-running the earth, and devouring his Iuel-coffer, as if it had beene an ordinarie peece of yron' (1.359.5–9).

67 **Saint Denis** first bishop of Paris, and patron saint of France

2.1.0.1 *band* the company of soldiers guarding the town; see Appendix 4.

4 **court of guard** station where sentinels wait in between tours of duty. The modern equivalent would be 'guardroom', but here the Sentinels are more likely to gather out of doors, around a fire.

5 **servitors** servants, or common soldiers – as opposed to the aristocratic commanders, whose amateurism the English are about to expose

7.1–2 This scene continues the identification of the tiring house wall with the outer walls of Orleans; the English arrive outside, on the main stage. F's SD does not necessarily imply that the generals carry the scaling ladders themselves, but it does

66 kings] royal kings *(Ard²)* France] France up-borne *Capell* 2.1] *(Actus Secundus. Scena Prima.)* 0.1 on the walls] *Ard²; aloft Cam²; to the Gate / Capell* French] *Capell* 5 SP] *Capell; Sent.* F SD] *Capell*

Enter TALBOT, BEDFORD *and* BURGUNDY, *with* [*three*]
scaling ladders.

TALBOT

Lord Regent, and redoubted Burgundy –
By whose approach the regions of Artois,
Wallon and Picardy are friends to us –   10
This happy night the Frenchmen are secure,
Having all day caroused and banqueted.
Embrace we then this opportunity
As fitting best to quittance their deceit,
Contrived by art and baleful sorcery.   15

BEDFORD

Coward of France! How much he wrongs his fame,
Despairing of his own arms' fortitude,
To join with witches and the help of hell.

BURGUNDY

Traitors have never other company.
But what's that Puzel, whom they term so pure?   20

allow it. The source presents the
event as exposing the easiness of
intimidating the French (cf. 37 SD –
38.3), so a farcically small-scale sur-
prise incursion, such as F's text presents, has its appeal. As a commercial
piece put together in times of plague,
and consequently of summer touring,
the play must have been designed to
accommodate staging with either a
large or a small cast, so I have preferred to leave the presence of extras
in these scenes *ad lib*. See Appendix 2
for discussion of cast size and doubling. F leaves open what happens to
the ladders – soldiers could take them
away, the commanders could push
them back as they shout (37 SD), or
they could remain, and the French
characters' leaping *over the walls*
(38.1), instead of using the ladders,

would further emphasize their panic.
Similarly, when Charles at 71 asks
how the English entered the town, the
effect of leaving the ladders on stage
would farcically underline his inepti-
tude and the transparency of his lie (if
that is what we take it to be) that he
was on guard duty and not sleeping
with Joan Puzel.

8   **Lord Regent** At this stage in the play,
and until his death, Bedford is the
regent – the King's substitute and
equivalent – in France.

10   **Wallon** the area of what is now southern Belgium, also called Wallonia

11   **secure** over-confident

14   **quittance** repay

16   **Coward of France** Charles, here
given a title that mockingly echoes
'Dolphin of France'

7.1 three] *this edn*   7.1–2   *with . . . ladders*] *with scaling Ladders: Their Drummes beating a Dead March.*
F; *and Forces, with scaling-ladders Ard²*   20 Puzel] *(Puzell);* Pucelle *Capell*

TALBOT

A maid, they say.

BEDFORD   A maid? And be so martial?

BURGUNDY

Pray God she prove not masculine ere long –
If underneath the standard of the French
She carry armour, as she hath begun.

TALBOT

Well, let them practise and converse with spirits.   25
God is our fortress, in whose conquering name
Let us resolve to scale their flinty bulwarks.

BEDFORD

Ascend, brave Talbot. We will follow thee.

TALBOT

Not altogether. Better far, I guess,
That we do make our entrance several ways: 30
That if it chance that one of us do fail
The other may yet rise against their force.

BEDFORD

Agreed; I'll to yond corner.

BURGUNDY   And I to this.

TALBOT

And here will Talbot mount, or make his grave.
Now, Salisbury, for thee and for the right   35
Of English Henry, shall this night appear
How much in duty I am bound to both.

---

25 **practise . . . spirits** implies the pursuit of occult arts
converse associate; this can mean
'have sexual intercourse'.
26 **fortress** Shaheen (33) points out that
'fortresse' is used in this biblical
phrase uniquely in the Geneva Bible,

citing 2 Samuel, 22.2–3: 'The Lord is
my rocke and my forteresse, and he
that delivereth me. God is my strength
. . . my hie towre and my refuge'. See
also Psalms, 31.3 and 18.2.
30 **several** separate

29 altogether] all together *Rowe*   33 yond] yon *Ard²*

[*The English*] *cry,* 'Saint George, a Talbot'
[*as they enter Orleans*].

1 SENTINEL

Arm, arm, the enemy doth make assault.

[*Exeunt French Sentinels.*]

The French leap over the walls in their shirts.
Enter several ways [*the*] BASTARD, ALENÇON, REIGNIER,
half ready and half unready.

ALENÇON

How now, my lords? What, all unready so?

BASTARD

Unready? Ay, and glad we scaped so well.   40

37 SD *they enter Orleans* Each mounts a
ladder to a different part of the upper
stage, with Talbot central.
38.1 *The French . . . shirts* In Hall, the
incidents presented in this scene take
place earlier, at the recapture of Le
Mans; Orleans itself was not recaptured
by the English. Talbot, Lord Scales and
Matthew Gough (an experienced soldier who had reconnoitred the town
and found that the French 'began to
waxe wanton and felle to riote') gathered and 'with al hast possible came to
the posterne gate, and alighted from
their horses, and about sixe of the
clocke in the mornyng they issued out
of the castle criyng sainct George,
Talbot. The French men whiche wer
scarce up, and thought of nothyng lesse
then of this sodain approchement,
some rose out of their beddes in their
shertes, and lepte over the walles, other
ranne naked out of the gates for savyng
of their lives, levyng behynde theim all
their apparell, horsses, armure and

riches' (Bullough, 3.53–4). Gough,
given his prominence in the sources, is
notable in his absence from this play (he
is mentioned in *2H6* at 4.5.10 and in the
opening SD of 4.7 where, as the court's
champion against Jack Cade and the
rebels, he enters, fights and is killed,
without uttering a word or, as far as one
can tell, doing anything that would
identify him). F's SD suggests non-
speaking 'extras' leaping on to the stage
(a drop of about ten feet; see
Introduction, p. 12) while the actors to
speak enter below, in the confusion. It is
unlikely that the *Sentinels* (38 SD) would
be *in their shirts*. For the fate of the ladders, by means of which Talbot and the
others entered the town, see 7.1–2n.
38.3 *half . . . unready* incompletely
dressed. F's SD most probably applies
to the state of each individual, each
entering in a comic confusion of hasti-
ly put-on arms, rather than suggesting
that *half* the group who enter are *ready*
and the others not.

37 SD *The English . . . Orleans*] *this edn*; *Cry, S. George, A Talbot. F, after 38; The English, having
scaled the walls, cry, 'St George!', 'A Talbot!'* Cam²; *The* English, *scaling the Walls, Cry, St. George!* A
Talbot! *Theobald; Cry, 'Saint George!' 'A Talbot!' The English scale the walls, and exeunt.* Ard²
38 SD–38.1 *Exeunt . . . shirts*] *this edn*; *The French Sentinels leap o'er the walls in their shirts and
exeunt. The English exeunt aloft.* Cam²; *Alarum. The French soldiers . . . shirts and exeunt.* Oxf
38.2 *ways*] *ways below* Cam²

REIGNIER

    'Twas time, I trow, to wake and leave our beds,

    Hearing alarums at our chamber doors.

ALENÇON

    Of all exploits since first I followed arms,

    Ne'er heard I of a warlike enterprise

    More venturous or desperate than this.   45

BASTARD

    I think this Talbot be a fiend of hell.

REIGNIER

    If not of hell, the heavens sure favour him.

ALENÇON

    Here cometh Charles. I marvel how he sped.

Enter CHARLES *and* JOAN.

BASTARD

    Tut, holy Joan was his defensive guard.

CHARLES

    Is this thy cunning, thou deceitful dame?   50

    Didst thou at first, to flatter us withal,

    Make us partakers of a little gain,

    That now our loss might be ten times so much?

JOAN

    Wherefore is Charles impatient with his friend?

    At all times will you have my power alike?   55

    Sleeping or waking, must I still prevail,

    Or will you blame and lay the fault on me?

    Improvident soldiers, had your watch been good,

    This sudden mischief never could have fallen.

---

48 **marvel** wonder (with a sense of the miraculous apt to Joan)

56 **still** always

58 **Improvident soldiers** Here, Joan Puzel could be talking to the Sentinels, who may have re-entered in the mêlée, or have jumped down during the assault. Or she could be telling off the commanders – deliberately ignoring their status in a way prepared for by the Sentinel's speech at the beginning of the scene (5–7). Alençon's response at 63–5 suggests this second option.

59 **fallen** befallen, happened

CHARLES

    Duke of Alençon, this was your default,   60

    That, being captain of the watch tonight,

    Did look no better to that weighty charge.

ALENÇON

    Had all your quarters been as safely kept

    As that whereof I had the government,

    We had not been thus shamefully surprised.   65

BASTARD

    Mine was secure.

REIGNIER   And so was mine, my lord.

CHARLES

    And for myself, most part of all this night

    Within her quarter and mine own precinct

    I was employed in passing to and fro

    About relieving of the sentinels;   70

    Then how, or which way, should they first break in?

JOAN

    Question, my lords, no further of the case

    'How, or which way?'; 'tis sure they found some place

    But weakly guarded, where the breach was made.

    And now there rests no other shift but this –   75

    To gather our soldiers, scattered and dispersed,

    And lay new platforms to endamage them.

---

62 **weighty charge** important duty

63, 68 **quarter(s)** apartments, but with a sense also of the body (as in 'hindquarters'), which is drawn on for sexual innuendo

65 **surprised** attacked

67–70 *Quarter, precinct, passing to and fro* and *relieving* all continue the vein of sexual innuendo set up by the other characters' suspicion that Joan and the Dolphin have been sleeping together.

68 **precinct** set of rooms

75 **shift** strategy, though possibly also with a pun on *shift* as undergarment, activated visually – Joan Puzel may be

wearing only a light shirt or smock, if we take her to have entered at 48.1 in the same state as the anonymous characters who enter at 38.1 and take the SD at 77.2 to apply to her and Charles as well as to the other French characters. But F's text allows for the possibility that they enter fully clothed, which would imply that they were on guard duty, as Charles claims, and not sleeping together, as the English (and the French courtiers) seem to assume.

77 **platforms** here used in the sense of 'A plan, design' (*OED* A *sb*. II 3a)

77 them.] *Capell;* them. *Exeunt. F*

Alarum. Enter [an English] Soldier, *crying, 'A Talbot, a Talbot';*
they fly, leaving their clothes behind.

SOLDIER
I'll be so bold to take what they have left.
The cry of 'Talbot' serves me for a sword –
For I have loaden me with many spoils,   80
Using no other weapon but his name.   *Exit.*

[**2.2**]   *Enter* TALBOT, BEDFORD, BURGUNDY [*with a*
Captain, *and Soldiers carrying the body of Salisbury*], *their drums*
beating a dead march.

BEDFORD
The day begins to break, and night is fled,
Whose pitchy mantle overveiled the earth.
Here sound retreat and cease our hot pursuit.
    [*They sound*] *retreat.*

2.2.0.1–3 ***with . . . march*** This stage
direction is based on that placed in F at
the English characters' entrance at
2.1.7.1–2, with the addition in this
context of Salisbury's funeral, for
which the *dead march* would seem to be
sounding. The SD in F may be a simple misplacing; but see Hattaway's
argument (Cam²) for retaining it in
that position. This scene creates a parallel to the start of the play, and so represents the English once again
attempting to recoup loss in heroic
ceremony. As Hall recounts, Salisbury
died after '.viij. daies' and then his
body was conveyed to England; but the
play, in using theatrical ritual to reca-
pitulate both the opening scene and
the recounted narrative of Talbot's
exhibition in the market-place of

Orleans, responds to Hall's expansion
of the event through metaphor, to
instate it as expressive of the decay of
England, symbolized by these imperilled and declining male bodies. 'What
detriment, what damage, what losse
succeded to the Englishe publique
wealthe, by the sodain death of this
valiaunt capitain, not long after his
departure, manifestly apered . . .
whiche thyng, although the Englishe
people like a valiant & strong body, at
the first tyme did not perceive, yet
after that thei felt it grow like a pestilent
humor, which successcively alitle and
litle corrupteth all the membres, and
destroyeth the body' (Bullough, 3.56).
3SD This signals the end of the battle
fought in the previous scene, and
might conventionally have ended it. It

77.1 *an English* Soldier] *Capell; a Souldier* F   **2.2**] *Capell*   0.1–2 *with . . . Salisbury*] *this edn; a*
Captain, *and Others. / Capell*   0.2–3 *their . . . march*] *this edn; after 2.1.7.2* F   3   SD *They sound*] *this*
edn; Retreat sounded. / Capell

TALBOT

Bring forth the body of old Salisbury,
And here advance it in the market-place, 5
The middle centre of this cursed town.
Now have I paid my vow unto his soul.
For every drop of blood was drawn from him
There hath at least five Frenchmen died tonight.
And that hereafter ages may behold 10
What ruin happened in revenge of him,
Within their chiefest temple I'll erect
A tomb wherein his corpse shall be interred,
Upon the which, that everyone may read,
Shall be engraved the sack of Orleans, 15
The treacherous manner of his mournful death,
And what a terror he had been to France.

would be possible to begin a new scene at 4, and this would make more literal sense of the location; the *retreat* would be sounded outside the walls, rather than from the town's *centre* (6), and the funeral would begin a new scene, set within Orleans. But this would require a large number of actors to enter for three lines, then exit, then re-enter immediately. The dramatists are, as so often in the play, overlapping and juxtaposing different kinds of stage action, and playing intelligently but freely with the audience's sense of the location of a scene. The funeral procession, entering to begin the scene, has to wait for the battle of the previous scene to be formally ended by the *retreat* until it can get under way, and the audience is allowed, until 5 tells us otherwise, to believe we are still outside the walls. Hence perhaps the confusion of F's compilers as to where to place the funeral (see 0.1–3n.).

6 **middle . . . town** So now the stage image has reversed – the main stage now represents the *centre*, not, as in the

previous scene, and perhaps the beginning of this one, the outside, of the town. F's 'Centure' is an unusual spelling; the word could be rendered as 'cincture' (Cam^2), suggesting the innermost circle of a walled town organized defensively as a concentric sequence. The word 'cincture' is not recorded in Shakespeare. OED attests to 'centure' as a common sixteenth-century spelling of *centre*.
    cursed cursèd
8 **was drawn** that was drawn
12 **their chiefest temple** Salisbury, as Hall relates, was buried in England (at Bisham; Bullough, 3.56). But Talbot's promise may be related to the burial of Bedford as described by Hall, an aspect of which event is transposed by the adaptors of the chronicle to Talbot's own death. See 4.4.162.
17 There is some sense in Ard^2's provision here of an exit for the funeral. But *train* (34) might suggest that the Countess's Messenger confronts the procession about to leave; the scene, as interrupted obsequies, echoes 1.1 in a

6 centre] *(Centure); cincture Cam^2* town.] town. *Dead March. Enter with the body of Salisbury. Ard^2*
17 France.] France. *Exit Funeral. Ard^2*

But, lords, in all our bloody massacre
I muse we met not with the Dolphin's grace,
His new-come champion, virtuous Joan of Aire,   20
Nor any of his false confederates.

BEDFORD
'Tis thought, Lord Talbot, when the fight began,
Roused on the sudden from their drowsy beds,
They did, amongst the troops of armed men,
Leap o'er the walls for refuge in the field.   25

BURGUNDY
Myself, as far as I could well discern
For smoke and dusky vapours of the night,
Am sure I scared the Dolphin and his trull,
When arm in arm they both came swiftly running,
Like to a pair of loving turtle-doves   30

---

lighter vein. Talbot may be taken aside by the Messenger, as the rest are about to leave with the funeral; then the other English commanders intervene, and their own attendance at the funeral is delayed. Alternatively, the Messenger's arrival may halt the general exit, which then takes place only at the end of the scene.

19 muse wonder (more normally, in silence)

Dolphin's grace This is most probably a sarcastic reference to the Dolphin himself, and to his (in English eyes) dubious title, in that *grace* was shifting, in the time the play was written, from being the mode of address to kings to that deemed apt to dukes and bishops; just conceivably it refers to Joan as his *grace*, in an overlap of the theological and erotic sense of the word, typical of the language used of her throughout the play.

20 *Joan of Aire Holinshed (3.163) gives Joan's father's name as 'James of Are'. She calls herself 'Joan of Aire' at 5.3.49, where again the connotations

of 'air' are exploited in a relation to virtue and innocence. 'Arc' is Rowe's version with no particular etymological justification. Warner notes interpretations of this name in terms of the Amazon's bow, and the archetypal female symbol of the curve, but the biblical idea of the 'ark' as the vessel of salvation is surely more immediately relevant here. F has 'Acre', a town in the Holy Land, the site of significant action in the Crusades, but this seems a simple misreading. See Appendix 1.

24 armed armèd

27 For given

28 trull low-class prostitute

30 turtle-doves *Turtle-doves* were an image of faithfulness in love, in that the male and female were thought to be true to each other for life and their cooing was interpreted as amorous. There are many examples in Shakespearean texts; for example, 'So turtles pair / That never mean to part', *WT* 4.4.154–5. The idea is proverbial: 'As true as a TURTLE to her mate' (Dent, T624).

20 Aire] *Ard²*; Acre *F*; Arc *Rowe*

That could not live asunder day or night.
After that things are set in order here
We'll follow them with all the power we have.

Enter a Messenger.

MESSENGER

All hail, my lords. Which of this princely train
Call ye the warlike Talbot, for his acts   35
So much applauded through the realm of France?

TALBOT

Here is the Talbot. Who would speak with him?

MESSENGER

The virtuous lady, Countess of Auvergne,
With modesty admiring thy renown,
By me entreats, great lord, thou wouldst vouchsafe   40
To visit her poor castle where she lies,
That she may boast she hath beheld the man
Whose glory fills the world with loud report.

BURGUNDY

Is it even so? Nay, then I see our wars
Will turn unto a peaceful comic sport,   45
When ladies crave to be encountered with.
You may not, my lord, despise her gentle suit.

TALBOT

Ne'er trust me then; for when a world of men
Could not prevail with all their oratory,

---

33 **with . . . have** *Power* is used in the
sense of 'military power'; so, 'with all
the soldiers available to us'.

43 **loud report** widespread rumour; also,
punningly, noisy explosions or gunfire

45 **comic sport** lighthearted game

46 **crave . . . with** want to be met; but
crave has the stronger sense of 'desire'

or 'be hungry for', and *encountered with*
has sexual overtones. It may also be the
case that *encountered* is a play on the
Countess's title, and possibly her sex;
Burgundy is, with typical suavity,
steering the play towards *comic sport*.

48 **Ne'er . . . then** mistrust me if I do
despise it

38 Auvergne] *(Ouergne)*   46 encountered] *(encountred)*

171

Yet hath a woman's kindness overruled.   50
And therefore tell her I return great thanks
And in submission will attend on her.
Will not your honours bear me company?

BEDFORD

No, truly, 'tis more than manners will:
And I have heard it said unbidden guests   55
Are often welcomest when they are gone.

TALBOT

Why then, alone (since there's no remedy)
I mean to prove this lady's courtesy.
Come hither, captain, you perceive my mind.   59
    [*The Captain comes forward; Talbot*] *whispers*
    [*to him*].

CAPTAIN

I do, my lord, and mean accordingly.   *Exeunt.*

[**2.3**]   *Enter* COUNTESS [of Auvergne, *and her* Porter].

COUNTESS

Porter, remember what I gave in charge;
And when you have done so, bring the keys to me.

PORTER Madam, I will.   *Exit.*

COUNTESS

The plot is laid. If all things fall out right
I shall as famous be by this exploit   5

---

50 overruled *OED v.* 3: 'To prevail over (a person) so as to change or set aside his opinion'

52 attend on visit, but with a sense of courtly deference

55–6 Dent, G475, cites these lines and relates them to 'Welcome when you go' (Dent, W259).

57 there's no remedy there's no alternative; cf. Dent, R71, R71.1.

58 prove test

59 perceive my mind understand my intention

60 mean intend

2.3.1 gave in charge ordered you to do

4 fall out work out

54 'tis] it is *Malone* 59 captain] Captain. *Whispers / Johnson* SD *The . . . Talbot*] *this edn to him*] *this edn* **2.3**] *Capell* 0.1 *and her* Porter] *Pope*

As Scythian Tomyris by Cyrus' death.
Great is the rumour of this dreadful knight,
And his achievements of no less account:
Fain would mine eyes be witness with mine ears,
To give their censure of these rare reports.   10

Enter Messenger *and* TALBOT.

MESSENGER

Madam, according as your ladyship desired,
By message craved, so is Lord Talbot come.

COUNTESS

And he is welcome. What? Is this the man?

MESSENGER

Madam, it is.

COUNTESS   Is this the scourge of France?
Is this the Talbot, so much feared abroad   15
That with his name the mothers still their babes?
I see report is fabulous and false.
I thought I should have seen some Hercules,

6 **Tomyris** one of the nine female worthies. See Introduction, p. 45. Tomyris was queen of Scythia, who avenged the suicide of her son while he was in captivity to Cyrus. She defeated the Persian king in battle, and then ritually insulted his corpse by pushing his face into a wineskin full of blood (Herodotus, 1.212–14). This behaviour seems more like that of Margaret towards York in *3H6* 1.4 than any actions of the Countess or Joan in this play.

7 **rumour** fame or reputation but with a sense that this might be false; *rumour* is fame's untrustworthy anti-type. See *2H4* Induction.
   dreadful fearsome

8 **of . . . account** equal or superior

9 **Fain** gladly, with pleasure

10 **censure** judgement

these rare reports Shaheen (34) finds in this a reference to the Queen of Sheba and Solomon, 2 Chronicles, 9.6: 'Howbeit I beleved not their reporte, until I came, and mine eyes had sene it'. See also 67n.

15 **abroad** in the sense of *OED* A *adv.* 2 *fig.*: 'current in the outside world'

16 **still** quieten

17 **fabulous** mythical (or, possibly, if *report* is personified, given to recounting myths)

18 **Hercules** The legendary Greek hero was famed not only for his physical prowess – the main emphasis in his citation here – but for his unfortunate relations with women. Omphale, who may well be on the Countess's mind, enslaved Hercules and made him dress as a woman and spin with her maids.

11 Madam] *om. Ard²*   desired] *om. Pope*   15 abroad] *Johnson;* abroad? *F*

A second Hector for his grim aspect
And large proportion of his strong-knit limbs.   20
Alas, this is a child, a silly dwarf:
It cannot be this weak and writhled shrimp
Should strike such terror to his enemies.

TALBOT

Madam, I have been bold to trouble you;
But, since your ladyship is not at leisure,   25
I'll sort some other time to visit you.

COUNTESS

What means he now? Go ask him whither he goes.

MESSENGER

Stay, my Lord Talbot, for my lady craves
To know the cause of your abrupt departure.

TALBOT

Marry, for that she's in a wrong belief,   30
I go to certify her Talbot's here.

The story is retold in Spenser's *FQ*,
5.5–7, where Artegall is captured 'by
guile' by Radigund, a woman warrior,
and made to work with her women, but
rescued by his lover, the virtuous
woman warrior, Britomart. Hercules'
wife, Deianeira, was tricked by a cen-
taur he had wounded into killing him
with a poisoned robe. Like other figures
with whom Talbot is linked, Hercules
was often listed as one of the nine worthies, though less frequently than some
of the others cited in this play.

19 **Hector** Like others to whom Talbot is
compared, Hector is doomed, though
as the defeated champion of Troy only
indirectly by a woman, Helen, on
whose behalf the war was fought.
More directly relevant here is the
fabled size of Homeric heroes, a super-
human attribute to which Talbot fails
to measure up. Hector is usually one of
the nine worthies.

20 **proportion** form

21 **silly** innocent; helpless
22 **writhled** 'Of persons, the skin, etc.:
Wrinkled; shrivelled, withered' (*OED*
1). The suggestion, in conjunction with
shrimp, and in the erotic context of the
scene, is of a small and detumescent
penis, an audience-pleasing joke easily
activated on stage by a knowingly aimed
downward glance from the actress (as
by Yvonne Coulette, RSC, 1977–8). In
the masque of the 'worthies' in *LLL*
Hercules is represented by the tiny page
Moth as '*a child, a shrimp*' (5.2.584). See
Introduction, p. 44.

26 **sort** assign
31 **her Talbot's here** This is F's punctuation; it leaves open the ambiguity as to
whether *her* is object of the verb *certify* or possessive of *Talbot* – he goes to
certify the presence of *her* Talbot.
There is a paradox, a riddle, in
Talbot's going out in order to prove his
presence, which the Countess registers
at 56–8.

26 you] you. *going* / *Capell*   27] *Pope; F lines* now? / goes? /

Enter Porter *with keys.*

COUNTESS
    If thou be he, then art thou prisoner.
TALBOT
    Prisoner? To whom?
COUNTESS   To me, bloodthirsty lord;
    And for that cause I trained thee to my house.
    Long time thy shadow hath been thrall to me;   35
    For in my gallery thy picture hangs.
    But now the substance shall endure the like,
    And I will chain these legs and arms of thine,
    That hast by tyranny these many years
    Wasted our country, slain our citizens   40
    And sent our sons and husbands captivate.
TALBOT   Ha, ha, ha.
COUNTESS
    Laughest thou, wretch? Thy mirth shall turn to
        moan.
TALBOT
    I laugh to see your ladyship so fond
    To think that you have aught but Talbot's shadow   45
    Whereon to practise your severity.
COUNTESS
    Why? Art not thou the man?
TALBOT
    I am indeed.
COUNTESS   Then have I substance too.

---

34 **trained** *OED v.*[1] II 4 *fig.* gives, for 'train', 'To draw by art or inducement': a metaphor from hunting – 'pieces of carrion or the like laid in a line or trail for luring certain wild beasts' (*OED* train *sb.*[1] II 7).
35 **thrall** slave, also suggesting enchantment (as in 'enthrall')

37 **the like** thralldom; or hanging?
41 **captivate** in captivity
48 **Then . . . substance** The shadow/substance distinction is recurrent in Shakespeare's reflections on history. See Introduction, pp. 60–1. There is a further sense here of magic, also often associated with the shadow/substance

43] *Pope; F lines* Wretch? / moane. /

TALBOT

No, no, I am but shadow of myself:
You are deceived, my substance is not here;   50
For what you see is but the smallest part
And least proportion of humanity.
I tell you, madam, were the whole frame here,
It is of such a spacious lofty pitch
Your roof were not sufficient to contain't.   55

COUNTESS

This is a riddling merchant, for the nonce.
He will be here, and yet he is not here:
How can these contrarieties agree?

TALBOT

That will I show you presently.
    Winds his horn. Drums strike up. A peal of ordnance.

     Enter Soldiers.

How say you, madam? Are you now persuaded   60
That Talbot is but shadow of himself?
These are his substance, sinews, arms and strength,
With which he yoketh your rebellious necks,
Razeth your cities and subverts your towns,

dichotomy both by Shakespeare and
by his dramatist colleagues. See for
example Greene's *Friar Bacon and
Friar Bungay*, 6.128–30.
53 **frame** structure; often used of the
human body and, less often, of an
army (*OED sb.* II 4c)
54 **pitch** height
56 **merchant** fellow; evoking the Elizabethan phrase 'to play the merchant
with', meaning 'to . . . get the better of'
(*OED* A *sb.* 1c)
 for the nonce at the moment, with an
undertone of scorn: 'He can play at
riddles too, can he?'

57 **yet** ambiguous between the senses of
the word in the phrases *and yet*, 'but',
and *yet . . . not*, 'not for a while'/'not yet'
59 **presently** This can mean 'immediately'. *OED adv.* 2a, 'At the present time;
at this time,' is the primary meaning
here, but the sense of immediacy is
also relevant to the action; perhaps we
can see here one meaning emerging
out of the other.
 SD *Winds* blows
 peal of ordnance burst of cannon-
fire; see 1.4.15n.
64 **subverts** in its literal, Latin-derived,
sense (*OED* 1) of 'raze to the ground'

59 That] That, madam, *(Steevens);* Lady, that *Keightley*

And in a moment makes them desolate.   65

COUNTESS

Victorious Talbot, pardon my abuse.

I find thou art no less than fame hath bruited,

And more than may be gathered by thy shape.

Let my presumption not provoke thy wrath,

For I am sorry that with reverence   70

I did not entertain thee as thou art.

TALBOT

Be not dismayed, fair lady, nor misconster

The mind of Talbot as you did mistake

The outward composition of his body.

What you have done hath not offended me;   75

Nor other satisfaction do I crave,

But only, with your patience, that we may

Taste of your wine and see what cates you have;

For soldiers' stomachs always serve them well.

COUNTESS

With all my heart – and think me honoured   80

To feast so great a warrior in my house.   *Exeunt.*

[**2.4**]   *Enter* RICHARD Plantagenet, WARWICK,
                    SOMERSET[, SUFFOLK, VERNON *and a* Lawyer].

66 **abuse** ill-usage
67 This line helps shape the scene as an
· analogue of the Solomon/Sheba encounter (See 10n.). See 2 Chronicles,
9.6: 'thou exceedest the fame that I
heard'. *Bruited* means 'spoken of'.
72 **misconster** misinterpret, misconstrue
78 **cates** provisions, usually festive
80 **honoured** honourèd
2.4.0.2 *SUFFOLK . . . **Lawyer** F's SD
omits Suffolk, but includes the name
'*Poole*' after '*Somerset*'. Poole is the
name by which Richard calls Suffolk
throughout the scene, in what is

probably, given the emphasis here on
birth and title, a deliberately contemp-
tuous choice of the English form of his
family name, which his ancestors
Frenchified to 'de la Pole' on their elevation from merchants to knights. See
Appendix 1. Capell's version of the
SD, by putting 'another' before
Lawyer, and by placing *Richard*, presumably in terms of strict social hierarchy, after the less controversially
aristocratic figures, implies that
Vernon and Richard are also lawyers.

2.4] *Capell*   0.2 SUFFOLK . . . Lawyer] *Capell (subst.); Poole, and others* F

RICHARD

Great lords, and gentlemen, what means this silence?
Dare no man answer in a case of truth?

SUFFOLK

Within the Temple Hall we were too loud;
The garden here is more convenient.

RICHARD

Then say at once if I maintained the truth;   5
Or else was wrangling Somerset in th'error?

SUFFOLK

Faith, I have been a truant in the law

2   **a case of truth** a dispute as to the *truth* of a particular argument (we do not know exactly what this quarrel is about); but also, potentially, an argument about *truth* in the sense of loyalty, which is what the quarrel turns into. See Introduction, pp. 62–4.

3   **Temple Hall** From at least the beginning of the fifteenth century, the quadrangles and lodgings of the 'Temple', to the west of the City of London, which had been, until their dissolution in the previous century, the property of the Knights Templar, have been the institutional centre of English law. As we see from the Gaoler's statement in the next scene (2.5.19), Richard is living in chambers in the Temple, a departure from history, since he had in fact remained well regarded at court: 'so long as Gloucester or Beaufort ruled he was not cold-shouldered by the king, for his lineage commanded respect from both statesmen' (Griffiths, 673). Richard had already inherited the dukedom of York in 1415, and was put by Henry V into the care of 'an old Lancastrian retainer' (Griffiths, 666), but after Henry's death, when York was twelve, he was brought closer and closer to the centre of power. In the play Richard's exile places him as seeking a legal education seldom undertaken by an aristocrat, and this is reflected in some of the more technical legal language he uses in this scene and later in the play. The play, ahistorically, emphasizes his isolation from, and opposition to, the court.

were This could mean that they enter from the *Temple Hall*, steered out by Suffolk, where they had been *too loud*. Alternatively, *were* could be subjunctive in mood, and so Suffolk could be preventing them entering the hall, saying that they would be too loud. In either case Suffolk's mood and intention are much less clear than Richard's.

5–6 **if I . . . error** There is no clue either in the play or in any likely source as to what this dispute was initially about. Though it comes to turn on the question of Richard's status, that question erupts in the course of a dispute whose starting point is forgotten. If (as here) F's punctuation is observed, Richard sets up two apparent alternatives which are actually the same – either Richard is right or Somerset is wrong. The effect is potentially farcical. It is just possible, however, that *wrangling* is a gerund form, and that Richard is challenging the others to say that *wrangling* [with] Somerset was an *error* on his part. But this, without 'with' or equivalent, would be an awkward and unusual form.

1] *Pope; F lines* Gentlemen, / silence? /   1+ SP] *this edn; Yorke. F; Plantagenet / Rowe*   6 th'error] error *Hudson (Dyce);* right *Johnson*

And never yet could frame my will to it,
And therefore frame the law unto my will.

SOMERSET

Judge you, my lord of Warwick, then, between us. 10

WARWICK

Between two hawks, which flies the higher pitch,
Between two dogs, which hath the deeper mouth,
Between two blades, which bears the better temper,
Between two horses, which doth bear him best,
Between two girls, which hath the merriest eye, 15
I have perhaps some shallow spirit of judgement:
But in these nice sharp quillets of the law,
Good faith, I am no wiser than a daw.

RICHARD

Tut, tut, here is a mannerly forbearance:
The truth appears so naked on my side 20
That any purblind eye may find it out.

SOMERSET

And on my side it is so well apparelled,
So clear, so shining and so evident,
That it will glimmer through a blind man's eye.

RICHARD

Since you are tongue-tied and so loath to speak, 25

8, 9 **frame** adapt, shape

11 **pitch** altitude

12 **the deeper mouth** Theseus in *MND* prides himself that his dogs are 'So flew'd, so sanded' (4.1.119–20). His dogs, like those of which Warwick is a connoisseur, hunt and retrieve their prey, and so need to be 'flewed', or deep-mouthed, in order to retain their prize. They are most probably a kind of beagle.

13 **temper** *OED sb*. II 5, 'The particular degree of hardness and elasticity or resiliency imparted to steel by tempering'

14 **bear him** hold its head up; deport itself

17 **quillets** 'a verbal nicety or subtle distinction' (*OED sb.*[2])

18 **daw** jackdaw; proverbial for stupidity (Dent, D49.1, D50)

21 **purblind** Though the more common meaning is 'partly blind' (cf. *VA* 679), Shakespeare usually uses it to mean completely blind; in *LLL* 3.1.174 and *RJ* 2.1.12 it is used of Cupid.

---

13 bears] shows *Cam²;* hath *Cam*

In dumb significants proclaim your thoughts.
Let him that is a true-born gentleman
And stands upon the honour of his birth,
If he suppose that I have pleaded truth,
From off this briar pluck a white rose with me.　　　　30
SOMERSET
　　Let him that is no coward nor no flatterer,

26 **significants** symbols, signifiers
27 **true-born** The meaning of the term 'truth' shifts throughout this scene. Here, in referring to social class, it paves the way for the *yeoman* insult later (81), but in these circumstances truth as 'loyalty', as a moral virtue, as honest attention to the real and as validated social status all overlap and so focus Richard's sense of the injustice done him.
28 **stands upon** affirms, and takes confidence from
30 **briar** This normally refers to a wild rose. The choice of the term here in reference to a rose-bush foregrounds danger – from the thorns – and wildness, the qualities that define the term when it is applied to plants of other species. In the original staging an artificial plant was presumably carried on to set the scene. It would be possible for the same plant to bear white and red flowers, but two plants, intertwined, may have been envisaged. In either case, this is not a formal garden, but a kind of accidental wilderness, like the action that springs from it. The red rose had been the symbol of the House of Lancaster since the thirteenth century: 'sprung from the same stem as Edward I's golden rose, [it] was a badge of the house of Lancaster from the time of Earl Edmund "Crouchback" (son of Henry III) who died in 1296' (Scott-Giles, 136); the white rose was less traditional as the symbol of York, adopted from the Mortimers in order to emphasize Richard's line of descent and so his claim to the throne. But there is little evidence that it was used as an identifying standard or badge.

For Scott-Giles 'the roses already existed as badges, the red rose being definitely that of the house of Lancaster. We must not think of the episode as having given rise to the roses as badges, but only as having focused their rivalry' (137). Yet there is no sense in the scene as written that the choice of the roses as badges is anything other than gratuitous; it is thus presented as a point of origin for the rose badges, not a ceremonial enactment of something already established. The unified rose, both white and red, was the Tudor emblem. In a context where the meaning of these events is (as for Hall) the eventual union of the two houses, it makes sense for the dramatists to establish the white rose as the Yorkist badge ahistorically early, and that is the function of this scene. Hall may be drawing on the role of the red rose and the white in alchemical tradition in order to strengthen the sense of the dynastic marriage between York and Lancaster, the climax of his narrative, as inevitable and beneficent; in that case the setting of this scene has a symbolic role, as the crucible of a disorder that eventually leads to a resolution perfected in marriage. But, as Gary Taylor has pointed out, it is only in this first play of the 'trilogy' that the rose badges are mentioned; in *2H6* and *3H6* there is no reference to them, (though the SDs to 3.11 of *True Tragedy* establish the convention, followed in all productions, of the wearing of symbolic roses). See Introduction, pp. 57–60.

But dare maintain the party of the truth,
Pluck a red rose from off this thorn with me.

WARWICK

I love no colours: and, without all colour
Of base insinuating flattery,   35
I pluck this white rose with Plantagenet.

SUFFOLK

I pluck this red rose with young Somerset,
And say withal I think he held the right.

VERNON

Stay, lords and gentlemen, and pluck no more
Till you conclude that he upon whose side   40
The fewest roses are cropped from the tree
Shall yield the other in the right opinion.

SOMERSET

Good Master Vernon, it is well objected:
If I have fewest I subscribe in silence.

RICHARD   And I.   45

VERNON

Then, for the truth and plainness of the case,
I pluck this pale and maiden blossom here,
Giving my verdict on the white rose side.

SOMERSET

Prick not your finger as you pluck it off,
Lest, bleeding, you do paint the white rose red   50

---

34 **colours** This can imply falsehood in
the sense of the cosmetic (*OED sb.*[1] III
11a, 'that which serves to conceal or
cloak the truth'), but it can also imply
the 'colours' of opposing sides in battle.
See *TN* 1.5.9–11, where the phrase
'fear no colours', according to Maria
(and Dent, C520), is proverbial.
Warwick's alteration of the phrase to
'love no colours' reveals that his earlier
desire to avoid taking sides has given

way to a belief in the rightness of
Richard's cause.
38 **held the right** was in the right
42 'shall concede the rightness of the
other's opinion'
44 **subscribe** give in; literally, write
under, give a signature to
45 The marked break in rhythm and
metre might imply that Richard is
pausing before he concedes (RP).

41 are cropped . . . tree] *(*cropt*); from the tree are cropp'd *Ard*[2]

And fall on my side so, against your will.

VERNON

If I, my lord, for my opinion bleed,

Opinion shall be surgeon to my hurt

And keep me on the side where still I am.

SOMERSET

Well, well, come on, who else?   55

LAWYER

Unless my study and my books be false,

The argument you held was wrong in you;

In sign whereof I pluck a white rose too.

RICHARD

Now, Somerset, where is your argument?

SOMERSET

Here in my scabbard, meditating that   60

Shall dye your white rose in a bloody red.

RICHARD

Meantime your cheeks do counterfeit our roses;

For pale they look with fear, as witnessing

The truth on our side.

SOMERSET   No, Plantagenet:

'Tis not for fear, but anger, that thy cheeks   65

Blush for pure shame, to counterfeit our roses –

And yet thy tongue will not confess thy error.

RICHARD

Hath not thy rose a canker, Somerset?

SOMERSET

Hath not thy rose a thorn, Plantagenet?

---

51 **fall . . . side** end up on my side (by
involuntarily staining the white rose red)
52 **opinion** personal judgement
53 **Opinion** public opinion
55 The short line could emphasize Somerset's undignified, almost comic impatience.
· 57 **wrong in you** If F's *in you* is correct,
it intensifies *wrong*. From the Lawyer's

57 in you] in law *Ard²*

point of view, then, Somerset has not
simply made a legal error, but revealed
a personal bias, which provokes the
Lawyer himself to forfeit professional
neutrality, in taking the rose. The
emendation in Ard² finds some support in 4.1.95.
60–1 **that / Shall** upon something that must
68, 71 **canker** disease, blight; cankerworm

RICHARD

    Ay, sharp and piercing to maintain his truth,   70

    Whiles thy consuming canker eats his falsehood.

SOMERSET

    Well, I'll find friends to wear my bleeding roses

    That shall maintain what I have said is true,

    Where false Plantagenet dare not be seen.

RICHARD

    Now, by this maiden blossom in my hand,   75

    I scorn thee and thy fashion, peevish boy.

SUFFOLK

    Turn not thy scorns this way, Plantagenet.

RICHARD

    Proud Poole, I will, and scorn both him and thee.

SUFFOLK

    I'll turn my part thereof into thy throat.

SOMERSET

    Away, away, good William de la Pole –   80

    We grace the yeoman by conversing with him.

WARWICK

    Now, by God's will, thou wrong'st him, Somerset:

    His grandfather was Lionel, Duke of Clarence,

    Third son to the third Edward, King of England;

    Spring crestless yeomen from so deep a root?   85

70, 71 **his** its

75 **maiden** White is the colour of virgin innocence.

76 **peevish** weakly defiant

78 **Poole** See 0.2n. and Appendix 1 for consideration of the form of the name.

81 **yeoman** 'A man holding a small landed estate; a freeholder under the rank of gentleman' (*OED* II 4a). It seems to be this insult, and the consequent reflection on Richard's father, rather than the undisclosed offstage argument, that triggers Richard's subsequent actions and the ensuing conflict. See 2.5.45–54.

83 **grandfather** Clarence was actually, in modern terms, Richard's great-great-grandfather, but the Elizabethans used terms for family relationship much more loosely – so adding to the confusion of later readers and audiences. See also *nephew*, 2.5.64. For relevant section of family tree, see Introduction, p. 57.

76 fashion] passion *Pope;* faction *Theobald*

RICHARD

   He bears him on the place's privilege,

   Or durst not, for his craven heart, say thus.

SOMERSET

   By him that made me, I'll maintain my words

   On any plot of ground in Christendom.

   Was not thy father Richard, Earl of Cambridge,   90

   For treason executed in our late king's days?

   And by his treason stand'st not thou attainted,

   Corrupted, and exempt from ancient gentry?

   His trespass yet lives guilty in thy blood,

   And till thou be restored thou art a yeoman.   95

RICHARD

   My father was attached, not attainted,

   Condemned to die for treason, but no traitor;

   And that I'll prove on better men than Somerset,

   Were growing time once ripened to my will.

   For your partaker Poole, and you yourself,   100

   I'll note you in my book of memory,

   To scourge you for this apprehension;

---

86 **bears him on** depends upon
place's privilege The use of arms is
forbidden within the precincts of the
Temple. Cf. 1.3.46n.

87 **craven** cowardly

88 **maintain** stand by

90 **Earl of Cambridge** See 2.5.2n., and
H5 2.2.

92 **attainted** a legal term; the consequence of receiving an 'attainder', by
which a person condemned to the
death penalty could neither transmit
nor inherit property or title, and lost
all civil rights

93 **exempt from** cut off from

96 **attached** attachèd; arrested and
charged. Richard is arguing that his
father's indictment did not incur a
penalty (an attainder) that would apply
to his descendants.

98 **prove** test, demonstrate

99 If the time were ripe for me to do so.

100 **partaker** supporter

101 **book of memory** Memory is often
presented through the metaphor of a
memorandum book in Renaissance
writing; see *Ham* 1.5.107–10, where
the context of the idea is, as here, a private intent of vengeance.

102 **apprehension** Five syllables; the
primary meaning is of 'idea' or 'con-
cept', that of Richard's father's
treachery, but other possible meanings, of physical attack or legal arrest,
make Richard's choice of word more
loaded.

---

91 executed] headed *Pope*   102 this apprehension] misapprehension *(Vaughan);* this reprehension
Theobald

Look to it well, and say you are well warned.

SOMERSET

Ah, thou shalt find us ready for thee still,

And know us by these colours for thy foes;   105

For these my friends, in spite of thee, shall wear.

RICHARD

And, by my soul, this pale and angry rose,

As cognizance of my blood-drinking hate,

Will I for ever, and my faction, wear

Until it wither with me to my grave   110

Or flourish to the height of my degree.

SUFFOLK

Go forward, and be choked with thy ambition:

And so farewell, until I meet thee next.   *Exit.*

SOMERSET

Have with thee, Pole. Farewell, ambitious Richard.   *Exit.*

RICHARD

How I am braved, and must perforce endure it.   115

WARWICK

This blot that they object against your house

Shall be whipped out in the next parliament,

Called for the truce of Winchester and Gloucester:

And if thou be not then created York,

---

105 **colours** red roses; insignia
106 **in spite of** despite; in contempt of
108 **cognizance** acknowledgement –
    another word from a legal vocabulary;
    also family badge (*OED* III 5)
111 **degree** rank
115 **braved** challenged
116–27 Warwick's prophecy seems to
    have no particular source or authori-
    ty behind it. But it does show that,
    however improvised the beginning of
    the scene, by the end of it those who
    take the white rose are acting with a

sense of the consequences of their
actions.
116 **object** urge as an objection against
117 **whipped** In British parliamentary
    practice party 'whips' supervise the
    voting of their members, but that
    sense, according to *OED* (*sb.* I 7a),
    dates from 1828; here the term has a
    simpler sense of correction through
    chastisement, *OED v.* II 11 *fig.* F2's
    'wipt' fits metaphor and context as
    easily.

117 whipped] *(*whipt*)*; wipt *F2*

I will not live to be accounted Warwick.   120
Meantime, in signal of my love to thee,
Against proud Somerset and William Poole
Will I upon thy party wear this rose.
And here I prophesy: this brawl today,
Grown to this faction in the Temple Garden,   125
Shall send between the red rose and the white
A thousand souls to death and deadly night.

RICHARD

Good Master Vernon, I am bound to you,
That you on my behalf would pluck a flower.

VERNON

In your behalf, still will I wear the same.   130

LAWYER

And so will I.

RICHARD   Thanks, gentle.
Come, let us four to dinner: I dare say
This quarrel will drink blood another day.   *Exeunt.*

---

120 The line is ambiguous. Warwick could be saying, 'I would rather die than keep my own title', so implying an offer of military support to Richard, or he could be reassuringly expressing confidence: 'You are only as likely to fail to gain your title as I am to lose mine'. Choice between the two would depend on interpretation of the character. See note on List of Roles.

125 **faction** formation of parties; dissension

131 **Thanks, gentle** It is particularly difficult to coerce this exchange into verse; but the raggedness of the effect of F's text is appropriate enough to the dramatic action. It may be that the compositor failed to decipher the Lawyer's proper name in the MS and

simply left it out, or there may have been a lacuna in the copy-manuscript at this point. See Introduction, p. 100. For what may be a parallel instance, see 1.4.94 and t.n.

132 **dinner** the main meal of the day, eaten at midday, by which time most of the day's business would be done. The scene as written thus takes place in the late morning; the ESC production set it after or during dinner – in the modern sense of a mid-evening dinner – with the participants in slightly dishevelled evening dress, glasses in hand. In that context the line suggests that the quarrelling group had broken away from a formal dinner which continued without them, and to which Richard and his supporters returned.

---

131 gentle] gentle sir *F2;* gentlemen *Ard²*

[**2.5**]   *Enter* MORTIMER, *brought in a chair, and* Gaolers.

MORTIMER

Kind keepers of my weak decaying age,
Let dying Mortimer here rest himself.
Even like a man new haled from the rack,
So fare my limbs with long imprisonment;
And these grey locks, the pursuivants of death,   5
Nestor-like aged, in an age of care,
Argue the end of Edmund Mortimer.
These eyes, like lamps whose wasting oil is spent,
Wax dim, as drawing to their exigent;
Weak shoulders, overborne with burdening grief,   10
And pithless arms, like to a withered vine

2.5.0.1 **Gaolers** For speculations as to
the Gaolers' comings and goings, see
Introduction, pp. 94–5.

2   **dying Mortimer** This scene expands
on a sentence of Hall's: 'Edmonde
Mortimer, the last Erle of Marche of
that name (whiche long tyme had been
restrained from his liberty, and finally
waxed lame) disceased without issue,
whose inheritaunce discended to lorde
Richarde Plantagenet, sonne and heire
to Richard erle of Cambridge, behed-
ed, as you have heard before, at the
toune of Southhampton' (Bullough,
3.47). For Mortimer's genealogical
position, see Introduction, p. 57.
Characteristically, the playwrights
amplify Hall's already schematized
presentation of history to move one
step further away from historical fact.
The historical Mortimer, the fifth Earl
of March, from whom Richard inherited his claim to the throne, was a
respected figure by the time of his
death. For more on the conflation of
various members of the Mortimer
family into this role, see notes to List of
Roles (p. 110). Here a figure is created
to join the sequence of maimed or ageing male figures, whom the play tends
to present as living memorials to

England's past. Shakespeare returns to
the events that Mortimer describes in
1H4, *2H4* and *H5*.

3   **haled** halèd: pulled; hauled
5   **pursuivants** A pursuivant is 'a junior
heraldic officer attendant on the heralds; also one attached to a particular
nobleman' (*OED* 1). So the signs of
age Mortimer has noted are notifying
officers of the approach of their more
powerful master, death.
6   **Nestor** Homeric hero proverbial for
his wisdom and great age. He appears
as a character in *TC*.
aged agèd
8   **wasting** lessening
9   **exigent** 'Last pinch; end, extremity'
(*OED* B *sb.*[1] I b)
10   **overborne** oppressed
11   **pithless** without vital force; 'pith' is
the structuring fabric of a plant form,
the thing that holds it together. In this
period it also applies to the marrow in
the centre of the bone, and also, as in
modern usage, in a metaphorical extension of meaning, to strength or force as
such. On one level Mortimer is simply
saying that he has difficulty moving his
arms, on another that his strength of
spirit has gone.

2.5] *Capell*   3 rack] *Pope;* Wrack F   6] *placed after 7 Oxf*   11 like to] are like *(Ard²)*

That droops his sapless branches to the ground.
Yet are these feet, whose strengthless stay is numb,
Unable to support this lump of clay,
Swift-winged with desire to get a grave,   15
As witting I no other comfort have.
But tell me, keeper, will my nephew come?

GAOLER

Richard Plantagenet, my lord, will come:
We sent unto the Temple, unto his chamber,
And answer was returned that he will come.   20

MORTIMER

Enough; my soul shall then be satisfied.
Poor gentleman, his wrong doth equal mine.
Since Henry Monmouth first began to reign –
Before whose glory I was great in arms –
This loathsome sequestration have I had;   25
And even since then hath Richard been obscured,
Deprived of honour and inheritance.
But now the arbitrator of despairs,
Just death, kind umpire of men's miseries,
With sweet enlargement doth dismiss me hence: 30
I would his troubles likewise were expired,
That so he might recover what was lost.

---

13 **strengthless stay** immobility caused
   by weakness, and (in another meaning
   of *stay*) impotent support
15 **winged** wingèd
16 **witting** knowing
17 **nephew** Richard, historically, was the
   nephew of an Edmund Mortimer who
   died as a respected servant of the
   crown; the rebel Mortimer was that
   Mortimer's uncle. Though the usual
   meaning of the term in this period is
   the same as the modern, it can be used
   more generally as a term for relative by
   blood or marriage (*OED* 3). This

would allow identification of the character with the rebel, but the scene
tends to suggest that the dramatists
have arrived at a composite figure. See
notes to List of Roles (p. 110).

23 **Monmouth** Henry V, born in Monmouth (see 3.1.200), and from
   Mortimer's point of view the inheritor
   of a title rightly his
24 **glory** rise to power, ascendancy
25 **sequestration** confinement, keeping
   apart
30 **enlargement** liberation
31 **his** Richard's

18, 33 SP] *this edn; Keeper. F*   19 unto his] to his *Rowe*

Enter RICHARD.

GAOLER

My lord, your loving nephew now is come.

MORTIMER

Richard Plantagenet, my friend, is he come?

RICHARD

Ay, noble uncle, thus ignobly used,   35

Your nephew, late despised Richard, comes.

MORTIMER

Direct mine arms – I may embrace his neck,

And in his bosom spend my latter gasp.

O tell me when my lips do touch his cheeks,

That I may kindly give one fainting kiss.   40

And now declare, sweet stem from York's great stock,

Why didst thou say of late thou wert despised?

RICHARD

First, lean thine aged back against mine arm,

And in that ease I'll tell thee my disease.

This day, in argument upon a case,   45

Some words there grew 'twixt Somerset and me,

Among which terms he used his lavish tongue

And did upbraid me with my father's death;

Which obloquy set bars before my tongue,

Else with the like I had requited him.   50

Therefore, good uncle, for my father's sake –

In honour of a true Plantagenet –

---

34 **friend** could be either the Gaoler or
   Richard
36 **late** lately, in relation to *despised*
   despised despisèd
38 **latter** last, as in 'latter end' (*OED* A
   adj. 3b), meaning death
40 **kindly** in token of kinship
43 **aged** agèd
44 **disease** discomfort; lack of ease

47 **lavish** loose
49 **obloquy** slander
   set . . . tongue rendered me speech-
   less, silenced me
52 **true** here both 'loyal' and 'true-bred',
   and so returning us to the indictment
   of Richard's father, the Earl of
   Cambridge. See 2.4.27n.

32.1 RICHARD] Richard Plantagenet *Rowe*   34 is he] is *Ard²*   35+ SP RICHARD] *(Rich.)*; *Plan.*
Rowe   37 arms –] *this edn*; Armes, *F*   40 kiss] kiss. *Embraces him Cam²*

189

And for alliance' sake, declare the cause
My father, Earl of Cambridge, lost his head.

MORTIMER

That cause, fair nephew, that imprisoned me,   55
And hath detained me all my flowering youth
Within a loathsome dungeon, there to pine,
Was cursed instrument of his decease.

RICHARD

Discover more at large what cause that was,
For I am ignorant and cannot guess.   60

MORTIMER

I will, if that my fading breath permit,
And death approach not ere my tale be done.
Henry the Fourth, grandfather to this King,
Deposed his nephew Richard, Edward's son,
The first begotten and the lawful heir   65
Of Edward, king, the third of that descent,
During whose reign the Percies of the north,
Finding his usurpation most unjust,
Endeavoured my advancement to the throne.
The reason moved these warlike lords to this   70

---

53 **for alliance' sake** to affirm political and familial loyalty
55 **That** the same
58 **cursed** cursèd
59 **Discover** reveal
60 **and cannot guess** Historically it is, of course, ridiculous that Richard would not know his family history. Theatrically, this is a crude cue to furnishing information to the audience that the 'real' characters themselves would 'really' already know. But the dramatists have invented Richard's exile from the court and stressed Mortimer's solitary confinement; the effect is to create a sense of repression and concealment, of the censoring and rewriting of history, more typical of the Renaissance (or

indeed of the twentieth century) than of the Middle Ages.
64 **his nephew Richard** Richard II, Henry IV's cousin – not, in modern terms, his nephew; see 2.4.83n.
66 **of that descent** Edward's father was Edward II, his father Edward I; so Edward III is both the third Edward and the third king in that line of descent.
67 **the Percies** Earls of Northumberland. Henry Percy, or Hotspur, was married to the sister of the rebel Edmund Mortimer, one of the three members of the Mortimer family who seem to have been amalgamated to create this character. See note on List of Roles (p. 110).

56 flowering] *(flowring)*

Was for that – young Richard thus removed,
Leaving no heir begotten of his body –
I was the next by birth and parentage:
For by my mother I derived am
From Lionel, Duke of Clarence, third son   75
To King Edward the Third, whereas he
From John of Gaunt doth bring his pedigree,
Being but fourth of that heroic line.
But mark: as in this haughty great attempt
They laboured to plant the rightful heir,   80
I lost my liberty and they their lives.
Long after this, when Henry the Fifth,
Succeeding his father Bolingbroke, did reign,
Thy father, Earl of Cambridge then – derived
From famous Edmund Langley, Duke of York –   85
Marrying my sister, that thy mother was,
Again, in pity of my hard distress,
Levied an army, weening to redeem
And have installed me in the diadem;

---

73 See genealogy, Introduction, p. 57.
74 **mother** a more accurate reference would be to his grandmother.
74 **derived** derivèd
76 **he** This is confusing, largely because of *doth* in 77, which suggests to the modern reader and audience that the person referred to exists in the present, and so could well be Henry VI, as occupying the throne that Mortimer feels to be his. But *he* could also refer to Henry IV, son of John of Gaunt, fourth son of Edward III. If so, the real topic of this part of his monologue is still Henry IV and his usurpation of Richard II's throne. Mortimer, in this reading, is moving into the present tense as he relives his past.
79 **haughty** In this period, the word can

simply mean 'noble', without the pejorative sense of 'arrogant' that predominates slightly later. Mortimer does not seem here to be criticizing the Percy uprising, or regretting his involvement in it.
80 **laboured** labourèd
81 **I . . . liberty** Though dramatically effective, this is historically inaccurate, as a compression of events and amalgam of historical figures. See note on Mortimer in List of Roles (p. 110).
86 **my sister** Anne Mortimer, who married Richard Earl of Cambridge. Historically this now makes 'our' Mortimer the nephew of the rebel Edmund, whose story the amalgamated dramatic character took on himself at 73.
88 **weening** expecting

71 Richard] King Richard *F2*   76 To . . . Third] Unto the third King Edward *(Ard²)*   he] the king *Oxf*; Bolingbroke *Pope*

But as the rest, so fell that noble earl,   90
And was beheaded. Thus the Mortimers,
In whom the title rested, were suppressed.

RICHARD

Of which, my lord, your honour is the last.

MORTIMER

True; and thou seest that I no issue have,
And that my fainting words do warrant death.   95
Thou art my heir. The rest, I wish thee gather:
But yet be wary in thy studious care.

RICHARD

Thy grave admonishments prevail with me.
But yet, methinks, my father's execution
Was nothing less than bloody tyranny.   100

MORTIMER

With silence, nephew, be thou politic.
Strong fixed is the house of Lancaster,
And, like a mountain, not to be removed.
But now thy uncle is removing hence,
As princes do their courts, when they are cloyed   105
With long continuance in a settled place.

RICHARD

O uncle, would some part of my young years

90 **as the rest** like the Percies and their
followers
95 **warrant** guarantee
96 **The rest . . . gather** 'gather together,
harvest, the rest of your inheritance';
also, 'work out the implications of
what I am saying to you'
101 **politic** strategically aware
102–3 a reminiscence, if a bitter one, of
Psalm 125.1: 'Even as the mount Sion:
which may not bee removed, but
standeth fast for ever'. Mortimer's verbal style includes several more vague
biblical echoes, especially of the books
of Job and of Samuel. See Shaheen,
34–5.
102 **fixed** fixèd

104–6 Both Tudor and medieval monarchs spent much of their time in
expensive 'progresses', taking a large
court with them through their domains.
For medieval royalty this had a more
direct political purpose, as it involved
overseeing and administering far-flung
and often unruly property. For
Elizabeth the progress was more a ceremonial demonstration of power, often
ruinously expensive for the nobility on
whom she billeted herself. The use of
the analogy here hints at Mortimer's
bitterness at an enforced immobility
designed to remind him he is not the
prince he attempted to become.
104 **removing hence** passing on

Might but redeem the passage of your age.
MORTIMER
Thou dost then wrong me, as that slaughterer doth
Which giveth many wounds when one will kill.   110
Mourn not, except thou sorrow for my good;
Only give order for my funeral.
And so farewell, and fair be all thy hopes,
And prosperous be thy life in peace and war.   *Dies.*
RICHARD
And peace, no war, befall thy parting soul.   115
In prison hast thou spent a pilgrimage
And like a hermit overpassed thy days.
Well, I will lock his counsel in my breast,
And what I do imagine – let that rest.
Keepers, convey him hence, and I myself   120
Will see his burial better than his life.
                    [*Exeunt Gaolers, bearing out the body of Mortimer.*]
Here dies the dusky torch of Mortimer,
Choked with ambition of the meaner sort.
And for those wrongs, those bitter injuries
Which Somerset hath offered to my house,   125
I doubt not but with honour to redress.
And therefore haste I to the parliament –

---

108 **redeem the passage** save you from
the increase
111 Mourn only for what was good in me;
but there is a possible meaning of
'Don't mourn unless you can turn it to
my advantage' – posthumously, that is,
in revenge.
117 **overpassed** lived beyond (as a hermit may be said to have given up life as
normally understood, and gone into a
kind of death in life); or, simply, lived
through to the end of

119 **imagine** used here in the archaic
legal sense of 'to conceive in the mind
as a thing to be performed; to devise,
plot, plan, compass', *OED v.* I 3
rest stay dormant
122 **dusky torch** figuratively, fading life;
possibly literally a firebrand present on
stage to denote the prison location
123 **ambition . . . meaner sort** ambition
of less noble men (i.e. the supporters
of Henry IV).

108 passage] passing *Ard²*   113 be all] befall *Theobald*   121 SD] *Capell; Exit. F*   122 dies] lies
(Warburton)

Either to be restored to my blood,
Or make my will th'advantage of my good.   *Exit.*

3.1   *Flourish. Enter* KING, EXETER, GLOUCESTER,
WINCHESTER, WARWICK, SOMERSET, SUFFOLK,
RICHARD Plantagenet. *Gloucester offers to put up a bill;
Winchester snatches it, tears it.*

WINCHESTER
Com'st thou with deep premeditated lines?
With written pamphlets, studiously devised?
Humphrey of Gloucester, if thou canst accuse,
Or aught intend'st to lay unto my charge,
Do it without invention, suddenly,   5
As I with sudden and extemporal speech
Purpose to answer what thou canst object.

GLOUCESTER
Presumptuous priest, this place commands my patience,

---

128 **restored** restorèd
blood family inheritance
129 **make . . . good** 'assert my will in
pursuit of my good (= title)'.
Whatever has been established in the
rest of the scene as to Richard's place
in the dynastic pattern, he here
speaks as a Machiavellian individual-
ist, who will seize an opportunity
given, or create one for himself,
whether his status is ratified by the
King or not.
3.1.0.3–4 *Gloucester . . . tears it*
According to Hall, the parliament was
called by Bedford, away from
London, at Leicester, where he 'openly rebuked the Lordes in generall,
because that thei, in the tyme of
warre, through their privie malice and
inwarde grudge, had almoste moved
the people to warre and commocion
. . . In this parliament the Duke of
Gloucester, laied certain articles to

the bishoppe of Wynchesters charge,
the whiche with the answeres herafter
do ensue' (Bullough, 3.49). There are
five main items laid to the Bishop's
charge, and they are drawn on by the
dramatists, who move the scene to
London to allow the incursion of the
two men's supporters. The formality
of the written presentation of these
charges is emphasized in Hall by the
way they are set out on the printed
page.
1 **lines** writing
5 **invention** fabrication; rhetorical composition
5, 6 **suddenly, sudden** in the sense of
OED A *adj.* 2a, 'unpremeditated'
8 **this place** Though historically Bedford
called the parliament at Leicester (see
0.3–4n.), the dramatists have moved the
action to London, so *this place* refers to
the palace of Whitehall.

129 my will] my ill *Theobald;* mine ill *Ard²*   3.1] *(Actus Tertius. Scena Prima.)*

Or thou shouldst find thou hast dishonoured me.
Think not, although in writing I preferred   10
The manner of thy vile outrageous crimes,
That therefore I have forged or am not able
Verbatim to rehearse the method of my pen.
No, prelate, such is thy audacious wickedness,
Thy lewd, pestiferous and dissentious pranks,   15
As very infants prattle of thy pride.
Thou art a most pernicious usurer,
Froward by nature, enemy to peace,
Lascivious, wanton – more than well beseems
A man of thy profession and degree.   20
And for thy treachery, what's more manifest,
In that thou laid'st a trap to take my life,
As well at London Bridge as at the Tower?
Beside, I fear me, if thy thoughts were sifted,
The King, thy sovereign, is not quite exempt   25
From envious malice of thy swelling heart.

WINCHESTER

Gloucester, I do defy thee. Lords, vouchsafe
To give me hearing what I shall reply.
If I were covetous, ambitious, or perverse –

---

13 **Verbatim** orally, without a written script
    rehearse repeat
16 **very** even
17 **usurer** Winchester is called by Hall 'the riche Cardinall' (see note on List of Roles pp. 108–9). His claim to poverty later in the scene (30) is broadly comic. The accusation of usury is another example of a tainting of the Cardinal's reputation by his association with Southwark. Foreign, especially Italian, money-lenders and merchants tended to gather there, and were the focus of xenophobic suspicion and attack. See Introduction,

pp. 19–21.
18 **Froward** perverse
20 **profession and degree** religious calling and rank
21–3 derived from Hall's 'articles of accusation': 'My saied lorde of Winchester, untruly and against the kynges peace, to the entent to trouble my said lord of Gloucester goyng to the kyng purposyng his death in case that he had gone that waie, set men of armes and archers, at thende of London bridge nexte Southwerke' (Bullough, 3.50).
25 **exempt** immune (for context, see 21)
26 **envious** malevolent; resentful

---

13 the method . . . pen] my method penn'd *Ard²*   29 If I were] If *Ard²*

As he will have me – how am I so poor?   30
Or how haps it I seek not to advance
Or raise myself, but keep my wonted calling?
And for dissension, who preferreth peace
More than I do? – except I be provoked.
No, my good lords, it is not that offends,   35
It is not that that hath incensed the Duke.
It is because no one should sway but he,
No one but he should be about the King;
And that engenders thunder in his breast
And makes him roar these accusations forth.   40
But he shall know I am as good –

GLOUCESTER   As good?
Thou bastard of my grandfather!

WINCHESTER
Ay, lordly sir; for what are you, I pray,
But one imperious in another's throne?

GLOUCESTER
Am I not Protector, saucy priest?   45

WINCHESTER
And am not I a prelate of the Church?

GLOUCESTER
Yes, as an outlaw in a castle keeps
And useth it to patronage his theft.

WINCHESTER
Unreverent Gloucester!

GLOUCESTER   Thou art reverend
Touching thy spiritual function, not thy life.   50

---

30 **so poor** See 17n.
33 **preferreth** urges; see also 111, *prefer*.
37 **because** in order that
   sway rule
42 **bastard** Winchester was the illegitimate son of John of Gaunt. See note on List of Roles (pp. 108–9).
47 **keeps** stays

48 **patronage** 'to give patronage to; to countenance, uphold, protect, defend' (*OED*)
49 **Unreverent** irreverent, disrespectful
   reverend deserving of respect
50 **Touching . . . function** in relation to your role as priest

31 it] that *(Ard²)* 32 myself, . . . calling?] *Cam;* my selfe? . . . Calling. *F*
41 good –] *F2;* good. *F* 49 reverend] *F3;* reverent *F*

WINCHESTER

Rome shall remedy this.

GLOUCESTER   Roam thither, then.

WARWICK [*to Gloucester*]

My lord, it were your duty to forbear.

SOMERSET

Ay, see the Bishop be not overborne.

Methinks my lord should be religious

And know the office that belongs to such.   55

WARWICK

Methinks his lordship should be humbler:

It fitteth not a prelate so to plead.

SOMERSET

Yes, when his holy state is touched so near.

WARWICK

State – holy or unhallowed – what of that?

Is not his grace Protector to the King?   60

RICHARD [*to the audience*]

Plantagenet, I see, must hold his tongue,

Lest it be said, 'Speak, sirrah, when you should:

51 **Rome** the Pope
remedy stressed on second syllable
52 SD *As *lord* is used elsewhere in addressing either Gloucester or Winchester, it is not absolutely clear who is addressed here, but Warwick, though largely on Gloucester's side, seems to be trying to calm both men down. Somerset's *Ay* (53) suggests he is agreeing with and amplifying Warwick's intervention.
53 **overborne** oppressed by greater force; cf. 5.1.60
54 Somerset is taking Winchester's side, but *my lord* here is still ambiguous. If he means Gloucester by it here, he is saying that Gloucester should pay Winchester's

office due religious reverence; if he means Winchester, he is affirming that Winchester understands his own *office*, and so can be trusted to act properly.
55 **office** duties
58 **when . . . near** when his status as a senior churchman is under such intense attack
58, 59 **state** status; social standing
62 **sirrah** a term to be used to address a servant, or social inferior; see 1.4.1, where the context, a father treating his young son as a trusted deputy, is affectionate. But here, just before his ennoblement, Richard's use of the term reveals his assumptions about the lords' attitude to him.

51 SP GLOUCESTER] *Hanmer, Capell; Warw. F*   52 SP] *Hanmer; not in F*   52 SD] *Capell; to Win. / Hanmer*   53 SP] *War. / Theobald*   53 Ay, see] *(I, see); Ay, so Sisson; I'll see Hanmer*   54 Methinks] *To Winchester Methinks Cam²*   61 SD] *this edn; Aside / Hanmer*

> Must your bold verdict enter talk with lords?'
> Else would I have a fling at Winchester.

KING

> Uncles of Gloucester and of Winchester,   65
> The special watchmen of our English weal,
> I would prevail – if prayers might prevail –
> To join your hearts in love and amity.
> O what a scandal is it to our crown
> That two such noble peers as ye should jar?   70
> Believe me, lords – my tender years can tell –
> Civil dissension is a viperous worm,
> That gnaws the bowels of the commonwealth.
>> *A noise within.* [*Gloucester's Men shout:*] 'Down with
>> the tawny coats'.
> What tumult's this?

WARWICK   An uproar, I dare warrant,

> Begun through malice of the Bishop's men.   75
>> *A noise again.* [*Gloucester's and Winchester's Men*
>> *shout:*] 'Stones, stones'.

Enter Mayor.

MAYOR

> O my good lords, and virtuous Henry,
> Pity the city of London, pity us:
> The Bishop and the Duke of Gloucester's men,
> Forbidden late to carry any weapon,
> Have filled their pockets full of pebble stones   80

---

63 **verdict** opinion (a legal term, characteristic of Richard's vocabulary)
64 **have . . . at** verbally attack
72 **viperous worm** venomous snake, from 'viper', the only poisonous snake native to the British Isles. According to Pliny (10.82) the female was killed by the young gnawing their way out of her body, an error which here creates a homology for the *commonwealth* destroyed by those it had nurtured within itself.

73 SD *Gloucester's Men shout*] *this edn*   74 What] *Capell; King.* What *F*   75 SD *Gloucester's . . . shout*] *this edn*   75.1] *Enter the Mayor of* London, *attended. / Capell*

And, banding themselves in contrary parts,
Do pelt so fast at one another's pate
That many have their giddy brains knocked out.
Our windows are broke down in every street,
And we, for fear, compelled to shut our shops.   85

Enter [Servingmen *of Gloucester and Winchester*] *in skirmish,*
with bloody pates.

KING
We charge you, on allegiance to ourself,
To hold your slaughtering hands and keep the peace.
Pray, uncle Gloucester, mitigate this strife.
1 SERVINGMAN   Nay, if we be forbidden stones, we'll fall
to it with our teeth.   90
2 SERVINGMAN   Do what ye dare, we are as resolute.
    Skirmish again.
GLOUCESTER
You of my household, leave this peevish broil
And set this unaccustomed fight aside.
3 SERVINGMAN
My lord, we know your grace to be a man
Just and upright, and for your royal birth   95
Inferior to none but to his majesty;
And ere that we will suffer such a prince,
So kind a father of the commonweal,
To be disgraced by an ink-horn mate,
We and our wives and children all will fight,   100
And have our bodies slaughtered by thy foes.
1 SERVINGMAN
Ay, and the very parings of our nails

85 **shops** workshops
99 **disgraced** disgracèd
99 **ink-horn mate** a low-status scribe (an
    ink-horn is a portable container for

ink), here applied contemptuously to
Winchester
102–3 **parings . . . field** 'nail clippings
    will serve as defensive stakes on a

81 in] into *(RP)*   82 pate] pates *Pope*   85.1 Servingmen . . . *Winchester*] *Capell*   87 slaughter-
ing] *(slaughtring)*

199

Shall pitch a field when we are dead.   *[They] begin again.*

GLOUCESTER

  Stay, stay, I say:

  And if you love me, as you say you do,   105

  Let me persuade you to forbear awhile.

KING

  O, how this discord doth afflict my soul.

  Can you, my lord of Winchester, behold

  My sighs and tears, and will not once relent?

  Who should be pitiful, if you be not?   110

  Or who should study to prefer a peace

  If holy churchmen take delight in broils?

WARWICK

  Yield, my lord Protector, yield, Winchester –

  Except you mean with obstinate repulse

  To slay your sovereign and destroy the realm.   115

  You see what mischief, and what murder too,

  Hath been enacted through your enmity:

  Then be at peace – except ye thirst for blood.

WINCHESTER

  He shall submit, or I will never yield.

GLOUCESTER

  Compassion on the King commands me stoop,   120

  Or I would see his heart out ere the priest

  Should ever get that privilege of me.

WARWICK

  Behold, my lord of Winchester – the Duke

  Hath banished moody discontented fury,

---

battlefield' (c.f. 1.1.116–19); and conceivably a secondary allusion to the myth of Cadmus and the dragon's teeth ('nail clippings will spring up as new soldiers'), Ovid, 3.97ff.

111 **prefer** See 33n.

114 **Except** unless
    repulse rebuff
121 **his** Winchester's (not the King's)
122 **privilege** pre-eminence
124 **moody** headstrong

103 SD *They] this edn; Begin the skirmish again Cam²* 113] My lord Protector, yield; yield, Winchester; *Ard², after Pope*

As by his smoothed brows it doth appear.   125
Why look you still so stern and tragical?

GLOUCESTER

Here, Winchester, I offer thee my hand.
[*Winchester ignores Gloucester's offered hand.*]

KING

Fie, uncle Beaufort, I have heard you preach
That malice was a great and grievous sin:
And will not you maintain the thing you teach,   130
But prove a chief offender in the same?

WARWICK

Sweet King! The Bishop hath a kindly gird.
For shame, my lord of Winchester, relent;
What, shall a child instruct you what to do?

WINCHESTER

Well, Duke of Gloucester, I will yield to thee.   135
Love for thy love and hand for hand I give.
[*He takes Gloucester's hand.*]

GLOUCESTER

Ay, but I fear me with a hollow heart.
See here, my friends and loving countrymen,
This token serveth for a flag of truce
Betwixt ourselves, and all our followers: 140

---

125 **smoothed** smoothèd
130 Romans, 2.21: 'Thou therefore, which teachest another, teachest thou not thy self? thou that preachest, A man shulde not steale, doest thou steale?'
132 **a kindly gird** a gentle but also a 'kind', in the sense of a 'fitting', rebuke, fitting to the nature or 'kind' of the rebuked; Warwick is congratulating the young King on the Christian aptness of his question to Winchester.
137 **a hollow heart** Both this line and Winchester's response to Gloucester's speech (142) could be marked as

asides, but this limits the choice available to actors and director. Gloucester's remark could, for example, be addressed directly to Winchester, but not be meant to be overheard by the King. Similarly, Winchester's 'as I intend it not' (142) could apply either to the gesture of reconciliation – and so be played conspiratorially to the audience as a disclaimer – or to the offence previously given; again, the line could be played as an ambiguous equivocation.
139 **token** symbol (their joined hands)

127 SD] *this edn; Winchester turns away Cam²*   136 SD] *this edn*   137 Ay] *Aside* Ay *Collier*

So help me God, as I dissemble not.

WINCHESTER

So help me God, as I intend it not.

KING

O loving uncle, kind Duke of Gloucester,

How joyful am I made by this contract.

Away, my masters, trouble us no more,   145

But join in friendship, as your lords have done.

1 SERVINGMAN   Content. I'll to the surgeon's.

2 SERVINGMAN   And so will I.

3 SERVINGMAN   And I will see what physic the tavern   149

affords.   *Exeunt [Servingmen and Mayor].*

WARWICK

Accept this scroll, most gracious sovereign,

Which in the right of Richard Plantagenet

We do exhibit to your majesty.

GLOUCESTER

Well urged, my lord of Warwick – for, sweet prince,

An if your grace mark every circumstance,   155

You have great reason to do Richard right,

Especially for those occasions

At Eltham Place I told your majesty.

---

143 'And', as suggested by Collier as an insertion between *uncle* and *kind*, would make the difference of including the King's great-uncle Winchester in his address. Otherwise only uncle Gloucester is addressed. Cf. 1.3.4, where *Gloucester* is clearly trisyllabic.

145 *my masters* polite or friendly as a way of addressing those of a lower social class

153 **exhibit** 'where a Deed, or other Writing is in a Suit in Chancery *exhibited* to be proved by Witnesses' (Jacob). Here, the King's assent 'proves' the written claim, which he should sign or seal or, as Jacob puts it, 'certify on the

Back of it'.

155 **mark** pay attention to

157 **occasions** considerations; pronounced as four syllables

157–8 The involvement of Gloucester in the reinstatement of Richard as Duke of York is a departure from the sources, but the dramatists want to strengthen the sense of tragic irony already present in Hall, by implicating Gloucester in the unwitting instigation of general disaster.

158 **Eltham Place** See 1.1.170n. Gloucester, in keeping the King at this relatively secluded location, strengthens his own influence over him.

142 So] *Aside* So *Pope*   God, as] God! *Aside* As *Cam²*   143 kind] and kind *Collier²*; most kind *(Steevens);* gentle *Pope*   150 SD *Servingmen and Mayor] this edn, after Capell*

KING

And those occasions, uncle, were of force.

Therefore, my loving lords, our pleasure is   160

That Richard be restored to his blood.

WARWICK

Let Richard be restored to his blood:

So shall his father's wrongs be recompensed.

WINCHESTER

As will the rest, so willeth Winchester.

KING

If Richard will be true, not that alone   165

But all the whole inheritance I give

That doth belong unto the house of York,

From whence you spring by lineal descent.

RICHARD

Thy humble servant vows obedience

And humble service till the point of death.   170

KING

Stoop then and set your knee against my foot:

And, in reguerdon of that duty done,

I girt thee with the valiant sword of York.

Rise, Richard, like a true Plantagenet,

---

161 Hall presents the reinstatement of Richard to the dukedom of York as a celebratory response to the apparently established peace, and places it at a later date. 'For joy wherof, the kyng caused a solempne feast, to be kept on Whitson sondaie, on the whiche daie, he created Richard Plantagenet . . . Duke of Yorke, not forseyng before, that this preferment should be his destruccion' (Bullough, 3.51). The dramatists' compression sharpens Hall's already graphically ironic shaping of events; in reality Richard was 'knighted, along with the young king,

by Bedford at the Leicester parliament. Richard was gradually being brought into English aristocratic society' (Griffiths, 667). Historically York, a teenager at this time, had remained part of the royal household, and retained the right to his title. He entered into his estates a little earlier (under twenty-one) than usual, and without all the usual formalities, most probably because of his closeness to the court; the parliament of 1433 sorted out the complex legal obligations.

161, 162 **restored** restorèd

172 **reguerdon** reward

165 alone] *F2;* all alone *F*   170 humble] gentle *Pope*   171 foot] foot *Plantagenet kneels Cam²*

And rise created princely Duke of York.   175

RICHARD

And so thrive Richard, as thy foes may fall:

And, as my duty springs, so perish they

That grudge one thought against your majesty.

ALL

Welcome, high prince, the mighty Duke of York.

SOMERSET [*to the audience*]

Perish, base prince, ignoble Duke of York.   180

GLOUCESTER

Now will it best avail your majesty

To cross the seas and to be crowned in France:

The presence of a king engenders love

Amongst his subjects and his loyal friends,

As it disanimates his enemies.   185

KING

When Gloucester says the word, King Henry goes –

For friendly counsel cuts off many foes.

GLOUCESTER

Your ships already are in readiness.

Sennet. Flourish. Exeunt all but Exeter.

EXETER

Ay, we may march in England or in France,

Not seeing what is likely to ensue: 190

This late dissension grown betwixt the peers

Burns under feigned ashes of forged love

And will at last break out into a flame:

As festered members rot but by degree,

Till bones and flesh and sinews fall away,   195

---

178 **grudge one thought** think one dis-
     contented thought
181 **avail** help
185 **disanimates** renders lifeless; dispirits

192 **feigned** feignèd
194 **festered** gangrenous
     by degree bit by bit

180 SD] *this edn; Aside / Rowe* 188 SD *all but*] *(Manet)* 194 festered] *(*festred)* degree]
degrees *Rowe*

So will this base and envious discord breed.
And now I fear that fatal prophecy,
Which in the time of Henry, named the Fifth,
Was in the mouth of every sucking babe –
That Henry born at Monmouth should win all,   200
And Henry born at Windsor lose all:
Which is so plain that Exeter doth wish
His days may finish ere that hapless time.   *Exit.*

3.2   *Enter* [JOAN] *Puzel, disguised* [*as a poor peasant*], *with*
          four Soldiers *with sacks upon their backs.*

JOAN
These are the city gates, the gates of Rouen,
Through which our policy must make a breach.
Take heed – be wary how you place your words;
Talk like the vulgar sort of market men

197–201 Hall presents the *fatal prophecy*
(197), somewhat sceptically, at the
moment of Henry's birth: 'when he
[Henry V] heard reported the place of
his nativitie, whether he fantasied
some old blind prophesy, or had some
foreknowledge, or els judged of his
sonnes fortune, he sayd . . . these
wordes . . . "I Henry borne at Mon-
moth shall small tyme reigne &
muche get, & Henry borne at
Wyndsore shall long reigne and al
lese, but as God will so be it"'
(Bullough, 3.42–3). The second
Henry here is Henry VI.
199 **sucking babe** Psalms, 8.2, 'Out of
the mouth of babes and sucklings'.
Also Matthew, 21.16, where Christ
uses the phrase of the wisdom of the
innocent when God speaks through
them.
203 **hapless** unlucky

3.2.0.1–2 This SD prepares for the stratagem that is used by Joan Puzel to gain
entry to Rouen. In Hall a similar trick
is used by the English 'Sir Fraunces
Arragonoys' to capture 'the Castle of
Cornyll' in 1441 (Bullough, 3.69).
Transferring the story to Joan Puzel
emphasises her trickster-like quality,
and her distance from chivalric codes
of behaviour, upheld consistently by
the English throughout the play. This
is another scene that uses all the available levels of stage space with, once
again, the architecture of the back of
the stage representing the outside of
the walls of an occupied town.
1   **Rouen** Throughout this scene and the
next, but not at 1.1.60 and 65, the
name of the town is pronounced as a
monosyllable; in F it is spelt 'Roan'.
2   **policy** cunning

---

201 lose] *(loose)*   **3.2**] *Capell; Scœna Secunda.* F   0.1 Puzel] *(Pucell);* La Pucelle *Rowe   as a poor
peasant*] *this edn*   1+ SP JOAN] *this edn; Pucell.* F   1+ Rouen] *(Roan)*

That come to gather money for their corn.   5
If we have entrance, as I hope we shall,
And that we find the slothful watch but weak,
I'll by a sign give notice to our friends
That Charles the Dolphin may encounter them.

SOLDIER

Our sacks shall be a mean to sack the city,   10
And we be lords and rulers over Rouen.
Therefore we'll knock.   [*They*] *knock.*

WATCH [*within*]

   Qui est là?

JOAN   *Paysans, les pauvres gens de France,*
Poor market folks that come to sell their corn.

WATCH [*within*]

Enter, go in – the market bell is rung.   [*Opens the gate.*]   15

JOAN

Now, Rouen, I'll shake thy bulwarks to the ground.

                                        Exeunt [*into the town*].

Enter CHARLES, [*the*] BASTARD, ALENÇON [*and* REIGNIER].

CHARLES

Saint Denis bless this happy stratagem,
And once again we'll sleep secure in Rouen.

---

5 **corn** wheat
7 **that** a rather stronger, more hopeful
   'if'
9 **encounter** engage with
13 ***Qui . . . France** 'Who is there?'
   'Peasants, the poor people of France.'
15 **the market bell** The market bell
   would be rung just before dawn, to
   warn would-be traders of the opening

of the market and, most probably here,
of their last chance to enter the town
before the gates were shut again. With
an irony typical of the play, the good-
natured leniency of the English watch
allows the French into the town when
strictly he should not, and they then
kill him (34).

---

10 SP] 1 *Sold. Ard²*, after *Capell; Souldier.* F   12 SD *They*] *this edn*   13 SD] *Capell*   13 *Qui est
là?*] *Malone; Che la.* F   *Paysans . . . France*] *this edn; Peasauns la pouure gens de Fraunce* F; Paysans,
pauvre gens de France *Rowe; Paysans, la pauvre gent de France / Sanders*   15 SD] *Hart; Guard
open / Capell; Opening the gate Cam²*   16 SD] *Exeunt.* 3.3. *Oxf   into the town*] *this edn* 16.1 *and*
REIGNIER] *Cam*

206

BASTARD

    Here entered Puzel and her practisants.

    Now she is there, how will she specify   20

    'Here is the best and safest passage in'?

REIGNIER

    By thrusting out a torch from yonder tower;

    Which, once discerned, shows that her meaning is,

    No way to that – for weakness – which she entered.

Enter [JOAN] *Puzel, on the top, thrusting out a torch, burning.*

JOAN

    Behold, this is the happy wedding torch   25

    That joineth Rouen unto her countrymen –

    But burning fatal to the Talbonites.

BASTARD

    See, noble Charles, the beacon of our friend;

    The burning torch in yonder turret stands.

CHARLES

    Now shine it like a comet of revenge,   30

    A prophet to the fall of all our foes.

---

19 **practisants** possibly a unique instance of this word; *OED* glosses it, giving this example only, as '?A plotter, conspirator . . . ; or ?performer of a stratagem (Schmidt)'. The word's very obscurity lends it sinister connotations, perhaps of magic rites.

24 This line gives Joan Puzel's 'meaning', the message she wishes the French soldiers to understand.

24.1 *on the top* This scene, like that of the English commanders on the tower at Orleans, 1.4, could exploit a structure higher than the back-stage gallery – a trumpeter's turret, for example.

See 1.4.21.1n.

25 **wedding torch** Hymen, the classical god of marriage, was usually depicted holding a torch; see the dumb-show in Kyd's *The Spanish Tragedy*, prior to Act IV. Here the reference continues the theme of an erotic relation between Joan and the Dolphin.

27 **Talbonites** followers of Talbot; an otherwise unknown word coined by Joan, perhaps mockingly. Or it could be a compositor's misreading of 'Talbotites'.

30 **shine it** let it shine

19+ Puzel] *(Pucell)*   20 specify] *Rowe;* specifie? *F*   21 Here] Where *Rowe*   24.1 Puzel] *(Pucell)*
27 Talbonites] Talbonites. *Exit Ard²;* Talbotites *Theobald*

207

REIGNIER

    Defer no time, delays have dangerous ends.

    Enter and cry 'The Dolphin' presently,

    And then do execution on the watch.

                     Alarum [and exeunt into the town].

           An alarum. [Enter] TALBOT *in an excursion*.

TALBOT

    France, thou shalt rue this treason with thy tears,   35

    If Talbot but survive thy treachery.

    Puzel, that witch, that damned sorceress,

    Hath wrought this hellish mischief unawares,

    That hardly we escaped the pride of France.

                     Exit. An alarum, excursions.

[Enter] BEDFORD, *brought in sick in a chair [by two attendants]*.
Enter TALBOT *and* BURGUNDY *without; within,* [JOAN] *Puzel,*
    CHARLES, *[the]* BASTARD *and* REIGNIER *on the walls*.

JOAN

    Good morrow, gallants; want ye corn for bread?   40

    I think the Duke of Burgundy will fast

    Before he'll buy again at such a rate.

    'Twas full of darnel: do you like the taste?

---

32 **Defer** put off
    delays . . . ends proverbial (Dent, D195)
33 **presently** immediately
34.1 *excursion* entrance at a run (used mainly in military contexts); Talbot is escaping from the town.
35, 48 **treason** trickery, but also, from the English point of view, treason in the criminal sense of rebellion against the (English) monarch

37 **damned** damnèd
38 **unawares** without the knowledge of the English
39 **hardly** with difficulty
39.3 REIGNIER . . . *walls* See casting notes, Appendix 2, for an argument for omitting Reignier from this scene.
43 **darnel** species of wild grass, *lolium temulentum*, which tends to grow with wheat

---

34 SD *and . . . town*] *this edn*   34.1 *Enter*] *Capell*   39 pride] prize *Theobald*   39.1 *Enter . . . by attendants*] *this edn*   39.2 BURGUNDY] *(Burgonie)*   Puzel] *(Pucell);* La Pucelle *Collier*

BURGUNDY

    Scoff on, vile fiend and shameless courtesan.

    I trust ere long to choke thee with thine own,   45

    And make thee curse the harvest of that corn.

CHARLES

    Your grace may starve perhaps before that time.

BEDFORD

    O let no words, but deeds, revenge this treason.

JOAN

    What will you do, good greybeard? Break a lance

    And run a-tilt at death within a chair?   50

TALBOT

    Foul fiend of France and hag of all despite,

    Encompassed with thy lustful paramours,

    Becomes it thee to taunt his valiant age

    And twit with cowardice a man half dead?

    Damsel, I'll have a bout with you again,   55

    Or else let Talbot perish with this shame.

JOAN

    Are ye so hot, sir? Yet, Puzel, hold thy peace;

    If Talbot do but thunder, rain will follow.

       The English whisper together in counsel.

    God speed the parliament: who shall be the speaker?

TALBOT

    Dare ye come forth and meet us in the field?   60

---

46 **harvest . . . corn** 'outcome of that strategy'

50 **run . . . death** charge with a lance to fight death, as if on horseback in a tournament

51 **hag** witch, with an emphasis on ugliness, ironizing *paramours* (52)
of all despite totally malicious

55 **bout** fight, but also sexual encounter

57 **Are . . . hot** Joan Puzel picks up on

bout to use the persistent sexual *double entendre* that conditions the presentation of her martial prowess to discomfort Talbot.

59 **speaker** 'The member of the House of Commons who is chosen by the House itself to act as its representative and to preside over its debates' (*OED* 3a). The position was established in the parliament of 1376–7.

49–50] *Pope; F lines* gray-beard? / Death, / Chayre. /   57 hot . . . Puzel] *this edn;* hot, Sir: yet *Pucell F;* hot? Yet, Pucelle *Pope*   58 SD *The English*] *Capell; They* F

JOAN

    Belike your lordship takes us then for fools,

    To try if that our own be ours or no.

TALBOT

    I speak not to that railing Hecate,

    But unto thee, Alençon, and the rest.

    Will ye, like soldiers, come and fight it out?   65

ALENÇON

    Seigneur, no.

TALBOT

    Seigneur, hang: base muleteers of France –

    Like peasant footboys do they keep the walls

    And dare not take up arms like gentlemen.

JOAN

    Away, captains; let's get us from the walls,   70

    For Talbot means no goodness by his looks.

    Goodbye, my lord. We came but to tell you that we

        are here.   *Exeunt from the walls.*

TALBOT

    And there will we be too, ere it be long,

    Or else reproach be Talbot's greatest fame.

    Vow, Burgundy, by honour of thy house,   75

    Pricked on by public wrongs sustained in France,

    Either to get the town again, or die.

    And I, as sure as English Henry lives,

    And as his father here was conqueror,

    As sure as in this late betrayed town   80

    Great *Cœur de Lion*'s heart was buried,

---

63 **Hecate** The goddess of witches. The name is pronounced as three syllables, accented on the first.
67 **muleteers** mule drivers (peasants, as opposed to aristocratic horsemen)
68 **footboys** page-boys, servants
    keep stay on
76 **Pricked** spurred

80 **betrayed** betrayèd
81 Richard I, called the 'Lionheart' (*Cœur de Lion*), died in 1199 in France. His heart was buried in Rouen, where there is a monument surviving. The rest of him is at Fontevrault.
    buried burièd

66, 67 *Seigneur*] *Cam²*; Seignior *F*; Signior *Ard²*   70 Away, captains] Captains, away *Rowe*   72] *this edn; F lines* you / here. /   75+ Burgundy] *(Burgonie)*   81 *Cœur de Lion*'s] *(Cordelions)*

So sure I swear to get the town or die.

BURGUNDY

My vows are equal partners with thy vows.

TALBOT

But ere we go regard this dying prince,

The valiant Duke of Bedford. Come, my lord,   85

We will bestow you in some better place,

Fitter for sickness and for crazy age.

BEDFORD

Lord Talbot, do not so dishonour me.

Here will I sit, before the walls of Rouen,

And will be partner of your weal or woe.   90

BURGUNDY

Courageous Bedford, let us now persuade you.

BEDFORD

Not to be gone from hence; for once I read

That stout Pendragon, in his litter sick,

Came to the field, and vanquished his foes.

Methinks I should revive the soldiers' hearts,   95

Because I ever found them as myself.

TALBOT

Undaunted spirit in a dying breast!

Then be it so: heavens keep old Bedford safe.

---

84 **regard** attend to

87 **crazy** fragile

93 **stout Pendragon** Geoffrey of Monmouth's *Historia Regum Britanniae*, Book 8, chs 21–3: 'he bade make a litter wherein he might be carried, seeing that his malady did hinder him of moving otherwise from place to place . . . Not until the day was far spent did victory declare for the Britons, and the Saxons turned tail . . . So overjoyed was the King at the issue of the battle, that whereas afore he was too weak to lift him up without help of another, he now raised him with a light effort and sate him upright in the litter as though

he were of a sudden restored unto health. Then with a laugh, he cried out in a merry voice: "These Ambrons called me the half-dead King, for that I was laying sick of my malady in the litter, and so in truth I was. Yet would I rather conquer them half-dead, than be conquered by them safe and sound and have to go on living thereafter. For better is death with honour than life with shame" ' (Bullough, 3.79–80). For more on Pendragon, his heraldic associations and relevance to Bedford's sense of his family heritage, see 1.1.11n.

94 **vanquished** vanquishèd

And now no more ado, brave Burgundy,
But gather we our forces out of hand   100
And set upon our boasting enemy.

Exeunt [all but Bedford and two attendants].

An alarum; excursions. Enter Sir John FASTOLFE *and a* Captain.

CAPTAIN
Whither away, Sir John Fastolfe, in such haste?
FASTOLFE
Whither away? To save myself by flight –
We are like to have the overthrow again.
CAPTAIN
What? Will you fly, and leave Lord Talbot?   105
FASTOLFE
Ay, all the Talbots in the world, to save my life.   *Exit.*
CAPTAIN
Cowardly knight, ill fortune follow thee.   *Exit.*

Retreat. Excursions. [JOAN] Puzel, ALENÇON *and* CHARLES
[*enter and*] *fly.*

BEDFORD
Now, quiet soul, depart when heaven please,

---

100 **out of hand** immediately (*OED* hand *sb.* B II 3a)
101 SD It would be feasible to include Bedford in the *Exeunt*, and so to take *carried in* at 112 SD as a delayed re-entry, but there is a point to be made, with an irony typical of the play, that his onstage death is marred in heroic effect by juxtaposition with Fastolfe's retreat, which he accidentally witnesses. The *excursions* (101.1) are entries by the

French from the doors at the back of the stage, which represents the town.
104 **have the overthrow** be defeated
108–10 This speech is shaped by biblical echoes, lines 108–9 by Luke, 2.29–30: 'Lord now lettest thou thy servant departe in peace, according to thy worde. For mine eyes have sene thy salvation'. The next line continues the biblically derived theme of the vanity of human endeavour with reference to

101 SD] *Cam, after Capell; Exit. F; Exeunt* BURGUNDY, TALBOT, *and Forces; leaving* Bedford *under the Guard of a* Captain, *and Others. / Capell; Exit with Burgundy and Forces into the town. / Dyce* 101.1+ FASTOLFE] *Theobald; Falstaffe F* 102 Sir John] John *Ard²* 105–6] *Hanmer lines* Ay, / life. / 107.1 Puzel] *(Pucell)* 107.2 *enter and*] *Malone (subst.)*

212

For I have seen our enemies' overthrow.

What is the trust or strength of foolish man?   110

They that of late were daring with their scoffs

Are glad and fain by flight to save themselves.

> *Bedford dies, and is carried in, by two, in his chair.*

An alarum. Enter TALBOT, BURGUNDY *and the rest.*

TALBOT

Lost – and recovered in a day again!

This is a double honour, Burgundy;

Yet heavens have glory for this victory.   115

BURGUNDY

Warlike and martial Talbot, Burgundy

Enshrines thee in his heart, and there erects

Thy noble deeds as valour's monuments.

TALBOT

Thanks, gentle duke. But where is Puzel now?

I think her old familiar is asleep.   120

Now where's the Bastard's braves and Charles his
    gleeks?

What, all amort? Rouen hangs her head for grief

That such a valiant company are fled.

Now will we take some order in the town,

Placing therein some expert officers,   125

And then depart to Paris to the King,

Jeremiah, 17.5, and Psalms, 146.3 and 118.8–9. In Hall, Bedford dies in Rouen, but later, in 1435.

112 **fain** willing

120 **familiar** a spirit who helps a witch or magician, often, in the accounts of sixteenth- and seventeenth-century commentators, taking the form of a small animal. The term is biblical; Saul asks the Witch of Endor: 'I pray thee, coniecture unto me by the familiar spirit, and bring me him up whome I shal name unto thee' (1 Samuel, 28.8).

121 **braves** challenges

gleeks A gleek is 'a gibe, jest, gird' (*OED sb.*[2] I).

122 **all amort** lifeless; derived from the French *à la mort*, meaning 'to the death'

124 **take some order** take control, establish order

125 **expert** experienced

115 Yet] Let *Dyce*[2]   119 Puzel] *(Pucel)*

For there young Henry with his nobles lie.
BURGUNDY

What wills Lord Talbot pleaseth Burgundy.
TALBOT

But yet before we go let's not forget
The noble Duke of Bedford, late deceased,   130
But see his exequies fulfilled in Rouen.
A braver soldier never couched lance,
A gentler heart did never sway in court.
But kings and mightiest potentates must die,   134
For that's the end of human misery.   *Exeunt.*

3.3   *Enter* CHARLES, [*the*] BASTARD, ALENÇON
                        [*and* JOAN] Puzel.

JOAN

Dismay not, princes, at this accident,
Nor grieve that Rouen is so recovered:
Care is no cure, but rather corrosive,
For things that are not to be remedied.
Let frantic Talbot triumph for a while,   5
And like a peacock sweep along his tail;
We'll pull his plumes and take away his train,
If Dolphin and the rest will be but ruled.
CHARLES

We have been guided by thee hitherto

---

131 **exequies fulfilled** funeral completed
132 **couched** couchèd; lower a spear to
   the position of attack (*OED v.*[1] I 7)
133 **sway** rule; have influence
3.3.1 **Dismay not** be not dismayed
   accident event
2 **recovered** recoverèd
3 'Worry solves nothing, it only eats
   away at things (like rust).' *Corrosive* is
   accented on the first syllable. Cf.

proverbial 'Past cure, past care' (Dent,
C921).
6 **peacock** Peacocks are an image of
   pride. Joan's own pride may recall the
   sarcastic ' "Fly pride", says the peacock' (*CE* 4.3.80).
7 **train** of the male peacock, his trailing
   tail feathers; of Talbot, his followers
   and military strength

3.3] *(Scaena Tertia.)* 0.2+ Puzel] *(Pucell)* 1+ SP JOAN] *this edn; Pucell. F* 2+ Rouen] *(Roan)*

And of thy cunning had no diffidence.   10
One sudden foil shall never breed distrust.

BASTARD

Search out thy wit for secret policies
And we will make thee famous through the world.

ALENÇON

We'll set thy statue in some holy place
And have thee reverenced like a blessed saint.   15
Employ thee then, sweet virgin, for our good.

JOAN

Then thus it must be – this doth Joan devise:
By fair persuasions mixed with sugared words
We will entice the Duke of Burgundy
To leave the Talbot and to follow us.   20

CHARLES

Ay marry, sweeting, if we could do that,
France were no place for Henry's warriors,
Nor should that nation boast it so with us,
But be extirped from our provinces.

ALENÇON

For ever should they be expulsed from France,   25
And not have title of an earldom here.

JOAN

Your honours shall perceive how I will work
To bring this matter to the wished end.   *Drum sounds afar off.*
Hark – by the sound of drum you may perceive

---

10 **diffidence** doubt, distrust
11 **foil** setback
12 **wit** intellect
  policies here in the sense of *OED sb.*[1]
  I 3, 'in bad sense, political cunning'
14–15 Jeanne's canonization as a saint of
  the Catholic Church did not take place
  until 1920; see Introduction, pp. 40–2.
15 **blessed** blessèd
16 **Employ thee** set to work

19 **entice . . . Burgundy** In the sources,
  Jeanne plays no part in Burgundy's
  change of sides. She has been captured
  by a joint force 'as well Englishe as
  Burgonions' four years earlier (Bullough, 3.61).
21 **sweeting** darling, sweetheart
24 **extirped** extirpèd; cut out
25 **expulsed** expelled
28 **wished** wishèd

18 sugared] *(sugred)*   19+ Burgundy] *(Burgonie)*

Their powers are marching unto Paris-ward.   30

        Here sound an English march [offstage].

There goes the Talbot with his colours spread,

And all the troops of English after him.

        French march [sounds offstage].

Now in the rearward comes the Duke and his:

Fortune, in favour, makes him lag behind.

Summon a parley. We will talk with him.   35

        Trumpets sound a parley.

CHARLES

A parley with the Duke of Burgundy.

      [*Enter* BURGUNDY.]

BURGUNDY

Who craves a parley with the Burgundy?

JOAN

The princely Charles of France, thy countryman.

BURGUNDY

What sayst thou, Charles? For I am marching hence.

CHARLES

Speak, Puzel, and enchant him with thy words.   40

30, 32 SD The difference between a French and an English march would not be especially marked in the fifteenth and sixteenth centuries, though the characteristic rhythm they shared – five beats followed by three silent beats, and so on, repeated – was different from the triple rhythms of other European armies. Charles I identified and sought to establish by law specifically English march-tunes. The dramatists here demand an identifiably English march, but perhaps the differentiation is largely in instrumentation, with the English using the trumpet and the French the fife, in improvised tunes over the basic beat (Grove, 'March').

31 **colours spread** banners flying

34 Fortune is on the French side, and so has temporarily separated Burgundy from his English allies.

38 **countryman** Joan Puzel's choice of term is provocative, since Burgundy and Charles are at this point equal leaders of separate states. See Introduction, pp. 42–3.

40 **enchant ... words** Though Joan herself is claiming no more than rhetorical skill here, comments such as this, and Burgundy's *aside* at 58, point up that overlap between rhetorical and magical power which makes it fitting to assign responsibility to her for an event presented much more matter-of-factly in the chronicles (see Bullough, 3.64).

30 SD *offstage*] *this edn; Enter, and pass over at a distance,* Talbot, *and his forces. / Capell*   32 SD *sounds offstage*] *this edn; Enter the Duke of* BURGUNDY *and Forces. / Capell*   36.1] *Ard²*

JOAN

Brave Burgundy, undoubted hope of France,
Stay, let thy humble handmaid speak to thee.

BURGUNDY

Speak on, but be not over-tedious.

JOAN

Look on thy country, look on fertile France,
And see the cities and the towns defaced   45
By wasting ruin of the cruel foe,
As looks the mother on her lowly babe
When death doth close his tender-dying eyes.
See, see the pining malady of France,
Behold the wounds, the most unnatural wounds,   50
Which thou thyself hast given her woeful breast.
O turn thy edged sword another way,
Strike those that hurt, and hurt not those that help:
One drop of blood drawn from thy country's bosom
Should grieve thee more than streams of foreign gore. 55
Return thee therefore with a flood of tears
And wash away thy country's stained spots.

42 **humble . . . thee** 1 Samuel, 25.24: 'let
thine handmaid speake to thee'. This is
less a quotation than a use, typical of
Joan, of a biblical echo susceptible of
erotic reading to strengthen her
rhetorical power.

44–51 Burgundy himself makes a very
similar speech in *H5* 5.2.23–67. Joan
has here been assigned some of the
arguments that Burgundy uses in Hall
'to sette a vayle, before the kyng of
Englandes iyes . . . that he, beyng not
only waxed faint, and weried, with
continual warre, and daily conflictes,
but also chafed daily, with complaintes
and lamentacion, of his people,
whiche, of the Frenchemen, suffered
losse and detriment, embraydyng and
rebukyng hym openly, affirmyng that
he onely was the supporter and
mainteyner, of the Englishe people,
and that by his meanes and power, the

mortall warre was continued and sette
forward . . . to advaunce and promote
their desires, & intentes, rather then to
restore kyng Charles his cosyn, to his
rightful inheritaunce' (Bullough,
3.64). See note on Burgundy in List of
Roles, and Introduction, pp. 42–3, 85.

47 **lowly** humble (picking up on 42), with
a sense also of scarce-grown, and possibly low in health; Joan is looking for
a language as emotive as possible, and
comically overdoing it.

48 **tender-dying** F's hyphenation, which
creates a composite word for 'dying
gently'; a comma instead of the
hyphen would make equal sense, with
a slightly different rhetorical effect.
Without either punctuation mark, *tender* could simply mean young. Again,
Joan is overdoing it.

52 **edged** edgèd

57 **stained** stainèd

217

BURGUNDY [*aside*]

    Either she hath bewitched me with her words,

    Or nature makes me suddenly relent.

JOAN

    Besides, all French and France exclaims on thee,   60

    Doubting thy birth and lawful progeny.

    Who join'st thou with but with a lordly nation,

    That will not trust thee but for profit's sake?

    When Talbot hath set footing once in France

    And fashioned thee that instrument of ill,   65

    Who then but English Henry will be lord,

    And thou be thrust out, like a fugitive?

    Call we to mind – and mark but this for proof –

    Was not the Duke of Orleans thy foe?

    And was he not in England prisoner?   70

    But when they heard he was thine enemy

    They set him free without his ransom paid,

    In spite of Burgundy and all his friends.

    See then, thou fight'st against thy countrymen

    And join'st with them will be thy slaughter-men.   75

    Come, come, return; return, thou wandering lord.

    Charles and the rest will take thee in their arms.

BURGUNDY [*aside*]

    I am vanquished: these haughty words of hers

    Have battered me like roaring cannon-shot

---

60 **exclaims on** shouts out against
61 **progeny** usually 'offspring'; here, more likely 'Lineage' (*OED* 5)
65 **fashioned . . . ill** 'made you into a tool of destruction'
72 **set him free** Historically this event happened five years later; Hall presents it as a consequence of Burgundy's reconcilement to the house of Orleans, and, though he presents some controversy as

to the size of the ransom paid, he is clear that Burgundy paid it, to end the family feud begun by 'the death of duke Lewes his [Charles's] father (whom duke Jhon, father to this duke Phillip, shamefully slewe, and cruelly murdered in the citee of Paris)' (Bullough, 3.67).
76 **wandering** straying; metaphorically, as morally lost
78 **vanquished** vanquishèd

58 Either] *Aside. Either Ard²* 78] *F lines* vanquished: / hers / I am] *Aside.* I am *Ard²* 79 battered] (*batt'red*)

And made me almost yield upon my knees. –   80
Forgive me, country, and sweet countrymen;
And, lords, accept this hearty kind embrace.
My forces and my power of men are yours.
So farewell, Talbot. I'll no longer trust thee.

JOAN

Done like a Frenchman: turn and turn again.   85

CHARLES

Welcome, brave Duke. Thy friendship makes us fresh.

BASTARD

And doth beget new courage in our breasts.

ALENÇON

Puzel hath bravely played her part in this
And doth deserve a coronet of gold.

CHARLES

Now let us on, my lords, and join our powers,   90
And seek how we may prejudice the foe.   *Exeunt.*

3.4   *Enter the* KING, GLOUCESTER, WINCHESTER,
        [Richard Plantagenet, *now* Duke of] YORK, SUFFOLK,
    SOMERSET, WARWICK, [VERNON *and* BASSET,] EXETER;
            to them, with his Soldiers, TALBOT.

TALBOT

My gracious Prince and honourable peers,
Hearing of your arrival in this realm
I have awhile given truce unto my wars
To do my duty to my sovereign.

---

83 **power** army
85 *Dyce's 'aside'* after *Frenchmen* has
often been adopted. In any event,
Joan's remark underlines her comic,
audience-pleasing role as an irreverent
outsider.

86 **fresh** new
88 **bravely** spectacularly well, impressively
91 **prejudice** injure

85 Done . . . turn] *Aside* Done *Capell; Aside* turn *Dyce*   90] *Pope; F lines* Lords, / Powers, /
3.4] *(Scoena Quarta.)*   0.1 *Enter*] *Flourish. Enter Oxf*   0.3 VERNON *and* BASSET] *Capell*

219

In sign whereof, this arm – that hath reclaimed   5
To your obedience fifty fortresses,
Twelve cities and seven walled towns of strength,
Beside five hundred prisoners of esteem –
Lets fall his sword before your highness' feet,
        [*Kneels.*]
And with submissive loyalty of heart   10
Ascribes the glory of his conquest got
First to my God, and next unto your grace.

KING

Is this the Lord Talbot, uncle Gloucester,
That hath so long been resident in France?

GLOUCESTER

Yes, if it please your majesty, my liege.   15

KING

Welcome, brave captain and victorious lord.
When I was young – as yet I am not old –
I do remember how my father said
A stouter champion never handled sword.
Long since we were resolved of your truth,   20
Your faithful service and your toil in war;
Yet never have you tasted our reward,
Or been reguerdoned with so much as thanks,
Because till now we never saw your face.
Therefore stand up, and for these good deserts   25
We here create you Earl of Shrewsbury,

3.4.6–8 **fifty . . . esteem** The figures are
    approximate (and aggrandize Talbot
    by ascribing to him the successes of
    other commanders); they are rounded
    up to conventionally resonant 'power-
    ful' numbers.
7   **walled** wallèd
9, 11 **his** refers to *this arm* (5) as a synec-
    doche for Talbot, emphasizing his mil-
    itary strength

17–18 Henry was nine months old when
    his father died, so if he remembers
    this, it is mystically, an access to a
    prophetic wisdom he is granted in
    3H6 (4.6.65–76). In this scene, his-
    torically, he would be four years of
    age.
20   **resolved** resolvèd; convinced
23   **reguerdoned** rewarded

9 SD] *this edn*   13 the Lord Talbot] the Talbot *Capell;* the fam'd Lord Talbot *Rowe*

And in our coronation take your place.

Sennet. Flourish. Exeunt all but Vernon and Basset.

VERNON

Now, sir, to you, that were so hot at sea,
Disgracing of these colours that I wear
In honour of my noble lord of York –   30
Dar'st thou maintain the former words thou spak'st?

BASSET

Yes, sir, as well as you dare patronage
The envious barking of your saucy tongue
Against my lord the Duke of Somerset.

VERNON

Sirrah, thy lord I honour as he is.   35

BASSET

Why, what is he? As good a man as York.

VERNON

Hark ye, not so; in witness, take ye that.   *Strikes him.*

BASSET

Villain, thou knowest the law of arms is such
That whoso draws a sword, 'tis present death –
Or else this blow should broach thy dearest blood.   40
But I'll unto his majesty, and crave

---

27 SD Basset was not present in the rose
garden scene, though Vernon was. The
point that the dramatists are making is
that the quarrel between masters, rather
like that between the Montagues and
Capulets in *Romeo and Juliet*, is spreading to their followers and moving further
and further away from its original cause.
Vernon and Basset's quarrel, as is con-
firmed at 4.1.89–107, began on board the
ship that brought the court to France.

28 **hot** angry

29 **Disgracing of** mocking; dishonouring
colours insignia (i.e. the white rose)

32 **patronage** 'countenance, uphold,
protect, defend' (*OED v.*)

33 **envious** malicious

38 **law of arms** 'that *Law* which gives
Precepts how to proclaim War, make
and observe Leagues and Treaties, to
assault and encounter an Enemy, and
punish Offenders in the Camp, &c . . .
when the *Law of Arms* and War do rule,
the Civil *Laws* are of little or no Force'
(Jacob). Here, the special context of the
war involves draconian penalties for
fights between soldiers on the same
side. Ironically, this allows their quarrel
to develop, rather than burn out.

39 **present** immediate, there and then

40 **broach** make flow (like opening a bottle)

---

27 SD *all but*] *(Manet)*   38] *Pope; F lines* knowest / such, /

I may have liberty to venge this wrong –
When, thou shalt see, I'll meet thee to thy cost.

VERNON

Well, miscreant, I'll be there as soon as you   44
And after meet you sooner than you would.   *Exeunt.*

4.1   *Enter* KING, GLOUCESTER, WINCHESTER, YORK,
SUFFOLK, SOMERSET, WARWICK, TALBOT, *Governor*
[*of Paris and*] EXETER.

GLOUCESTER

Lord Bishop, set the crown upon his head.

WINCHESTER

God save King Henry, of that name the Sixth.

GLOUCESTER

Now, Governor of Paris, take your oath:
That you elect no other king but him,

---

44 **miscreant** evil-doer, with a sense of heretic or unbeliever

4.1.1 **Lord Bishop** At this point historically, and in Hall, Winchester is already a cardinal, but in this play he is still, given Henry V's refusal to endorse the appointment, officially a bishop, whatever his claim to higher status (and despite his premature appearance as cardinal in 1.3). Gloucester is not present at the coronation in Hall. His opening line is both a typical attempt to take control of the coronation, and a taunt at Winchester, at the gap between his ambitions and their endorsement by the rest of the English court. See 1.3.36n.

set the crown Henry's coronation in Paris was a magnificent affair designed to compete with the displays of power put on by his rivals of Valois and Burgundy; the gesture of a coronation

in France answers Charles's defiant coronation at Reims, though by all accounts the event itself was somewhat chaotic (see Griffiths, 187–90, Huizinga, 47–8, and Introduction, p. 44). Henry's claim is to a double crown, one of France, one of England and Wales. 'When the devine servise was finished . . . the kyng departed toward the palaice, havyng one croune on his hed, and another borne before hym, and one scepter in his hand, & the second borne before hym' (Bullough, 3.62).

3 **Governor of Paris** The BBC production, has the Governor repeat Gloucester's last line (8), as if it *were* the oath (cf. 5.3.169–75), before Fastolfe enters, and the ESC production replaces Fastolfe with Lucy as the bearer of bad news, and so loses the garter scene. See Appendix 3.

4 **elect** assent to

4.1] *(Actus Quartus. Scena Prima.)*   0.1 *Enter*] Flourish. Enter Oxf   0.2–3 *Governor . . .* EXETER]
this edn; and Gouernor Exeter F; Exeter, *the Governor of* Paris *and others. /* Pope   2 sixth] Sixth!
Winchester crowns King Henry Cam²   3 oath] oath, *Governor kneels / Capell*

Esteem none friends but such as are his friends,   5
And none your foes but such as shall pretend
Malicious practices against his state:
This shall ye do, so help you righteous God.

[*Exit Governor.*]

Enter FASTOLFE.

FASTOLFE

My gracious sovereign, as I rode from Calais
To haste unto your coronation,   10
A letter was delivered to my hands,
Writ to your grace from the Duke of Burgundy.

TALBOT

Shame to the Duke of Burgundy, and thee.
[*Tears the emblem of the Garter from Fastolfe's leg.*]

---

6 **pretend** intend, profess
13 SD **Tears . . . leg* This event did not
coincide with the coronation, either
historically or in Hall, and Fastolfe's
failure was seen as an uncharacteristic
aberration. According to Hall, as a consequence of Fastolfe's withdrawal from
the battle of Meuns (repeated as an
instance of comic cowardice in this
play at the siege of Rouen, in the
invented scene with the English captain, 3.2.102–7), 'the Duke of Bedford,
in a great anger, toke from hym the
Image of sainct George, and his Garter,
but afterward, by meane of frendes,
and apparant causes of good excuse by
hym alledged, he was restored to the
order again, against the mynd of the
lorde Talbot' (Bullough, 3.59–60). The
most likely placing for this moment of
stage action seems to be here, but
Talbot's *have done* (16) could refer to
the making of the vow, rather than the
action. If this were the case then the

removal of the Garter follows the
King's speech at 45. On this depends
how much onstage authority the King
is to be given at his coronation. As the
rest of his speech implies, the King is
attempting to take command. If
Talbot, having made his case, waits for
the King's word, his act is then more
clearly an attempt to confirm the
meaning of the symbol of the Garter in
relation to the King, and not simply an
angry disruption of the ceremony. If
the SD is placed as here, as in previous
editions, Talbot acts impulsively and
disruptively in 'the presence'. The
Order of the Garter (see 33–44) was
founded by Edward III and reaffirmed
by Henry V, who in 1417 gave its
knights precedence 'over all other officers, subject to the Crown of England'
(Fox-Davies, 34). So Fastolfe has
offended against, and Talbot is impulsively confirming, a central part of
English heroic and aristocratic identity.

---

8 SD] *this edn*; *Exeunt Gov and Train / Capell* 8.1 FASTOLFE] *Theobald; Falstaffe F; Sir John Falstaff Ard²; FASTOLF Cam²* 9 SP] *Theobald; Fal. F* 12 the Duke] *(th'Duke)* 13 SD] *this edn*

I vowed, base knight, when I did meet thee next
To tear the Garter from thy craven's leg,   15
Which I have done, because unworthily
Thou wast installed in that high degree.
Pardon me, princely Henry, and the rest:
This dastard, at the battle of Patay, –
When but in all I was six thousand strong,   20
And that the French were almost ten to one –
Before we met, or that a stroke was given,
Like to a trusty squire, did run away;
In which assault we lost twelve hundred men.
Myself and divers gentlemen beside   25
Were there surprised and taken prisoners.
Then judge, great lords, if I have done amiss;
Or whether that such cowards ought to wear
This ornament of knighthood, yea or no?

GLOUCESTER

To say the truth, this fact was infamous   30
And ill beseeming any common man,
Much more a knight, a captain and a leader.

TALBOT

When first this order was ordained, my lords,
Knights of the Garter were of noble birth,
Valiant and virtuous, full of haughty courage,   35

---

15 **craven's** coward's
17 **installed** installèd. The knights of the
   Garter were (and are) literally
   'installed', in that they are awarded the
   right to a 'stall', or official seat, in the
   Garter Chapel at Windsor.
19 **dastard** coward
   *__Patay__ F's *Poictiers* (Poitiers) must be
   an error, if an accidentally ironic one,
   given that Poitiers was the site of an
   English victory under Edward III. For
   a description of the Patay incident, see
   1.1.110–40, where, probably con-

tributing to the confusion, the battle is
not named.
20 **but in all** only in total
23 **trusty squire** *Trusty* and *squire* both
   tend to be condescending, arch or down-
   right sarcastic terms in Shakespeare.
30 **fact** in the sense of *OED* 1c, 'An evil
   deed, a crime', referring here to
   Fastolfe's retreat
31 **common man** man without any
   special title or status
35 **haughty** ambitious (not, here, pejorative)

15 leg] leg, *plucking it off* / Capell   19 Patay] *Malone (Capell); Poictiers* F

Such as were grown to credit by the wars;
Not fearing death nor shrinking for distress
But always resolute in most extremes.
He then that is not furnished in this sort
Doth but usurp the sacred name of knight,   40
Profaning this most honourable order,
And should (if I were worthy to be judge)
Be quite degraded, like a hedge-born swain
That doth presume to boast of gentle blood.

KING

Stain to thy countrymen, thou hear'st thy doom: 45
Be packing, therefore, thou that wast a knight.
Henceforth we banish thee on pain of death.

[Exit Fastolfe.]

And now, my lord Protector, view the letter
Sent from our uncle, Duke of Burgundy.

GLOUCESTER

What means his grace, that he hath changed his style?   50
No more but, plain and bluntly, 'To the King'.
Hath he forgot he is his sovereign?
Or doth this churlish superscription
Pretend some alteration in good will?
What's here? *I have upon especial cause,*   55
Moved with compassion of my country's wrack,
Together with the pitiful complaints
Of such as your oppression feeds upon,
Forsaken your pernicious faction

---

36 **were . . . credit** had proved their worth
38 **most extremes** the utmost danger
39 **furnished . . . sort** qualified in this way
43 **quite degraded** completely demoted
   hedge-born swain peasant, from a
   homeless family (so, born under a
   hedge). See Dent, H361.1.
44 **gentle** noble, well-born

46 **Be packing** go away
50 **style** manner of address
53 **churlish superscription** curt, grudging, ill-mannered address (*'To the King'*)
54 **Pretend** aim at; portend
56 *wrack* ruin
59 *pernicious faction* evil gang

38 most] worst *Hanmer*   47 SD] *F2 (Exit Falstaffe.)*   48 my lord] *F2;* Lord *F*   54 Pretend]
Portend *Rowe²*

225

And joined with Charles, the rightful King of France.   60
O monstrous treachery: can this be so,
That in alliance, amity and oaths
There should be found such false dissembling guile?

KING

What? Doth my uncle Burgundy revolt?

GLOUCESTER

He doth, my lord, and is become your foe.   65

KING

Is that the worst this letter doth contain?

GLOUCESTER

It is the worst – and all, my lord, he writes.

KING

Why then, Lord Talbot there shall talk with him
And give him chastisement for this abuse.
How say you, my lord, are you not content?   70

TALBOT

Content, my liege? Yes: but that I am prevented,
I should have begged I might have been employed.

KING

Then gather strength and march unto him straight.
Let him perceive how ill we brook his treason
And what offence it is to flout his friends.   75

---

60 *the rightful King* Burgundy's change of
side (depicted in this play at 3.3.36–89)
took place four years later than the
coronation, in 1435. The play builds on
Hall's account of the Duke's letter and
the English response to it. 'This letter
was not alitle looked on, nor smally
regarded of the kyng of England, and
his sage counsaill: not onely for the
waightines of the matter, but also for
the sodain chaunge of the man, & for
the straunge superscripcion of the letter, which was: To the high and might-
ie Prince, Henry, by the grace of GOD

Kyng of Englande, his welbeloved
cosyn: Neither namyng hym kyng of
Fraunce, nor his sovereigne lorde,
accordyng as, (ever before that tyme) he
was accustomed to do' (Bullough, 3.65).

62 **alliance** family relationship
69 **abuse** insult
71 **Content** 'content to fight Burgundy'
   prevented forestalled, by being
   assigned a task he had already decided
   to ask for.
73 **straight** straightaway, immediately
74 **brook** tolerate
75 **flout** mock

70 How . . . lord,] My lord, how say you, *Pope*

TALBOT

I go, my lord, in heart desiring still

You may behold confusion of your foes.   [*Exit.*]

Enter VERNON *and* BASSET.

VERNON

Grant me the combat, gracious sovereign.

BASSET

And me, my lord, grant me the combat too.

YORK

This is my servant: hear him, noble prince.   80

SOMERSET

And this is mine: sweet Henry, favour him.

KING

Be patient, lords, and give them leave to speak.

Say, gentlemen, what makes you thus exclaim,

And wherefore crave you combat? Or with whom?

VERNON

With him, my lord, for he hath done me wrong.   85

BASSET

And I with him, for he hath done me wrong.

KING

What is that wrong whereof you both complain?

First let me know and then I'll answer you.

BASSET

Crossing the sea from England into France,

This fellow here with envious carping tongue   90

Upbraided me about the rose I wear,

---

76 **still** always
77 **confusion** defeat.
77 SD An exit for Talbot is necessary here (*I go*, 76), to give the actor time to arm himself in preparation for the next scene (and in obedience to a royal

command).
80 **servant** a member of a household, not necessarily a menial position, and not one of the family. See note on List of Roles (pp. 110–11).
90 **envious** malicious

77 SD] *Rowe*

Saying the sanguine colour of the leaves
Did represent my master's blushing cheeks
When stubbornly he did repugn the truth
About a certain question in the law,   95
Argued betwixt the Duke of York and him –
With other vile and ignominious terms.
In confutation of which rude reproach
And in defence of my lord's worthiness
I crave the benefit of law of arms.   100

VERNON

And that is my petition, noble lord:
For though he seem with forged quaint conceit
To set a gloss upon his bold intent,
Yet know, my lord, I was provoked by him,
And he first took exceptions at this badge,   105
Pronouncing that the paleness of this flower
Bewrayed the faintness of my master's heart.

YORK

Will not this malice, Somerset, be left?

SOMERSET

Your private grudge, my lord of York, will out,
Though ne'er so cunningly you smother it.   110

KING

Good Lord, what madness rules in brainsick men,
When for so slight and frivolous a cause
Such factious emulations shall arise?
Good cousins both, of York and Somerset,
Quiet yourselves, I pray, and be at peace.   115

---

94 **repugn** *OED* 1c: 'stand *against* something'
100 'I beg for permission to break the
normal rules of a country at war, and
settle this by combat.' The two men
compete, somewhat farcically, to gain
moral advantage, by having the King
grant this *benefit* to each of them first.
102 **forged** forgèd

103 **set . . . upon** give a better appearance
to
105 **took exceptions at** objected to
107 **Bewrayed** revealed
110 **smother** as in covering a fire, but to
preserve, not to extinguish it
111 **brainsick** feverish; deluded
113 **factious emulations** divisive rivalries

YORK

    Let this dissension first be tried by fight,

    And then your highness shall command a peace.

SOMERSET

    The quarrel toucheth none but us alone;

    Betwixt ourselves let us decide it then.

YORK

    There is my pledge; accept it, Somerset.   120

       [*York throws down his gauntlet.*]

VERNON

     Nay, let it rest where it began at first.

BASSET

    Confirm it so, mine honourable lord.

GLOUCESTER

    Confirm it so? Confounded be your strife

    And perish ye with your audacious prate.

    Presumptuous vassals, are you not ashamed   125

    With this immodest clamorous outrage

    To trouble and disturb the King and us?

    And you, my lords, methinks you do not well

    To bear with their perverse objections –

    Much less to take occasion from their mouths   130

    To raise a mutiny betwixt yourselves.

    Let me persuade you take a better course.

EXETER

    It grieves his highness. Good my lords, be friends.

KING

    Come hither, you that would be combatants.

---

120 SD **throws down . . . gauntlet* as a challenge to combat; see *R2* 1.1.69, 4.1.25.

123 **Confounded** *OED* Confound *v.* 1b 'To overthrow, defeat or bring to nought'

124 **prate** thoughtless talk

126 **immodest** improper

129 **bear with** tolerate

    perverse obstinate, self-willed

    objections four syllables; expressions of disapproval

120 SD] *this edn*   133] *Pope; F lines* Highnesse, / Friends. /

Henceforth I charge you, as you love our favour,   135
Quite to forget this quarrel and the cause.
And you, my lords; remember where we are –
In France, amongst a fickle wavering nation.
If they perceive dissension in our looks,
And that within ourselves we disagree,   140
How will their grudging stomachs be provoked
To wilful disobedience and rebel!
Beside, what infamy will there arise
When foreign princes shall be certified
That for a toy, a thing of no regard,   145
King Henry's peers and chief nobility
Destroyed themselves and lost the realm of France!
O think upon the conquest of my father,
My tender years, and let us not forgo
That for a trifle that was bought with blood.   150
Let me be umpire in this doubtful strife.
    [*Takes the red rose from Basset.*]
I see no reason, if I wear this rose,
That anyone should therefore be suspicious
I more incline to Somerset than York:
Both are my kinsmen, and I love them both.   155
As well they may upbraid me with my crown
Because, forsooth, the King of Scots is crowned.
But your discretions better can persuade

---

135 **charge** order
138 **fickle . . . nation** a familiar English
    stereotype of France; see 3.3.85n.
140 **within** among
141 **grudging** complaining, but also,
    ominously, 'slight symptom of an
    approaching illness' (*OED vbl. sb.* 2)
142 **wilful . . . rebel** Shaheen (37) notes
    that this echoes the title of the Anglican
    homily 'Against Disobedience and
    Wilfull Rebellion'. The *Homilies* 'set

out by the aucthoritie of the Quenes
Maiestie' ('The Seconde Tome', 1563)
were set sermons on various topics, to
be read at church services.
144 **be certified** know for certain
145 **toy** frivolity
149 **forgo** forsake, give up
151 **doubtful** giving cause for apprehen-
    sion; uncertain
157 **forsooth** indeed, truly (ironic)
158 **discretions** ability to make distinctions

151 SD] *this edn*   152 rose] rose, *Putting on a red rose / Johnson*

Than I am able to instruct or teach:
And therefore, as we hither came in peace,   160
So let us still continue peace and love.
Cousin of York, we institute your grace
To be our regent in these parts of France:
And, good my lord of Somerset, unite
Your troops of horsemen with his bands of foot,   165
And like true subjects, sons of your progenitors,
Go cheerfully together and digest
Your angry choler on your enemies.
Ourself, my lord Protector and the rest
After some respite will return to Calais,   170
From thence to England – where I hope ere long
To be presented, by your victories,
With Charles, Alençon and that traitorous rout.
    Flourish. Exeunt all but York, Exeter, Warwick [and] Vernon.
WARWICK
My lord of York, I promise you the King
Prettily, methought, did play the orator.   175
YORK
And so he did, but yet I like it not,
In that he wears the badge of Somerset.
WARWICK
Tush, that was but his fancy. Blame him not.
I dare presume, sweet prince, he thought no harm.

---

162 **institute** appoint
166 **true . . . progenitors** The phrase is addressed to Somerset as well as York, deflecting any tactlessness in the reference to York's father as among the *true subjects*.
167–8 **digest . . . choler** Henry's primary meaning is 'take out your anger', with *digest* in the sense of 'disperse', but the physiological sense of *digest* and the Elizabethan sense of *choler* as a physical 'humour', a force within the body, suggest that the aggression will remain inter-

nal to the 'body' of the English nobility.
173 **rout** disorderly gang, but also with the (from the English point of view) hopeful sense of 'chaotic retreat'
SD **Flourish* F places this at York's exit (181), a confusion presumably implying that either the compositor of F (despite his provision of *Manet*), or the author of the manuscript from which he worked, thought that York, Warwick and Exeter leave here, the King and the rest later. Conventionally only the royal exit would require a *Flourish*.

163 these] the *Ard²*   173 SD *Flourish*] Theobald; *after 181* F   all but] *(Manet)*

YORK

> An if I wist he did – but let it rest; 180
> Other affairs must now be managed. *Exeunt all but Exeter.*

EXETER

> Well didst thou, Richard, to suppress thy voice;
> For had the passions of thy heart burst out
> I fear we should have seen deciphered there
> More rancorous spite, more furious raging broils, 185
> Than yet can be imagined or supposed:
> But howsoe'er, no simple man that sees
> This jarring discord of nobility,
> This shouldering of each other in the court,
> This factious bandying of their favourites, 190
> But that it doth presage some ill event.
> 'Tis much when sceptres are in children's hands,
> But more when envy breeds unkind division –
> There comes the ruin, there begins confusion. *Exit.*

[**4.2**] *Enter* TALBOT *with Trumpet and Drum, before Bordeaux.*

TALBOT

> Go to the gates of Bordeaux, trumpeter;
> Summon their general unto the wall.
> > [*Trumpet*] *sounds* [*for parley*].

180 *An . . . **did** if I thought he did
181 **managed** managèd
184 **deciphered** revealed
185 **broils** disturbances
188 **jarring discord** harsh, clashing
190 **factious bandying** see *OED* bandying, *vbl. sb.* 3: 'To toss from side to side, like a tennis-ball'; here in a game of teams, or 'factions'.
191 **event** outcome
192 According to Shaheen (37), 'Shakespeare's passage seems to be based on Hall's paraphrase of Isaiah, 3.4:

"Saiying by hys prophet Esay: I shall geue you children to be your princes, and enfantes without wysedom, shall haue the gouernaunce of you" '.
193 **unkind** unnatural
194 **confusion** destruction
4.2.0.1 *Trumpet and Drum* The trumpeter and drummer may either remain on stage with Talbot to the end of the scene, or exit after the trumpeter plays (an offstage drum is required at 38 SD).
2 **general** refers to the populace or their representatives. Talbot expects them to

180 An . . . wist] *Capell (*And if*); And if I wish *F*; And if, iwis, *Theobald* 181 SD *Exeunt all but] *Cam; Exeunt. / Flourish. Manet *F* 191 that] sees *Ard² (H. Brooks); at *(Vaughan); fears *(RP)* 4.2] *Capell*

Enter Captain *aloft.*

English John Talbot, captain, calls you forth,
Servant in arms to Harry, King of England.
And thus he would: open your city gates,   5
Be humble to us, call my sovereign yours
And do him homage as obedient subjects,
And I'll withdraw me and my bloody power.
But if you frown upon this proffered peace
You tempt the fury of my three attendants,   10
Lean famine, quartering steel and climbing fire,
Who, in a moment, even with the earth
Shall lay your stately and air-braving towers,
If you forsake the offer of their love.

CAPTAIN

Thou ominous and fearful owl of death,   15
Our nation's terror and their bloody scourge,
The period of thy tyranny approacheth.
On us thou canst not enter but by death:

assemble to receive his message, as *obedient subjects* (7). Though the character who subsequently arrives on the walls is called *'Generall'* in F's SD, in terms of military hierarchy F's later 'captain' is more accurate. He is the Captain of the troops in Bordeaux – the 'general' would in strict terms be the Dolphin himself. That the scene (musicians apart) is between two men (unless one takes F's 'Captaines' at 3 to imply the presence of further, silent figures on the walls) only intensifies the mood of an intimation of death, while also freeing the maximum number of actors for the next scene, where, owing to mismanagement, they are ironically impotent to help Talbot.

5 **would** wishes

11 **quartering** cutting the human body into quarters (the punishment for treason, in the Middle Ages and Renaissance)
12 **even** level
13 **air-braving** high, challenging the sky
15 **owl of death** In many cultures owls are regarded as harbingers of death. There are many such references in Shakespeare. See, for example, *Mac* 2.2.3: 'It was the owl that shriek'd, the fatal bellman'. Here the Captain identifies Talbot as thus *ominous* to the French, though in a situation where his message in itself reverses the situation; it is he who is *ominous* to Talbot.
17 **period** 'Completion, end of any course' (*OED sb.* II 5a)

2 SD *Trumpet . . . for parley*] *this edn*   2.1 Captain] *this edn; Generall F; General and Others / Malone*   3 captain] *Oxf;* Captaines *F*   calls] *F2;* call *F*   7 And do] Do *(Cam²)*   14 their] our *Hanmer;* his *(Cam¹)*   15 SP] *(Cap.);* Gen. / *Theobald*

For I protest we are well fortified
And strong enough to issue out and fight. 20
If thou retire, the Dolphin well appointed
Stands with the snares of war to tangle thee.
On either hand thee there are squadrons pitched
To wall thee from the liberty of flight;
And no way canst thou turn thee for redress 25
But death doth front thee with apparent spoil
And pale destruction meets thee in the face.
Ten thousand French have ta'en the sacrament
To rive their dangerous artillery
Upon no Christian soul but English Talbot. 30
Lo, there thou stand'st a breathing valiant man
Of an invincible unconquered spirit:
This is the latest glory of thy praise
That I, thy enemy, due thee withal;
For ere the glass that now begins to run 35
Finish the process of his sandy hour,
These eyes that see thee now well coloured
Shall see thee withered, bloody, pale and dead.

Drum afar off.

21 **well appointed** well prepared
22 **snares** traps, usually in the form of nooses, used to catch small animals. The Captain introduces, in an unflattering form, the hunting analogy that underlies the subsequent battle scenes.
23 **either hand thee** either side of thee
25 **redress** help
26 **apparent spoil** visible ruin
28 **sacrament** the sacrament of Holy Eucharist, or Communion, taken as the most solemn way of binding an oath. Cf. *R3* 5.5.18–19: Richmond 'And then as we have ta'en the sacrament, / We will unite the White Rose and the Red'.

29 **rive** thrust (more usually used of knife or spear than of *artillery*)
dangerous artillery The development of superior artillery was a decisive factor in the French defeat of the English. See Introduction pp. 15–16, and Appendix 4.
34 **due thee withal** pay as is due
35 **glass** hourglass. Shakespeare's infrequent use of the idea is always linked to the allegorical personification of Time, whose emblem it is. See *Son* 126.2, *WT* 1.2.306, 4.1.16, *AW* 2.1.165–6.
37 **coloured** colourèd

29 rive] rove *Cam¹ (Hart)*

Hark, hark; the Dolphin's drum, a warning bell,
Sings heavy music to thy timorous soul,   40
And mine shall ring thy dire departure out.   *Exit.*

TALBOT

He fables not. I hear the enemy.
Out, some light horsemen, and peruse their wings.
O negligent and heedless discipline –
How are we parked and bounded in a pale –   45
A little herd of England's timorous deer
Mazed with a yelping kennel of French curs.
If we be English deer, be then in blood:
Not rascal-like to fall down with a pinch,
But rather, moody-mad and desperate stags,   50
Turn on the bloody hounds with heads of steel
And make the cowards stand aloof at bay.
Sell every man his life as dear as mine

39 **warning bell** continues the idea of presages of death. See 15n.
40 **heavy** ominous
41 **dire departure** dreadful death
45 **parked . . . pale** 'enclosed and limited'. (A *pale* is a fence, or some other sort of physical boundary.) Nobles and royalty of this and later periods kept deerparks for hunting.
46 **England's timorous deer** Earlier, 1.5.25–6, Talbot contrasts the reputation of the English as hunting dogs with their actual cowardice in fleeing Joan – 'whelps'. Here again the English are the hunted rather than the hunters; see Introduction, pp. 50–2.
47 **Mazed with** bewildered, confused by
48 **in blood** another hunting term, meaning (a) noble blood as inherited identity; (b) bloody battle. See *LLL* 4.2.3–4 and Ard[3] note, where it is glossed (of a deer) as 'in prime condition'.
49 **rascal-like** a play on two meanings of the word *rascal*, the still current use of

it to describe a disreputable or untrustworthy person, and the obsolete sense of 'the young, lean, or inferior deer of a herd' (*OED* A *sb.* 4)
with a pinch at the first threat
50 **moody-mad** reckless with rage
51 **heads of steel** a metaphor that brings together the English soldiers' armour and the deer's antlers
52 **aloof at bay** a deceptively complex phrase. *Aloof* means 'at a distance', *at bay* 'trapped at close quarters'. The context here, though, is the continuing hunting metaphor, so the sense of *bay* may well be that of *OED sb.*[4] II, 'The chorus of barking raised by hounds in immediate conflict with a hunted animal; *hence* the final encounter between hounds and the prey they have chased'. Talbot hopes his men will keep their baying enemies *aloof*, if only as a temporary assertion of English honour.

41 SD] *Exeunt General and others aloft Cam[2], after Malone*   43 wings.] wings. *Exit one or more* / *Oxf*
50 moody-mad and] *Capell;* moodie mad: And *F*

And they shall find dear deer of us, my friends.
God and Saint George, Talbot and England's right,   55
Prosper our colours in this dangerous fight.   [*Exit.*]

[**4.3**]   *Enter a Messenger that meets* YORK.
              Enter YORK *with Trumpet and many Soldiers.*

YORK

Are not the speedy scouts returned again,
That dogged the mighty army of the Dolphin?

MESSENGER

They are returned, my lord, and give it out
That he is marched to Bordeaux with his power
To fight with Talbot; as he marched along,   5
By your espials were discovered
Two mightier troops than that the Dolphin led,
Which joined with him and made their march for
      Bordeaux.

YORK

A plague upon that villain Somerset,
That thus delays my promised supply   10
Of horsemen, that were levied for this siege.
Renowned Talbot doth expect my aid,
And I am louted by a traitor villain,

---

54 **my friends** This could be spoken to
the musicians with '*trumpet and drum*',
or to military extras unspecified by F,
but need not be; as with the order to
the horsemen (43) Talbot addresses
the audience; the play thus releases the
soldiers for the next scene, and emphasizes Talbot's isolation in the face of
his realization of defeat. It also forms
an emotive high-point of that 'recruitment' of the audience into Talbot's
militia commented on by Nashe in

Piers Penniless; see Introduction, p. 1.
4.3.0.1 **Messenger** one of York's own
officers
0.2 To emphasize by contrast the isolation
of Talbot in the previous scene, F's
SD specifies *many Soldiers.*
3 **give it out** report
6 **espials** spies
discovered discoverèd
10 **promised** promisèd
12 **Renowned** renownèd
13 **louted** treated contemptuously, mocked

---

56 SD] *this edn; Exeunt F2*   **4.3**] *Capell*   5 Talbot . . . along.] *F2; Talbot* as he marched along. *F*
8 Bordeaux.] Bordeaux. *Exit. Ard²*   13 louted] flouted *(Johnson)*

And cannot help the noble chevalier.
God comfort him in this necessity.   15
If he miscarry, farewell wars in France.

Enter another messenger[, Sir William LUCY].

LUCY

Thou princely leader of our English strength –
Never so needful on the earth of France –
Spur to the rescue of the noble Talbot,
Who now is girdled with a waste of iron   20
And hemmed about with grim destruction.
To Bordeaux, warlike Duke, to Bordeaux, York,
Else farewell Talbot, France and England's honour.

YORK

O God, that Somerset, who in proud heart
Doth stop my cornets, were in Talbot's place;   25
So should we save a valiant gentleman
By forfeiting a traitor and a coward.
Mad ire and wrathful fury makes me weep,
That thus we die while remiss traitors sleep.

LUCY

O send some succour to the distressed lord.   30

YORK

He dies, we lose, I break my warlike word.

---

14 **chevalier** pronounced as three syllables, stressed on first and third. The
choice of the French word is ironically
pointed, in that York (25) has aimed to
furnish Talbot with cavalry, claiming
later that Somerset fails to release the
horse-troops for Talbot and his use.
Historically, the outdated English cavalry
strategy was especially vulnerable to
the artillery attack that secured French
victory.

20 **waste** 'Waist' is another possible

reading of F's 'waste', in the light of
girdled, so emphasizing the physical
constriction of Talbot's situation, but
waste conveys the desolation, the lack
of hope facing him on all sides.

25 **cornets** companies of cavalry.

28 **makes** The verb is in the singular
because *wrathful fury* is simply an
emphatic restatement of *mad ire*, and
so only one thing is being described.

29 **remiss** careless

16.1 Sir . . . LUCY] *Theobald*   17 SP] *Theobald; 2. Mes. F*   20 waste] waist *Steevens*   30, 34, 47 SP]
Theobald; Mes. F   30 distressed] *(*distrest*)*   31 He dies] *Aside* He dies *Cam²*

237

We mourn, France smiles; we lose, they daily get,
All long of this vile traitor Somerset.

LUCY

Then God take mercy on brave Talbot's soul,
And on his son, young John, who two hours since   35
I met in travail toward his warlike father.
This seven years did not Talbot see his son,
And now they meet where both their lives are done.

YORK

Alas, what joy shall noble Talbot have,
To bid his young son welcome to his grave.   40
Away, vexation almost stops my breath,
That sundered friends greet in the hour of death.
Lucy, farewell; no more my fortune can
But curse the cause I cannot aid the man.
Maine, Blois, Poitiers and Tours are won away,   45
Long all of Somerset and his delay.

                                    Exeunt [all but Lucy].

LUCY

Thus, while the vulture of sedition

33 **long of** because of
36 **travail** Later emphasis on the motif of
   'birth' at the imminent death of John
   justifies retention of F's form of the
   word. It compresses the senses of
   'travel' and 'work' with the birth pangs
   that create a new 'John' in a heroic
   identity conferred by his affirmation
   of his relation to his father. See also
   4.4.35, 129 and 158.
37 **This seven years** proverbial (Dent,
   Y25). The play adapts and confuses
   the historical time scheme to such an
   extent that it is impossible to judge
   duration exactly. The point here is that
   Talbot has missed his son's growth
   into manhood. Traditionally the stages
   in human life were reckoned in sevens,
   so the implication is that Talbot is

meeting a son of twenty-one whom he
last saw at fourteen, or perhaps more
likely, given that this is the start of
John's military career, a fourteen-year-
old he had last seen at seven.
43–4 **no . . . But** 'in my present circumstance I can do no more than'
44 **the cause** i.e. Somerset
46 **Long all of** only because of
47–8 **vulture . . . Feeds** In classical
   mythology, Prometheus was punished
   for his disobedience towards Zeus, the
   king of the Olympian gods, by an eagle
   that fed on his liver. But in this case
   the *vulture* is a cherished pet, fed *in*, to
   some extent on, the *bosom*, or heart, of
   the *commanders*. A similar, if less well-
   known myth, which the dramatists
   may have conflated with that of

36 travail] *(trauaile); travel F3*   46 SD] *Collier subst. Exit. F*

238

Feeds in the bosom of such great commanders,
Sleeping neglection doth betray to loss
The conquest of our scarce-cold conqueror,   50
That ever-living man of memory,
Henry the Fifth. Whiles they each other cross,
Lives, honours, lands and all hurry to loss.

Enter SOMERSET *with his army*   [4.4]
[and a Captain of Talbot's].

SOMERSET

It is too late, I cannot send them now.
This expedition was by York and Talbot   55
Too rashly plotted. All our general force
Might with a sally of the very town

Prometheus, has Tityus, the rebellious son of Zeus, as the victim of a liver-consuming *vulture*.

49 **neglection** negligence
50 **scarce-cold** In historical terms, thirty-one years had passed between Henry V's death and Talbot's. But the play persistently compresses and reshapes historical continuities; see Introduction, pp. 23–5. Lucy's remark applies, hyperbolically, to Henry's fame, as with *ever-living* in the next line. A confusion of the time scheme, in the interest of linking the two deaths, is made easier by the limited amount of attention given in the play so far to Henry VI, and a certain vagueness about his age.
52 **cross** thwart
53.1 F, which is not divided into scenes at this point, marks no exit for *another Messenger*, identified in York's last speech as *Lucie* (43). Similarly, there is no exit marked for the first messenger. In presenting both of Lucy's encounters with the rival commanders as one scene, rather than the customary two, I

may violate geographical probability, but this would be unlikely to trouble the original audience of the play, and it does produce a more cogent and emblematically telling shape to the scene, an option taken in the 1977 RSC production. Exits added to facilitate a scene division reduce Lucy's choric authority and dilute the power of the action. When played as one scene, York's and Somerset's exits and entrances become tellingly symmetrical. Two later scenes provide analogies to this non-realistic bipartite structure. Both 5.2 and 5.3 flout geographical realism to set up a significant comparative diptych, setting Joan in the first instance in apposition to Margaret, in the second to Winchester. See 0.1n. and Introduction, pp. 102–3. Ard² gives '*Scene iii continued / conj. this edn*' in the textual notes, while following the conventional scene division in the text.
56 **general force** whole army
57 **sally** sudden attack; sortie
   the very town the town itself, even without reinforcements

53 loss] loss. *Exit. / Capell*   53.1] SCENE IV. – *Other Plains in the same. Enter* Somerset, *and Forces; a Captain of* Talbot's *with him / Capell*

Be buckled with: the over-daring Talbot
Hath sullied all his gloss of former honour
By this unheedful, desperate, wild adventure.   60
York set him on to fight and die in shame,
That, Talbot dead, great York might bear the name.
CAPTAIN [*to Somerset*]
Here is Sir William Lucy, who, with me,   [10]
Set from our o'ermatched forces forth for aid.
SOMERSET
How now, Sir William, whither were you sent?   65
LUCY
Whither, my lord? From bought and sold Lord Talbot
Who – ringed about with bold adversity –
Cries out for noble York and Somerset
To beat assailing death from his weak regions;
And whiles the honourable captain there   70
Drops bloody sweat from his war-wearied limbs
And, in advantage lingering, looks for rescue,
You, his false hopes, the trust of England's honour,   [20]
Keep off aloof with worthless emulation.
Let not your private discord keep away   75
The levied succours that should lend him aid,

---

58 **buckled with** engaged in fight
65 **whither** an odd question; it is more
important to Somerset to establish
whether Lucy was sent to him or to
York and so to determine which of
them will be seen to have failed him.
Lucy's response is tactful evasion.
Somerset would hardly be happy to
know that Lucy went first to York.
69 **regions** Rowe emends to 'legions'.
Regions would mean the territory surrounding Talbot, *weak* referring to his
loosening grip on it; this is not elegant,
but neither is 'legions', an aggrandize-
ment of the number of Talbot's troops,
and of his (if we take that choice of

word) quasi-imperial relation to them.
71 **bloody sweat** Luke, 22.44: 'But being
in an agonie . . . his sweate was like
droppes of blood'. Talbot is thus implicitly compared to Christ, of whom the
phrase is used on the eve of *his* death.
72 **in advantage lingering** holding on to
his last chance. Oxf's emendation to
'unadvantaged, lingering' misses the
point; Talbot *has* the advantage but, with
his weakening army, will not be able to
hold on to it without reinforcements.
73 **trust** in the sense of *OED sb.* 6,
'trustee', a legal term
76 **levied succours** specially recruited
auxiliary forces

62 name.] name. *Enter Sir William* LUCY *Capell* 63 SD] *this edn* 65, 66 whither] *(whether)*
69 regions] legions *Rowe* 72 in . . . lingering] *(lingring); unadvantaged, ling'ring Oxf*

While he, renowned noble gentleman,
Yield up his life unto a world of odds.
Orleans the Bastard, Charles, Burgundy,
Alençon, Reignier, compass him about,   80
And Talbot perisheth by your default.

SOMERSET

York set him on, York should have sent him aid.

LUCY

And York as fast upon your grace exclaims,   [30]
Swearing that you withhold his levied host,
Collected for this expedition.   85

SOMERSET

York lies. He might have sent, and had the horse.
I owe him little duty and less love,
And take foul scorn to fawn on him by sending.

LUCY

The fraud of England, not the force of France,
Hath now entrapped the noble-minded Talbot.   90
Never to England shall he bear his life,
But dies betrayed to fortune by your strife.

SOMERSET

Come – go – I will dispatch the horsemen straight: [40]
Within six hours they will be at his aid.

LUCY

Too late comes rescue: he is ta'en or slain,   95
For fly he could not, if he would have fled;
And fly would Talbot never, though he might.

---

77 **renowned** renownèd
78 **a world of odds** overwhelming odds
84 **his levied host** the forces he levied
86, 88 **sent**, **sending** While this may refer to *sending* the required cavalry, it seems more likely to point to the failure of communication between the two men at a simpler, more trivial level: out of pique, they have refused to *send* messages to each other.
86 **horse** cavalry
88 'and disdain to flatter York by helping to remedy the consequences of his mistake'

78 Yield] Yields *F2*   79 Charles] Charles and *F2*   80 Reignier] *(Rowe); Reignard F*   84 host] horse *Hanmer (Theobald)*   94 aid] *(*ayde*);* side *Ard²*

SOMERSET

    If he be dead – brave Talbot, then, adieu.

LUCY

    His fame lives in the world, his shame in you.   *Exeunt.*

[4.4]   *Enter* TALBOT *and his son* [JOHN].

TALBOT

    O young John Talbot, I did send for thee

    To tutor thee in stratagems of war,

    That Talbot's name might be in thee revived

    When sapless age and weak unable limbs

    Should bring thy father to his drooping chair.   5

    But – O malignant and ill-boding stars –

    Now thou art come unto a feast of death,

    A terrible and unavoided danger.

    Therefore, dear boy, mount on my swiftest horse,

    And I'll direct thee how thou shalt escape   10

    By sudden flight. Come – dally not, be gone.

JOHN

    Is my name Talbot? And am I your son?

---

99 This could be marked as an 'aside', or Somerset and Lucy could be directed to exit separately, each at the end of his line, if it seems unlikely that Lucy is speaking directly to Somerset. F's *Exeunt*, however, makes sense in terms of the stage space for which the play was written: if the two men exit at opposite sides of a laterally organized stage and at speed, Lucy's line may well be unheard by Somerset (see Introduction pp. 10–12).

4.4.1 young John Talbot In Hall, Talbot, his son and, among others omitted in the play, 'his bastard sonne Henry Talbot' (Bullough, 3.73) take the town of Castillon, and then return to defend it when they hear of a French force besieging it; but they encounter 'iii .C. peces of brasse, beside divers other small peces, and subtill Engynes to the Englishmen unknowen, and nothing suspected, they lyghted al on fote, the erle of Shrewesbury only except, which because of his age, rode on a litle hakeney, and fought fiercely with the Frenchmen' (Bullough, 3.72). Hall goes on to present the argument between Talbot and John in much the same terms as does the play.

5 **drooping chair** chair for a feeble (*drooping*) person, here Talbot imagining himself in a peaceful old age

11 **dally not** do not delay

4.4.] *this edn;* IV.v. *Capell*   0.1 JOHN] *Oxf*

And shall I fly? O, if you love my mother,
Dishonour not her honourable name
To make a bastard and a slave of me.   15
The world will say, 'He is not Talbot's blood,
That basely fled when noble Talbot stood'.

TALBOT

Fly, to revenge my death if I be slain.

JOHN

He that flies so will ne'er return again.

TALBOT

If we both stay we both are sure to die.   20

JOHN

Then let me stay and, father, do you fly.
Your loss is great – so your regard should be;
My worth unknown – no loss is known in me.
Upon my death the French can little boast;
In yours they will, in you all hopes are lost.   25
Flight cannot stain the honour you have won;
But mine it will, that no exploit have done.
You fled for vantage, everyone will swear;
But if I bow they'll say it was for fear.
There is no hope that ever I will stay   30
If the first hour I shrink and run away.
Here on my knee I beg mortality,
Rather than life preserved with infamy.   [*He kneels.*]

TALBOT

Shall all thy mother's hopes lie in one tomb?

JOHN

Ay, rather than I'll shame my mother's womb.   35

---

22 **regard** care
28 **for vantage** in strategy, to get to a
   better position for attack
29 **bow** bend, yield
31 **shrink** retreat

32 **beg mortality** ask for death
33 SD* It was customary in Elizabethan
   domestic ceremonial for a child to kneel
   for its parent's blessing.

33 SD] *this edn*

TALBOT

Upon my blessing I command thee go. [*John rises.*]

JOHN

To fight I will, but not to fly the foe.

TALBOT

Part of thy father may be saved in thee.

JOHN

No part of him but will be shame in me.

TALBOT

Thou never hadst renown, nor canst not lose it.   40

JOHN

Yes, your renownèd name: shall flight abuse it?

TALBOT

Thy father's charge shall clear thee from that stain.

JOHN

You cannot witness for me, being slain.

If death be so apparent then both fly.

TALBOT

And leave my followers here to fight and die?   45

My age was never tainted with such shame.

JOHN

And shall my youth be guilty of such blame?

No more can I be severed from your side

Than can yourself yourself in twain divide.

Stay, go, do what you will, the like do I;   50

For live I will not, if my father die.

TALBOT

Then here I take my leave of thee, fair son,

---

41 **renowned** renownèd
42 **charge** order
44 **apparent** obvious. There is perhaps a pun available on 'a parent'; death is poised to become young Talbot's parent, in the sense of cancelling his father's authority, and giving him a new birth in an heroic identity.

46 **My age** my whole life; but it also draws attention to Talbot's declining years, and possibly also to his heroic status, as the *age*, the now departing era of English chivalry, for which he stands.
tainted stained

36 SD] *this edn*   39 shame] sham'd *Hudson (Walker)*

Born to eclipse thy life this afternoon.
Come, side by side together live and die,
And soul with soul from France to heaven fly.   55
                              Alarum. Exit [*Talbot*].

[*Enter* ALENÇON, BASTARD *and* BURGUNDY *in*]   **[4.6]**
excursions, wherein Talbot's son is hemmed about [*by the three*
Frenchmen, as he goes after his father], *and* TALBOT
[*re-enters and*] *rescues him.*

TALBOT

Saint George and victory! Fight, soldiers, fight.
The regent hath with Talbot broke his word
And left us to the rage of France his sword.
Where is John Talbot? Pause, and take thy breath.
I gave thee life, and rescued thee from death.   60
JOHN

O twice my father, twice am I thy son:
The life thou gav'st me first was lost and done,
Till with thy warlike sword, despite of fate,
To my determined time thou gav'st new date.   [9]
TALBOT

When from the Dolphin's crest thy sword struck fire   65
It warmed thy father's heart with proud desire

55.3–4 *TALBOT *re-enters* F marks no
  exit for John; the scene makes sense as
  a continuous action, presenting on
  stage the fight described in lines
  60–81. See Introduction, pp. 17–18. I
  take it that *side by side* (54) need not be
  taken entirely literally; even if the
  Talbots start to exit together, an
  immediate French excursion could
  separate them.
57 **The regent** York

64 **determined** fated
  date limit
65 **crest** the plumed top of Charles' helmet; John's sword has hit it sharply
  enough to strike sparks from the metal.
  There is also a sense in *crest* of pride –
  of a peacock, for example, and of the
  crown, presumably represented on the
  helmet, which the English seek to deny
  the Dolphin.

55 SD] *this edn; Exeunt. SCENE VI. – A Field of Battle. Loud Alarums. / Capell* 55.1 *Enter . . .
in*] *this edn* 55.2–3 *by . . . father*] *this edn* 55.4 *re-enters and*] *this edn*

Of bold-faced victory. Then leaden age,
Quickened with youthful spleen and warlike rage,
Beat down Alençon, Orleans, Burgundy,
And from the pride of Gallia rescued thee.   70
The ireful bastard Orleans, that drew blood
From thee, my boy, and had the maidenhood
Of thy first fight, I soon encountered,
And, interchanging blows, I quickly shed   [19]
Some of his bastard blood, and in disgrace   75
Bespoke him thus: 'Contaminated, base
And misbegotten blood I spill of thine,
Mean and right poor, for that pure blood of mine
Which thou didst force from Talbot, my brave boy'.
Here, purposing the Bastard to destroy,   80
Came in strong rescue. Speak, thy father's care:
Art thou not weary, John? How dost thou fare?
Wilt thou yet leave the battle, boy, and fly,
Now thou art sealed the son of chivalry?   [29]
Fly, to revenge my death when I am dead;   85
The help of one stands me in little stead.
O, too much folly is it, well I wot,
To hazard all our lives in one small boat.
If I today die not with Frenchmen's rage,
Tomorrow I shall die with mickle age.   90
By me they nothing gain, an if I stay,
'Tis but the shortening of my life one day;

In thee thy mother dies, our household's name,
My death's revenge, thy youth and England's fame.   [39]
All these, and more, we hazard by thy stay;   95
All these are saved, if thou wilt fly away.

JOHN

The sword of Orleans hath not made me smart:
These words of yours draw life-blood from my heart.
On that advantage, bought with such a shame,
To save a paltry life and slay bright fame?   100
Before young Talbot from old Talbot fly,
The coward horse that bears me fall and die!
And like me to the peasant boys of France,
To be shame's scorn, and subject of mischance.   [49]
Surely, by all the glory you have won,   105
An if I fly I am not Talbot's son.
Then talk no more of flight, it is no boot:
If son to Talbot, die at Talbot's foot.

TALBOT

Then follow thou thy desperate sire of Crete,
Thou Icarus; thy life to me is sweet.   110
If thou wilt fight, fight by thy father's side,

---

97 **smart** feel pain
99–100 'Shall I save my own life at the cost of your death and my reputation?'
103 **like me** liken me, see me as equivalent to
107 **boot** benefit
109–10 **Then . . . Icarus** According to classical legend, Icarus was the son of Daedalus, the architect and inventor who, among other things, designed and built for King Minos of Crete the labyrinth, in which the King housed the Minotaur (cf. 5.2. 209–10), the offspring of his wife Pasiphae and a bull. Daedalus escaped from Crete flying on wax and feather wings which he had

made himself. But his son Icarus, in following him, flew too near the sun, the wax in his wings melted and he fell into the sea. Though often in this period Icarus is an emblem of overweening ambition (Marlowe's *Dr Faustus*, for example, Prologue, 20–2), here the reference is inflected to emphasize the loyalty shown in John's imitation of his father. This was possibly suggested by Hall's use of the labyrinth metaphor to present Talbot's sense of his fate: 'the erle . . . perceivynge the imminent jeopardy and subtile labirynth' (Bullough, 3.73).

---

99 On that] Out on that *Theobald;* On what *Hanmer*   109 desperate] *(desp'rate)*

And, commendable proved, let's die in pride. *Exeunt.*

Alarum. Excursions. Enter old TALBOT *led* [4.7]
[*by a* Servant].

TALBOT

Where is my other life? Mine own is gone.

O where's young Talbot? Where is valiant John?

Triumphant death, smeared with captivity, 115

Young Talbot's valour makes me smile at thee.

When he perceived me shrink and on my knee,

His bloody sword he brandished over me

And like a hungry lion did commence

Rough deeds of rage and stern impatience. 120

But when my angry guardant stood alone,

Tendering my ruin and assailed of none, [10]

Dizzy-eyed fury and great rage of heart

Suddenly made him from my side to start

---

112 **commendable** worthy of praise
112.1–2 This entry SD in previous editions has been presented as the beginning of the last scene of the fourth act. However, since F starts to mark new scene divisions from '*Scena secunda*', (5.1 in this edition), the action of Talbot's death and the French reaction to it could be regarded as the '*Scena prima*' of a new act (Act 5). This would make sense of F's final act of one scene only – which would then become, not '*Actus Quintus*' but '*Scena Quinta*', the fifth scene of a fifth act. But it is more appropriate, and consistent with this edition's practice, to regard Talbot's death as the climax of a long continuous scene. See Introduction, pp. 101–3.
  old TALBOT In calling Talbot *old* and by having him led by a *Servant* rather than by the expected soldiers, F underlines the pathos of the situation,

by presenting him as an aged father, rather than as a commander.
115 Talbot addresses death, whom he imagines smeared with his own blood and that of his dead son.
120 **impatience** defiance
121 **guardant** guardian, or protector (*OED sb.* B). Here the word may pick up on the *lion* image in the heraldic context, where the word would be used of 'a beast. Having the full face towards the spectator' (*OED* A *adj.*2).
122 **Tendering** The sense here is multiple; to tender means; 'to mitigate' (*OED v.*[2] 2b); 'to be concerned or solicitous about' (*OED v.*[2] 3a); 'to have regard or respect to as something to be dreaded and avoided' (*OED v.*[2] 3e). All these meanings are relevant to Talbot's sense of his son's actions.
123 **Dizzy-eyed** wild-eyed

---

112 proved] *(prou'd)*   SD *Exeunt*] *Rowe; Exit.* F   112.1] IV. vii *Pope*   112.2   *by a* Servant] *Cam*
122 Tendering] *(*Tendring*)*

Into the clustering battle of the French,   125
And in that sea of blood my boy did drench
His over-mounting spirit, and there died
My Icarus, my blossom, in his pride.

Enter [Soldiers] with JOHN Talbot, *borne.*

SERVANT

O my dear lord, lo where your son is borne.

TALBOT

Thou antic death, which laugh'st us here to scorn,   130
Anon from thy insulting tyranny,
Coupled in bonds of perpetuity,   [20]
Two Talbots, winged, through the lither sky
In thy despite shall scape mortality.
O thou, whose wounds become hard-favoured death,   135
Speak to thy father ere thou yield thy breath:
Brave death by speaking, whether he will or no;
Imagine him a Frenchman, and thy foe.
Poor boy, he smiles, methinks, as who should say,
'Had death been French, then death had died today'.   140

---

125 **clustering battle** fast-increasing group of soldiers
126 **drench** drown
128 **Icarus . . . pride** This further reference to the Icarus story presents the blood of the battle as the sea in which John/Icarus drowns, and so transforms the story from a tale of rash accident to one of heroic resolve. *Pride* here is morally neutral, meaning 'at the height of his glory'. See 109–10n.
129 **borne** As so often in scenes between Talbot and John there is a pun available here: borne/born, a compression of the birth-in-death idea.
130 **antic** Death is an 'antic', a mocking jester (cf. *R2* 3.2.162).

131 **Anon** soon, in a moment
132 **bonds of perpetuity** eternal bonds
133 **winged** wingèd
    lither 'supple . . . yielding' (*OED* A *adj.* 4)
134 **In thy despite** in despite of you
135 **become hard-favoured death** suit ugly death
137 **Brave** challenge
140 **death had died** death would have died. Cf. John Donne's 'Holy Sonnets', 640.14: 'And death shall be no more, Death thou shalt die'; also *Son* 146.14, 'And death once dead, there's no more dying then'. The source is 1 Corinthians, 15.26.

125 clustering] (clustring) 128.1 *Soldiers*] *Alexander* 130 antic] (antique) 137 whether] (whither)

Come, come, and lay him in his father's arms;
My spirit can no longer bear these harms. [30]
Soldiers, adieu. I have what I would have,
Now my old arms are young John Talbot's grave. *Dies.*

Enter CHARLES, ALENÇON, BURGUNDY, [*the*] BASTARD
and [JOAN] Puzel.

CHARLES

Had York and Somerset brought rescue in 145
We should have found a bloody day of this.

BASTARD

How the young whelp of Talbot's, raging wood,
Did flesh his puny sword in Frenchmen's blood.

JOAN

Once I encountered him, and thus I said:
'Thou maiden youth, be vanquished by a maid'. 150
But with a proud majestical high scorn
He answered thus: 'Young Talbot was not born [40]
To be the pillage of a giglot wench'.
So, rushing in the bowels of the French,
He left me proudly, as unworthy fight. 155

BURGUNDY

Doubtless he would have made a noble knight.
See where he lies inhearsed in the arms
Of the most bloody nurser of his harms.

---

147 **wood** mad
153 **giglot wench** light-hearted girl (with the implication of lower social class, and dubious sexual morality)
154 **the bowels . . . French** the centre of the French forces
155 **as unworthy fight** not worth fighting
157 **inhearsed** inhearsèd; enfolded, held as in a hearse
158 **bloody nurser** Talbot is physically 'nursing' John, but he is also, at least from the point of view of those who

did not witness his attempt to persuade John to escape, the cause and maintainer, so the *nurser*, of John's injuries. He is *bloody* literally and in his commitment to bloodshed, blood becoming equivalent of the nurse's milk in that it feeds the heroic. The visual image here is that of the *pietà*, the dead Christ in his mother's arms. Here it is presented in ironic relation to the Marian ideas that condition the presentation of Joan Puzel, and it continues the complex of

144 SD] *Dies. Actus Quintus. Scœna Prima. F2* 144.2 JOAN] *this edn; Pucell F* 149+ SP JOAN] *this edn; Puc., Pucel. F*

BASTARD

Hew them to pieces. Hack their bones asunder,
Whose life was England's glory, Gallia's wonder.   160

CHARLES

O no, forbear. For that which we have fled
During the life, let us not wrong it dead.   [50]

Enter [Sir William] LUCY [*with a French Herald*].

LUCY

Herald, conduct me to the Dolphin's tent,
To know who hath obtained the glory of the day.

CHARLES

On what submissive message art thou sent?   165

LUCY

Submission, Dolphin? 'Tis a mere French word:
We English warriors wot not what it means.
I come to know what prisoners thou hast ta'en,
And to survey the bodies of the dead.

CHARLES

For prisoners ask'st thou? Hell our prison is.   170

associations and meanings which place the story of Talbot and his son in a context of birth, death and the idea of patriarchal descent.

162 **let . . . dead** The source here appears to be a threat to the tomb of Bedford at Rouen, related by Hall: 'when kyng Lewes the .xj. sonne to this kyng Charles, which recovered again Normandy, did well advise and behoulde, certayne noblemen in his company, havyng more youthe then discrecion, and more envie in their hartes, then consideracions of their parentes, counsailed hym to deface and plucke doune the tombe, and to cast the deede carcasse into the feldes: affirmyng, that it was a greate dishonor, bothe to the kyng and to the realme, to se the enemie of his

father, and theirs, to have so solempne & riche memorial. Kyng Lewes aunswered again, saiyng: what honor shall it be to us, or to you, to breake this monument, and to pull out of the ground and take up, the deed bones of hym, whom in his life, neither my father, nor your progenitors, with all their power . . . wer once able, to make flie one foote backeward' (Bullough, 3.65–6).

166 **mere** primarily in the now nearly obsolete sense of 'purely' or 'absolutely', but also with the belittling modern sense of 'only', 'no more than'

167 **wot** know

170 **Hell . . . is** They have killed the English, rather than captured them, and have sent them to hell, so no other prison is necessary.

162.1] *Capell (subst.)*   164] *Pope lines* know / day. /   To know who] Who *Hanmer*

But tell me whom thou seek'st.

LUCY

But where's the great Alcides of the field? –   [60]
Valiant Lord Talbot, Earl of Shrewsbury,
Created for his rare success in arms
Great Earl of Washford, Waterford and Valence,   175
Lord Talbot of Goodrig and Urchinfield,
Lord Strange of Blackmere, Lord Verdon of Alton,
Lord Cromwell of Wingfield, Lord Furnival of
    Sheffield,
The thrice victorious Lord of Falconbridge,
Knight of the noble order of Saint George,   180
Worthy Saint Michael and the Golden Fleece,
Great marshal to Henry the Sixth   [70]
Of all his wars within the realm of France.

JOAN

Here's a silly stately style indeed:
The Turk, that two and fifty kingdoms hath,   185

---

172 **Alcides** another name for the hero Hercules, used also at 2.3.18 as comparison to Talbot

173–83 Cairncross (Ard[2]) gives a possible source of this epitaph as 'Roger Cotton's *Armor of Proofe*, 1596 (Miss J. Pearce in *MLN*, 59.327–9)'. The context of this is an argument for dating 'Shakespeare's revision' of existing material, but it is of course likely that Cotton is repeating a formula that could have existed in many sources now lost. The historical Talbot was created Earl of Waterford when he became Governor of Ireland, but the other titles were inherited; the syntax allows Lucy to blur the distinction, and strictly speaking the list has little to do with 'rare success in arms'.

175 **Washford** Wexford, in the south-east of Ireland

184 **style** title, style of address

185 **The Turk** Turkish rulers were proverbial for grandiloquence and pomposity; there are many examples in plays of this period, most notably Bajazet in Marlowe's *1 Tamburlaine*. But there is a more precise reference, pointing up the pettiness of the internal strifes of Christendom. In the same year as Talbot's defeat, as Hall notes, 'yet a greater detryment hapned in the same season to the whole flocke of Christen people. For Machumet, called the great Turk, beseaged the citie of Constantynople in Grece . . . and . . . toke it perforce' (Bullough, 3.74). *H5* adds another layer to the irony here: when Henry woos Katherine he hopes that their child –

---

172 But where's] Where is *Rowe*   176 Goodrig] Goodrich *Oxf*   178 Lord Cromwell . . . Furnival] Cromwell of Wingfield, Furnival *Ard*[2]   181 Worthy . . . Michael] – Worthy . . . Michael – *(Cam[2])* 182 Henry] our King Henry *F2*

Writes not so tedious a style as this.
Him that thou magnifiest with all these titles
Stinking and fly-blown lies here at our feet.

LUCY

Is Talbot slain, the Frenchmen's only scourge,
Your kingdom's terror and black Nemesis?   190
O, were mine eyeballs into bullets turned,
That I in rage might shoot them at your faces.   [80]
O, that I could but call these dead to life,
It were enough to fright the realm of France.
Were but his picture left amongst you here   195
It would amaze the proudest of you all.
Give me their bodies that I may bear them hence
And give them burial as beseems their worth.

JOAN

I think this upstart is old Talbot's ghost,
He speaks with such a proud commanding spirit.   200
For God's sake let him have him: to keep them here,
They would but stink, and putrefy the air.   [90]

CHARLES

Go, take their bodies hence.

LUCY   I'll bear them hence;
But from their ashes shall be reared

to be Henry VI – will 'take the Turk by
the beard' (5.2.206–7).

188 **fly-blown** implying that flies have
started to swarm around the corpse
and to lay their eggs in it

190 **Nemesis** the Greek word for divine
punishment, often seen to follow
hubris, or pride, here the misplaced
pride of the French. It was often personified, usually as a female figure.

195 **his picture** There is a reminiscence
here of the Countess of Auvergne

scene, and the shadow/substance distinction instigated by her possession of
his picture, and Talbot's demonstration of where the 'substance' of his
power lies. See 2.3.35–65.

196 **amaze** startle, confuse

198 **beseems** suits

199 **upstart** insolent man (with the implication that he is not socially entitled to
the confidence his manner suggests)

202 **putrefy** corrupt, turn rotten

187 magnifiest] *(*magnifi'st*)*   197 may bear] bear *Ard²*   201 have him] have 'em *Theobald*   203–4
I'll . . . reared] *Pope; one line F*   204 ashes] ashes, Dauphin, *Pope;* noble ashes *(Ard²)*

253

A phoenix that shall make all France afeared. 205

CHARLES

So we be rid of them, do with him what thou wilt.
And now to Paris, in this conquering vein.
All will be ours, now bloody Talbot's slain. *Exeunt.*

[5.1] *Sennet. Enter* KING, GLOUCESTER *and* EXETER.

KING

Have you perused the letters from the Pope,
The Emperor and the Earl of Armagnac?

GLOUCESTER

I have, my lord, and their intent is this:
They humbly sue unto your excellence
To have a godly peace concluded of 5
Between the realms of England and of France.

KING

How doth your grace affect their motion?

GLOUCESTER

Well, my good lord, and as the only means
To stop effusion of our Christian blood
And 'stablish quietness on every side. 10

KING

Ay marry, uncle, for I always thought
It was both impious and unnatural

---

205 **phoenix** According to myth there is only ever one phoenix bird at any one time, but it regenerates itself from the ashes of its funeral pyre, in the deserts of Arabia, so it is an emblem of the survival of individual worth in defiance of the logic of natural survival.

207 **this conquering vein** Perhaps there is a hint of, though not an exact verbal reference to, Marlowe's *Tamburlaine* here.

5.1.2 **The Emperor** Hall mentions a peace-making intervention of the Emperor Sigismund and Pope Eugenius IV in 1435, which, while it failed to negotiate any agreement between the English and the French, did seem to have prompted Burgundy's change of sides (Bullough, 3.63).

5 **a godly peace** Bullough gives the source of this phrase as Holinshed (3.63n.).

7 **affect their motion** like their proposal

205 afeared] afeard. *Exeunt Lucy and Attendants with the bodies. Ard², after Capell* 206 rid of them] rid *Capell* him] them *F2* 208 SD *Exeunt*] *Rowe; Exit. F* 5.1] *Capell* (V.i); *Scena secunda. F*

That such immanity and bloody strife
Should reign among professors of one faith.

GLOUCESTER

Beside, my lord, the sooner to effect   15
And surer bind this knot of amity,
The Earl of Armagnac – near knit to Charles,
A man of great authority in France –
Proffers his only daughter to your grace
In marriage, with a large and sumptuous dowry.   20

KING

Marriage, uncle? Alas, my years are young,
And fitter is my study and my books
Than wanton dalliance with a paramour.
Yet call th'ambassadors and, as you please,
So let them have their answers every one.   25
I shall be well content with any choice
Tends to God's glory and my country's weal.

Enter WINCHESTER *and three* Ambassadors [*among them the papal* Legate *and an ambassador from the Earl of Armagnac*].

13 **immanity** monstrous cruelty (*OED* 2)
17 **near knit** closely tied
17–19 **Earl . . . only daughter** Gloucester or the playwrights part company with the chronicles here. As Hall records, Armagnac's motivation was to secure Henry's support against Charles, who seized the Earl and his daughters in retaliation (Bullough, 3.70–1). The Earl declared his support for Charles in 1433, but was never wholly reliable. Henry here is offered the chance of a match with 'one of the daughters of the greatest of the southern French nobility . . . Such a match might give to English Gascony the kind of security which direct military aid

from England could not . . . It was certain, on the other hand, to anger King Charles' (Griffiths, 461–2). Hall mentions several daughters; Gloucester is exaggerating the special nature of the Earl's offer. Or perhaps at this point the play reflects the account of Holinshed, who mentions only one daughter (Bullough, 3.623–4).
20 **sumptuous** rich
23 **wanton . . . paramour** pleasure with a lover
27 **weal** good government
27.2 *papal* **Legate** brings both a letter of intercession and – at last – confirmation of Winchester's elevation to a cardinal's seat.

17 knit] kin *Pope*   25 one] one. *Exit Attendant Cam*² 27.1] *Enter* WINCHESTER *in Cardinal's habit, a Legate and two Ambassadors. Ard*², *after Capell; among . . . Armagnac*] *this edn*

255

EXETER

What, is my lord of Winchester installed
And called unto a cardinal's degree?
Then, I perceive, that will be verified   30
Henry the Fifth did sometime prophesy:
'If once he come to be a cardinal
He'll make his cap co-equal with the crown'.

KING

My lords ambassadors, your several suits
Have been considered and debated on.   35
Your purpose is both good and reasonable,
And therefore are we certainly resolved
To draw conditions of a friendly peace,
Which by my lord of Winchester we mean
Shall be transported presently to France.   40

GLOUCESTER [*to the Ambassador of the Earl of Armagnac*]

And for the proffer of my lord your master,
I have informed his highness so at large
As, liking of the lady's virtuous gifts,
Her beauty and the value of her dower,
He doth intend she shall be England's queen.   45

KING

In argument and proof of which contract,

---

29 **degree** rank
31–3 Exeter, as Henry V's brother and so
a memorialist of the last reign, takes on
a choric function here, in order to
mark Winchester's finally unambiguous assumption of a cardinal's status
and to remind us, as he had at
3.1.197–203, of a 'prophecy' made by
Henry V. According to Hall, 'knowyng
the haute corage, and the ambicious
mynde of the man, prohibited hym on
his allegeaunce once, either to sue for
or to take, meanyng that Cardinalles

Hattes should not presume to bee egall
with Princes' (Bullough, 3.51–2).
31 **sometime** once
33 **cap** reference to *the cardinal's hat* (cf.
1.3.36), but put in a belittling form.
'To set one's cap at' something is to
aim at it.
34 **your several suits** your individual
requests
40 **presently** at once
42–3 **so . . . As** so fully that
46 **In argument** as demonstration

28 What] *aside* What *Munro*   41 SD] *this edn*

Bear her this jewel, pledge of my affection.
    [*Gives the Ambassador a ring.*]
And so, my lord Protector, see them guarded,
And safely brought to Dover, wherein shipped,
Commit them to the fortune of the sea.   50
                        Exeunt [all but Winchester,
                        who keeps back the papal Legate].

WINCHESTER

Stay, my lord legate. You shall first receive
The sum of money which I promised
Should be delivered to his holiness
For clothing me in these grave ornaments.

LEGATE

I will attend upon your lordship's leisure.   55

WINCHESTER

Now Winchester will not submit, I trow,
Or be inferior to the proudest peer;
Humphrey of Gloucester, thou shalt well perceive
That neither in birth or for authority
The Bishop will be overborne by thee.   60
I'll either make thee stoop and bend thy knee,
Or sack this country with a mutiny.   *Exeunt.*

---

49 **wherein shipped** *Wherein* is an awkward way of referring to a town, so
F4's 'where, inshipped' is possible,
though an unusual form; *OED* cites F4
as its main example of the verb 'inship'
for embark, so the argument is somewhat circular.

52 **promised** promisèd

55 But, if, as in F, the Legate remains on
stage, he must be out of earshot of
Winchester.

60 **overborne** See 3.1.53 and 4.4.129.
The pun (born/borne) becomes possible here, as Winchester may reflect on
his own illegitimate, and Gloucester's
legitimate, birth.

47 SD] *this edn*   49 wherein shipped] where, inshipped *F4*   50.1–2 *all . . . Legate] Capell subst.*
55 leisure.] leisure. *Exit / Dyce*   59 neither] nor *Pope*

[5.2]   *Enter* CHARLES, BURGUNDY, ALENÇON,
          [*the*] BASTARD, REIGNIER *and* JOAN.

CHARLES

These news, my lords, may cheer our drooping spirits:
'Tis said the stout Parisians do revolt
And turn again unto the warlike French.

ALENÇON

Then march to Paris, royal Charles of France,
And keep not back your powers in dalliance.   5

JOAN

Peace be amongst them if they turn to us;
Else ruin combat with their palaces.

Enter Scout.

SCOUT

Success unto our valiant general
And happiness to his accomplices.

CHARLES

What tidings send our scouts? I prithee, speak.   10

SCOUT

The English army, that divided was
Into two parties, is now conjoined in one
And means to give you battle presently.

CHARLES

Somewhat too sudden, sirs, the warning is;

5.2.2 stout sturdy
   Parisians do revolt But, technically,
   in this play at least, the oath of allegiance to Henry has not been explicitly sworn – unless one takes this line in
   itself as evidence that it was. See
   4.1.3n. and 5.3.169–72n.
4 royal Charles It is important to the
   play's sense of the weakening of

English power that Charles becomes
increasingly apparent as the *de facto*
King of France, despite the English
unwillingness to recognize his title.
See also 1.1.92n.
5 dalliance wasteful delay
7 ruin combat with let forces of
   destruction attack
13,15 presently immediately

5.2] *Capell; Scœna Tertia.* F   0.2 JOAN] *(Ione); La Pucelle Cam*   7 combat with] come within
Ard²   12 is now conjoined] now conjoins *(Ard²)*

But we will presently provide for them.   15
BURGUNDY

I trust the ghost of Talbot is not there.

Now he is gone, my lord, you need not fear.
JOAN

Of all base passions, fear is most accursed.

Command the conquest, Charles, it shall be thine:

Let Henry fret, and all the world repine.   20
CHARLES

Then on, my lords, and France be fortunate.   *Exeunt.*

Alarum. Excursions. Enter JOAN Puzel.   [5.3]

JOAN

The regent conquers and the Frenchmen fly.

Now help, ye charming spells and periapts,

And ye, choice spirits that admonish me   24

And give me signs of future accidents.   *Thunder.*

You speedy helpers, that are substitutes

Under the lordly monarch of the north,

20 **repine** complain

22 **regent** York

23 **periapts** written charms, inscribed on a bandage and wrapped around a part of the body which they were deemed to protect. Henslowe's diary contains a formula, written in a hand other than Henslowe's, for a periapt to grant wishes: '+ wryte these wordes in virgins parchement wth the blood of a batt vppon tewseday morning betwixt v or vj in the morning or at nighte . halia J K.turbutzi & tye yt abowt thy left arme and aske what ye will have' (Henslowe, 40).

25 **signs . . . accidents** coded prophecies of events. The historical Jeanne at her trial was accused of witchcraft, and both Holinshed and Hall hint at a connection of Joan with magic, though their attitude seems basically sceptical. This moment in the play has disappointed critics by

seeming to make too unambiguous an identification of Joan's powers with the forces of darkness. See Introduction, pp. 33–6.

26 **substitutes** deputies

27 **lordly . . . north** name for the devil derived from Isaiah, 14.13: Lucifer sets up his throne 'upon the mount of the Congregacion in the sides of the North'. Nashe, *Piers Penniless*, gives a more detailed account of demonic ecology: 'The second kind of Devils which he most imploieth, are those Northerne *Marcij*, called the spirits of revenge, & the authors of massacres, and seedesmen of mischiefe' (Nashe, 1.230.19–21). The Rose playhouse was so oriented that those of the audience who faced the stage directly (in most performances probably the majority) faced north-north-west. This was

21 SD–21.1 *Exeunt . . . Puzel*] *(Exeunt. Alarum. Excursions. / Enter Ione de Pucell); Exeunt, marching.*
SCENE III – *The same. Under* Angiers. *Enter / Capell*

259

Appear, and aid me in this enterprise.

Enter Fiends.

This speedy and quick appearance argues proof
Of your accustomed diligence to me.   30
Now, ye familiar spirits, that are culled   [10]
Out of the powerful regions under earth,
Help me this once, that France may get the field.
   They walk, and speak not.
O hold me not with silence over-long:
Where I was wont to feed you with my blood,   35
I'll lop a member off and give it you
In earnest of a further benefit
So you do condescend to help me now.
   They hang their heads.
No hope to have redress? My body shall
Pay recompense if you will grant my suit.   40
   They shake their heads.
Cannot my body nor blood sacrifice   [20]
Entreat you to your wonted furtherance?

presumably in order to make the most
efficient use of available light, but it
also suggests where Puzel's devils
might appear – 'above' and/or from
the back of the platform, or through a
trap from *under earth* (32).
29–30 **argues proof / Of** establishes
31 **familiar spirits** See 3.2.120n.
32 **powerful regions** Some editions have
emended F's 'regions' to 'legions' in
reference to Mark, 5.9, 'My name *is*
Legion: for we are manie', but the
point is probably simpler; F's *regions*
refers to the infernal environs where
the spirits dwell. See also 4.3.69n.
33 **get the field** gain control of the battle
36 **lop** chop

37 **In earnest of** as a token of
38 **So** If, provided that
   condescend literally, 'come down vol-
untarily' (*OED v.* I); this may have
some relevance to the placing of the
demons on stage (28.1) but, more likely, reflects the Fiends' awareness of
their superior powers.
39 **redress** help
41 **blood sacrifice** Actresses, Janet
Suzman in *The Wars of the Roses*, for
example, have represented Joan cutting herself at this point, but the *sacrifice* she refers to could equally well be
the death of her enemies.
42 **wonted furtherance** usual assistance

29 speedy and quick] speed and quick *Dyce;* speedy quick *Pope*   32 regions] legions *Singer*
(Warburton)

Then take my soul – my body, soul, and all –
Before that England give the French the foil.   *They depart.*
See, they forsake me. Now the time is come   45
That France must vail her lofty-plumed crest,
And let her head fall into England's lap.
My ancient incantations are too weak,
And hell too strong for me to buckle with.   49
Now, France, thy glory droopeth to the dust.   *Exit.*

Excursions: BURGUNDY *and* YORK [*enter and*] *fight hand to hand.*
French [*enter with* JOAN *and*] *fly.* [*York captures Joan Puzel.*]

YORK

Damsel of France, I think I have you fast.   [30]
Unchain your spirits now with spelling charms
And try if they can gain your liberty.
A goodly prize, fit for the devil's grace.
See how the ugly witch doth bend her brows   55
As if, with Circe, she would change my shape.

---

46 **vail** lower
plumed plumèd
48 **ancient** This leaves it open whether her
spells have an ancient provenance, and
so link her into the classical tradition of
witches such as Erichtho and Medea, or
whether she simply means 'usual',
'often-used'. See Introduction, pp.
33–9.
49 **buckle with** engage with
50.1 BURGUNDY *and* YORK Both Hall
and Holinshed are clear that the capture of Joan was a joint Anglo-
Burgundian initiative. If it is to be
Burgundy who fights York, rather than
Joan herself, that will emphasize his
change of sides earlier in the play.
After her intimations of defeat in the
scene with the *Fiends* Joan Puzel has
either simply stopped bothering to
fight, or lost her demonic power, so

that Burgundy must now attempt to
protect her. The BBC version has York
pursue Burgundy, and kill him at
Joan's feet, which is nonsensical on any
reading of the history, but understand-
able as an attempt to make sense of a
somewhat confusing SD.
52 **with spelling charms** by casting
spells
54 **devils grace** devil's favour. *OED*
describes 'divel', the spelling of the
word in F, as obsolete; but as a spoken
form at least it is still current in Irish
English.
55 **bend her brows** frown in concentra-
tion
56 **Circe** In Homer's *Odyssey* (10,
133–574) she transforms some of
Odysseus' men to swine, before being
defeated by the hero.

50.1 *enter and*] *this edn*   50.2] *The French fly, leaving* LA PUCELLE *in* YORK's *power* / *Tucker Brooke*
enter . . . and] *this edn*   *York . . . Puzel*] *this edn*   54 devil's] *(divels)*

JOAN

    Changed to a worser shape thou canst not be.

YORK

    O, Charles the Dolphin is a proper man;

    No shape but his can please your dainty eye.

JOAN

    A plaguing mischief light on Charles and thee,   60

    And may ye both be suddenly surprised   [40]

    By bloody hands, in sleeping on your beds.

YORK

    Fell banning hag, enchantress, hold thy tongue.

JOAN

    I prithee, give me leave to curse awhile.   64

YORK

    Curse, miscreant, when thou com'st to the stake.   *Exeunt.*

Alarum. Enter SUFFOLK *with* MARGARET *in his hand.*

SUFFOLK   '

    Be what thou wilt, thou art my prisoner.   *Gazes on her.*

---

59 **dainty** choosy

60–2 Joan Puzel's prophecy here is without force, as would be particularly clear in York's case to an audience that knew *3H6*. There York is killed after military defeat at the hands of Margaret and her forces, in a ritual that grotesquely parodies his designs on the crown (*3H6* 1.4).

62 **in** while

63 **Fell** ominous; ugly
    banning cursing

65 **miscreant** wrongdoer, with a sense of heretic or unbeliever

65.1 *Enter . . . Margaret* This 'capture' of Margaret by Suffolk is invented by the dramatists – according to Hall, Suffolk, 'extendyng his commission to the uttermoste, without assent of his associates, imagened in his phantasie, that the nexte waie to come to a perfite peace,

was to move some mariage, betwene the Frenche kynges kynsewoman, and kyng Henry his sovereigne: & because the Frenche kyng had no doughter of ripe age . . . he desired to have the Lady Margaret, cosyn to the Frenche kyng, and doughter to Reyner duke of Anjow, callyng hymself kyng of Scicile, Naples, and Hierusalem, havyng onely the name and stile of the same, without any peny profite, or fote of possession' (Bullough, 3.71). Though it is not clear at this point in Hall's narrative what the nature of Suffolk's interest in Margaret is, Hall's planting of the word 'desired' sets up an innuendo that the play expands on. Their encounter is a conflation of the military and the erotic, in symmetrical apposition to the capture of Joan by York.

65 SD] *Exeunt.* 5.5 *Oxf*

O fairest beauty, do not fear nor fly,

For I will touch thee but with reverent hands;

I kiss these fingers for eternal peace

And lay them gently on thy tender side.   70

Who art thou? Say, that I may honour thee.   [50]

MARGARET

Margaret my name, and daughter to a king,

The King of Naples – whosoe'er thou art.

SUFFOLK

An earl I am, and Suffolk am I called.

Be not offended, Nature's miracle;   75

Thou art allotted to be ta'en by me.

So doth the swan her downy cygnets save,

Keeping them prisoner underneath his wings.

Yet, if this servile usage once offend,

Go, and be free again as Suffolk's friend.   *She is going.*   80

O stay: [*to himself*] I have no power to let her pass.   [60]

My hand would free her, but my heart says no.

As plays the sun upon the glassy streams,

Twinkling another counterfeited beam,

So seems this gorgeous beauty to mine eyes.   85

Fain would I woo her, yet I dare not speak.

I'll call for pen and ink and write my mind.

69 **these fingers** The fingers could be either Margaret's, or Suffolk's own. If Margaret's, then Suffolk is demonstrating that she is free to go if she wishes. If his, the opposite is intended, but he conveys that holding on to her is a kind of reverence.

77 **swan** known not only for its aristocratic grace, but also for its ferocity in protecting its young. The shift from *her* to *his* in line 78 is the effect of Suffolk bringing the analogy closer to himself, and thus creating a hermaphroditic amalgam, both enticing and threaten-ing to Margaret, of feminine 'protectiveness' and a male imprisoning force.

81 SD *Suffolk speaks to himself until 121, after Margaret begins to mock him, imitating his self-absorption. See Introduction, p. 99.

87 There is a parallel here with *E3*, and a similarly illicit wooing, the King's of the Countess of Salisbury, where the wooer finds writing an easier medium than speech (2.1.48–184). Writing interacts here, as so often in this play, with the idea of the 'counterfeit', to create a sense of delusive and narcissistic self-projection.

68 reverent] *Hanmer;* reverend *F*   69–70 *lines reversed in Capell*   71 thou? Say,] *Oxf ;* thou, say? *F*   77 her] his *Oxf*   78 his] her *F3*   81+ SD *to himself*] *this edn; Aside / Pope*

Fie, de la Pole, disable not thyself:
Hast not a tongue? Is she not here?
Wilt thou be daunted at a woman's sight?   90
Ay. Beauty's princely majesty is such   [70]
Confounds the tongue, and makes the senses rough.

MARGARET
Say, Earl of Suffolk – if thy name be so –
What ransom must I pay before I pass?
For I perceive I am thy prisoner.   95

SUFFOLK [*to himself*]
How canst thou tell she will deny thy suit
Before thou make a trial of her love?

MARGARET
Why speak'st thou not? What ransom must I pay?

SUFFOLK [*to himself*]
She's beautiful, and therefore to be wooed:
She is a woman, therefore to be won.   100

MARGARET [*to herself*]
Wilt thou accept of ransom, yea or no?   [80]

SUFFOLK [*to himself*]
Fond man, remember that thou hast a wife.
Then how can Margaret be thy paramour?

MARGARET [*to herself*]
I were best to leave him, for he will not hear.

SUFFOLK [*to himself*]
There all is marred; there lies a cooling card.   105

---

88 **de la Pole** For this form of Suffolk's name, and the contrast to York's use of 'Poole' in the rose garden scene, see 2.4.0.2n. and Appendix 1.
disable not thyself do not disparage yourself
92 **makes . . . rough** blunts the senses
97 **make . . . of** attempt to win

99–100 a commonplace, with many parallels in plays of this period. See, for example, *Tit* 1.1.582–4 (Ard³; other edns 2.1.82–5) and *R3* 1.2.227–8.
102 **Fond** foolish
wife Suffolk had married Alice, the second wife, and widow, of Salisbury.
105 **cooling card** according to *OED* card

89 here?] heere thy prisoner? *F2;* prisoner here *Ard²;* here to hear *Oxf*   92 makes . . . rough] mocks the sense of touch *Collier;* Makes the senses nought. *(Vaughan)*   104, 106 SD [*to herself*] *this edn; Aside / Theobald*   104 I were] 'Twere *Pope*

MARGARET [*to herself*]

   He talks at random: sure the man is mad.

SUFFOLK [*to himself*]

   And yet a dispensation may be had.

MARGARET

   And yet I would that you would answer me.

SUFFOLK [*to himself*]

   I'll win this Lady Margaret. For whom?

   Why, for my king. Tush, that's a wooden thing.   110

MARGARET

   He talks of wood: it is some carpenter.   [90]

SUFFOLK [*to himself*]

   Yet so my fancy may be satisfied,

   And peace established between these realms.

   But there remains a scruple in that too:

   For though her father be the King of Naples,   115

   Duke of Anjou and Maine, yet is he poor

   And our nobility will scorn the match.

MARGARET

   Hear ye, captain? Are you not at leisure?

SUFFOLK [*to himself*]

   It shall be so, disdain they ne'er so much.

   Henry is youthful, and will quickly yield.   120

---

sb.[2] 2a, 'apparently a term of some unknown game, applied *fig.* or punningly to anything that "cools" a person's passion or enthusiasm'

107 **dispensation** a dissolution of the marriage, to be granted by the Pope in the period of the events dramatized, and in the late sixteenth century by 'the *Archbishop* of *Canterbury*' (Jacob); ironically, given Suffolk's purpose

110 **wooden thing** *OED* I 2 *fig.* b 'dull or dead as the sound of wood when struck'. The word *king* has no force for Suffolk in his present state of mind.

113 **established** establishèd

114 **scruple** cause for doubt

115–16 For Reignier's titles, see note on List of Roles (pp. 112–13).

118 **captain** Margaret is addressing Suffolk by a provocatively unflattering title; this is his rank within the army, but one might expect her to acknowledge his aristocratic status.

119 **disdain** disapprove

106 random] (randon)

[*to Margaret*] Madam, I have a secret to reveal.   [100]
MARGARET [*to herself*]
   What though I be enthralled? He seems a knight,
   And will not any way dishonour me.
SUFFOLK
   Lady, vouchsafe to listen what I say.
MARGARET [*to herself*]
   Perhaps I shall be rescued by the French,   125
   And then I need not crave his courtesy.
SUFFOLK
   Sweet madam, give me hearing in a cause.
MARGARET [*to herself*]
   Tush, women have been captivate ere now.
SUFFOLK
   Lady, wherefore talk you so?
MARGARET
   I cry you mercy, 'tis but *quid* for *quo*.   130
SUFFOLK
   Say, gentle princess, would you not suppose   [110]
   Your bondage happy, to be made a queen?
MARGARET
   To be a queen in bondage is more vile
   Than is a slave in base servility;
   For princes should be free.
SUFFOLK   And so shall you,   135
   If happy England's royal king be free.
MARGARET
   Why, what concerns his freedom unto me?

---

122 SD *Margaret continues talking to
   herself until 130.
   enthralled Margaret plays between a
   literal (enslaved) and a metaphorical,
   erotic (spellbound), sense.
127 **cause** serious proposition – with

legal and business connotations
128 **captivate** captivated; see 122n. She is
   transforming the hazards of her immediate situation into a courtly love game.
130 *quid* for *quo* one thing for another,
   fair exchange.

121 SD] *this edn* 122, 125, 128 SD] *this edn; Aside / Theobald* 129 Lady] Lady, sweet lady
(Walker); Nay, hear me, lady *Capell*

SUFFOLK

    I'll undertake to make thee Henry's queen,

    To put a golden sceptre in thy hand

    And set a precious crown upon thy head,   140

    If thou wilt condescend to be my –

MARGARET   What?   [120]

SUFFOLK

    His love.

MARGARET

    I am unworthy to be Henry's wife.

SUFFOLK

    No, gentle madam; I unworthy am

    To woo so fair a dame to be his wife –   145

    And have no portion in the choice myself.

    How say you, madam, are ye so content?

MARGARET

    An if my father please, I am content.

SUFFOLK

    Then call our captains and our colours forth,

    And, madam, at your father's castle walls   150

    We'll crave a parley to confer with him.   [130]

              Sound [trumpets, at Suffolk's command].

Enter REIGNIER *on the walls.*

144–6 **unworthy . . . portion** Suffolk reverses his ostensible meaning in 144–5 (*unworthy*) by the addition of his next line (146).

150 **castle walls** There has been no sense till now that the action takes place anywhere near Reignier's castle. The layout of the scene thus becomes more diagrammatic than realistic; the stage architecture, possibly used for spectac-ularly 'diabolic' effect at 23–44 now becomes the castle in Anjou (at some distance from the place of Joan's capture at Compiègne). The shift in theatrical style creates a bathetic dwindling of the action from an epic to a comic/erotic 'fabliau' theatrical style (see Introduction, p.14).

151 **confer with** speak to

149 forth,] forth. *Enter Captains, Colours, and Trumpeters Oxf* 151 SD *trumpets*] *this edn; Trumpet sounds a parley: Is answer'd from within. / Capell at Suffolk's command] this edn*

　　See, Reignier, see, thy daughter prisoner.

REIGNIER

　　To whom?

SUFFOLK　　　　To me.

REIGNIER　　　　　　　　Suffolk, what remedy?

　　I am a soldier, and unapt to weep,

　　Or to exclaim on fortune's fickleness.　　　　　　　155

SUFFOLK

　　Yes, there is remedy enough, my lord.

　　Consent – and for thy honour give consent –

　　Thy daughter shall be wedded to my king,

　　Whom I with pain have wooed and won thereto,

　　And this, her easy-held imprisonment,　　　　　　160

　　Hath gained thy daughter princely liberty.　　　　　[140]

REIGNIER

　　Speaks Suffolk as he thinks?

SUFFOLK　　　　　　　　　　Fair Margaret knows

　　That Suffolk doth not flatter, face or feign.

REIGNIER

　　Upon thy princely warrant I descend

　　To give thee answer of thy just demand.　　　　　165

　　　　　　　　　　　[*Exit Reignier from the walls.*]

SUFFOLK

　　And here I will expect thy coming.　　　　*Trumpets sound.*

Enter REIGNIER.

---

154 **unapt** not inclined

157 **and . . . consent** Suffolk emphasizes
that Reignier will gain status (*honour* in
that sense) from the apparently dishonourable trading of his daughter.

160 **easy-held** comfortable. He draws
attention, probably for Margaret's

benefit, to the ambiguously erotic and
aggressive act of his taking hold of her
(cf. 65.1–70).

163 **face** 'To show a false face' (*OED v.* I k)

164 **Upon . . . warrant** given a guarantee
sanctioned by your king, or by a high-
ranking noble such as Suffolk

165 SD] *Capell (subst.)*　166 coming.] coming, Reignier. *Capell*　166.1] *Enter* REIGNIER *below. /
Capell*

REIGNIER

Welcome, brave earl, into our territories.

Command in Anjou what your honour pleases.

SUFFOLK

Thanks, Reignier, happy for so sweet a child,

Fit to be made companion with a king.   170

What answer makes your grace unto my suit?   [150]

REIGNIER

Since thou dost deign to woo her little worth

To be the princely bride of such a lord –

Upon condition I may quietly

Enjoy mine own, the country Maine and Anjou,   175

Free from oppression or the stroke of war –

My daughter shall be Henry's, if he please.

SUFFOLK

That is her ransom. I deliver her,

And those two counties I will undertake

Your grace shall well and quietly enjoy.   180

REIGNIER

And I – again in Henry's royal name,   [160]

As deputy unto that gracious king –

Give thee her hand for sign of plighted faith.

SUFFOLK

Reignier of France, I give thee kingly thanks,

Because this is in traffic of a king.   185

And yet methinks I could be well content

---

167 Reignier's offer of hospitality does not imply a handing over of his *territories* to the English forces – rather it confirms his possession of them. From the English point of view, Anjou is not his at all; so his use of *our* could be heard as provocative.

169 **happy for** fortunate in

172 **her little worth** her lowly state

175 **country . . . Anjou** contiguous provinces of France. *Country*, like *counties* (179), is less politically specific than in modern usage. It refers simply to a tract of land.

185 **in traffic . . . king** in a king's business – or 'in the selling of a king'

175 country] countries *Capell;* county *Malone*   186 And yet] *Aside.* And yet *Rowe*

To be mine own attorney in this case.
I'll over then to England with this news,
And make this marriage to be solemnized.
So farewell, Reignier; set this diamond safe   190
In golden palaces, as it becomes.   [170]

REIGNIER

I do embrace thee, as I would embrace
The Christian prince King Henry were he here.

MARGARET

Farewell, my lord. Good wishes, praise and prayers
Shall Suffolk ever have of Margaret.   195

    [Exit Reignier.] She is going [after him, when Suffolk stops her].

SUFFOLK

Farewell, sweet madam; but hark you, Margaret –
No princely commendations to my king?

MARGARET

Such commendations as becomes a maid,
A virgin and his servant, say to him.

SUFFOLK

Words sweetly placed, and modesty directed.   200
But, madam, I must trouble you again –   [180]
No loving token to his majesty?

MARGARET

Yes, my good lord: a pure unspotted heart,
Never yet taint with love, I send the King.

SUFFOLK

And this withal.   *Kisses her.*   205

---

187 to represent myself in this negotiation (rather than the King)
190 **set** a metaphor from 'setting' a jewel
in precious metal
191 **as it becomes** as is fitting
200 **modesty** An emendation to 'modestly' might make more immediate sense,
but this is not nonsensical as it stands

– *modesty* is parallel here to *words*; the
effect, at least, of modesty is *directed* to
Suffolk with all the strategic force that
words and actions can possess. Suffolk
is charmed by the effect without being
wholly taken in by it.
204 **taint** touched, stained
205 **withal** in addition

195 SD *Exit . . . Reignier] this edn after . . . her] this edn* 196 madam] maid *Ard²* 200 modesty]
modestly *F2* 205 SD] *(Kisse her.)*

MARGARET

That for thyself. I will not so presume

To send such peevish tokens to a king.   [*Exit.*]

SUFFOLK

O wert thou for myself! But Suffolk, stay,

Thou mayst not wander in that labyrinth:

There Minotaurs and ugly treasons lurk.   210

Solicit Henry with her wondrous praise,   [190]

Bethink thee on her virtues that surmount,

Mad natural graces that extinguish art;

Repeat their semblance often on the seas,

That when thou com'st to kneel at Henry's feet   215

Thou mayst bereave him of his wits with wonder.   *Exit.*

[**5.3**]   *Enter* YORK, WARWICK, Shepherd *and* [JOAN] Puzel.

YORK

Bring forth that sorceress condemned to burn.

SHEPHERD

Ah, Joan, this kills thy father's heart outright.

Have I sought every country far and near

---

207 **peevish** feeble

209 **labyrinth** For the source of this idea
in Hall, see 4.4.109–10n. Where earlier the focus was on the maker of the
labyrinth, Daedalus, and on Icarus his
son, here the aspect of the myth in
focus is that of illegitimate and 'unnatural' relationship, as typified by
Pasiphae's love for a bull, whose offspring, the *Minotaur*, the labyrinth was
constructed to hide. Suffolk's primary
meaning is, of course, that he is lost in
a maze of transgressive erotic feeling.

211 **Solicit** seek to persuade
    her wondrous praise dazzling praise
    of her

212 **surmount** excel

213 **Mad** Both metre and sense are better without *Mad*; this syllable may be
the start of a first thought in the
manuscript ('maidenly', perhaps),
only half erased and then mistakenly
set by the printer. But this is speculation as *natural* can be disyllabic, and
the idea that Suffolk finds Margaret's
flirtatiousness attractively, even
gracefully, wild has its appeal.

214 **Repeat their semblance** recall their
appearance

216 **bereave** deprive

5.3.3 **country** region

---

207 SD] *this edn; Exeunt* Reignier *and* Margaret. *Capell*   213 Mad] And *Capell;* 'Mid *Collier²;*
Maid *Cam (Perring)*   5.3] *Capell*   0.1] *(Pucell); Enter* YORK, WARWICK, *and Others. / Capell;*
Enter YORK, WARWICK, *a* SHEPHERD, LA PUCELLE *guarded, and others Cam²*   1 burn.] burn. *Enter*
LA PUCELLE *guarded and a* Shepherd. *Ard², after Capell*

271

And – now it is my chance to find thee out –
Must I behold thy timeless cruel death?   5
Ah, Joan, sweet daughter Joan, I'll die with thee.

JOAN

Decrepit miser, base ignoble wretch,
I am descended of a gentler blood.
Thou art no father, nor no friend of mine.

SHEPHERD

Out, out! My lords, an please you, 'tis not so.   10
I did beget her, all the parish knows.
Her mother liveth yet, can testify
She was the first fruit of my bachelorship.

WARWICK

Graceless, wilt thou deny thy parentage?

YORK

This argues what her kind of life hath been –   15
Wicked and vile, and so her death concludes.

SHEPHERD

Fie, Joan, that thou wilt be so obstacle.
God knows, thou art a collop of my flesh,
And for thy sake have I shed many a tear.
Deny me not, I prithee, gentle Joan.   20

JOAN

Peasant, avaunt! [*to York*] You have suborned this man

---

5   **timeless** untimely
7   **miser** wretch
8   **gentler** more noble
9   **friend** as well as the modern sense,
    this means 'relation' here; Joan Puzel
    claims that the Shepherd is not of her
    kindred, and hostile to her.
10 **an please you** if you please
13 **my bachelorship** Though the word
    'bachelor' can refer to any kind of
    novice or apprentice, irrespective of
    marital status (in this character's case
    to his time as a trainee shepherd) its

overlap with the more familiar sense of
'unmarried man' may ribaldly link the
play's broader concern with legitimacy
to the issue of Joan Puzel's sexually
and socially anomalous status.

17 **obstacle** Though this might appear to a
    modern reader as a malapropism for
    'obstinate', *OED* 3a gives several citations
    of it as an adjective, meaning 'stubborn'.
18 **collop** slice, lump (normally used of
    meat)
21 **avaunt** go away
    suborned employed

7+ SP JOAN] *this edn; Pucel., Pucell., Puc., Pue., Pu. F*   21 SD] *this edn*

Of purpose to obscure my noble birth.

SHEPHERD

'Tis true, I gave a noble to the priest
The morn that I was wedded to her mother.
Kneel down and take my blessing, good my girl.   25
Wilt thou not stoop? Now cursed be the time
Of thy nativity. I would the milk
Thy mother gave thee when thou suck'st her breast
Had been a little ratsbane for thy sake –
Or else, when thou didst keep my lambs a-field,   30
I wish some ravenous wolf had eaten thee.
Dost thou deny thy father, cursed drab?
O burn her, burn her, hanging is too good.   *Exit.*

YORK

Take her away, for she hath lived too long,
To fill the world with vicious qualities.   35

JOAN

First let me tell you whom you have condemned:
Not me begotten of a shepherd swain,
But issued from the progeny of kings;
Virtuous and holy, chosen from above
By inspiration of celestial grace   40
To work exceeding miracles on earth.
I never had to do with wicked spirits;
But you, that are polluted with your lusts,

---

23 **a noble** 'A former English gold coin, first minted by Edward III' (*OED* B *sb.*[1] 2a). It would represent a significant sum to the Shepherd. He may have misunderstood what Joan has said, or he may be mocking her.

25 **take my blessing** Joan's refusal to kneel offers a contrast to the meeting between Talbot and John at 4.4.33.

26, 32 **cursed** cursèd

29 **ratsbane** poison used to kill rats, most often arsenic

30 **keep** guard

32 **drab** physically dirty woman, with a sense of prostitute

37 **me** *me* for the expected I is grammatically possible in the period; however, Malone's conjecture of 'one', combining the appeal of easy sense and more expected grammar, has much to recommend it. In secretary hand the misreading of 'one' as 'me' would be easy.

37 me] one *Collier (Malone)*

Stained with the guiltless blood of innocents,
Corrupt and tainted with a thousand vices,   45
Because you want the grace that others have,
You judge it straight a thing impossible
To compass wonders but by help of devils.
No – misconceived, Joan of Aire hath been
A virgin from her tender infancy,   50
Chaste and immaculate in very thought,
Whose maiden-blood, thus rigorously effused,
Will cry for vengeance at the gates of heaven.

YORK

Ay, ay: away with her to execution.

44 **blood of innocents** Again, Joan uses a biblical diction to bolster her case. The phrase itself is from Jeremiah, 2.34, 'in thy wings is founde the blood of the soules of the poore innocents', but there is a reminiscence also of Herod's massacre of the innocents, the occasion of an important Christian feast-day. See Matthew, 2.16.

48 **compass wonders** achieve miracles
by help of devils An echo here of the Pharisees' disbelief of Jesus's miracles: 'the Pharises said, He casteth out devils, through the prince of devils' (Matthew, 9.34).

49 ***No – misconceived, Joan** misconceivèd. A difficult line, as the various editorial attempts to punctuate it reveal. Joan claims that York's charges of sexual looseness are unjustified (*misconceived*); however, the word may carry further connotations of bastardy and thus relate to her repudiation of the Shepherd's claim to be her natural father. **Joan of Aire** One of many variants on Joan's name that run through the text here has connotations of 'pure as air', and one can assume that that is why she has chosen it.

49–50 **hath . . . infancy** One can read this statement as Joan saying that she has been a virgin from a precociously

early age – a hyperbolic and self-defeating exaggeration of her female virtue, along the lines of the old Hollywood joke about knowing the actress Doris Day (famous for roles that cast her as the unyielding independent woman) *before* she was a virgin. Or, in a less comic reading of the role, Joan merely asserts that she has retained the innocence of infancy into her adulthood.

52 **maiden-blood** Joan uses a trope of martyrdom, derived from the death of Abel (Genesis, 4.10: 'the voyce of thy brothers blood cryeth vnto me from the grounde'). But in relation to her sexualized language of the body this becomes suggestive both of the breaking of the hymen and of menstrual blood, especially in F's hyphenated form. The historical Jeanne did not menstruate, something taken as a token of either saintliness or unnaturalness, according to the side taken by the commentator. Jeanne's hymen may have been broken, presumably through exercise and horse-riding, but a tribunal of noble ladies examined her and declared her virgin. The evidence presented at the trial tends to feed, as here in the play, into an area of sexualized speculation and fantasy (Warner, 19–21).
rigorously effused ruthlessly shed

49 No – misconceived,] *this edn;* No misconceyued, *F;* No, misconceived *F4;* No. Misconceived! *Steevens;* No, misconceivers: *Capell*   Aire] Arc *Rowe*

WARWICK

And hark ye, sirs: because she is a maid,   55
Spare for no faggots, let there be enough.
Place barrels of pitch upon the fatal stake
That so her torture may be shortened.

JOAN

Will nothing turn your unrelenting hearts?
Then, Joan, discover thine infirmity,   60
That warranteth by law to be thy privilege.
I am with child, ye bloody homicides:
Murder not then the fruit within my womb,
Although ye hale me to a violent death.

YORK

Now heaven forfend, the holy maid with child?   65

WARWICK

The greatest miracle that e'er ye wrought.
Is all your strict preciseness come to this?

YORK

She and the Dolphin have been ingling.

60 **discover** reveal
61 **warranteth . . . privilege** is guaranteed by law to ensure exemption from the death penalty (as being pregnant)
63 **fruit . . . womb** reference to the Virgin Mary, taken up and underlined in the next three lines. Elizabeth at the visitation said to the Virgin 'Blessed art thou among women, because the frute of thy wombe is blessed' (Luke, 1.42).
65 **heaven forfend** literally 'may God prevent'; but weaker in colloquial use, 'surely not'
67 **strict preciseness** careful morality. Puritans were known as 'precisians'.
68 ***ingling** fondling, caressing. F has 'iugling', which could be modernized as 'juggling, a common sixteenth-century term often used by Protestants to denigrate Catholic claims

to work miracles. Shakespeare uses it in this sense in *KJ* 3.1.169, 'juggling witchcraft', in reference to the sale of pardons. Here the 'juggling' would refer to the pregnancy of a virgin (65–6). 'Ingling', however, is a more directly sexual reference with homosexual overtones relevant to Joan's sexual ambiguity. It has precedents in Nashe's *Four Letters Confuted*, '*Thou protests it was not my person thou mislikt* (I am afraide thou wilt make mee thy Ingle)', Nashe, 1.326.1–2). This sequence is an expansion of Holinshed: 'But herein (God helpe us) she fullie afore possest of the feend, not able to hold hir in anie towardnesse of grace, falling streight waie into hir former abominations, (and yet seeking to eetch out life as long as she might,) stake not (though the shift

56 enough] *(*enow*)*   61 to be thy] thy *Hanmer*   68 ingling] *Oxf*; iugling *F*

I did imagine what would be her refuge.

WARWICK

Well, go to, we'll have no bastard live;   70
Especially since Charles must father it.

JOAN

You are deceived, my child is none of his.
It was Alençon that enjoyed my love.

YORK

Alençon, that notorious Machiavel?
It dies, an if it had a thousand lives.   75

JOAN

O give me leave, I have deluded you.
'Twas neither Charles, nor yet the Duke I named,
But Reignier, King of Naples, that prevailed.

WARWICK

A married man, that's most intolerable.

YORK

Why, here's a girl! I think she knows not well –   80
There were so many – whom she may accuse.

WARWICK

It's a sign she hath been liberal and free.

YORK

And yet, forsooth, she is a virgin pure.
Strumpet, thy words condemn thy brat and thee.
Use no entreaty, for it is in vain.   85

JOAN

Then lead me hence – with whom I leave my curse.

---

were shamefull) to confesse hir selfe a
strumpet, and (unmaried as she was)
to be with child.' (Bullough, 3.77).
74 **Machiavel** *The Prince* (1513–15) was
the major work of political theory of
Niccolò Machiavelli, and its interpretation as a scandalously atheistic and
amoral text made him a byword for
unscrupulous political individualism,
especially in English drama of this
period (cf. *3H6* 3.2.193).
75 **an if** if
82 **liberal and free** generous and easy-
going; licentious

70 we'll] we will *F2*   74 Machiavel] *Pope;* Macheuile *F*

May never glorious sun reflex his beams
Upon the country where you make abode,
But darkness and the gloomy shade of death
Environ you, till mischief and despair   90
Drive you to break your necks, or hang yourselves.   *Exit.*

Enter [the] Cardinal [of WINCHESTER*].*

YORK

Break thou in pieces, and consume to ashes,
Thou foul accursed minister of hell.

WINCHESTER

Lord Regent, I do greet your excellence
With letters of commission from the King.   95
For know, my lords, the states of Christendom,
Moved with remorse of these outrageous broils,
Have earnestly implored a general peace
Betwixt our nation and the aspiring French;

87–91 Given English weather, this prophecy is more impressive in its bravado than in any special knowledge it implies, and so, like Joan's curse on Charles and York (5.2.60–2), represents the waning of her powers, after her informative familiars have left her. Some productions – the BBC's *Age of Kings*, for example – have shaped this moment into an ominous presage of the future civil war.

87 **reflex** *OED v.* 2b: 'To throw, cast (beams) *on* a place'

91 SD Joan would presumably be guarded throughout this scene.

91.1 This is F's position for the Cardinal's entry. It allows Winchester to be on stage for York's curse on Joan, which might then be seen to have application to him as an equivalent figure of diabolical Catholicism.

Some other editions move the SD to 93.

93 **accursed** accursèd
   minister servant

96–9 Winchester's speech derives from Hall, but what he reports is presented there as a general view. The implied context is the contemporaneous attack on Constantinople by the Turks: 'all christendom lamented the continuall destruccion of so noble a realme, and the effusion of so muche Christen bloud, wherfore . . . all the princes of Christendom, so muche labored and travailed, by their orators and Ambassadors, that the frostie hartes of bothe the parties, wer somewhat mollified' (Bullough, 3.71).

97 **remorse of** pity for
   outrageous broils shocking disorders

91 SD] *Exit, guarded. / Theobald*   91.1] *after 93 Capell*

277

And here at hand the Dolphin and his train   100
Approacheth, to confer about some matter.

YORK

Is all our travail turned to this effect?
After the slaughter of so many peers,
So many captains, gentlemen and soldiers
That in this quarrel have been overthrown   105
And sold their bodies for their country's benefit,
Shall we at last conclude effeminate peace?
Have we not lost most part of all the towns,
By treason, falsehood and by treachery,
Our great progenitors had conquered?   110
O Warwick, Warwick, I foresee with grief
The utter loss of all the realm of France.

WARWICK

Be patient, York. If we conclude a peace
It shall be with such strict and severe covenants
As little shall the Frenchmen gain thereby.   115

Enter CHARLES, ALENÇON, [*the*] BASTARD [*and*] REIGNIER.

CHARLES

Since, lords of England, it is thus agreed
That peaceful truce shall be proclaimed in France,
We come to be informed, by yourselves,
What the conditions of that league must be.

100–1 **the Dolphin . . . Approacheth**
This episode is most closely paralleled
historically by the 'greate diete . . . to
be kept at the citee of Tours', in Hall
the setting of Suffolk's courtship of
Margaret (Bullough, 3.71). *2H6*
(1.3.50–4) places his winning of her at
Tours, as part of a chivalric tournament. This play presents the event

more ironically at 5.2.66–216. Here,
the entry of Winchester, like
Margaret's, directly after an exit of
Joan's, provides a parallel sense of
unease; there is some suggestion, in his
ushering in of the French, of his stage-
managing of events.
118 **informed** informèd

---

101 some matter] the same *Ard²*   102 travail] *(trauell)*   114 severe] several *Ard² (Vaughan)*

YORK

    Speak, Winchester, for boiling choler chokes   120

    The hollow passage of my poisoned voice

    By sight of these, our baleful enemies.

WINCHESTER

    Charles, and the rest, it is enacted thus:

    That, in regard King Henry gives consent,

    Of mere compassion and of lenity,   125

    To ease your country of distressful war

    And suffer you to breathe in fruitful peace,

    You shall become true liegemen to his crown.

    And Charles, upon condition thou wilt swear

    To pay him tribute and submit thyself,   130

    Thou shalt be placed as viceroy under him

    And still enjoy thy regal dignity.

ALENÇON

    Must he be then as shadow of himself –

    Adorn his temples with a coronet,

    And yet in substance and authority   135

    Retain but privilege of a private man?

    This proffer is absurd and reasonless.

CHARLES

    'Tis known already that I am possessed

    With more than half the Gallian territories,

---

120 **choler** one of the four bodily humours, according to Renaissance psychopathology; it is fiery, and it causes and is the expression of anger.

122 **baleful** sinister; poisonous; deadly

123 **Charles** The first time that an English character calls the Dolphin by his Christian name, rather than by the title that defines him as still waiting to assume the throne that the English claim as their own, but to which, from the French point of view, he has already acceded. In calling him 'Charles', Winchester may implicitly accept him as King of France, and so increase the other English characters' suspicion of himself.

125 **mere** pure

128 **liegemen** men sworn to obey a superior, in return for his protection

131 **viceroy** 'One who acts as the governor of a country . . . in the name and by the authority of the supreme ruler' (*OED* 1)

132 **still** continue to

136 **privilege** legal status

139 **Gallian** French

121 poisoned] prisoned *Theobald*

And therein reverenced for their lawful king.   140
Shall I, for lucre of the rest unvanquished,
Detract so much from that prerogative
As to be called but viceroy of the whole?
No, lord ambassador; I'll rather keep
That which I have, than, coveting for more,   145
Be cast from possibility of all.

YORK

Insulting Charles, hast thou by secret means
Used intercession to obtain a league
And, now the matter grows to compromise,
Stand'st thou aloof upon comparison?   150
Either accept the title thou usurp'st –
Of benefit proceeding from our king,
And not of any challenge of desert –
Or we will plague thee with incessant wars.

[*The French turn to talk among themselves.*]

REIGNIER

My lord, you do not well in obstinacy   155
To cavil in the course of this contract.
If once it be neglected, ten to one
We shall not find like opportunity.

ALENÇON

To say the truth, it is your policy
To save your subjects from such massacre   160

141–3 Must I forfeit my right as *lawful king* of half of France, and accept a role secondary to Henry in order to gain control of the other half (which I have not yet won back)?

146 **cast** expelled

147–8 **secret means . . . league** York seems to be suggesting that Charles has conspired, possibly through Winchester's means, with the Pope and the Emperor, as heads of the Catholic Church and the state, to form a league against England. But his accusations are typically vague.

149 **grows to compromise** is reaching final agreement

150 Do you withdraw from negotiation, now you compare your position with ours?

152 **Of . . . from** by the kindness of

153 **of any . . . desert** as yours by any right or merit

156 **cavil** raise points of detail

154 SD] *this edn*   155 My lord] *To the Dauphin aside.* My lord *Hanmer*

And ruthless slaughters as are daily seen
By our proceeding in hostility:
And therefore take this compact of a truce –
Although you break it, when your pleasure serves.

WARWICK

How sayest thou, Charles? Shall our condition stand?   165

CHARLES

It shall:
Only reserved you claim no interest
In any of our towns of garrison.

YORK

Then swear allegiance to his majesty:
As thou art knight, never to disobey   170
Nor be rebellious to the crown of England –
Thou nor thy nobles to the crown of England.
So, now dismiss your army when ye please.
Hang up your ensigns, let your drums be still,   174
For here we entertain a solemn peace.   *Exeunt.*

5[.4]   *Enter* SUFFOLK *in conference with the* KING,
GLOUCESTER *and* EXETER.

KING

Your wondrous rare description, noble earl,
Of beauteous Margaret hath astonished me.
Her virtues, graced with external gifts,
Do breed love's settled passions in my heart;
And like as rigour of tempestuous gusts   5
Provokes the mightiest hulk against the tide,

163 **compact** agreement
167 **Only reserved** the only reservation being
168 **towns of garrison** fortified towns, with a military presence

175 **entertain** accept
5.4.0.1 *conference* conversation
4 **settled** steady
5–6 as the strength of stormy winds propels even the largest ship against the tide

164 pleasure serves.] pleasure serves. *Aside to the Dauphin / Pope*   165 How . . . stand?] *Pope; F lines Charles? / stand? /*   sayest] *(sayst)*   172 England.] England. *Charles and the rest give tokens of fealty. / Johnson*   5.4] *this edn;* V. v *Capell; Actus Quintus.* F

So am I driven, by breath of her renown,
Either to suffer shipwreck or arrive
Where I may have fruition of her love.

SUFFOLK

Tush, my good lord, this superficial tale   10
Is but a preface of her worthy praise:
The chief perfections of that lovely dame –
Had I sufficient skill to utter them –
Would make a volume of enticing lines
Able to ravish any dull conceit.   15
And, which is more, she is not so divine,
So full replete with choice of all delights,
But with as humble lowliness of mind
She is content to be at your command –
Command, I mean, of virtuous chaste intents –   20
To love and honour Henry as her lord.

KING

And otherwise will Henry ne'er presume.
Therefore, my lord Protector, give consent
That Margaret may be England's royal queen.

GLOUCESTER

So should I give consent to flatter sin.   25
You know, my lord, your highness is betrothed
Unto another lady of esteem;
How shall we then dispense with that contract,
And not deface your honour with reproach?

SUFFOLK

As doth a ruler with unlawful oaths,   30

7 **breath** report; a metaphor carried
over from the idea of the wind blowing
the sails of a ship – literally
Margaret's, metaphorically Henry's
heart
15 **any dull conceit** even the least lively
imagination

22 Henry will never assume he has the
right to do otherwise.
25 **sin** Henry's breaking of his promise to
the Earl of Armagnac
27 **another lady** the daughter of the Earl
of Armagnac; see 5.1.41–5.
28 **contract** contràct

11 of] to *F2*   24 Margaret] *(Marg'ret)*

Or one that, at a triumph having vowed
To try his strength, forsaketh yet the lists
By reason of his adversary's odds.
A poor earl's daughter is unequal odds
And therefore may be broke without offence.   35

GLOUCESTER

Why, what, I pray, is Margaret more than that?
Her father is no better than an earl,
Although in glorious titles he excel.

SUFFOLK

Yes, my lord, her father is a king,
The King of Naples and Jerusalem,   40
And of such great authority in France
As his alliance will confirm our peace,
And keep the Frenchmen in allegiance.

GLOUCESTER

And so the Earl of Armagnac may do,
Because he is near kinsman unto Charles.   45

EXETER

Beside, his wealth doth warrant a liberal dower,
Where Reignier sooner will receive than give.

SUFFOLK

A dower, my lords? Disgrace not so your king
That he should be so abject, base and poor
To choose for wealth, and not for perfect love.   50
Henry is able to enrich his queen,
And not to seek a queen to make him rich;
So worthless peasants bargain for their wives,
As market-men for oxen, sheep or horse.

---

35 **broke** broken with, repudiated
40 **King of Naples** See note on Reignier in
List of Roles (pp. 112–13).
42 **alliance** relation to us

46 **warrant . . . dower** guarantee a large
payment to the King on marriage to
his daughter (as was customary)

39 my] my good *F2*   46 warrant a] warrant *F2*

283

Marriage is a matter of more worth   55
Than to be dealt in by attorneyship:
Not whom we will, but whom his grace affects,
Must be companion of his nuptial bed.
And therefore, lords, since he affects her most,
Most of all these reasons bindeth us: 60
In our opinions she should be preferred.
For what is wedlock forced but a hell,
An age of discord and continual strife?
Whereas the contrary bringeth bliss,
And is a pattern of celestial peace.   65
Whom should we match with Henry, being a king,
But Margaret, that is daughter to a king?
Her peerless feature, joined with her birth,
Approves her fit for none but for a king.
Her valiant courage and undaunted spirit   70
(More than in women commonly is seen)
Will answer our hope in issue of a king.
For Henry, son unto a conqueror,
Is likely to beget more conquerors,
If with a lady of so high resolve   75
As is fair Margaret he be linked in love.

---

55 **Marriage** pronounced as three syllables, but in the English rather than the
   French way, i.e. with the stress on the
   first syllable
56 **by attorneyship** by a go-between
57, 59 **affects** desires
60 That 'he affects her most' is the decisive factor.
62 **forced** forcèd
68 **joined** joinèd
68–72 The play echoes Hall here, with a
   hint of the trouble yet to come, given
   the imbalance between Margaret's
   combination of masculine and feminine force, and her husband's more

negative and inert mode of androgyny:
'This woman excelled all other, as well
in beautie and favor, as in wit and polli-
cie, and was of stomack and corage,
more like to a man, then a woman'
(Bullough, 3.102). Suffolk's argument
is that she will, as good breeding-stock,
compensate for Henry's weakness, to
produce a son´ fit to be king. When a
son was eventually born, Yorkist gossip
put about that it was Suffolk's. See
notes on Henry and Margaret in List of
Roles (pp. 110, 113).
72 **issue** birth; offspring
75 **resolve** resolution, courage

55 Marriage] But marriage *F2*   60 Most] It most *Rowe;* Which most *Cam¹;* That most *Ard²*
72 Will . . . our] Answer our *Pope;* Will answer *Hudson (Steevens)*

Then yield, my lords, and here conclude with me
That Margaret shall be queen, and none but she.
KING
Whether it be through force of your report,
My noble lord of Suffolk, or for that   80
My tender youth was never yet attaint
With any passion of inflaming love,
I cannot tell; but this I am assured –
I feel such sharp dissension in my breast,
Such fierce alarums both of hope and fear,   85
As I am sick with working of my thoughts.
Take therefore shipping post, my lord, to France.
Agree to any covenants, and procure
That lady Margaret do vouchsafe to come,
To cross the seas to England and be crowned   90
King Henry's faithful and anointed queen.
For your expenses and sufficient charge,
Among the people gather up a tenth.
Begone, I say, for till you do return
I rest perplexed with a thousand cares.   95
And you, good uncle, banish all offence:
If you do censure me by what you were,
Not what you are, I know it will excuse
This sudden execution of my will.

---

81 **attaint** touched; corrupted
84 **such sharp dissension** such painful conflict – ironically, given the *dissension* depicted in *2H6* and *3H6*. It is as if the King is giving painful birth to future events – which in a sense he is.
86 **working . . . thoughts** turning things over in my mind
87 **post** as fast as possible
92 **sufficient charge** enough cash
93 **a tenth** A 'tithe' (or *tenth*) of income or produce was, on biblical authority, the Church's right: 'all the tithe of the land

. . . is the Lords' (Leviticus, 27.30–2). The King could exercise a similar prerogative, which was often used on occasions like this, when a sudden cause of expenditure presented itself. The practice was much resented, and can be read ominously here, as a potential cause of unrest, especially since Margaret herself brings no dowry.
95 **perplexed** perplexèd
96 **banish all offence** cast away all disapproval
97 **censure** judge

82 love] *F2;* Ioue *F*   90 To cross] Across *Hudson (Walker)*

And so conduct me where, from company,   100
I may revolve and ruminate my grief.   *Exit.*

GLOUCESTER

Ay, grief, I fear me, both at first and last.
Exeunt Gloucester [and Exeter].

SUFFOLK

Thus Suffolk hath prevailed, and thus he goes,
As did the youthful Paris once to Greece,
With hope to find the like event in love –   105
But prosper better than the Trojan did.
Margaret shall now be queen, and rule the King:
But I will rule both her, the King and realm.   *Exit.*

---

101 **revolve** turn around in my mind
   grief suffering. Sorrow as such is not
   necessarily meant here, but that is
   what Gloucester means by *grief* in the
   next line.
104 **Paris** the *Trojan* prince who was led
   on by Venus to kidnap Helen from her

husband Menelaus, and so began the
Trojan war
105 **the like event** the same outcome, as
   far as sexual satisfaction is concerned.
   Suffolk's hope that his story will end
   more happily in other respects is seriously misplaced.

102 SD *and Exeter*] *Capell*

APPENDIX 1

NAMES, NAMING
AND WORDPLAY

Several names – especially those of the French characters – are highly unstable in F. This may well, as Gary Taylor has argued in the case of Joan Puzel (Taylor, 154–7), reflect collaborative authorship, though it might of course equally well reflect the uncertainty of a single dramatist, and of the scribes and compositors who worked with whatever text he left in the thirty-year gap between performance and first printing, as to the spelling and pronunciation of French words. None of the choices that I outline below can be established uncontroversially. In the end, I have chosen, between well-supported alternatives, the version of the name that seems to me best to serve the play, in the context of my reading of its tone and aims, as described in the Introduction (pp. 25–6).

I have decided not to use, as other editions have, 'Pucelle' and 'Dauphin'. These modernized forms would be in line with the general Arden policy of modernization of all but proper names. Arguably, Pucelle/Puzel is a kind of proper name. But my reason for adopting Puzel and Dolphin is that they draw attention to the play as a satirical distortion of history, particularly in relation to the French. Richard Proudfoot has remarked to me privately that 'an imaginable theatrical alternative might be to give the monoglot English the forms "dolphin" and "puzel" to signify their xenophobic rejection of anything so deferential to the foe as correct French pronunciation (analogous with Winston Churchill's celebrated "Naazi" instead of "Naatzi" for Nazi)', adding that obviously there was no textual justification for this. What is attractive theatrically cannot always be rendered editorially; F does not distinguish between the pronunciation of the English and that of

287

the French (who are, after all, represented by English actors for an English audience), so a consistent choice must be made.

The names below are presented in the order and form in which they occur in the 'List of Roles'.

The Duke of SUFFOLK (William de la Pole)

F spells the name as *Poole* in 2.4; at 5.2.88 it is spelled *Pole*, most likely reflecting the spelling preferences of the two compositors who set the text. Nonetheless some significance may be sought in the distinction. The family of Suffolk were descended from merchants of Hull, called 'Poole', who later frenchified their name into the form Pole that Suffolk adopts. Richard Plantaganet, in an argument that, wherever it started, ends up as a squabble about social status, mocks Suffolk, in a way that Somerset tries to deflect:

RICHARD
    Proud Poole, I will, and scorn both him and thee.
SUFFOLK
    I'll turn my part thereof into thy throat.
SOMERSET
    Away, away, good William de la Pole –
    We grace the yeoman by conversing with him.
                                        (2.4.78–81)

Retention of the *Poole* form here seems congruous with the tone of mockery. I have accordingly decided to introduce a differentiation between the forms. When Suffolk names himself, in the scene of the wooing of Margaret, he uses the more sophisticated form, 'de la Pole' (5.2.88). I have given this form also to his supporter Somerset. Sinister and malicious puns on 'pool' and 'poll' (meaning head) are made available to signal the inglorious end that Suffolk meets in *2 Henry VI* – decapitation, by the sea – with a further pun available in the name of his killer, water/Walter/Gualtier (*2H6* 4.1.32–9). Cercignani is sceptical of the Poole/Poll pun, but it seems unlikely that Elizabethan pronunciation can be pinned down so precisely as to rule out a reading that makes clear dramatic sense (Cercignani, 190, 222).

Sir John FASTOLFE

The Folio text of *1 Henry VI* spells the name of this character Falstaffe. His historical original is, however, Sir John Fastolfe. The Folio spelling Falstaffe is, of course, also that of the popular character well known from the two parts of *Henry IV*, *Henry V* and *The Merry Wives of Windsor* (all written some four to seven years after our play).

George Walton Williams has argued that the compilers of the First Folio assimilated the spelling of the name in *1 Henry VI* to that of the popular later figure, pointing out that Fastolfe, the spelling of the sources, ought to be retained (Williams, 308–12). The difference in spellings produces two different puns, differently apt to the different figures: 'l' could often be silent (see 'Dolphin' below), so the character in *1H6* might be called 'fast off'; the drunken and ageing amorist in the later plays has his name spelt in a way that suggests 'fall staff' – if the option of pronouncing the 'l' were to be taken. The major reason for adopting Williams's suggestion is that the two figures are clearly distinct. The character in this play is neither fat nor a drunkard, nor an amateur criminal.

CHARLES, *Dolphin of France*

This edition adopts F's spelling 'Dolphin' within the dialogue. F *Henry V* uses this form also in SPs and SDs, but in *1H6* 'Charles' predominates; 'Dolph.' and 'Dolphin' are only used in SPs and SDs in 1.2, from 47 onward, and in 1.5. In each case the character has been called 'Dolphin' in the dialogue a few lines before.

The word *dauphin* is French for 'dolphin', the sea-mammal, and was already in use in English in the sixteenth century as a term for the French prince. 'Dauphin' is the modern English spelling of the title, but it would lose an intriguing and possibly significant reference to the heraldic dolphin. In both senses the word was generally spelled with an 'l' in French and English in the sixteenth century. The dolphin was the heraldic symbol of the Comte de Vienne, a province on the Rhone, up which, presumably, dolphins might at that time have swum. In 1349 the impoverished holder of the title sold it to the King of France, Philip IV. From then on it became the title of the heir to the French throne (Larousse, 'Dauphin', 'Dauphin d'Auvergne').

T.W. Craik (Ard³) registers F's invariable use of the form 'Dolphin' in *Henry V* but has modernized it to 'Dauphin'. 'Dolphin' seems apt to the more playful, ironic *1 Henry VI* in its congruity with the heraldic and beast-fable references that multiply through the play. As with Jeanne la Pucelle/Joan Puzel, it may even be that the play offers consciously grotesque parodies of historical figures rather than serious attempts at historical reconstruction. Talbot draws attention, with 'Dolphin or dog-fish', to the zoological aspect of the title, and so the Dolphin is pulled into the animal/hunting analogies which dominate the French battle scenes (1.4.106). The animal characteristics invoked a certain levity and a capacity for survival combined, as when Cleopatra says of Antony 'His delights were dolphin-like' (*AC* 5.2.87–8). Audiences hearing Antony as 'dauphin-like' (a phonetic option in the period) might have reflected that Antony, like Charles here, from the English point of view at least, had never achieved truly legitimate power.

REIGNIER, Duke of Anjou and Maine,
King of Naples and Jerusalem

Though Oxford modernizes 'Reignier' to 'René', it seems to make more sense to keep to the anglicized spelling more or less consistently used in F. At 4.3.80 however, the Folio renders the name as 'Reignard', a perhaps revealing interaction of the historical King's name with the proverbial name ('Reynard') of the wily fox of European tradition. A similar identification is implied by the spelling used in Elizabeth Cary's 'History of the Life, Reign and Death of Edward II', when she refers to 'Margaret . . ., daughter of Reynard that styled himself King of Naples and Jerusalem' (Cary, 225).

JOAN Puzel

F varies significantly in its description of this character; see
Introduction, pp. 25–6). Gary Taylor, in the service of his arguments about authorship, presents the following table of forms in F.

Compositors	Spelling	Frequency	Reference
A	*Puzel*	11	Act I
A	*Puzel.* (prefixes)	11	Act I
B	*Puzell*	1	II.i
B	*Ioane.* (prefixes)	2	II.i
A, B	*Pucell*	13	III.ii–V.vi
A, B	*Pucell.* (prefixes)	14	III.ii–V.vi
A	*Pucel*	1	III.ii
B	*Pucel.* (prefixes)	4	IV.vii–V.vi
B	*Puc.* (prefixes)	9	IV.vii–V.vi
B	*Pue.* (prefix)	1	V.vi
B	*Pu.* (prefix)	1	V.vi

Taylor identifies the most significant differential as the medial 'z'
or 'c', and counts 25 of the first, all in the first two acts, and 42 of
the second, all in the last three (Taylor, 154–5). But there are
problems with Taylor's computation in his summary. I take it
that Compositor B's two '*Ioane.*'s have been added in to the 'z'
account by accident. 23 is the correct total, and the table here is
accurate. More problematically, though the total of 42 is accurate if we include *Pue.* as a misreading of *Puc.*, the counting here
is wrong. F, to my eye, has 18 *Pucell.* prefixes, which would give
46 instances, as the other figures in the table are accurate. The
overall point of course, still stands.

He says of all these spellings that they 'would be represented
by the modern "pucelle"' (154). I am not so sure. 'Pucelle' was
the title the historical Jeanne bestowed on herself, and the word,
as Marina Warner has pointed out (Introduction, pp. 25–6),
combines the idea of chastity with that of incipient sexuality. In
sixteenth- and seventeenth-century English this ambiguity

coarsens, in that the word, whether spelt in French style with 'c' or in English with 'z', would more usually mean a prostitute. If the alternatives for spelling the medial consonant – 'z' or 'c'/'ss' – were to be taken as identical, and their identity collapsed into the modern French 'pucelle', then in Talbot's 'Puzel or pussel, Dolphin or dog-fish, / Your hearts I'll stamp out with my horse's heels' (1.4.106–7) the distinction between the first two terms would have been inaudible to an Elizabethan audience, and therefore the line would have to be rendered in a modernized edition as 'Pucelle or pucelle'. Obviously that would be nonsensical, and the two terms must be sounded differently, in a way that suggests distinct, even opposed meanings. In this edition's 'Puzel or pussel' the different sounds of the medial consonants provide the distinction. However, because a theatre audience – either modern or Elizabethan – might not pick up a clear sense of each word, shouted out by Talbot in the heat of battle, the emotive effect is primary, and that also constructs the 'puzzle' – we puzzle at what Talbot, in his puzzlement, is trying to define.

The spelling 'Puzel' belongs in Taylor's computation to the writer he identifies persuasively as Nashe. In F 'Puzel' only becomes 'Pucelle' after Talbot has named her 'pussel' (1.4.106) – and, in fact, after compositor B's sole setting of the 'z' form in 2.1.

The retention of the 'z' spelling is designed to help the modern reader define the nature of the role. The first use of the word in the modern sense of 'puzzle' – with a stronger connotation of 'confusion' or 'bewilderment' – is not recorded as a noun by *OED* until around 1599, some years after the first performance of this play, in a phrase by Francis Bacon referring to 'the pusle of businesse'. The *OED* does record somewhat earlier uses of the word as a verb. *Robert Dudley's Voyage to the West Indies* by Captain Wyatt (*c*. 1595) is cited by *OED* as the first appearance of the verb ('whilst we weare theare pusled . . . Baltizar . . . dropped overborde'). The *OED* also gives as an early example

Shakespeare's *Hamlet* (Ard²), 3.1.78–80, 'the dread of something after death . . . puzzles the will' – where 'puzzles', meaning
'bewilders so as to make incapable of proceeding' (Ard²), is variously spelt in the First Quarto as 'pusles', in the Second Quarto
as 'puzels' and in the Folio as 'Puzels'. Normally in English the
noun form appears before the verb; but then perhaps the
pucelle/puzel word *is* that pre-existing noun, and its development into a verb is equivalent to cousin/cozen giving rise to the
verb 'to cozen', i.e. to trick someone by assuming a cousin-like
intimacy with them. In any case it seems to me to serve the play
better if all the possible meanings are presented through the
adoption of a form of the word where their overlap with each
other is preserved. (In addition, Leslie Fiedler (52), not entirely
convincingly, suggests that the Italian *puzzare* lies behind the
name to provide an 'evocation of the "burning, scalding,
stench"' he finds epitomized in 'Lear's diatribe against
women'.)

Variants of other elements in the character's name, as they
occur in dialogue, seem to result from the conflation of two
sources – Hall, and Holinshed's more sensationally elaborated
account. In Holinshed, for example, she is 'called Jone Are, by the
name of hir father (a sorie sheepheard) James of Are' (Bullough,
3.75), while in Hall she is, on the occasion of her first victory, at
Orleans, labelled '*Pucelle*' (Bullough, 3.57), and then at the time
of her trial as 'Jone the Puzell'. F adopts the nonsensical 'of Acre'
for Joan at 2.2.20, the resonant 'of Aire' at 5.3.49; I have used the
latter for both, as the first could easily be a misreading of the
manuscript, if the dot of the 'i' had become hard to see or, conversely, was large enough to be misread as the capping stroke on
a 'c'. For more thoughts on these lines, see 2.2.20n. and 5.3.49n.

From F's unstable set of versions on the possibilities of naming
her, I have tried to make a choice which closes down the fewest
possibilities in the reading of a character constructed as an insol-
uble enigma. 'Ioane', as we can see from Taylor's table, occurs
only twice in a speech prefix, but there is a case for arguing that,

when a character is well known, whether from the play itself or from other sources, it does a disservice to the reader to render that character unrecognizable (as she might be if I had adopted, as originally planned, just 'Puzel'), and so I have adopted 'Joan Puzel' – a recurrent form in F's SDs – with 'Joan' as the SP, and Puzel as the form of the 'p-word' as it occurs in the text, apart from Talbot's 'pussel'; this is the method I have chosen to highlight this particular puzzle.

General Editors' Note

While it is the policy of the third series of the Arden Shakespeare to leave to the volume editor final decisions on points which have been debated during the editorial process, it is also understood that the General Editors have the right to comment on any such decision about which they have expressed and continue to harbour reservations.

They believe that the decision of the editor of *1 Henry VI* to retain in his modernized text two F spellings may give rise to complications, to which they wish to draw the attention of users of the edition. The complications are brought into sharp focus at 1.4.106, where Talbot jests sardonically on the titles of his two leading opponents: in F the line reads '*Puzel* or *Pussel*, Dolphin or Dog-fish' (TLN 581), usually modernized to 'Pucelle or pussel, Dauphin or dogfish', but in this edition to 'Puzel or pussel, Dolphin or dogfish'.

1. 'Puzel' is the spelling of Joan's sobriquet found in the opening act of Folio *1H6*; later in the play it is superseded by 'Pucel(l)', which occurs twice as often as the 'z' form. The first objection to adopting 'Puzel', then, is simply that it is the minority form in F (possibly reflecting the spelling preference of one of a team of collaborating playwrights, possibly no more than an attempt to render the French pronunciation of 'pucelle' in phonetic English form). Rejection of the conventional modernization 'Pucelle' has two inconveniences: it deprives the French characters of an intelligible French epithet for their saviour, Joan 'the Maid'; and it

further imposes on them the necessity of adopting a derogatory English alternative. That the French word 'pucelle' was also used derogatorily in English, as well as in its literal sense of 'virgin', is amply attested in the period, so that it can equally be used by the French as a term of honour and by the English as an insult (cf. Jonson, *The Underwood*, 49, 'Epigram on the Court Pucell', Jonson, 8.222–3). In Talbot's line at 1.4.106, adoption of F's '*Puzel*' for the first of his two terms leads to a blurring of his defamatory intent: if 'puzel' excludes the sense 'virgin' and is itself already an insult (*OED* 2, 'A drab, a slut, a courtesan. *Obs.*'), then little is added by contrasting it with 'pussel' (*OED*, 'a dirty slovenly person, esp. woman, a slattern'). As Dr Burns acutely observes (Introduction, p. 26), with reference to the masculine Joan, 'The woman in man's clothes wielding a sword is a pucelle with a pizzle, and therefore a puzzle': the progression is not, however, valid or meaningful if 'puzel' is used to replace 'pucelle' as the first term in this formulation.

2. 'Dolphin' (or 'Daulphin', *KJ* 3.1.311) is the spelling of the title of the crown prince of France found throughout the First Folio. In the sixteenth and earlier seventeenth centuries, English spellings of this title and of the aquatic mammal from whose name it derives were not clearly differentiated and both always included the 'l'. That differentiation – the one now in standard usage – began in the 1670s, when English orthography, retaining 'dolphin' for the sea beast, followed French precedent and assigned 'dauphin' to the prince. Kökeritz (311) and Cercignani (354) both class 'dolphin' as a word in which in Shakespeare's time the sounding of the 'l' was optional: other words in Shakespeare similarly spelt in the early editions with optional 'l' include 'sa(l)vage', 'alab(l)aster' and 'sa(l)tiers', which are habitually modernized without it. *2H6* 4.1.31–8 offers the relevant analogue of 'Walter/water' (whether or not the 'l' is sounded being crucial to the prophecy that Suffolk will die 'by water'), while the variable modern English pronunciation of the name Ralph is reflected in the currency of the two spellings, 'Ralph'

and 'Rafe'. To print 'Dolphin' rather than 'Dauphin' restricts the range of possibility by requiring that the 'l' should always be sounded, as in standard modern English, and precluding the alternative pronunciation 'daw-fin'. (The French pronunciation 'doe-fa(n)' is not under consideration here.) Were the modernization 'Dauphin' (adopted by other editors) to be retained, then Talbot's sardonic pun would gain force if he alone – and only, perhaps, at 1.4.106 – were to use the pronunciation 'doll-fin' (necessary for the pun with which he validates his scathing comparison of the 'king of fish' to a fish of the cheapest and humblest kind).

RP, GWW

APPENDIX 2

CASTING

In preparing a casting chart for an Elizabethan production, I have worked on the assumption of an available group of fourteen men and two 'boys'. All the speaking roles can be accommodated without any particular difficulty, even taking into account a performer's appearance in consecutive scenes. When I have suggested a change of roles between adjacent scenes, this is allowed for by the character entering and/or exiting some way into each scene, and by one of the two roles being 'anonymous', such as a messenger. This is not to undervalue the difficulty of anonymous roles; many would benefit from the skills of an accomplished rhetorician. The French Captain who predicts Talbot's imminent death (4.2.15–41) or the three Messengers of 1.1 are cases in point. The Elizabethan stage may well have had 'extras' of some kind, to swell ceremonial scenes, but a casting plan of this kind does suggest that spoken roles could be shared out among a cast used to doubling; in the context of a more modern, 'star-conscious' style of casting it may seem odd that the actors playing, say, Gloucester and Winchester should come in with the occasional small role, but it provides one way of making the play work with a company of this size. In assigning these 'one-interjection' roles I am not assuming any great precision; they can be distributed among the five or six actors available for them at any one point more or less ad lib. An exception here is Talbot, for whom there is no other suitable role but the Scout who signals the French defeat (5.2.8). The only other actor available to play this latter role is Somerset. Though one should treat with extreme caution the idea that doubling creates a significant relation between the roles doubled (it is the very condition of this kind of doubling that the audience agrees to *overlook* the individual identity of the actors), there are moments when a play may draw attention to the effect. Burgundy's 'I trust the ghost of Talbot be not there' (5.2.16), on the Scout's exit, may well be one of them.

The casting of the 'boy' players can be arranged to give two performers an equal amount to do. I have adopted Hattaway's suggestion that Henry is played by a boy (see Introduction, pp. 30, and note on List of Roles), who can then be assumed to play Margaret and the Gunner's Boy as well. Joan Puzel doubles the Countess. I would suggest, in contradiction of my general caveat regarding how much one can read into doubling, that in the case of transvestite performance a different kind of audience awareness comes into play. So when the Joan Puzel actor turns up to 'seduce' Talbot as a feminine and sexually challenging sorceress, or when the actor who played a pre-pubescent or only just pubescent King then impersonates that King's dangerously seductive nemesis, the challenges that sexuality and gender offer to 'history' are underlined. The term 'boy' is unsatisfactory for the actors who played female roles, not least in the kind of rather dubious sentimentality it can bring to a discussion of these performers and the assumed response of the audience to the roles they played. The tradition of transvestite performance with which most Shakespeare editors of the past have been familiar has been that of the English public schools and universities, and this has been read back on to the boys/adolescents/young-to-youngish men of the Renaissance staging with confusing, even sometimes rather unsettling, results. But I adopt it as a convenient way of labelling the transvestite performers. The two performers posited here require a sharp comic ability to foreground sexual difference and sexual knowingness, with pathos in Henry's case, athleticism in Joan Puzel's and ambiguities of innocence and experience in both.

One other role, John Talbot, obviously belongs to a younger actor, but not one playing any transvestite roles in this play. (Frank Benson at Stratford in 1906 cast a young woman in the role, and a young man as Henry – contemporary reviewers suggested the casting should have been reversed.) John Talbot's most convenient double is Suffolk, a role that fits well on a younger performer with persuasive rhetorical skills, and an attractive presence. I take these to be the three junior members of the company, with Henry as the youngest, while Gloucester, Bedford/Mortimer/Lucy/Shepherd, Winchester, Warwick and Exeter provide a solid older contingent, with Bedford as perhaps the most senior – the portfolio of roles I have ended up with for him seems attractive for an experienced actor. Four characters have the most conspicuous roles, with seven scenes each for Gloucester and Winchester, eight for Joan and nine for Talbot.

As one works the plan out, clear parameters determine the assignment of all the roles except one-scene messengers or servants. Fourteen of the total of sixteen speaking performers are on stage in the first two scenes, and pairs of consecutive scenes, like 3.1 and 3.2, can between them employ the whole company, so these provide a solid basis from which to work outwards in assigning roles. Important two- or three-scene roles (Fastolfe, Lucy, Vernon and Basset, for example) can be assigned from within only a limited group of actors: Lucy from the actors playing the older English nobility, the other three from within the French contingent. In the case of Lucy, who appears only in 4.4, the choice of double is between Bedford, Gloucester, Winchester and Exeter, but the last three appear in the immediately subsequent scene (5.1), so the role is assigned here to the Bedford actor. Alençon, the Dolphin and the Bastard form a comic group whose sparring relationship transposes well into the more dangerous context of the rivalry of the minor English nobles. Reignier is a more intermittent presence among the French, a fact which the doubling chart makes easier to explain. If he takes on the Mayor and Fastolfe his long absences are accounted for, and he plays a group of roles ideal for a middle-aged actor who has good rapport with the audience and an ability to combine wiliness and apparent cowardice. All the roles seem to offer that cowardice/good-sense juxtaposition to which audiences always respond, and on which Shakespeare was to expand with his development of the Falstaff figure. F has marked Reignier to appear at 3.239.3. He is silent (which is very unlike him) and 'on the walls' and makes no other appearance in a lengthy and busy battle scene. I would suggest that this is an error, perhaps transmitted from an unemended state of the playhouse manuscript.

Following the chart through, one can see at least the possibility of an egalitarian sharing of work and audience attention, across a cast that ranges widely in age but not, it would seem, in levels of rhetorical adeptness. Financial stringency, at least in Britain, has made audiences and actors much more used to this kind of doubling since the 1970s – most classical productions are ingenious, energetic and low-budget affairs (outside, that is, the often less satisfactory large-stage work of one or two more lavishly funded companies). So, however much one may regret the political and economic reasons for this return to a practice similar to that of the companies and writers that Henslowe employed, a renewed familiarity with doubling helps us to appreciate the skill of the devisers of *1 Henry VI* in a way which a more hierarchical, star-oriented tradition of casting would obscure.

In presenting this chart with a cast of around fourteen to sixteen, I follow Ringler's argument for those numbers worked out for *A Midsummer Night's Dream* (Ringler, 126). *1 Henry VI* could, if desired, be performed with large forces at the Rose, and T.J. King points to a cast of thirty for this play: fifteen 'major' players, two boys and thirteen 'minor' players. His thesis is governed by the assumption that actors playing major roles did not take on minor ones, and that theatres employed a fluctuating number of small-part and walk-on actors (King, table 35). But we should bear in mind that Ringler's figures are for a later play and a different company (the Lord Chamberlain's men). Scott McMillin, while pointing out that the companies he discusses consisted of twelve adult actors, draws attention to the number of Strange's and Queen's Men's plays (including *1 Henry VI* and

Friar Bacon and Friar Bungay) which introduce twenty or more characters within the first 500 lines (McMillin, 57). As my chart demonstrates, this can be accommodated with sixteen players, but it might point to the desirability of a larger cast, in the Rose if not on tour.

Finally, the reader should bear in mind that the chart is designed around the play as it has been edited. Scene divisions, some role designations and some interpretations of roles (for instance, that of John Talbot as an older adolescent/young adult with fighting skills) are necessarily editorial and thus inevitably open to question. This makes the chart one of the more ludic areas of an edition; its value is in suggesting possibilities, not in establishing historical 'facts'.

Silent roles are marked on the chart by an asterisk.

Actor	1.1	1.2	1.3	1.4	1.5	2.1	2.2	2.3	2.4	2.5	3.1
1	Bedford					Bedford	Bedford			Mortimer	
2	Gloucester		Gloucester			English soldier					Gloucester
3	Exeter			Gunner			Countess's M	Countess's M			Exeter
4	Warwick*		1 Warder	Gargrave					Warwick		Warwick
5	Winchester		Winchester			Sergeant		Porter			Winchester
6	Somerset*		2 §Warder	Messenger			English Capt.	English Capt.	Somerset		Somerset
7	1 Messenger			Salisbury					Richard (York)	Richard (York)	Richard (York)
8	2 Messenger		Servingman			Sentinel			Suffolk		Suffolk
9	3 Messenger		Woodville	Glansdale		Burgundy	Burgundy			Gaoler	Servingman
10		Charles	Servingman		Charles	Charles			Lawyer		Servingman
11		Alençon	Servingman		Alençon	Alençon			Vernon		Servingman
12		Reignier	Mayor		Reignier	Reignier					Mayor
13		Bastard	Officer			Bastard					Servingman
14				Talbot	Talbot	Talbot	Talbot	Talbot			
Boy 1		Joan			Joan	Joan		Countess			
Boy 2				Gunner's Boy							King

3.2	3.3	3.4	4.1	4.2	4.3	4.4	5.1	5.2	5.3	5.4
Bedford			Governor of Paris*		Lucy	Lucy			Shepherd	
		Gloucester	Gloucester		York's Messenger		Gloucester			Gloucester
		Exeter	Exeter			Servant	Exeter			Exeter
		Warwick	Warwick		Talbot's Captain				Warwick	
		Winchester	Winchester				Winchester		Winchester	
English Capt.		Somerset	Somerset		Somerset		Papal Legate			
		York	York		York	John T.		York	York	
Watch	Burgundy	Suffolk	Suffolk	French Captain				Suffolk		Suffolk
Burgundy	Charles					Burgundy		Burgundy		
Charles	Alençon					Charles		Charles	Charles	
Alençon		Vernon	Vernon			Alençon		Alençon	Alençon	
Fastolfe			Fastolfe				Ambassador*	Reignier	Reignier	
Bastard	Bastard	Basset	Basset			Bastard		Bastard	Bastard	
Talbot		Talbot	Talbot	Talbot		Talbot		Scout		
Joan	Joan					Joan		Joan	Joan	
		King	King				King	Margaret		King

APPENDIX 3

NINETEENTH- AND TWENTIETH-CENTURY ADAPTATIONS

Twentieth-century performance tradition, in so far as there is one for this play, is of incorporating it into a 'cycle' of at least the other *Henry VI* plays, sometimes in a presentation of the chronological span from *Richard II* to *Richard III*. Performances of *1 Henry VI* as an uncut text have been extremely rare: the 'trilogy' was performed at Stratford-upon-Avon in 1906, directed by Frank Benson (see Introduction, p. 67); at the Old Vic, London, directed by Robert Atkins in 1923; and again at the Old Vic by the Birmingham Repertory Theatre Company, directed by Douglas Seale, in 1957.

The most notable recent production was given as the first part of the three-play cycle by the Royal Shakespeare Company (RSC) under Terry Hands's direction at Stratford and London in 1977 and 1978 respectively. (For a vivid and detailed account of the production, predicated enthusiastically on the idea of the plays as a 'trilogy', see Daniell, 247–75). Audience and critical reaction was largely enthusiastic and the plays were seen to have justified themselves as a three-part epic, but, according to Lois Potter, it 'left others longing for the clarity and consistency of the Barton–Hall version' (Potter, 171). Hands's production was strongly cast and performed in a fast-moving kinetic style with a bleak bare stage, harsh lighting and strip-cartoon-like leather and metallic costumes (designed by Farrah) which were to become an easily parodiable RSC hallmark, but which in this case served the play well. Part One, as it becomes in this context, was not skimped or condescended to, but was presented as a kind of extrovert prologue to the more internalized and emotionally demanding material of the next two parts. On the occasions when all three parts were staged in one day, the event was a marathon for both actors and audience. At a performance attended by the present editor one or two of the actors who had been busily doubling roles throughout were so exhausted at the end of a twelve-hour performing day of fighting and brawling that they had to be exempted from taking part in the botched and weary dance with which, at the closing lines of *3 Henry VI*, the director wittily parodied the celebratory cliché that ended so many RSC productions of the time; they were reduced to holding on to prominent pieces of furniture in order to simply stay upright.

Financial considerations have effectively vetoed the stage revival of a largely unknown play with, by modern conventions, a larger than usual cast. In the production of the play in 1982 in the BBC complete Shakespeare series, Jane Howell used the same 'full-scale repertory company' for all three *Henry VI* plays and for *Richard III*; 'planning the sequence and its casting became a months-long, intricate affair' (Willis, *BBC*, 170) and the sequence was filmed in a continuous period on a large single set built in a converted warehouse. This enabled her to present a coherent performance of a largely uncut text. Directorial intention is very evident here, and it pulls in two contradictory ways. The opening intelligently draws on the Marian musical tradition of Henry V's time to use a singer at Henry's funeral in a chanson of the death of Christ. This is a framing device of the whole BBC presentation of the tetralogy, in that *Richard III* ends with a blasphemous *pietà* in which the camera pans up from a pile of bodies made from all the actors who appeared in the sequence to a hysterically laughing Margaret cradling Richard's naked corpse. The actor singing the opening number is revealed later to be playing Henry VI. Distinct from this religious sense of the trilogy overall, Howell's production presents the action of *1 Henry VI* as 'childish'; 'it struck me . . . that the behavior of the lords of

England was a lot like children – prep school children' (Howell, quoted in Willis, *BBC*, 167). The design of her production is that of an adventure playground on an impoverished council estate *c*. 1970, all recycled demolition doors and planks, with pink and blue paint slapped on them, and the battles are a semi-improvised sequence of running on and shouting. The problem – and for this commentator it makes the production unwatchable in more than small sections at a time – is that a kind of amateurishness in much of the acting and filming pushes the performance across the line between the childlike and the merely childish. The effect is one of under-rehearsal, cut-price designs and some outstandingly ludicrous wigs. With the exception of the handling of asides (see Introduction, pp. 97–8), it has been filmed with disappointingly little awareness of the potential of television to make sense of the structure of the text. In this it stands in strong contrast to two earlier TV adaptations, the filmed version of the Royal Shakespeare Company's *The Wars of the Roses* (1965) and the BBC's *The Age of Kings* (1960).

Later stage productions of the Henry VI material – the RSC's *The Plantagenets* (1988–9) and the English Shakespeare Company's (ESC) *House of Lancaster* and *House of York* (1986) – have returned to the practice of Peter Hall and John Barton in *The Wars of the Roses* by using parts of *1 Henry VI* in the first half of a restructured diptych, as sections in a presentation of the eight history plays from *Richard II* to *Richard III*. The process of reworking began much earlier, with Edmund Kean's plundering of material from all three plays to create, in 1817, a tragic role for himself as the title-role in *Richard, Duke of York*, to be performed as a precursor to his *Richard III*. Though the title-page of a later reprint (1852) describes it 'as adapted by Edmund Kean', the literary work was done by J.R. Merivale, a friend of Lord Byron. The first three scenes of Act one use material from *1 Henry VI* to build up Richard Plantagenet and to give a basis for his future actions: first comes a compressed version of the rose-plucking scene, with a more 'melodramatic' ending –

　　　War. This blot shall be wiped out before the king,
Who, if he bids thee not arise as York,
I will not live to be accounted Warwick.
– Meet me an hour hence, and we'll to the council.
　　　Plant. *First to my uncle's prison, aged March,*
There drink fresh spirit from his fast bleeding wrongs.
Thence, in an hour's space, will I call for thee.
　　　　　　　　　　　　　　　　　(Merivale/Kean, 7)

The next scene is the death of Mortimer, again compressed, and
ending with a 'stronger' exit for Richard:

　　　Plant. And peace – no war – befall thy parting soul!
In prison hast thou spent thy pilgrimage,
And like a hermit, overpast thy days!
Here lies the dusky torch of Mortimer,
Choak'd with th'ambition of a meaner race.
Fortune, not reason, rules the state of things;
Reward goes backward, Honour on his head –
As cedars beaten with continual storms,
So great men flourish. –
Man is a torch borne in the wind – a dream
But of a shadow, summ'd with all his substance:
And as great seamen using all their wealth
And skill in Neptune's deep invisible paths,
In tall ships richly built and ribb'd with brass,
To put a girdle round about the world;
When they have done it, (coming near their haven)
Are fain to give a warning piece, and call
A poor stay'd fisherman, that never past
His country's sight, to waft and guide them in;
So, when we wander furthest through the waves
Of glassy glory, and the gulphs of state,
Topp'd with all titles, spreading all our reaches,
As if each private arm would sphere the earth,

> *We must to Virtue for her guide resort,*
> *Or we shall shipwreck in our safest port.* *
>
> (Merivale/Kean, 9–10)

The asterisk at the end of that passage points to a footnote: 'The passages printed in Italics are those borrowed from the works of contemporary authors, or introduced for the sake of necessary connexion. The above is from Chapman's *Bussy D'Amboise*'. All the plays Merivale drew on for these extra flourishes 'had recently been reprinted in C.W. Dilke's *Old English Plays* (1815–16), probably the only place where they could be read' (Merivale/Kean, vi).

The next scene is another fairly accurate digest of Richard's instatement into his dukedom, ending on a speech which again puts together a nautical metaphor with garbled Shakespearean echoes and lines from other characters (here Suffolk's persuasion of the King to marry Margaret), becoming sarcastic in its transposition:

> *York*. An if I wis, he did – but let that rest.
> *Men must have these lures when they hawk for princes,*
> *And wind about them like a subtle river,*
> *That, seeming only to run on his course,*
> *Doth search yet as he runs, and still finds out*
> *The easier parts of entry on the shore,*
> *Gliding so slily by, as scarce it touch'd,*
> *Yet still eats something in it. –*
> *Give me a spirit that on life's rough sea*
> *Loves to have his sails fill'd with a lusty wind,*
> *Even till his sailyards tremble, his masts crack,*
> *And his rapt ship run on her side so low*
> *That she drinks water, and her keel ploughs air . . .* *
> *Hark! heard you not that shout? It doth proclaim*
> *The coming of that peerless bride of Anjou.*
> *Come, Warwick, to the bridal – haste we to greet*
> *Our most victorious Lord Ambassador,*
> *Who brings this princely treasure home with him.*
> *True, our most pious king was first betroth'd*

> *Unto another – old Armagnac's daughter,*
> *Our chiefest hope in France – But what of that?*
> The best earl's daughter is unequal odds,
> Matched with the heiress of a throneless king.
> And, for a dower, let's not disgrace our prince
> To think that he should be so base and poor,
> As chuse for wealth and not for perfect love.
> Not whom we will – but whom his grace affects
> Must be companion of his nuptial bed.
> *– But come, my lord, we're too long out of th'sun.*
>
> (Merivale/Kean, 14–15)

The asterisk here is to signal a borrowing from 'Chapman's *Byron's Conspiracy*'.

Inevitably every adaptation implies a reading of the play that says as much of the historical and theatrical context of the adaptation as it does of the original text. Later adaptations also reveal the presuppositions of the theatrical idiom of the time as to what constitutes a dramatic climax and what allows the protagonist to project a heroic presence, and this in turn begs the questions – who is the protagonist, what is the heroic? Structurally, different styles at different periods imply different ideas about what builds continuity, what an audience demands as a line through a complex set of events, what it will recognize as narrative logic. Behind the adaptations lies the assumption that *1 Henry VI* is itself confused; this too reveals as much about the preconceptions of the adapters as it does about the text.

In Peter Hall's introduction to the published text of *The Wars of the Roses* he justifies 'the ultimate literary heresy: Shakespeare cut, rewritten, and rearranged' by saying that 'there is a difference between interfering with the text of mature Shakespeare and with the text of the *Henry VI*'s. These plays are not only apprentice work, uneven in quality; we cannot be sure that Shakespeare was their sole author . . . some [scholars] hold that his contribution was as a collaborator or reviser'. Hall also cites his conviction that the plays do not work in unadapted form. 'I have seen the original version played twice . . . Shakespeare's voice is heard sporadically, and his vision, sharp and intense in some scenes, is swamped by the mass of Tudor history in others. All the same' – as he goes on immediately to say – 'I was doubtful about publishing our version. Our production was conceived with a knowledge of the whole text. If we cut an important passage, we only did so in the conviction that its values were being expressed in other ways . . . I therefore feel it is dangerous for anybody to use our text as the basis for another production . . . what follows is . . . what we found meaningful in the 1960's in Shakespeare's view of history. Its value is ephemeral, and its judgements are inevitably . . . of the decade which produced it and us' (Barton & Hall, vii–ix). John Barton's essay 'The Making of the Adaptation' agrees with Hall but adds more cautiously (and fortuitously, given the later success of the uncut Hands version), 'the obvious defence [i.e. of the adaptation] that they [the *Henry VI* plays] are much inferior to Shakespeare's best work, begins to look suspect when one remembers that other plays in the canon, such as *Titus Andronicus*, *Pericles* and *Timon of Athens*, have been similarly dismissed only to be proved viable in the theatre after all'. He goes on to observe that the compression was 'the response to theatrical pressure . . . [the] decision was strictly practical . . . we have perforce to be cautious about the number of rarities we include in our repertory' (Barton & Hall, xv).

Barton then explains, presenting his argument by reproducing an exchange of memos between himself and Hall, that the material of the French scenes of the original *1 Henry VI* is compressed into the first part of his *Henry VI* in order to emphasize their importance as setting up, through the opposition of the 'witchcraft' of Joan and 'a great and pious soldier, Talbot', what they call 'the curse on England' (Barton & Hall, xx).

This is also underlined in the opening of the text – a voice, that of Henry V, reads from his will, as presented in the sources, while the audience looks at the unattended hearse. The extract ends: '*What I have gotten, I charge you keep it. I command you*

defend it. And I desire you to nourish it'. After that Barton's alterations and cuts are largely in the service of compression and
pace. While not on the scale of Kean and Merivale's alterations,
they show a similar concern with forging scenic continuity. In
doing so they refer back to *Henry V* and try to construct a more
stable structure of prophecy, foreknowledge and memory than
that of the more quizzical and fluid original. Barton's additions
tend also to give individual figures more dignity. 'Charles *the
Dauphin*' says at the start of scene 2 (after the first four lines of
his original speech):

> Yet learn we, lords, from all that is forepast,
> Not to o'ervalue now our present fortune:
> The English thought at fatal Agincourt
> That France was like to be their own for ever;
> But Henry's death turn'd fortune's wheel about,
> And that same wheel must shortly turn again.
>
> (Barton & Hall, 5)

This and other emendations – Joan at the end of this scene claiming that 'My spirits swear to me, / That are all-potent and
infallible, / That fate hath put a curse on England's house'
(Barton & Hall, 8), or Bedford's dying *sententia*,

> Such is the history of all ambition,
> Now up, now down: how happy then am I
> To die at such an hour of England's glory.
> Old Bedford, close thine eyes and take thy rest:
>
> (Barton & Hall, 16)

– resemble Merivale's in their imposition of greater reflectiveness
on the characters as a means to a clearer continuity of action and,
like his, tend to the slightly ludicrous tone of invented folk wisdom.
Two long invented exchanges bring one closer to what is distinctive
in the Barton & Hall adaptation. Bedford, brooding on history and
class with a worried and disgruntled Talbot earlier in the scene,
remarks:

> Ah, Talbot, thou and I are simple men:
> All our ambition is for England's good.
> But for the rest, albeit their words are ours,
> Of England and of true inheritance,
> They do but sanctify their inward malice,
> Which is a vile abuse of those true sanctions
> That, under God, do tend on government.
>> (Barton & Hall, 14)

His prescience here moralizes the structure of the play. In the next scene, an invented council meeting allows Hall and Barton to establish what they identify as the dominant image of their trilogy: the council table, here organized and introduced by Henry, later to be hacked up by Richard III's thugs; the scene also allows more prominence to Henry (in contrast to the Merivale/Kean version where he becomes almost invisible), here played by a 'star' adult actor, David Warner.

> Good uncle, do you sit upon my right, –
> You on my left, my lord of Winchester, –
> For you shall be my chiefest counsellors.
>
> (They take their seats at the council-table)
>
> So, so, my lords.
>> (Barton & Hall, 19)

Hall and Barton's interest is primarily in political process; as I have suggested above, their inventions are largely in the interest of continuity, and *1 Henry VI* takes its place as a stage in the disintegration of the English state, leading to the tyrannical destruction of any semblance of a consensus under Richard III. In their version Winchester is identified throughout with the written and Gloucester with the spoken, and the dialogue, especially that of 3.1, is reassigned to suit this, a conscious revision of the play as F presents it, but in the direction of the anti-literacy prejudice of working-class characters in *2 Henry VI* and *Julius Caesar*. Though the production is costumed and set in a carefully realized Middle Ages of warlike iron, heavy and unglamorous fabrics, dark council chambers and muddy battle-fields, it was widely read at the time as a commentary on both the international and the domestic politics of its day.

As with the other adaptations discussed in this appendix, I present a scene-by-scene breakdown of the way *The Wars of the Roses* uses material from *1 Henry VI*.

The Wars of the Roses: Henry VI

1 A speech based on Henry V's will, read in voice-over. Then the interrupted funeral, with only one messenger. Bedford touches the coffin, and exits with 'farewell my master . . .'

2 The French outside Orleans. The Dauphin is more thought-ful and philosophical than F's version, with new lines (including musings on fortune's wheel) to accommodate this. Joan is introduced; at the end of the scene she refers to a 'curse set on the English', which she has learnt of from 'my spirits . . . that are all potent and infallible'.

3 The rose garden. Warwick's conciliatory lines are cut, and at the end of the scene he appoints himself Richard Plantagenet's patron, offering to see the issue of his title through 'the council'. The character is thus merged with the Warwick of the subsequent *Henry VI* plays.

4 A spectacularly decrepit Mortimer (clutching a crumpled bit of paper, presumably to represent his 'claim') declares to Richard Plantagenet, 'thou art my heir'.

5 Talbot tries to rally the English outside Orleans. The French fly their colours over Orleans. Joan shouts, 'a child, a silly dwarf' (a phrase taken from the Countess of Auvergne (2.3.24)), over the battlements at a retreating Talbot.

Bedford meets Talbot and Burgundy and they take Orleans. But Bedford has a kind of seizure at the base of his ladder, and stays behind to watch the battle. He dies, after some more of Barton's philosophical musings, at the end of the scene.

6 The King receives petitions, the first Richard's, then one from Winchester; in a reversal of the Gloucester/Winchester scene at 3.1, Gloucester challenges Winchester to accuse him verbally, rather than in writing. Then the nobles move from around the throne to a council table, where Gloucester, in a wholly invented sequence, devises and tries to enforce a voting system for the peers, with the King expressing his reluctance to take supreme power.

7 The English recover Orleans. Joan woos Burgundy.

8 The coronation.

9 Talbot, with a sizeable group of soldiers, outside Bordeaux.

10 York and Exeter (replacing Lucy).

11 Somerset and Exeter.

12 Talbot and his son. As in F, the fight is omitted, and they fall to cannon fire. Talbot's death; the French enter to discover his body.

13 The King and Gloucester discuss peace and the Armagnac marriage.

14 The French go into battle. Joan invokes invisible demons, lying face down on the battlefield. She slices into her hand to offer them blood, then rolls on her back to offer them her throat and bosom. She recovers to fight York, and defeats him, but he is rescued by his soldiers.

15 Suffolk and Margaret.

16 Joan dragged to the stake. York gloats that 'Now is Lord Talbot utterly revenged', and laughs. Winchester turns up for the peace treaty. The scene ends on an invented dialogue for York and Warwick, where Warwick outlines a military policy, building on York's role in France, to enable his taking of the English throne.

17 Suffolk persuades Henry to marry Margaret, as part of a largely invented scene concerned with Gloucester's authority and his relation to the King.

The place of the military action in this kind of adaptation is less prominent than in F. In *The Wars of the Roses* it is a symptom of 'the curse on England'.

The implied parallel with the decline of British military and colonial power in the mid-twentieth century was made more explicit in the ESC's later presentation of a chronological history cycle, from *Richard II* to *Richard III*, where again the material of *Henry VI* was cut down into two plays, here called *House of Lancaster* and *House of York*. Apart from *Richard II*, performed in early nineteenth-century costume, presumably as if it were a reminiscence of a lost 'romantic' England, the costume and setting were largely those of 1980s Britain. Margaret Thatcher and her Conservative government's attempt to revive a patriotic fervour in the campaign to recapture the Falkland Islands, one of Britain's few remaining fragments of empire, was clearly on the mind of the director, Michael Bogdanov – indeed the 'Margaret' of the play (June Watson) developed into a visual and vocal reminder of the Margaret of the politics of the time, a point not lost on the production's audiences, and tending, as did the mixture of modern costume and barbaric violence, to weight the show towards satire and a vicious black humour. Talbot in this context is a reminder of old values, values that pre-date the 'Falklands' patriotism of the preceding *Henry V*. At the start of *House of York* Cade and his followers (Cade played by the same actor, Michael Pennington, as played Henry V) revive the violent Union Jack-waving patriotism of the earlier play as mob violence and hooliganism, thus offering a commentary on the continuity between the 'Falklands factor' and increasing problems in Thatcher's Britain of racist and nationalistic rioting. Talbot (Michael Fenner), in contrast, is in Edwardian (Boer War) uniform, and the wars in France (with trenches and barbed wire) are visually reminiscent of the First World War. With eye-patch and moustache, and officer-class accent, he seems like a kind of quotation (as, to a less obvious extent, does Joan, with chain mail over her battledress), a hero from a *Boy's Own* adventure, or a cartoon character. Unexpectedly, this largely comic performance modulates into one of the most moving and fully realized versions of the scenes with John. Both pathos and parody mark him as a figure from a near-forgotten past – both conceptually and in physical staging. Bogdanov takes the military action far more seriously than do Barton and Hall. The following breakdown of the action, and any lines quoted, are transcribed from the commercially available video, recorded live at the Grand Theatre, Swansea, and issued in 1990.

Henry VI: House of Lancaster

1 The funeral, with only one messenger. (Identified later as Lucy, the same actor takes all the messenger roles in the English–French action, including Fastolfe, though without inheriting the 'cowardly' part of that role.)

2 Joan meets the French.

3 The rose garden.

4 Gloucester and Winchester quarrel in front of the King (but without their followers). Richard is made Duke of York, but with more overt opposition from Somerset than in F: 'His father was a foul ignoble traitor. Can he reap honour from his father's shame?'

5 Talbot tries to rally the soldiers, and mourns a composite dead English commander called 'Lancaster'. Joan defeats him, apparently by hypnosis. (See Introduction, p. 32).

6 Talbot wins Orleans.

7 Burgundy and Talbot in alliance. Then Burgundy is left alone for an invented, meditative soliloquy:

> Now Burgundy, betide thyself a while.
> For what ails France, and Burgundy, what thee?. . .
> . . . fair France bleeds, its fertile fields should flower . . .
> My country calls me, honour calls me. Aye –
> Heaven help Burgundy.

Joan enters and persuades him to join the French.

8 Coronation.
9 Talbot calls Burgundy to the walls of Bordeaux – 'Traitor! . . . false Burgundy, unto the walls come forth' – so it is Burgundy who announces Talbot's death.
10 York and Lucy.
11 Somerset and Lucy.
12 Talbot and John.
13 John's fight with the French commanders, performed at length (see Introduction, pp. 17–18). At the end of the scene Talbot is felled by a pistol shot from offstage.
14 Death of the Talbots. John is dragged on stage on a Union Jack.
15 Margaret and Suffolk. Their scene is framed by a wordless rape attempt by three English soldiers on a woman who, though wearing a skirt, looks initially as if she might be Joan, and who at the end of the scene runs across the stage before Joan enters.
16 Joan's invocation to the demons is changed to 'Help gracious lady, appear to me, give sign / And help me in this enterprise', and is reduced to an admission of defeat, a rhetorical demonstration of powerlessness (see Introduction, p. 33). Then York throws a net over her.
17 The peace treaty. At the end, Joan, in the background, is 'necklaced' – another contemporary image, the practice of rival groups in South Africa of assassination by putting a burning tyre round the victim's neck. At the front of the stage the English sip whisky.
18 Henry is persuaded to marry Margaret. At the end, Winchester enters as Cardinal. Gloucester has the last pessimistic word on this, conflating some of Exeter's lines and some of his own from scenes cut earlier.

The Plantagenets, Adrian Noble's two-part adaptation of the *Henry VI* plays for the RSC in 1988, was comparatively apolitical. Its style was pictorial, with the text freely adapted ('The first stages of the adaptation were done in collaboration with Charles Wood' – Noble, xii) to provide a fluid, cinematic sequence of images, where the transitions were as telling as the scenes themselves. Henry's coffin, for example, sinks into the ground towards the end of the first scene, and there emerges from the same trap a group of marching English soldiers, as if they were the survival of his spirit. (This fluidity necessitates a more complex labelling of scenes in my breakdown.) The medievalism of the design was more colourful than that of *The Wars of the Roses*, using light synthetic fabrics and gold where the earlier productions stressed the weight and harshness of the material world of the plays. John Bury, Hall and Barton's designer, was recognized as taking a 'Brechtian' approach in terms of that strand of Brecht's work developed by the Berliner Ensemble which emphasizes materiality and historical specificity. The 'storybook' spectacle of *The Plantagenets* represented something different from either this or the ESC's montage of contemporary media-derived references; as far as *1 Henry VI* goes, the effect was lightweight, vivid and kinetic.

To be fair to the production as a whole, one should remember that *The Plantagenets* was a free-standing diptych, where *1 Henry VI* could not acquire the significance it did in the larger cycles, and so it operated as an audience warm-up, an extrovert prologue to the claustrophobically violent action of the civil war. Within the politics of the RSC, the aim was to develop younger actors within an ensemble. While this pays off for those – especially Henry (Ralph Fiennes) and Margaret (Penny Downie) – who can develop characters across both parts, performances of the *1 Henry VI* material were – at least on the evidence of the RSC's in-house video recording – too often shallow and disengaged. As with the 1982 BBC version (but neither the ESC nor the earlier RSC versions, which succeeded in this respect), the realization that the style of the piece is more ironic than monumentally 'heroic' triggered a collapse into some lazy acting, both trivial and camp.

The Plantagenets, Stratford, 1988

1 The funeral. Two messengers. The coffin sinks down into the stage halfway through the scene; in the following scene a group of English soldiers come out of the same trap, as if representing Henry's legacy, his mission 'reborn'.

2 'March' – a scene invented out of the 'Is Talbot slain' section of F's first scene (1.1.141). The soldiers march on the spot 'towards' the audience. Bedford joins them at the end of the scene.

3 The rose garden. The Gloucester/Winchester riots erupt (wordlessly and, from an audience point of view, probably inexplicably) at the end of the scene, to underline the point that 'this quarrel will draw blood'.

4 The death of Mortimer.

5 The King opens parliament. Gloucester and Winchester clash.

6 An extended 'action' scene (located in the published text, rather oddly, in '*The cathedral garden of France*').

   (a) The French enter (on high gold hobby-horses) but are beaten back. Joan's imminent arrival is signalled.

   (b) Talbot meets Salisbury and tells him about his captivity. Talbot hears 'tumult in the heavens', signalled by a loud offstage shout of 'Dauphin' from Joan, which leads into . . .

   (c) Joan confronts the Dauphin and Reignier.

7 (a) The French defeat Talbot, and fly their flags over Orleans.

   (b) Talbot, Bedford and Burgundy scale the walls. Vernon and Basset challenge each other.

   (c) The French leap over the walls. They are frightened off by 'Watkins', an English soldier, who takes their discarded robes.

   (d) Talbot and his troops celebrate victory and mourn Bedford.

   (e) Joan woos Burgundy, initially from offstage.

8 Henry's coronation in Paris. He takes the red rose.

9   Talbot outside Harfleur. His death is presaged by the Bastard of Orleans.
10 Somerset and York fail to help Talbot. Messages are delivered and moralized on by Exeter and 'Watkins'.
11 Talbot and son; son killed rapidly, French stay on stage till six of them spear Talbot, at the end of his dying speech. French prepare for battle.
12 Joan re-enters, abandoned by her fellow commanders. She invokes the demons (the dead on the battlefield) with some initial success. Then she is captured and burnt, while shouting the names of demons (see Introduction, p. 33).
13 Peace treaty – marriage plans – but (as the prompt-book has it) 'the UNITED ARMY dividing into white and red roses again'.
14 Suffolk, Margaret and Reignier. Margaret is cloaked, scared and hungry. The scene is played in front of Joan's body, which has remained on stage since her burning.
INTERVAL
15 Part of Suffolk's 'selling' of Margaret to Henry, to preface her entry into the English court.

Finally, a pioneering adaptation, made especially for television. While actors and reviewers discussing the later productions tend to find analogies in TV serials and 'soap opera', the BBC's *Age of Kings* (1960), an adaptation of the history plays into a Sunday-afternoon serial in half-hourly episodes, was highly influential in British television in the formation both of a kind of serious issue-based 'soap opera' and of serial adaptations of classics, still current genres on British television at the time of writing. Set and camera work were technically extremely limited, but the restrictions of pioneering work within a new medium and the participation of actors who went on to be some of the most significant of their generation (Sean Connery turns up as Hotspur, for example; Judi Dench as Katherine of France) help to create a witty and imaginative version that makes this for me the most successful of all adaptations in finding the text's potential as a vivid and subversively entertaining popularization of English history.

The Age of Kings, Episode 9: The Red Rose and the White

1 The funeral (with three messengers).
2 Joan is introduced.
3 Winchester and Gloucester fight over the Tower.
4 The rose garden.
5 Winchester and Gloucester at court. Their followers riot, Richard is made Duke of York.
6 Coronation (but not in France – on the same set, with no congregation). The Armagnac marriage is proposed.
7 Joan in defeat invokes the demons (seen within a close-up of her eyes; see Introduction, p. 34).
8 Suffolk captures Margaret, and works out a deal with Reignier.
9 Joan's 'trial' – with the shepherd, and ending in a spectacular burning.
10 The peace treaty.
11 Suffolk persuades Henry to marry Margaret.

APPENDIX 4
MILITARY HIERARCHY AND THE CONDUCT OF WAR

A major part of this play is concerned with warfare; the language of war, its conduct and the social structure it creates are central to it. This appendix identifies and seeks to elucidate military matters relevant to understanding the play, matters often passed over in editions (and always in productions) as an ahistorical sense of warfare is unconsciously brought into play. Warfare and the issues of military command in *1 Henry VI* were highly topical at the time of its first performances, and may well have made a major contribution to its success. Campaigns in the Low Countries and in Ireland replicated many of the difficulties facing the English forces in *1 Henry VI*. Elizabeth's army was undergoing a process of change which took it from a mode of organization continuing from the late medieval feudal army to a modern structure already in place in most of its European rivals. The military tactics and terms used in the play are common to both periods, but an audience would have been aware of the increasing obsolescence and inefficiency of medieval practices, shown by the play to be ineffective; such practices were under debate by polemicists and in the Privy Council at the time of the play's performance. In addition to being over-stretched and inefficiently structured, Elizabeth's army faced difficulties of generalship; Elizabeth inherited the feudal tradition that the monarch was the general, but as a woman she had to depute this responsibility to noblemen of her choice, and her choice was rarely successful. Finally, a much-debated topic of the late Elizabethan period was the relation of firepower and artillery to traditional arms. These issues – the constitution of an army, generalship and structures of command, tactics and arms – will be discussed here in order both to clarify the play's terminology and to illustrate its topicality; its analysis of English failure and defeat is a contribution to an urgent debate of the 1580s and 1590s.

What is an army?

Bedford in the first scene of the play seems to refer to a standing army on which he can draw at will:

> Ten thousand soldiers with me I will take,
> Whose bloody deeds shall make all Europe quake.
>
> (1.1.155–6)

But this is bravado. A medieval army would have been dependent on ad hoc levies by feudal laws, supplemented increasingly by mercenaries. Elizabeth's government, in a series of bills put through parliament between 1588 and 1601, sought to establish a mode of recruitment that was better organized and regulated. This was not only a matter of maintaining campaigns abroad; another function of the army was to control the population at home, partly by keeping the young male population occupied, partly by having a standing army as a threat against insurrection. This meant, ironically, that the better soldiers were kept at home, and foreign campaigns suffered as a result (Cruickshank, 6–7).

Generals and captains

Normally, the general was the head of the nation's forces, and was usually the monarch. When it was necessary for someone other than the monarch to deputize, he was, in theory at least, 'directly controlled by the instructions from the queen or Privy Council, or both' (Cruickshank, 42–4). As a child, Henry is in the same position as Elizabeth was as a woman, and the chain of command becomes confused and open to dispute. Bedford impulsively takes the command on himself at 1.1.85, confirming his resolve when Gloucester challenges him (1.1.99–102). It would seem that there has been no general in the hiatus after Henry V's death. After Bedford's death, at the Paris coronation (4.1.162–8), Henry unwisely joins York and Somerset in a joint generalship, as a means of reconciling them, while passing over the properly humble 'captain', Talbot. Historically the two men were lieutenant-generals (Fowler, 125), but the play does not use this term, and so heightens rather than resolves the confusion; Lucy addresses York at 4.3.17 as 'Thou princely leader of our English strength'. Margaret, at the end of the first scene of *3 Henry VI* (1.1.251–6), appoints herself general in her husband's stead. Richard of Gloucester's confidence that 'A woman's general; what should we fear?' (*3H6* 1.2.68) turns out to be misplaced, with fatal results for his father York. In *1 Henry VI* Joan Puzel seems to take over the role from the Dolphin, but again a woman cannot officially be a general; this leaves her vulnerable, dependent on results, and gives the Dolphin an alibi for what may happen if it goes wrong. All these unstable 'generalships' can be seen as refractions of the contemporary situation, given Elizabeth's position. In *Richard III* Richmond is careful to characterize himself not as a 'general' but as God's 'captain' (5.3.108), so marking the hiatus in which England, until Richmond becomes king, has no true general. (At two cruxes in this play, where it may look as if 'general' is being used in the modern military sense, the word may include a quite different sense, as 'generalities' or as 'the general' – the people (see 1.1.73n., 4.2.2n.)).

This play ignores most of the intermediary ranks between the general and the fighting troops. This gap, an area of confusion between the rank of general and that of captain, has a point to make about contemporary attempts to reform military organization. The absence or lack of development of such ranks, and so of efficient lines of communication, was a major problem for the Elizabethan army. 'The gap between the higher command and the captains had to be filled somehow. The first step was the creation of the sergeant-major, sergeant-general, or sergeant-major-major' (Cruickshank, 50). The ordinary sergeant, like the one seen at the start of 2.1, giving two discontented French Sentinels their orders, is responsible for organization within the basic unit of an armed force, the 'band', each led by its captain. The term could be used of a temporary responsibility; Alençon is 'captain of the watch' when the English (unhistorically) recapture Orleans, and so gets the blame from the Dolphin. Joan Puzel addresses the other French commanders, including the Dolphin, as 'captains' after her recapture of Orleans (3.2.70), a token perhaps of her confidence here in her generalship. At 3.4.16 King Henry calls Talbot 'captain', after he has laid his sword at the King's feet; the gesture of submission demonstrates Talbot's willingness to accept the King as his general, rather than (now that Bedford is dead) taking on the role himself, but the play maintains the sense of a hiatus in leadership by leaving open the question of who exactly is in charge. In the Irish and Dutch campaigns contemporary with the play, captains were frequently accused of exploiting their powerful position as sole intermediary between the men in their band and the government to defraud both financially, which – combined with large-scale desertions – did much to destabilize the Irish campaign from within (Cruickshank, 54–5). After the 1580s, the English army adopted the European model of organization into regiments (Cruickshank, 51–2), but this comparatively new and still not fully developed structure is not reflected in the play.

The play presents various unnamed captains as subsidiary figures, who accompany the named aristocratic commanders; the one who appears with Talbot and speaks one line at 2.2.60 could appear also as the challenger of Fastolfe at 3.2.102–7, and also as the Captain who in 4.3 has left his 'o'ermatched forces' to seek help from Somerset. Whether separate or conflated, such captains are not necessarily of lower social class than the named characters, nor in a subsidiary relation to them, though this is how modern productions, adopting implicitly or explicitly a more modern style of military hierarchy, tend to present them. At the same time, feudal obligations complicate a purely military structure: the Captain who helps Talbot play his trick on the Countess (2.2.59–60) addresses him as 'my lord' and may well be of his 'family' or local clan, like the Servant who leads him on wounded at 4.4.112.1–2.

Tactics: arms and artillery

1 Henry VI tracks in its military action the changes in warfare which, having led to the English defeat in the Hundred Years' War, were still controversial for the audience of the play. In it we see traditional English weaponry, continuing use of which was still advocated by late Elizabethan commentators, overtaken by technological developments. In the first scene Talbot is described as adopting, without success, a classic English strategy:

> No leisure had he to enrank his men.
> He wanted pikes to set before his archers,
> Instead whereof sharp stakes plucked out of hedges
> They pitched in the ground confusedly,
> To keep the horsemen off from breaking in.
>
> (1.1.115–19)

The longbow was associated with the English victories of Edward III and Henry V, where, protected by the 'harrow' of pikes (Bennett, 15), the 'stakes' that Talbot did not have time to fix in the ground, the bowmen confronted French horsemen with weaponry of a force and efficiency that, in Edward III's time, they had never before encountered. The collapse of traditional English strategy in this play – without the pikes to protect them from cavalry charges, the English bowmen are vulnerable, their weaponry made to seem almost farcically cumbersome – begins, ominously, a sequence of defeats which figure the historical circumstance that it is now the French who have the technological upper hand. The development and deployment of firearms by the French speeded up the final stages of English defeat. In the interests of instating the event as an icon of an heroic past, the play ignores or at least does not specify the part-technological, part-improvised means of Talbot's death – he was shot by a culverin, a sort of small hand-held cannon, then finished off with an axe (Fowler, 110) – but some productions have, to good effect, used the first part of this at least in killing Talbot with firearms (see Introduction, p. 17, and Appendix 2), and the French Captain on the walls of Bordeaux

warns him that 'Ten thousand French have ta'en the sacrament /
To rive their dangerous artillery' on him (4.2.28–9). Gunpowder
and explosions are consistently associated with the French, in a
context that draws on an association with cheating, even devilry.
The effect of the cannon shot, cheekily set off by the Gunner's
Boy in 1.4, is echoed and amplified a little later in the scene by the
pyrotechnically achieved thunder and lightning that accompanies
Joan Puzel, disrupting Talbot's defiant response to the killing of
his fellow commanders, and creating a confusion between the natural, the portentous and the tactical:

> Wretched shall France be only in my name.
> *Here an alarum, and it thunders and lightens.*
> What stir is this? What tumult's in the heavens?
> Whence cometh this alarum and the noise?
>
> (1.4.96–8)

Like other aspects of the military action of the play, the controversy between bow and gun was highly topical. Firearms were
supplanting bows for military purposes, and in 1588 the Council
embarked on a series of measures to establish the manufacture of
gunpowder, hitherto imported (Cruickshank, 126). But archery
was established in English life, not simply through nostalgia, but
as an important manufacture, and as an officially approved leisure
occupation for that part of the young male population on whose
potential for disruption much legislation was focused, and the
issue was debated in government and in a series of pamphlets
(Cruickshank, 104–9).

Similarly, the organization of the play as a sequence of sieges
points to contemporary debates on tactics in Ireland and the
Low Countries. One effect of this on the play is an emphasis on
food and eating – ironically the English besiegers run out of supplies before the well-supplied French towns they attack, as we
are told in the first and second scenes (1.1.157–61; 1.2.9–12). In
1435 the historical Fastolfe had advised a shift from siege warfare to a kind of 'scorched earth policy', 'brenning and

destroying all the lands as they pass' (Fowler, 165). This advice was ignored, and *1 Henry VI* demonstrates the difficulties of siege warfare and the problems of supply lines in a way particularly pertinent to campaigns in Ireland at the time, where shortfalls in supplies accelerated the rapid desertion rate of English soldiers, and a shift to policies like Fastolfe's became the norm in an increasingly destructive campaign (Cruickshank, 76).

ABBREVIATIONS AND REFERENCES

Quotations and references to Shakespeare's plays and poems other than *King Henry VI, Part 1* are from Arden, third series, and *The Riverside Shakespeare*, second edition (Boston, Mass., and New York, 1997). Biblical quotations are from the 'Geneva Bible' (facsimile of the 1560 edn, with an introduction by Lloyd E. Berry (London, 1969)). Bullough's extracts from Hall and Holinshed have been corrected against the original editions. In all references, place of publication is London unless otherwise stated.

ABBREVIATIONS

ABBREVIATIONS USED IN THE NOTES

*	precedes commentary notes involving readings that are not found in F
ed.	edited
edn	edition
facs.	facsimile
introd.	introduced by
ms	manuscript
repr.	reprinted
rev.	revised by
SD	stage direction
sig.	signature
SP	speech prefix
subst.	substantially
this edn	a reading adopted for the first time in this edition
TLN	through line numbering in *The First Folio of Shakespeare* ed. Charlton Hinman
trans.	translated by
vol.	volume

WORKS BY AND PARTLY BY SHAKESPEARE

AC	*Antony and Cleopatra*
AW	*All's Well That Ends Well*
AYL	*As You Like It*
CE	*The Comedy of Errors*
Cor	*Coriolanus*
Cym	*Cymbeline*
E3	*The Reign of King Edward III*
Ham	*Hamlet*
1H4	*King Henry IV, Part 1*
2H4	*King Henry IV, Part 2*
H5	*King Henry V*
1H6	*King Henry VI, Part 1*
2H6	*King Henry VI, Part 2*
3H6	*King Henry VI, Part 3*
H8	*King Henry VIII*
JC	*Julius Caesar*
KJ	*King John*
KL	*King Lear*
LLL	*Love's Labour's Lost*
Luc	*The Rape of Lucrece*
MA	*Much Ado About Nothing*
Mac	*Macbeth*
MM	*Measure for Measure*
MND	*A Midsummer Night's Dream*
MV	*The Merchant of Venice*
MW	*The Merry Wives of Windsor*
Oth	*Othello*
Per	*Pericles*
PP	*The Passionate Pilgrim*
R2	*King Richard II*
R3	*King Richard III*
RJ	*Romeo and Juliet*
Son	*Sonnets*
STM	*Sir Thomas More*
TC	*Troilus and Cressida*
Tem	*The Tempest*
TGV	*The Two Gentlemen of Verona*
Tim	*Timon of Athens*
Tit	*Titus Andronicus*
TN	*Twelfth Night*
TNK	*The Two Noble Kinsmen*
TS	*The Taming of the Shrew*
VA	*Venus and Adonis*
WT	*The Winter's Tale*

REFERENCES

EDITIONS OF SHAKESPEARE COLLATED

Alexander	*William Shakespeare: The Complete Works*, ed. Peter Alexander (1951)
Ard[1]	*The First Part of King Henry the Sixth*, ed. H. C. Hart (1909)
Ard[2]	*The First Part of King Henry VI*, ed. Andrew S. Cairncross (1962)
Cam	*Works*, ed. William George Clark, William Aldis Wright, 9 vols (Cambridge and London, 1863–6)
Cam[1]	*Henry VI, Part 1*, ed. J. Dover Wilson (Cambridge, 1952)
Cam[2]	*The First Part of King Henry VI*, ed. Michael Hattaway (Cambridge, 1990)
Capell	*Comedies, Histories, and Tragedies*, ed. Edward Capell, 10 vols (1767–8)
Collier	*Works*, ed. John Payne Collier, 8 vols (1842–4)
Collier[2]	*Works*, ed. John Payne Collier, 6 vols (1858)
Dyce	*Works*, ed. Alexander Dyce, 6 vols (1857)
Dyce[2]	*Works*, ed. Alexander Dyce, 9 vols (1864–7)
F	*Comedies, Histories and Tragedies*, The First Folio (1623)
F2	*Comedies, Histories and Tragedies*, The Second Folio (1632)
F3	*Comedies, Histories and Tragedies*, The Third Folio (1663)
F4	*Comedies, Histories and Tragedies*, The Fourth Folio (1685)
Hanmer	*Works*, ed. Thomas Hanmer, 6 vols (Oxford, 1743–4)
Hudson	*Works*, ed. Henry N. Hudson, 20 vols (Boston and Cambridge, Mass., 1886)
Johnson	*Plays*, ed. Samuel Johnson, 8 vols (1765)
Keightley	*Plays*, ed. Thomas Keightley, 6 vols (1864)
Kittredge	*Works*, ed. George Lyman Kittredge (Boston, Mass., 1936)
Malone	*Plays and Poems*, ed. Edmond Malone, 10 vols (1790)
Munro	*Works*, ed. F. J. Furnivall and John Munro, 40 vols (1908)
Oxf	*Works*, ed. Stanley Wells, Gary Taylor, John Jowett and William Montgomery (Oxford, 1986)
Pope	*Works*, ed. Alexander Pope, 6 vols (1723–5)
Riv	*The Riverside Shakespeare*, textual editors G. Blakemore Evans and J.J.M. Tobin, 2nd edn (Boston, Mass., and New York, 1997)
Rowe	*Works*, ed. Nicholas Rowe, 6 vols (1709)
Rowe[2]	*Works*, ed. Nicholas Rowe, 8 vols (1714)
Sanders	*Henry VI, Part 1*, ed. Norman Sanders (Harmondsworth, 1981)
Singer	*Dramatic Works*, ed. Samuel Weller Singer, 10 vols (1856)
Sisson	*Works*, ed. Charles Jasper Sisson (1954)
Staunton	*Works*, ed. Howard Staunton, 3 vols (1858–60)

Steevens	*Plays*, ed. Samùel Johnson and George Steevens, 10 vols (1773)
Theobald	*Works*, ed. Lewis Theobald, 7 vols (1733)
Theobald[4]	*Works*, ed. Lewis Theobald, 7 vols (1757)
Tucker Brooke	*1 Henry VI*, ed. C.F. Tucker Brooke (1918)
Warburton	*Works*, ed. William Warburton, 8 vols (1747)

OTHER WORKS CITED

Astington	John H. Astington, 'The origins of the *Roxana* and *Messalina* illustrations', *SS43* (1991), 149–69
Baldwin	T.W. Baldwin, *On Act and Scene Division in the Shakespere First Folio* (Urbana, Ill., 1965)
Barton & Hall	John Barton and Peter Hall, *The Wars of the Roses* (1970)
Bate, *Genius*	Jonathan Bate, *The Genius of Shakespeare* (1998)
Bate, *Romantics*	Jonathan Bate, *The Romantics on Shakespeare* (Harmondsworth, 1992)
Bennett	Matthew Bennett, 'The development of battle tactics in the Hundred Years War', in *Arms, Armies and Fortifications in the Hundred Years War*, ed. Anne Curry and Michael Hughes (Woodbridge, 1994), 1–21
Berry	Edward I. Berry, *Patterns of Decay: Shakespeare's Early Histories* (Charlottesville, 1975)
Bevington	David M. Bevington, 'The domineering female in *1 Henry VI*', *SSt*, 2 (1966), 51–8.
Bloom	Harold Bloom, *Shakespeare and the Invention of the Human* (New York, 1998)
Bullough	Geoffrey Bullough (ed.), *Narrative and Dramatic Sources of Shakespeare*, 8 vols (1957–75), vol. 3 (1960)
Camden	William Camden, *Remains Concerning Britain*, first pub. 1605, ed. R.D. Dunn (Toronto 1984)
Campbell	Lily B. Campbell, *Shakespeare's 'Histories': Mirrors of Elizabethan Policy* (1964)
Carson	Neil Carson, *A Companion to Henslowe's Diary* (Cambridge, 1988)
Cary	Elizabeth Cary, Viscountess Falkland, 'History of the Life, Reign and Death of Edward II', in *Renaissance Women: The Plays of Elizabeth Cary; The Poems of Aemilia Lanyer*, ed. Diane Purkiss (1994)
Cercignani	Fausto Cercignani, *Shakespeare's Works and Elizabethan Pronunciation* (Oxford, 1981)
Chambers	E. K. Chambers, *William Shakespeare: A Study of Facts and Problems*, 2 vols (Oxford, 1930)
Chambers, *Stage*	*The Elizabethan Stage*, 4 vols (Oxford, 1923)
Chanson de Roland	*La Chanson de Roland*, ed. Luis Cortes (Paris, 1994)

Chaucer, *Riv*	*The Riverside Chaucer*, ed. F.N. Robinson, rev. Larry D. Benson (Oxford, 1988)
Contention	*The First Part of the Contention*, 1594 (Oxford, 1985)
Corbin & Sedge	Peter Corbin and Douglas Sedge (eds), *The Oldcastle controversy: Sir John Oldcastle Part I, and The Famous Victories of Henry V* (Manchester, 1991)
Cox	John D. Cox, 'Devils and power in Marlowe and Shakespeare', *Yearbook of English Studies*, 23 (1993), 46–64
Cruickshank	C.G. Cruickshank, *Elizabeth's Army* (Oxford, 1966)
Daniell	David Daniell, 'Opening up the text: Shakespeare's *Henry VI* plays in performance', in *Themes in Drama, 1: Drama and Society* (Cambridge, 1979)
Dent	R.W. Dent, *Shakespeare's Proverbial Language: An Index* (Berkeley, Calif., and London, 1981)
Discorsi	Niccolò Machiavelli, *Discorsi sopra la prima deca di Tito Livio* (1513–17), ed. Sergio Bertelli (Milan, 1960)
Ditié	Christine de Pisan, *Ditié de Jehanne d'Arc*, ed. Angus J. Kennedy and Kenneth Varty (Oxford, 1977)
Dobson	Michael Dobson, *The Making of the National Poet: Shakespeare, Adaptation and Authorship, 1660–1769* (Oxford, 1992)
Donne	John Donne, *The Divine Poems*, ed. Helen Gardner (Oxford, 1952)
Eccles	Christine Eccles, *The Rose Theatre* (1990)
Edelman	Charles Edelman, *Brawl ridiculous: Swordfighting in Shakespeare's Plays* (Manchester, 1992)
Edward III	*see* Melchiori
Edwards	Thomas Kyd, *The Spanish Tragedy*, ed. Philip Edwards (1959; repr. Manchester, 1977)
ELN	*English Language Notes*
ELR	*English Literary Renaissance*
Fenwick	Henry Fenwick, 'The Production', in *Henry VI, Part 1: The BBC TV Shakespeare* (1983)
Fiedler	Leslie Fiedler, *The Stranger in Shakespeare* (1973)
Foakes	R.A. Foakes, 'The discovery of the Rose theatre: some implications', *SS 43* (1991), 141–9
Fowler	Kenneth Fowler, *The Age of Plantagenet and Valois: The Struggle for Supremacy 1328–1498* (1967)
Fox-Davies	Arthur Charles Fox-Davies, *A Complete Guide to Heraldry* (1925)
FQ	Edmund Spenser, *The Faerie Queene*, ed. A.C. Hamilton (1977)
French	Marilyn French, *Shakespeare's Division of Experience* (1982)

Friar Bacon and Friar Bungay	Robert Greene, *Friar Bacon and Friar Bungay*, ed. J.A. Lavin (1969)
Friedman	Winifred H. Friedman, *Boydell's Shakespeare Gallery* (New York, 1976)
Froissart	*The Chronicle of Froissart translated by Sir John Bourchier, Lord Berners, annis 1523–25*, introd. W.P. Ker, 6 vols (1901–3)
Gabrieli & Melchiori	*Sir Thomas More*, ed. Vittorio Gabrieli and Giorgio Melchiori (Manchester, 1990)
Ginzburg	Carlo Ginzburg, *Ecstasies: Deciphering the Witches' Sabbath* (1989), trans. Raymond Rosenthal (Harmondsworth, 1992)
Golding	*The XV Books of P. Ovidius Naso, Entitled Metamorphosis*, trans. Arthur Golding (1567; repr. 1904 and 1961)
Greene	Robert Greene, *Greene's Groatsworth of Wit, Bought with a Million of Repentance* (1592 facs. edn, Menston, 1969)
Greg	W.W. Greg, *The Shakespeare First Folio: Its Bibliographical and Textual History* (Oxford, 1955)
Griffiths	R.A. Griffiths, *The Reign of King Henry VI: The Exercise of Royal Authority 1422–1461* (1981)
Grigson	Jane Grigson, *Fish Cookery* (1973)
Grove	*The New Grove Dictionary of Music and Musicians*, ed. Stanley Sadie (1980)
Hall	Edward Hall, *The Union of the Two Noble and Illustrious Families of Lancaster and York* (1548, repr. (1809)
Hardin	Richard F. Hardin, 'Chronicles and mythmaking in Shakespeare's Joan of Arc', *SS42* (1990), 25–35
Henslowe	*Henslowe's Diary*, ed. R.A. Foakes and R.T. Rickert (Cambridge, 1961)
Herodotus	*Histories*, Loeb edn, 4 vols, trans A.D. Godley (1920–4)
Holinshed	Raphael Holinshed, *Chronicles of England, Scotland, and Ireland*, 2nd edn (1587; repr. 6 vols, 1808)
Homer, *Iliad*	Loeb edn, 2 vols, trans. A.T. Murray (1924)
Homer, *Odyssey*	Loeb edn, 2 vols, trans. A.T. Murray, rev. George E. Dimock (1995)
Homilies	*The Book of Homilies*, vol. 1 (1547), vol. 2 (1563)
Honigmann	E.A.J. Honigmann, *Shakespeare: The Lost Years* (Manchester, 1985)
Hotson	Leslie Hotson, *Shakespeare's Wooden O* (1959)
Howard & Rackin	Jean E. Howard and Phyllis Rackin, *Engendering a Nation: A Feminist Account of Shakespeare's English Histories* (1997)
Howard-Hill	Trevor Howard-Hill (ed.), *Shakespeare and 'Sir Thomas More': Essays on the Play and its Shakespearean Interest* (Cambridge, 1989)
Huizinga	Johan Huizinga, *The Waning of the Middle Ages: A Study of the Forms of Life, Thought and Art in France and the Netherlands in the XIVth and XVth Centuries* (1924; repr. Harmondsworth, 1972)

Hunter	G.K. Hunter, 'Afterword: Notes on the genre of the history play', in *Shakespeare's English Histories: A Quest for Form and Genre*, ed. J.W.L. Velz (Binghamton, NY, 1996), 229–40
Jackson	Gabriele Bernhard Jackson, 'Topical ideology: witches, Amazons, and Shakespeare's Joan of Arc', *ELR*, 18 (1988), 40–65
Jacob	Giles Jacob, *A New Law-Dictionary. 2nd edition. Corrected, with Large Additions* (1732)
Johnson	David J. Johnson, *Southwark and the City* (Oxford, 1969)
Jones	Emrys Jones, *The Origins of Shakespeare* (Oxford, 1977)
Jonson	*Ben Jonson*, ed. C.H. Herford and Percy and Evelyn Simpson, 11 vols (Oxford, 1925–52)
Kahn	Coppélia Kahn, *Man's Estate: Masculine Identity in Shakespeare* (Berkeley, 1981)
Kastan	David Scott Kastan, *Shakespeare and the Shapes of Time* (1982)
Kean (see also Merivale/Kean)	*Richard, Duke of York* (1852)
King	Thomas James King, *Casting Shakespeare's Plays: London Actors and their Roles, 1590–1642* (Cambridge, 1992)
Kökeritz	Helge Kökeritz, *Shakespeare's Pronunciation* (New Haven, 1953)
Kyd	*The Spanish Tragedy*, *see* Edwards
Larousse	*Grand Larousse Encyclopédique* (Paris, 1960–4)
Leggatt	Alexander Leggatt, 'The death of John Talbot', in *Shakespeare's English Histories: A Quest for Form and Genre*, ed. J.W.L. Velz (Binghamton, NY, 1996), 11–30
Locrine	*The Lamentable Tragedy of Locrine*, 1595 in C.F.T. Brooke, ed., *The Shakespeare Apocrypha* (Oxford, 1908)
Lucan	*Pharsalia (The Civil War)*, Loeb edn, ed. and transl. J.D. Duff (1928)
Lucan (Marlowe)	*Lucan's First Book*, in *Christopher Marlowe, The Complete Poems and Translations*, ed. Stephen Orgel (Harmondsworth, 1971)
Mandeville	Sir John Mandeville, *Mandeville's Travels*, ed. M.C. Seymour (Oxford, 1967)
Marlowe	Christopher Marlowe, *Tamburlaine, Parts I and II, Doctor Faustus, A- and B-Texts, The Jew of Malta, Edward II*, ed. David Bevington and Eric Rasmussen (Oxford and New York, 1995)
Melchiori	*King Edward III*, ed. Giorgio Melchiori (Cambridge, 1998)
Merivale/Kean	*Richard, Duke of York* (1817), facs. edn with introduction, T.J.B. Spencer (1971)
Midgeley	Mary Midgeley, *Beast and Man: The Roots of Human Nature* (1979; rev. 1995)

N & Q	*Notes and Queries*
Nashe	*The Works of Thomas Nashe*, ed. R.B. McKerrow, rev. F.P. Wilson, 5 vols (Oxford, 1958)
Noble	Adrian Noble, *The Plantagenets* (1989)
OED	*The Oxford English Dictionary*, 2nd edn (Oxford, 1989)
Ormrod	W. M. Ormrod, 'The domestic response to the Hundred Years War', in *Arms, Armies and Fortifications in the Hundred Years War*, ed. Anne Curry and Michael Hughes (Woodbridge, 1994)
Osberg	Richard Osberg, 'The Jesse tree in the 1432 London entry of Henry VI: messianic kingship and the rule of justice', *Journal of Medieval and Renaissance Studies*, 16 (1986), 213–32
Ovid	*Metamorphoses*, Loeb edn, 2 vols, trans. Frank Justus Miller (1916)
Parker	Patricia Parker, *Shakespeare from the Margins: Language, Culture, Context* (Chicago, 1996)
Pinches	J.H. and R.V. Pinches, *The Royal Heraldry of England* (1974)
Plato	*Phaedrus*, Loeb edn, trans. Harold North Fowler (1914)
Pliny	*Naturalis Historia*, Loeb edn, 10 vols, trans. H. Rackham and others (1938–62)
Plutarch	*Lives*, Loeb edn, 10 vols, trans. Bernadotte Perrin (1914–26)
Plutarch (North)	*The Lives of the Noble Grecians and Romans . . . by Plutarch*, trans. Sir Thomas North (1579)
Potter	Lois Potter, 'Recycling the early histories: *The Wars of the Roses* and *The Plantagenets*', *SS43* (1991), 171–81
Rackin	Phyllis Rackin, *Stages of History: Shakespeare's English Chronicles* (1991)
Raysor	Samuel Taylor Coleridge, *Shakespearean Criticism*, ed. Thomas Middleton Raysor, 2 vols, 2nd edn (1960)
REED	*Records of Early English Drama: Chester*, ed. Lawrence M. Clopper (Manchester and Toronto, 1979)
Riggs	David Riggs, *Shakespeare's Heroical Histories: 'Henry VI' and its Literary Tradition* (Cambridge, Mass., 1971)
Ringler	William Ringler, Jr, 'The number of actors in Shakespeare's plays', in *The Seventeenth Century Stage*, ed. G.E. Bentley (London and Chicago, 1968), 110–39
Ripley	George Ripley, *The Compound of Alchemy* (1591)
Roberts	Gareth Roberts, *The Mirror of Alchemy: Alchemical Ideas and Images in Manuscripts and Books from Antiquity to the Seventeenth Century* (1994)
Rosador, 'Magic'	Kurt Tetzeli von Rosador, 'The power of magic: from *Endimion* to *The Tempest*', *SS43* (1991)
Rosador, 'Sacralizing'	Kurt Tetzeli von Rosador, 'The sacralizing sign: religion and magic in Bale, Greene, and the early Shakespeare', *The Yearbook of English Studies*, 23 (1993), 30–45

Rosen	Barbara Rosen (ed.), *Witchcraft*, Stratford-upon-Avon Library, 6 (1969)
RP	Richard Proudfoot, private communication
Rutter	Carol Chillingham Rutter (ed.), *Documents of the Rose Playhouse* (Manchester, 1984)
Schanzer	Ernest Schanzer, 'Thomas Platter's observations on the Elizabethan stage', *N&Q* (November 1956), 465–7
Scot	Reginald Scot, *The Discovery of Witchcraft* (1584), ed. Brinsley Nicholson (1886)
Scott-Giles	C.W. Scott-Giles, *Shakespeare's Heraldry* (1950)
Shaheen	Nasseeb Shaheen, *Biblical References in Shakespeare's History Plays* (Newark, NJ, 1989)
Shaw	George Bernard Shaw, *Saint Joan: A Chronicle Play* (1926)
Sir Thomas More	*see* Gabrieli & Melchiori
Spanish Tragedy	*see* Edwards
SS	*Shakespeare Survey*
SSt	*Shakespeare Studies*
Stowe	*A Survey of London by John Stowe*, repr. from the text of 1603, introd. Charles Lethbridge Kingsford, 2 vols (Oxford, 1908)
Suetonius	*The Lives of the Caesars*, Loeb edn, 2 vols, trans. J.C. Rolfe (1914)
Tacitus	*Annals*, Loeb edn, trans. John Jackson, 4 (1937)
Taylor	Gary Taylor, 'Shakespeare and others: the authorship of *Henry the Sixth, Part One*', *Medieval and Renaissance Drama in England*, 7 (1995), 145–205
Taylor & Jowett	Gary Taylor and John Jowett, *Shakespeare Reshaped, 1606–1623* (Oxford, 1993)
Tillyard	E.M.W. Tillyard, *Shakespeare's History Plays* (1944)
True Tragedy	*The True Tragedy of Richard Duke of York*, 1595 (Oxford, 1958)
Vaughan	Henry H. Vaughan, *New Readings and Renderings of Shakespeare's Tragedies* (1886)
Virgil	*Eclogues*, Loeb edn, trans. H. Rushton Fairclough (1932)
Walker	W.S. Walker, *A Critical Examination of the Text of Shakespeare, with Remarks on his Language and that of his Contemporaries, together with notes on his Plays and Poems*, ed., with a preface, W.N. Lettsom, 3 vols (1860)
Warner	Marina Warner, *Joan of Arc: The Image of Female Heroism* (1981)
Watt	R.J.C. Watt, 'The siege of Orleans and the cursing of Joan: corruptions in the text of *Henry VI Part 1*', *ELN*, 33:3 (1996), 1–6
Williams	George Walton Williams, 'Fastolf or Falstaff', *ELR*, 5 (1975), 308–12

Willis   Deborah Willis, 'Shakespeare and the English witch-hunts: enclosing the maternal body', in *Enclosure Acts: Sexuality, Property, and Culture in Early Modern England*, ed. John Michael Archer and Richard Burt (Ithaca, 1994)

Willis, *BBC*   Susan Willis, *The BBC Shakespeare Plays: Making the Televised Canon* (Chapel Hill, NC, 1991)

Wright   Celeste Turner Wright, 'The Elizabethan female worthies', *Studies in Philology*, 43 (1946), 628–43.

INDEX

Individual characters from this and other plays are not listed in the index. When a character is mentioned (Henry V, for example) the reference is to the historical or legendary personage.